PRINCE MICHAEL OF GREECE, related to every
royal family in Europe, knows the secret worlds of
the wealthy, privileged, and powerful. Already
famous as a writer in Europe for his biographies of
Napoleon and Louis XIV, he has now taken the
story of Aimée Dubuc de Riverie, the extraordinary
cousin of the Empress Josephine, who vanished into
the footnotes of history, and created an international
bestseller.

SULTANA

PRINCE MICHAEL
OF GREECE

Translated from the French
by Alexis Ullmann

AVON
PUBLISHERS OF BARD, CAMELOT, DISCUS AND FLARE BOOKS

AVON BOOKS
A division of
The Hearst Corporation
1790 Broadway
New York, New York 10019

The Harper & Row edition contains the following Library of Congress Cataloging in Publication Data:

Michael, Prince of Greece, 1939-
  Sultana.

  1. Turkey—History—Selim III, 1789-1808—Fiction. I. Title.
PR9115.9.M54S9   1983   823'.914   82-48685

First Avon Printing, May, 1984

from M. to M.

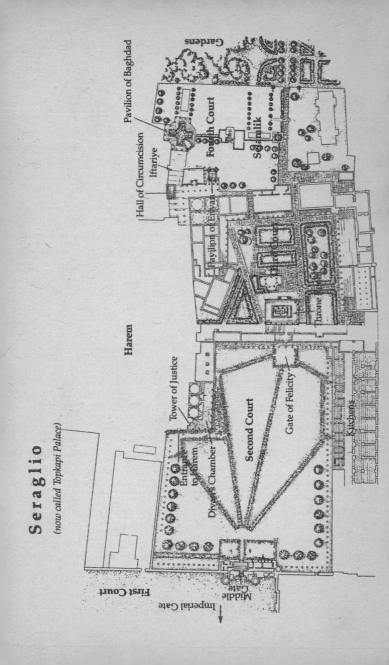

Seraglio
(now called Topkapi Palace)

First Court

Imperial Gate

Middle Gate

Harem

Tower of Justice

Entrance to Harem

Divan's Chamber

Second Court

Gate of Felicity

Kitchens

Third Court

Throne

Pavilion of Erivan

Hall of Circumcision

Iftariye

Fourth Court

Selamlik

Pavilion of Baghdad

Gardens

Harem

Gate of Death

Apartment of Selim III

Kiosk of Osman III

Terrace (of Kiosk of Osman III)

Apartment of Abdul Hamid

"Harem Gardens"

Cage

Gozdes' Courtyard

Golden Way

Fourth Court

Mabeyn

Sultan's Hall

Court of the Valideh

Apartment of the Valideh

Court of the New Women

Black Eunuchs' Court

Third Court

Tower of Justice

Entrance to Harem

Second Court

PART 1

FROM MARTINIQUE TO CONSTANTINOPLE

CHAPTER 1

I FAR PREFER this new residence of mine to the Seraglio, where I spent so many years. When I return there I am harassed by painful and sometimes tragic memories, whereas here light streams in through the casements. I am also grateful for the fact that from here I cannot see Constantinople, though it is close by. Constantinople . . . it is History, it is my past. From my windows I can see my peaceful flower garden, the marble terrace down by the water, the sailing ship drifting majestically on the Bosporus, surrounded by caïques. It is spring outside my palace—the spring of 1816—but in my soul and in my body it is forever midwinter. My Greek doctor can lie to me all he wants. I know I have only a few months left to live. I am forty-three years old, and consumption kills women far younger than I. Before I see the gates of death I wish to tell my story, to bear witness for myself and for those I love. I have spread around me the old diaries which will help me write those memories; and on my knees I hold the gold-and-agate writing case that my beloved gave me long ago.

3

Now that the island of my birth has drifted far away on the waters of time, far away in time and space, I retain a few images set in the gold of my memory; and at times I recollect them like gems which a melancholy hand draws, one by one, from the jewel box.

Euphemia David—the she-devil! She knew it all from the very beginning, and her bedeviled tongue, as long as life itself, knew better than any other how to spell the dictates of destiny. Where is she now, that old black witch? And you, lovely cousin Josephine, companion of my happy childhood—where are you? If I am to recall you today, from so far away, I have no choice but to retrace my steps to that scorching afternoon of my ninth year, to that luminous clearing, to that hut where you dragged me, Josephine, in secret and in spite of myself. It was you, the elder, who chose the day and the moment: the hour of the afternoon nap seemed the best to trick the household's vigilance and ensure the success of our escapade. And yes, you were right: we slipped out of bed, and we slipped out of the slumbering house and drew away into the trees without alerting a soul.

There was not a breath of air in Martinique. It was the hottest day of that hottest summer of 1781. A steely ocean—not a wave, not a ripple—reflected a leaden sky. Poisonous fumes rose from the half-drained swamps around the bay of Fort-de-France. Cane field and coffee field, stretching as far as the eye could see, were deserted. It was the hour when black and white alike took refuge in their houses and huts to seek slumber: the torpor of the afternoon nap, when all the island lies low, struck motionless as if by enchantment. There was no one to see us, no one and nothing to disturb us—except, from time to time, a rustle in the tall grass, the flight of a snake or a small rodent.

I was hot, I was afraid, I wanted to go home. But you would not listen to my complaints, Josephine. You wanted to know the future, and for this reason you had to find Euphemia David. She was famous on the island. It was said she was the daughter of an Irish sailor who had raped a slavewoman one drunken night. The white planters shrugged when she was mentioned—but they also sent her small presents once in a while, just in case; there were no real skeptics on Martinique. And the blacks shook with dread at the sound of her name and threatened one another with her power, as if she were a sort of werewolf: "Baron Samedi's daughter will come for you . . . the Devil's daughter!"

I walked on in the fire of that afternoon, I followed you on that path leading to Euphemia David; but I did so only to please you, Josephine. The idea did not appeal to me at all.

We reached the limits of the plantation. For a moment we hesitated before crossing the sandy road and risking our way under the giant amaryllis of the place known as Croc-Souris. It was reputed to be crawling with snakes, those little beige-and-brown snakes with flat rectangular heads, whose bite causes a quick and painful death. We jumped every time something cracked in the underbrush. But you weren't the kind who turns back; and you had to know what would come of the sweet glances you exchanged with that Englishman of yours. The canopy of entwined branches weighed on us, seemed to cut off both air and light. We stumbled on through darkness and palpable heat. I thought that life itself had been stifled in the thick and mysterious silence. There was no sign, no sound, no turtledove or macaw to be heard. And suddenly out of this silent nothingness rose a slight murmur, at first vague and indistinct. Then it grew a little more intricate, a little more precise, and finally we understood we were hearing human voices in song. And then, as we emerged from the trees into a clearing, we found ourselves facing Euphemia David's hut—a poor shack thrown together of wood and straw, patched and sagging, half hidden in the luxuriant shadows of the fronds. The monotonous, unsettling threnody still wafted from the hut and this time it was you, Josephine, who froze to the spot, who were afraid, who would not go on. And it was I, so much younger than you, who had to push you, who had to exhort you to walk the last yards to the hut's crude doorway.

We were blinded, coming in from the light; all we could see were vague shapes sitting on the earthen floor.

"Don't be afraid, my pretty Creoles. Come closer, come closer."

The voice sounded young and lilting, and carried an enticing hint of irony. But neither of us could move.

"Come on, come close, my pretty ones. I don't spit snakes. No pit is going to open under your feet, I promise. Come closer—I can't see you."

Now the voice was gentler. Already our eyes were growing accustomed to the darkness, and we could distinguish a score of silhouettes of black men and women, sitting on mats laid out in a circle. We had interrupted their song and now they sat stock-still, their gaze fixed on the ground before them. Only one had lifted her head to look at us; it was Euphemia. Although she was hunched over, one could see that she was tall and very skinny. For a black woman she had a peculiarly hooked nose and light eyes, no doubt inherited from her Irish father. She stared at the both of us in turn. Suddenly she hunched her shoulders even more, and a wave of dread swept over her glistening, sweating face. "Why have you come here? What are you looking for?"

Her voice had fallen now and thickened, and she seemed short of breath and spoke very quickly. Josephine made an effort to regain her composure, and said: "The future. They say you can see the future." She deposited before Euphemia the ritual gifts, a sack of ground coffee and a sugarloaf, and continued: "I want to know whether the man I love will love me forever and whether I shall marry him."

The old seer's face grew solemn. She peered intently at Josephine.

"So young and already curious about the future," she muttered. "Isn't the present enough for you, young lady?"

"I want to know," Josephine insisted, a note of fear still lingering in her voice.

"I won't hide the truth, little one, since you insist. But you must be prepared to hear that it may not be as you wish."

Euphemia's voice had grown raspy and hollow. It sounded as if its very nature had changed, as if it were no longer her own voice, but the oracle's.

"A dark-haired man, a foreigner, an Englishman, is thinking of you. You love each other, but you will never marry. You must renounce that dream at once if you believe me. Yet other dreams—

you can't even imagine them now—will come true in their own time. I see a fair-haired man. He is promised to a relative of yours who is soon to die. That man will be your first husband."

Euphemia grabbed Josephine's hands, turned their palms upward, and drew them close to her eyes. She spoke again in an astounding cascade of silvery notes, of pearly prophecy:

"You will marry twice. Your first husband will take you to France. You will be happy for a few years, but then you will separate, and he will die a tragic death, leaving you two small children. Your second husband will be small in stature, and also poor and unknown. Yet he will become immensely famous, the whole world will ring with his name, and he will submit many nations to his power. At his side you will be . . . a queen."

Here Euphemia hesitated, as if her pale eyes were waiting for a more definite image to form.

"No, not a queen. Something . . . more than that. You shall be more than a queen. But often, while you live in glory on that highest of peaks, surrounded by honors, you will long for the simple peaceful life that is yours now, here in Martinique. And I see—alas—that having dazzled the world, you will die abandoned and alone."

And that was all. Euphemia fell silent, head bowed as if crushed by the omen. Josephine, wide-eyed, seemed frozen to stone. I had listened to all this quite calmly, but I had grown curious as to what strange effect my own hands would produce in Euphemia. With a feeling of defiance, I stepped forward and showed her my upturned palms. "And what about me—what do you think will become of me? Tell me! I won't believe you, but just tell me."

Euphemia slowly lifted her gaze and looked at me. She took my hands and held them firmly in hers, but did not examine them. Her face was drenched in sweat.

I smiled, and challenged her again: "Well, don't you see anything?"

She forced her head back and shut her eyes, and again her voice was possessed by that strange metallic sonority, which made one think that the future was actually being forged and hammered inside her throat. "Within a few years your parents will send you to France. In the course of a voyage, your ship will be seized by pirates, who will carry you away, a prisoner. You will survive a shipwreck.... You will earn the love of an unhappy ruler.... You will command a great empire.... You will have a son. How strange! That son will be neither your son nor that ruler's. And he will reign, and his reign will be filled with glory; but I see the steps of his throne are covered with the blood of regicide. And in spite of the tremendous power you shall wield, you will never know public honors and recognition. You will live in a magnificent palace, but you will live there a recluse, unable ever to leave it."

Euphemia let go of my hands, and her body bent forward, as if broken by the effort. She seemed incapable of uttering another word.

Two future sovereigns, we ran back to the house of the Tashers de la Pagerie, Josephine's parents, as fast as we could. We still hoped to slip through a service door and return to our rooms and our beds without being caught. Unfortunately we had lost all notion of time at Euphemia's, the grownups had long since risen from their naps, and our absence had been discovered. Instead of the splendor and the honors Euphemia had predicted, we were greeted by a storm of reproof. I found Zinah, my black "da," standing in the middle of my room, her hands on her hips, wearing an air of severity worthy of the Day of Judgment. I had no sooner entered than she pelted me with a hail of questions.

"Where have you been, you naughty child? Why did you go out in this heat? And with whom?"

And without once pausing for breath, she reeled off a long string of threats and reproaches. "A young lady doesn't go out on the open road alone! You should be ashamed of yourself, giving me such a fright! I'm going to tell your parents, and they'll send you away to a convent! You've behaved like a slave child!"

Zinah was a nineteen-year-old girl, tall and graceful, who had been given to me at my birth. She was at once my governess, my servant, and my confidante. Her devotion was boundless, and I must have displeased her indeed if she called me a slave child—words that in her mind were the worst possible insult. I was not going to let it pass.

"That's not true," I answered, chin high. "One day I shall rule over a huge empire! I will do everything I want to do, and you will have to obey me!"

And I spilled out the whole incredible story of the shipwreck, the pirates, the ruler's love, the throne, and the blood. Zinah stared at me wide-eyed, as if I were possessed by demons.

"Oh, you poor girl! You've gone mad from the heat!"

A similar scene was unfolding a few doors down the hall, where Josephine faced her mother, who had just been informed of our escapade. Neither the visit to Euphemia nor the prediction which made future sovereigns of us was designed to soften Madame Tasher's mood, which was always at its worst when she awoke from her nap.

"Would you mind speaking like a well-brought-up girl and not mashing your words like a darkie!" she yelled, choking with indignation. "In this heat! To see that Negress! With all those slaves and snakes! To have your future told! And on top of that you took your guest, Aimée, an eight-year-old girl! Are you at least aware of your thoughtlessness? You're crazy, my girl—the child is crazy! She'll drive us all crazy!"

Aghast at our inconceivable audacity, Madame Tasher de la Pagerie called the entire household to arms, and a few moments later, Josephine and I appeared before a sort of solemn court-martial in one of the drawing rooms downstairs. Both of Josephine's parents were there, as well as mine and my little sisters. I could not help noticing that my father—the only one of our judges who might be inclined to leniency—was having trouble muffling his amusement.

I must admit that we had indeed committed a truly abominable crime. Our visit to Euphemia was doubly reprehensible in that we had broken, by lending weight to her words, the rules of our religion as well as those of society. Josephine's eyes were full of tears; she shifted her weight from leg to leg, twisted her fingers in the hem of her dress, and stammered muddled answers to her parents' questions. I concentrated on standing straight, on staring our judges in the eye, and maintained a righteous silence.

"More than a queen! And Aimée the ruler of an empire! How can you believe such nonsense?" said Madame Tasher. "I don't know who deserves the whipping—you crazy little girls or that old crank Euphemia David!"

A shudder spread among the group of black servants at the back of the room. Whip Euphemia David, the daughter of Baron Samedi!

"Yes, I'll have her whipped!" repeated Madame Tasher, enraged. Josephine saw that her mother's anger was cresting, and treacherously tried appeasement. "But, Maman, I don't believe her. I assure you we were only playing. I know very well these are nothing but fairy tales and lies!"

Oh, that Judas! I could understand that she did not want to believe the prediction that she would not marry her Englishman, William Fraser. But I despised her for letting our dream down. I hated her for denying the reality of Euphemia's world. I raised my voice against everyone, and shouted: "Well, I believe them!"

I saw my father bend toward my mother's ear and consult with her briefly. Then, since a show of severity was called for, since I had to be punished one way or another for my insolence, my mother suppressed a note of regret in her voice and said, "Well, for today at least our future ruler will have to pass the time on bread and water."

"Go ahead and punish me! One day I'll rule an empire, and then you'll have to be proud of me!"

"She's as stubborn as a mule, that one." My father laughed. "Our ancestor Pierre Dubuc wouldn't have disowned her—a real little Norman girl!"

Such was my father: a supportive and sensitive man, proud of the resurgence in his children of certain character traits which had guided the fortunes of the Dubuc family. He took a special pleasure in telling the story of the rise of Pierre Dubuc, the first of the line, who to my mind was a legendary hero. Born of a modest Norman family, Pierre Dubuc had joined the army at the age of fourteen.

After a few years spent fighting for his king—or rather for Cardinal Richelieu, the real power behind the throne—he came home with the rank of lieutenant. His contact with the lesser nobility in the army had made him ambitious, and the war had brought out in him a naturally bellicose streak. Once home, he quarreled with the Chevalier de Piancourt, and after challenging him to a duel on the flimsiest of pretexts, killed him.

Cardinal Richelieu, however, took a dim view of dueling, and had made it an offense punishable by death. After the duel with Piancourt, only one course of action was left open to Pierre Dubuc: to board the first outbound ship and leave France. In the nearby port of Dieppe he found a three-master ready to set sail for the West Indies. Pierre Dubuc unceremoniously climbed aboard, joining a group of young adventurers hungry for land and new horizons.

He disembarked at Saint Kitts a few weeks later. The French governor there, Monsieur d'Esnambuc, recognized the young man's worth at once, and sent him posthaste to assist the efforts of those who were then busy colonizing Martinique.

There again Dubuc soon proved himself to be an excellent soldier. He fought impartially against the Dutch and the British, since both coveted the West Indies. Once the region was pacified, he settled in the eastern part of Martinique and started its first sugarcane plantation and its first sugar mill, and launched the first attempts at the cultivation of cocoa.

He founded a family and a fortune, both of which grew apace, and in 1701 King Louis XIV decided to ennoble him. Having accumulated wealth, a large family, and rank, the enterprising Norman died a happy man.

Less than a century later, the numerous branches of his descendants had spread all over the island. Great landowners all, they held the power and controlled the economy. The Dubucs de Bellefonds, the Dubucs de Sainte Preuve, the Dubucs Beaudoin—all connected families—assembled as often as possible, organizing receptions and celebrations whenever any important event—a birth, a wedding, a funeral—allowed it.

One such gathering took place a year after our trek to Euphemia David's and its unpleasant aftermath. In the meantime my mother had given birth to a long-awaited first son. On that afternoon he was christened, like my sisters and myself before him, by Curé Trepsac at the Robert church. To celebrate, a banquet was organized for our guests on the lawn in front of the manor, while another was provided for the servants, down by the sugar mill. At dusk the paths were lit with scented torches and hundreds of multicolored lanterns were hung from the trees, cutting a swath of light down to Robert bay, which, that night, was ablaze with the lights of merchant ships lolling at anchor. Thousands of candles had been set on the tables, their flames flickering in a gentle Atlantic breeze. That evening I felt the fire of joy burning in our hearts and lighting up our eyes. And I especially beamed: my aunt Elizabeth had just given me my first piece of jewelry, a necklace of red and pink coral beads.

The only one who seemed downhearted in the midst of all this rejoicing was my cousin Josephine. She had grown and changed a good deal in the past months. She had developed languid airs and complained that she was forbidden to see that young man she had been in love with for so long. We were sitting a little way off from the crowd, sharing our latest secrets. Josephine spoke sadly, emphasizing points with little movements of her delicate white hands. Our conversation was interrupted by her little sister Marie-Françoise, who had not passed up a single opportunity to tease us since the Euphemia David affair.

"Here they are! The empresses! Everybody come and pay their respects!"

Half a dozen children ran to Marie-Françoise's call, forsaking piles of pastries and cake for the game. They laughed, shrieked, and pushed us and each other about until my aunt Elizabeth Dubuc de Bellefonds intervened and dispersed them with a few harsh words and a kick or two. Josephine was in tears, and refused to be consoled; I was bruised and scratched and covered with dirt, because I had fought our tormentors with all my strength.

My aunt Elizabeth was a smooth, elegant woman for whom I felt a kind of veneration. I accepted her remarks and her criticism more easily than anyone else's. "Really, Aimée," she said, "you shouldn't put yourself in such a state. Your cousins aren't nasty, you know that. I think it's you and Josephine who provoke them with all your airs and graces."

"But it's true, Auntie Elizabeth: Euphemia said that one day I would rule an empire!"

"Well, I'm not saying you couldn't," she remarked, smiling. "But if you kept your plans secret you wouldn't expose yourself to such unpleasant scenes. . . . I even hear that you have made yourself a court of black urchins, and that down at the grove . . ."

"But I'm only playing, Auntie. All children invent games."

I blushed, I trembled with shame and rage. So my games, my little empress games, were known as far as Bellefonds! Aunt Elizabeth calmed me with another smile and an indulgent caress, and left to join the adults.

Regardless of what I had told Aunt Elizabeth, the big grove of kapok trees at the juncture of four cane fields was indeed my kingdom. I had adopted the habit of taking refuge there whenever I had troubles or felt the need to talk to myself. I did not mind the rats and the snakes which inhabited the tall grass. No one disturbed me there. It was my palace, where I awaited my subjects, dressed in my court robes of blue silk brocaded with gold (a bedcover I "borrowed" from my mother). I wore a dashing plume of pink and white feathers on my head. Since I did not dare plunder my mother's jewelry box, I improvised with flowers, fashioning bracelets and necklaces out of gardenias entwined with fuchsia; the sumptuous corolla of a magnolia served as a tiara. My throne was a felled tree. From it I held audience to a handful of mystified black children.

"On your knees, Maximin! On your knees, Ti-Médas, and you too, Bocoyo! Dody, Apoline, Dorothy! Pay homage to your sovereign!"

And they obeyed.

"Repeat after me: We swear allegiance to our beloved Queen Aimée the First!"

Obediently, they bowed and pledged allegiance.

Since I did not wish to rule over an ignorant people, I shared my enlightenment with my subjects. Once they had taken the oath, I would pass on to them the learning I acquired at the Convent of the Ladies of Providence, where I went to school.

Some of the disciplines taught there, such as singing and dancing, bored me deeply; others, such as lessons in deportment, I thought grotesque. But I showed great interest in more serious matters—spelling, grammar, arithmetic—and I was fascinated by history and geography. Therefore it was these last topics which I inflicted most readily on my docile and silent court. The kapok grove echoed with illustrious names, with stories of murders, of plots, of tumultuous reigns, and with the names of exotic places, with their fascinating barbarous syllables. Once they were sufficiently educated, I fictionally dispatched my ambassadors to the capitals of the greatest empires—to Persia, China, Japan, Turkey. . . .

But there was no question of distant travels in reality; even the plans to send me to France to continue my education were endlessly postponed. At this time the two great naval powers of the world, England and France, were locked in a struggle for hegemony. Britain was waging a sort of naval guerrilla war on French shipping, and crossing the Atlantic was a dangerous proposition.

At home, my father secretly took pleasure in the impossibility of my departure. But the fateful moment came at last, and he had to resign himself to our long-dreaded and inevitable separation. The two rival powers had just signed the Treaty of Versailles, so that traffic across the ocean had recovered its former ease, its former speed and frequency. There was no longer anything preventing my sailing to France. Furthermore, my aunt Elizabeth was herself going to join her daughter Marie-Anne, and proposed to take me with her and my uncle Guy. If this offer broke my father's heart, it made me literally jump for joy. Not only was I at last to discover France, that ever promised land, but I was also to see again my favorite, my beloved cousin Marie-Anne. She was all the more dear to me for her recent misfortune: she had just lost her young husband, a sad event which had in part prompted the Bellefonds' decision to settle close to their daughter, in Nantes.

The day came in May 1785—a day my youthfulness and enthusiasm had looked forward to for so long, not thinking of the pain it would cause my parents. It was spring in Martinique, a season of enchantment, of sweet breezes and clear, luminous afternoons. They were all assembled on the wharf: my father, trying to conceal his sorrow under an overly joyful manner; my mother, busying herself until the last minute with material details; and my brother, my sisters, the servants and slaves—even old Nina, Zinah's grandmother, for naturally Zinah was coming with me.

She stood at my side on the deck of the *Vendée Royale* while, all sails on, the ship drew away from the shores of my childhood. I can still see it: the bay with the busy blacks milling against the white walls of the huts, the newly erected buildings of Fort-de-France, the dark hills speckled with the red light of sunset, their exuberant vegetation pierced, here and there, by the taller, bolder, palm trees. This beloved setting, which I had never before seen from a distance, stood out against the deep blue of the sky, and slowly grew smaller until at last it toppled silently over the horizon.

"Zinah, listen—do you think we'll be shipwrecked?"

"You're still thinking of shipwrecks, you silly child?"

I did not insist; yet I knew that as far as Josephine was concerned, Euphemia had spoken the truth: She had married not her Englishman but the man promised to her sister, who had since died, Viscount Alexandre de Beauharnais. I squeezed closer to Zinah. She was a small part of my island, a large part of my childhood. It seemed to me that at her side no serious danger could threaten me.

CHAPTER 2

We landed at Bordeaux on the eighteenth of July, less than two months later. My uncle and aunt considered this something of a record. I alighted on French soil a little shaken and disappointed: we had not been shipwrecked. Could it be that Euphemia had lied, that the words I had naively believed for so long might turn out to have been no more than the ravings of a diseased mind?

These pointless thoughts were soon swept away by a torrent of impressions of this new country I had heard so much about, which I had dreamed of so often. Everything astonished me as I walked the wide paved streets between tall buildings in this immense town. All the novelty astounded and enchanted me, and gave rise to endless comments, comparisons, and giggles. There were the old ladies' hoop skirts, their giant crinoline petticoats, a fashion left over from the reign of Louis XV, which, luckily, Martinique's climate had spared us. There were the fantastic hairstyles faithfully copied from Paris, precarious constructions of false hair, lacework, feathers, stuffed animals, and various other extraordinary objects. There were the fine swords the gentlemen wore at their side, which looked so pathetically thin and useless after the sabers and cutlasses of Martinique. But what shocked me more than anything else was the bustle, the speed at which the inhabitants of Bordeaux hurried about their lives, running rather than walking, in the grip of some ineffable urgency, as if they had decided to end each and every day as quickly as possible. This frantic pace, for someone freshly arrived from the indolent rhythm of the tropics, seemed at first the most disconcerting aspect of life in France.

Aunt Elizabeth and Uncle Guy planned to take their time and reach Nantes by a roundabout bucolic route. In order to enjoy the full variety of France's beauty, they meant to make as many stops as they wanted—and we had at least one cousin in every city of the realm.

Thus Marseille was the first big town for which we headed. The Bellefonds wanted to visit their Saint-Aurins and their De Trets cousins there, and spend the winter months with them under clement Mediterranean skies.

We left Bordeaux under sheets of water. The autumn rains had begun early that year, and we traveled through ceaseless torrential downpours. I found the flat, monotonous countryside, which rolled by our window with its endless vineyards and well-aligned trees, completely charmless. I realize now, thirty years later, how difficult it was for me to appreciate the beauty of a countryside so different from what I was accustomed to; and now it is with nostalgia that I look back on the lands of France, discovered under such difficult conditions.

Our carriage pitched through oceans of mud. We arrived in Montauban, our first stop, drenched to the bone, sneezing and shivering. My dear Zinah had turned that shade of gray which in her denoted dread and exhaustion. As for myself, I felt as if I had shriveled from the cold. To complete our misfortune, the inn where we stopped offered no great comfort. It was filled with treacherous drafts. Nor could we expect even a decent meal; the bailiff of Toulouse had dined there the night before, and his train had all but emptied the larder. We had to make do with leek soup before trying to find rest between humid sheets as cold as a shroud.

But our troubles had only begun. The following morning, still shivering and half starved as we prepared to leave, we were informed of a change of plans. Aunt Elizabeth had given orders to unhitch the horses; Uncle Guy was sick. Aunt Elizabeth thought he had a slight chill, which a little rest and a few precautions would cure. Three days later, alas, Uncle Guy was at death's door. Pneumonia had drained all the strength of his constitution, unused to the rigors of a European climate.

It was my first real encounter with death. True, my infant sister Rose had died, years before, in Martinique. But I had been very young then, and my parents had shielded me from the tragedy. Now, in this strange land, in these unwelcome surroundings, there was no question of my being spared. Nothing could come between me and my aunt's ordeal and I was well placed to experience the full extent of our situation. Uncle Guy was dying, and leaving us defenseless and alone in the middle of nowhere. The doctor who was called proved to be a pompous and ignorant man, powerless to alleviate Guy's suffering. As for the innkeeper, he cared far more for the reputation of his house than for his guests, and tried to force us to take our dying man away. Failing that, he managed to extort, on various pretexts, large sums of money from Aunt Elizabeth.

And then one morning, after several days of struggle, I discovered a new element in this tragedy, its worst, its most shocking aspect: resignation. The room where Aunt Elizabeth watched over her husband already reeked of death. Both seemed to have accepted it, just as the priest, who was brought from a neighboring parish to administer the last rites, accepted it. Then came the end, the intolerable end. Despite the poverty of the setting, it was a solemn scene. Summoning his last reserves of strength, Uncle Guy gasped for breath. Yet he managed, with a terrible effort, to murmur a parting phrase to each of us. To me he said: "Always be good, always be generous, my child. Don't forget to be obedient to your aunt, and cherish her as she deserves to be cherished." Then he fell silent. Aunt Elizabeth moved closer to him and wordlessly, hand in hand, they waited for death.

My beloved Uncle Guy, that sweet and noble man, died on the

evening of January 2, 1786. His death left me bewildered, a prey to contradictory emotions, torn between grief and revulsion at the injustice of this death, of all death. And I was terribly puzzled by my aunt's attitude. It seemed to me that tears or cries or any manifestation of grief would have been preferable to the icy dignity with which Madame de Bellefonds faced her bereavement. She was by nature a maternal and loving woman; and now her eyes remained dry, and, for the first time, her behavior felt strange and foreign to me.

I did not know yet—or perhaps I had forgotten—that the aristocracy did not think it proper to exhibit one's emotions, particularly if they were deeply felt. In any case, I was lost and alone. During those days filled with silence and sadness I wore mourning, it seemed, for my childhood, for my illusions.

My last memories of Montauban are quite as grim: a hasty makeshift funeral was held at dawn in an empty, freezing church. A humble coffin of raw wood, a procession consisting of a few bowed servants, Aunt Elizabeth, stiff in midnight blue silk, the grotesque negotiations with the priest, who did not want a foreigner in his graveyard. The service over, with Aunt Elizabeth still in her ball gown, now her widow's weeds, we climbed into the carriage and, under torrential rain, left Montauban forever.

Of course there was no longer any question of taking our time to see France. We wanted to join Marie-Anne as soon as we could. It took us ten days to retrace our steps to Bordeaux, and again as long to reach Nantes.

The reunion of mother and daughter, both of them widows, was not the happy occasion they had awaited for more than a year. It was not joy but grief which threw them into each other's arms on the steps of Hotel Montfraboeuf, Marie-Anne's house. Although life had not spared her, her features remained unchanged in their reflection of a noble soul. At twenty the widow of Count Montfraboeuf and now in mourning for her father, Marie-Anne nevertheless exuded a tranquil strength, a sort of solace to which Aunt Elizabeth and I gratefully abandoned ourselves.

And so, day by day, I regained spirit and confidence under Marie-Anne's wing. Her elegantly built mansion stood behind the old cathedral, on a long promenade bordered by lindens. Inside, her furnishings were the latest in refinement. From story to story, from room to room, there was nothing but neoclassical woodwork; draperies, curtains, and portieres of red and blue and gold damask, white on gold, yellow on yellow, green on green; gilded furniture, marquetry, and precious bronzes from Paris. From the dressers, tables, and mantelpieces rose a forest of delicate porcelain—Sevres, Meissen, China, East India Company. In the big parlor I found myself in front of Marie-Anne's portrait by Madame Vigée-Lebrun, the Queen's official portraitist.

The luxury dazzled us. Never, I told cousin Marie-Anne, had I imagined such an extraordinary assemblage of riches. She smiled, and said:

"And I am neither the only one, nor the richest. The whole of Nantes is awash in gold!"

"Is Brittany really that prosperous?"

"On the contrary. Brittany is still one of the most impoverished provinces of the realm, dear Aimée—but Nantes, the old capital, has recently become the world headquarters of the slave trade."

"Do the slaves my father buys travel through here?"

"Of course. Sometimes I wonder how God looks upon the buying and selling of human beings . . . and yet our holy mother the Church condones the trade in pagans."

"Is all of Nantes's prosperity due to the slave trade?"

"And to related industries. Here are made all the trinkets for the African kings who sell their subjects to European traders. And the construction of a new factory or warehouse in the low city is inevitably followed by that of a new mansion on the hill. Prosperity is remodeling our old town."

I could see that Marie-Anne was right. The dark medieval streets that wound around the cathedral were being gutted and replaced with wide and airy planted boulevards. These were lined by vast houses of white stone, hung with rococo balconies.

In spite of its splendors, Nantes did not truly seduce me. Perhaps my reticence had something to do with its pale walls, its gray cobblestones, its slate roofs, its winter mists; all this contrasted sharply with the highly colored, exuberant landscapes I had always known.

After taking us around the city in an effort to console and entertain us, Marie-Anne invited to her house our Nantes kin. The family gossip and familiar stories at these reunions with her sisters and cousins did much to revive Aunt Elizabeth. It was said that the handsome Chevalier François de Laurencin, whose constant attendance I had noticed, was quite in love with Marie-Anne. The old ladies chattered away, and whenever a particularly spicy tidbit was served up for their enjoyment, their murmurs intensified, until they sounded like wasps swarming frantically around a honey cake. I would draw closer, perk up my ears, and, unnoticed, catch upsetting little stories as they flew by. "Poor Josephine! I must say that her husband, that Alexandre de Beauharnais, is a sorry character. What, haven't you heard? But her misfortune must be the worst-kept secret in the world, my dear. . . . Besides, it was clear from the start that . . . very handsome, yes, but worldly, capricious, dissolute. . . . Sometimes he drowns her in passionate letters and at other times he insults her grossly. Not to mention his roving eye, my dear—oh, yes, very unfaithful. They say he even keeps a . . . *creature.*"

And, passing from the particular to the general, the conversation would turn to affairs of state. It was the time when the affair of the Queen's jewels had reached such proportions that the scandal threatened to shake the monarchy and blemish Marie-Antoinette, that queen so exposed to court intrigues and already soiled by all sorts of suspicious rumors and slander. A high-flying adventuress, Countess de la Motte, who had pinched the most expensive necklace in the world . . . A cardinal, the great chaplain of France, arrested in the Palace of Versailles itself . . . And behind the scenes a magus—Cagliostro—affiliated with secret societies . . . A sensational case. The French aristocracy was delighted by the Queen's troubles, and more or less openly stoked the fires of scandal.

Then the conversation at Marie-Anne's would veer back to the particular, which, I confess, interested me more than "the case of the Queen's jewels." "Do you know that Josephine's husband, handsome Alexandre, has become involved in it himself? There he is, making speeches, demanding limitations on the King's power, a constitution in the British manner. . . . I mean, really, my dear, what next?" But the sorry state of the kingdom did not prevent them from nibbling at the dainty little pastries they were served, nor from biting a few backs while they were at it. I was aghast at what I had just heard about Josephine. Alexandre de Beauharnais, her unworthy, unfaithful husband—might he not be that man whose tragic death Euphemia had predicted, one lovely morning in the summer of 1781, at Croc-Souris?

But I must have been by nature a carefree young girl. It seemed that I always cheered up and shed my somber thoughts. Besides, there was always Marie-Anne's support. She continued to provide us with ceaseless distractions in order to amuse us and make us forget the dramatic circumstances of our arrival in France. After inviting half of Nantes in to her house to meet us, she drew us out again to meet Nantes. She wanted us to see a play at the Nouveau Théâtre. I had already heard a good deal about Saint-Huberti, the most celebrated actress in the realm. That evening she was to play Racine's Phèdre. I listened anxiously to the debate on the suitability of taking a girl of my age to the theater. Luckily Marie-Anne was on my side, and in the end she prevailed.

Long before the curtain went up I was already wide-eyed, admiring the theater's giant portico, the extensive gilding, the frescoes, the Nantaises' naked shoulders and their lovely dresses and jewels. During the performance I felt myself transported by Racine's verse, and fascinated by Phèdre's destiny. But Saint-Huberti's acting disappointed me; I thought it overdone, and her makeup excessive.

Was it that night, my first night out at the theater, that I was accosted? It happened during the intermission. Marie-Anne had fallen into conversation with an acquaintance, and for a moment I was left alone, absorbed in contemplation of one of the frescoes.

"Are you an angel?" I heard. "A sylph? I beg you, miss, which are you?"

A lord, comfortable and elegant, dressed in the latest English fashion—all the rage in France at the time. His enticing smile retained a trace of innocence, but the piercing and yet glaucous blue gaze transfixed me. Having startled me into utter paralysis, he pressed his advantage: "Would you allow me to be your guide, my child?"

I was still too astonished to react.

"Will you allow me to invite you to supper after the play?"

I searched desperately for an answer, and found only a weak excuse. "I shall have to ask my cousin. . . ."

"Then ask her, miss, ask her—but accept my invitation."

It was then Marie-Anne intervened and saved me. "It ought to be clear to you, sir, that the child is far too young to accept invitations . . . and the attentions of strangers." Thereupon she dragged me away with unaccustomed abruptness.

Later I learned from Marie-Anne that he was Saint-Huberti's husband, a sort of adventurer, a man with a reputation throughout Europe for intrigue. It was said he corresponded with the King of Sweden, with the Queen of Naples, with the Russian Emperor. Count d'Antraigues, I confess, made me daydream. Thinking back, some thirty years later, I can gauge the innocence of the child I was.

After a few months of this life spent between social events in Nantes and short trips in the surrounding countryside, Marie-Anne must have thought that the desired results had been obtained. Her mother had overcome her grief, and I was no longer the little savage who had arrived on the *Vendée Royale* that spring. Now she found me sufficiently adapted to civilization to put me in the hands of the nuns who would undertake to finish my education.

The Convent of the Visitation had been built in the middle of the previous century. Its various wings were harmoniously disposed around lovely flower-planted courtyards, and its cloisters were conducive to solitary walks and meditation. The dormitories where the younger girls slept, like the bedrooms reserved for the older ones, were spacious and gaily decorated, with blue or pink printed wallpaper depicting pastoral scenes. There was only one problem: what to do about Zinah. The rules of the convent did not allow a governess to stay on at her charge's side, and I categorically refused to be separated from her. Endless negotiations followed as we tried to find a compromise suitable to both sides. Finally Mother Marie-Agnès suggested that Zinah be hired as a gardener's aide; she would sleep in a little pavilion at the end of the vegetable garden, and would be allowed to attend my private lessons. As for the rest, Zinah and I knew very well that we would break all these rules, and that she would slip into my dormitory as often as possible to kneel by my bed and whisper late into the night.

Mother Marie-Agnès was a friend of Marie-Anne's, and the latter had specifically entrusted me to her care. Like most of the nuns, she was of noble birth, and nobility was as much an attribute of her soul as of her blood. Her extreme thinness exaggerated her height, and the deep blue of her eyes was enhanced by a ruddy complexion. Her clipped accent, utterly unaffected, would have made her seem distant had she not been so accessible and understanding. She was by nature hard on herself and lenient with others, and her piety was too sincere to be stained with intolerance. Although she had none of the frivolity of the worldly, fashion-conscious nuns around her, she maintained friendships outside the convent and kept abreast of events in the world at large. We made friends immediately.

The convent's schedule was fairly strict. We were up at seven in winter, six-thirty in spring. After hasty ablutions we said our prayers, ate breakfast, went to mass. Classes began at eight: catechism, Latin, spelling. Mostly it was a question of learning by heart, which bored me to tears.

Our daily activities were punctuated with devotions, with aspersions of holy water, and the rhythm of our lives was that of little future nuns. To this day I remember the prayer that droned on our lips for hour after hour:

> "Long live Jesus, of kings the King,
> Who redeemed me on the cross,
> Whose love and praise I sing,
> Whose life for us was lost . . ."

The convent's rule contained certain bans and restrictions which weighed on me heavily. It was forbidden, for instance, to keep animals of any sort, whereas in Martinique I had lived surrounded by my cats and my parakeets; I had even had my own anthill. There was an unwritten regulation forbidding close friendships between the girls, or between pupils and teachers. Those who showed too much interest in or affection for each other were immediately separated. Worst of all, I hated the drab uniform I was forced to put on every morning: a close-fitting pleatless black dress, lightened only by a white collar. My hair was held by a white headband, and a short veil, also white, covered my face.

The well-intentioned women who looked after us—and they were, after all, quite stupid—were more intent on saving our souls than on educating us. They would have been very happy to see some of us take the veil. Paradoxically, they tolerated and even encouraged the practice of giving "tea parties." I myself hated these affairs, and always had to be dragged to them by force. They were childish imitations of afternoon teas in worldly drawing rooms. The older girls, at the age of thirteen, were permitted to receive, under the watchful eye of one of the nuns, suitors approved by their parents. There was little for me to enjoy at these reunions, where the younger girls aped the older ones, who in turn played at being adults, and the main purpose was to gorge on pastries and chatter in the most frivolous manner imaginable.

Unlike some of the other nuns, Mother Marie-Agnès eschewed proselytizing. "A vocation," she would say, "is born spontaneously. It cannot be inspired by others." On the other hand, she would not allow me to avoid my companions' "tea parties." "You have no right to judge or to ignore the other pupils, even if they are less studious than you. Furthermore, these reunions will put you in the presence of good manners, which will do you no harm, and which, you will discover, are a useful and powerful weapon in life."

I proved to be a disciplinary problem, just as I had at the convent in Martinique. One day I was caught reading "The Story of the Good King Saint Louis" while the chaplain instructed us, at great length, on the topic of grace. "But I can't help it—I'm interested only in what I like" I told Mother Marie-Agnès.

"Even useless things are worth learning," she answered. "You set a bad example, and you were rude to our chaplain. You shall be punished"—and for a whole month she deprived me of visiting rights, which cost me dearly. I respected her for her strictness, and yet her compassion never failed to move me. Only she could tell when I was seized by homesickness and shed secret tears for my island and my family. Then she would become almost maternal. "I renounced my family when I entered the convent, and I severed all ties with them in order to devote myself entirely to the service of God. Perhaps that allows me to understand your nostalgia."

Whenever that nostalgia became too painful, I could always take refuge in the music room with Zinah, where Monsieur Jolibois gave me harp lessons. Monsieur Jolibois was an endearing sight, if not a particularly aesthetic one. He had a big nose on which rested several warts and a pair of glasses. His complexion was very blotchy, and whenever he became heated with emotion he would remove his wig, fan himself with it, and hang it on the doorknob. He wore, invariably, a spotted brown waistcoat and loose stockings which bunched up around his ankles. Monsieur Jolibois was not a paragon of elegance. He was nevertheless a competent and dedicated musician, who did his best to infect me with his passion for the harp. Furthermore, he did not restrict himself to music; he had certain proud pretensions to erudition, and did not hesitate to speak to me, between scales, of authors forbidden by the nuns and the chaplains. He even slipped me secret volumes by Voltaire, Montesquieu, Rousseau. I was such an avid reader that I accepted these loans with gratitude, not realizing what subversive intentions lurked behind my harp teacher's kindness. His task was made even easier by the fact that I had been brought up to respect certain institutions unconditionally. I had always been secluded within my own milieu, and remained completely ignorant of the world.

Unbeknownst to the nuns, my harp lessons gradually turned into conversations, in the course of which Monsieur Jolibois gave free rein to his revolutionary fervor and his penchant for sedition. It is strange to think that I had to meet a man who, after all, liked me personally, to learn about class hatred. "If I'd had a daughter I would have wanted her to be like you, Miss Aimée," he would say. And yet I remember vividly our last lesson: I can still see him gesticulating wildly, lost in his diatribes, practically foaming with bitterness. "The Queen is a hussy, and the King an imbecile ridden by the nobility, who seek only to grow richer on the sweat of the people."

I rose to my feet, enraged, and interrupted him. "Monsieur Jolibois, I forbid you to speak of Their Majesties in that way. As for the aristocrats, you know very well that many of them, including my aunts and my cousins, devote their entire lives to alleviating the sufferings of the poor."

Monsieur Jolibois's face turned scarlet. "The people have no use for your charity. The people spit on your charity. They've had their fill of hunger and oppression. May the day come soon when they rise against the aristocracy."

"On that day we will fight back," I said, causing Monsieur Jolibois to lose all restraint. He shook, he shouted, he stuttered with rage.

"We shall free ourselves of you. We'll force you to spit up everything you stole from us. We shall slaughter you down to the last one, you and your kind!"

Suddenly Monsieur Jolibois had begun to address me with the familiar *tu*. This lack of respect shocked me more than his fiercest threats. For a moment I was struck dumb. When I regained the use of my tongue, I said, "I see, Monsieur Jolibois, that I shall no longer need your lessons." He slunk away without another word, shuffling his music sheets clumsily.

Zinah was fuming. "We must tell Mother Marie-Agnès everything," she said. "He is a cruel man."

"He is an unhappy man," I answered, "and we shall not denounce him."

The doors leading out of the convent opened for me in the spring of 1788, when Marie-Anne's engagement to Chevalier François de Laurencin became official. She had decided to take me to

Paris, where she was to pick up her trousseau. Zinah, of course, was coming with us.

Paris welcomed us in the last rainy days of April. Since the hotels and inns were all filled with foreign visitors, it was decided that we would live at the house of our uncle Jean Dubuc de Ramville, who had recently retired to his lands in the provinces. Most of his furniture and servants had followed him to Touraine, so that our footsteps echoed sadly in the long corridors and almost empty rooms.

Soon after our arrival, Marie-Anne took me to see Mademoiselle Bertin, the most famous couturiere in Paris, if not in all Europe. Still young, but ambitious, authoritarian, and very hard-working, Mademoiselle Bertin had secured for herself the reputation of a tyrant in the most frivolous aspects of Parisian life. Through fashion she imposed her rule on all rich and titled women. I learned that the extraordinary hairstyles I had seen so poorly copied in Bordeaux originated from Mademoiselle Bertin's workshops. Her most recent decree was simplicity. She had decided to dress the ladies in ordinary clothes hitherto worn only by shopkeepers' wives and workers. No more satins or silks for the daytime, no more printed flowers—nothing but linens, striped cottons, bayadere. I myself could not resist the intoxication of those workshops, where clients' and seamstresses' little hands feverishly fingered rainbows of cloth, ribbons, and other accessories.

My attention was drawn away from this colored whirlwind by the presence of a beautiful little girl who was standing a little way off, crying silently. The woman with her—obviously her mother—had chosen for her a green dress which did not suit her at all. She made no protest other than her silent, resigned tears. But Mademoiselle Bertin, for whom bad taste was a crime, would not let this go by, and an argument flared up between the two women. Marie-Anne took advantage of their involvement to tell me surreptitiously that the loud mother was the Marquise de Coigny. The little girl's name was Fany. Rose Bertin, from the full height of her authority, claimed loudly that the green dress was completely unsuited to Fany. The furious Marquise de Coigny insisted that she knew better than anyone what her daughter should wear. Throughout the long argument over her small person, Fany continued to weep silently, and I felt deep sympathy and compassion for her.

Luckily things went differently when the time came to fit me. Marie-Anne wisely left the initiative to Mademoiselle Bertin.

"But she's lovely! Simply lovely! Now, girls, bring me the Toulouse model for the child!"

Mademoiselle Bertin seized me by the shoulders, and a swarm of dressmakers' apprentices surrounded me. Immediately I found myself wrapped in the folds of the Toulouse model, a very simple cotton dress checkered in periwinkle blue and forget-me-nots. The image in the mirror was most flattering, and I remember thinking that Rose Bertin's pretentious dictatorship might be justified by the sureness of her touch. Even Queen Marie-Antoinette consulted her daily and left in Bertin's able hands everything from the choice of her dresses to the smallest accessories of her outfits.

Marie-Antoinette—how much I had heard about that good-natured and inexperienced queen! Marie-Anne had promised to take me to Versailles, where I would be presented to the Queen. This honor, the prerogative of any young woman of noble birth, had been stripped of its formerly crushing protocol. The Queen now received her subjects informally in her retreat at the Petit Trianon.

It had been quite different a few years before, when solemn presentations, huge balls, and masquerades were daily fare at Versailles. But the present rulers, who were more timid and less social, had put an end to such luxurious pleasures, and the nobility had practically abandoned the palace in its search for entertainment; so much so that when at last I saw it, I had the feeling I was entering Sleeping Beauty's castle. We met only a few sleepy footmen and idle courtiers. The Queen, we were told, could be found, as usual, at the Petit Trianon. There we faced no guards, no gates—just a gentleman who emerged from a thicket and politely asked us for our names. We were indeed awaited. Madame de Villeneuve, a distant cousin of ours who was a lady-in-waiting to the Queen, had secured an audience for us. It was she who guided us through the peaceful alleys of the park, spouting advice and recommendations all the while. I don't think I have ever again been as nervous.

At last, at a bend in the path, we came to a modest but elegant pavilion: the Petit Trianon. A few steps, a dollhouse's vestibule, a door swinging open. We stood on the threshold of an unpretentious drawing room, simply furnished and rather small, almost austere except for the abundance of flowers; exuberant bouquets covered every table. A score of men and women chatted informally, the men dressed in unembroidered cloth, the women in plain hostess gowns.

Madame de Villeneuve bowed before a woman in white sitting at a loom. "Madame, would Your Majesty allow me to remember Countess Montfraboeuf to her."

Despite the simplicity of her attire, despite her thirty-three years of age, Marie-Antoinette outshone all the woman around her, including those who were younger and more beautiful than she. It was, I think, that extraordinarily fresh complexion, that blend of natural splendor and welcoming grace which made her so radiant, and the melancholy gaze of her blue eyes that made her so seductive.

She interrupted her work at the loom, turned to Marie-Anne, and said, "Madame de Montfraboeuf, I was as sad upon hearing of your husband's death as I am pleased now to hear of your engagement. May you be happy. . . ."

Marie-Anne bowed respectfully, and spoke to the Queen: "Madame, would Your Majesty add to her kindness by allowing me to introduce my young cousin, Aimée Dubuc de Riverie?"

I stepped forward and, as was the custom, curtsied deeply and began to reach for the hem of her dress. But the Queen interrupted this gesture and held out her hand for me to kiss.

"Mademoiselle Dubuc de Riverie, I am told you come from Martinique. I have heard much about the beauty of your island, and I would so like to see it. . . . Unfortunately it does not seem likely that I will. But write to your parents and your friends and tell them that the King and I are grateful to the Frenchmen who maintain their country's prestige so far away across the seas. . . . Send them our wishes for health and prosperity."

The Queen awarded me one last smile. Then, after bowing again, we backed up to the door. The ordeal was over.

Outside again in the park, I felt relief slightly tinged with disappointment. Where was all the pomp I had expected? Instead I had found casual courtiers, few servants (there were more of them in attendance on us in Martinique than on the Queen of France), no precious objects, whitewashed paneling, ungilded square furniture. Marie-Anne's house seemed far more luxurious; it is true that starkest classicism was in fashion then, and that provincial cities were a little behind the times. Nevertheless my child's imagination did not think of such simplicity as befitting a queen. Marie-Antoinette's image was certainly not the one I would choose to project if one day, as Euphemia had promised, fate granted me a throne. . . .

I could not speak of my mixed emotions to Marie-Anne. She was a loyal soul who respected her queen without reservations, and my criticism would only have saddened her. It was not until a few days later that I was able to unburden myself—to Josephine, whom I had joined at last. Marie-Anne had refused to come with me. She was exasperated by Josephine's flightiness, the disorder of her life, her inability to make a decision. If she condemned Josephine's husband Beauharnais for abandoning her, she also criticized Josephine for her frivolity and her insatiable hunger for worldly pleasures. I tried to defend Josephine; to me she was more than a cousin—a faithful friend, a harmless, kind woman, incapable of meanness of any sort. Despite Marie-Anne's disapproval, I insisted on going to Fontainebleau, where Josephine rented a house, and I went there only with Zinah. Josephine's warm welcome convinced me that I had been right.

In spite of our long separation, we immediately regained the complicity and intimacy we had shared before, on the island. I told her how the Queen's lack of authority had upset me, how I had been surprised by the rustic life she led at the Trianon. Josephine did not agree with me, understanding as she did that a queen might want to spare herself some of the rigors of protocol, that she might prefer to be loved, or not enjoy the official aspects of her rank.

"But that is what being a queen is like!" I said. "And if she doesn't like her job, then she'll fail!"

The word "job" was perhaps not the perfect one, and Josephine, teasing, laughed. "And where did you acquire such rigid opinions, young lady?"

"Well, I've had enough time to reflect on the duties of a queen ever since . . ."

At last Josephine understood, and burst into laughter. "Oh, my dear mad little cousin. It's so nice to see you again! So you still think about all those fables. . . . How I envy you! Euphemia, the old witch, might have been right about you. In my case she was completely wrong. Life, alas, has taken care of *my* dreams. . . ."

There was no doubt that her current tribulations justified some bitterness. She had just separated from her husband, the unfaithful, unpredictable Alexandre de Beauharnais, and had been forced to take financial charge of her two small children, Hortense and Eugène. She lived as modestly as possible in Fontainebleau, but even so she could not help incurring debts. At one point there had been talk of her returning to Martinique with Hortense, but she had not been able to secure enough money to book passage.

"I should have kept my Englishman—you remember, William Fraser. Perhaps I would have been happier. But my family insisted that I marry Beauharnais—and then I was infatuated with him. I don't hold any grudge against him, but I am unhappy. It is true that I enjoy society, but once I dreamed of a peaceful life, with my children and a husband who would have loved me as much as I loved him. . . ."

Josephine's sadness, her resignation, her lack of bitterness, brought tears to my eyes.

"Don't cry, little Aimée. There are many who deserve your tears more than I."

There were—and they interrupted our conversations incessantly. Ladies of the impoverished provincial nobility and even ruined commoners often dropped in to visit—or rather to beg. Because she had been presented at court, and because she was on good terms with powerful people, it was universally supposed that Josephine wielded great influence. She promised each petitioner that she would write to Versailles to put forth a request—and she fulfilled her promises. Because she came from the West Indies, it was thought she was rich. Discreetly she slipped borrowed sovereigns into the hands and pockets of her visitors, and had others distributed to the poor who came and went in her pantry. It is true that Josephine could not do without company, but her generosity under strained circumstances moved me deeply. Perhaps it was that very virtue which enabled her to maintain her constant high spirits. She flitted gaily from guest to guest, and burst into laughter at their slightest show of wit.

"Life is always beautiful, little Aimée," she whispered.

"Life is always beautiful," grumbled Zinah when we left Fontainebleau. "Perhaps your cousin would think otherwise if she didn't have the Chevalier de Coigny for her lover."

"Good for her if she has a lover," I answered. "And all the better if he's young and handsome. Josephine has never harmed anyone, and she deserves all the solace she can have. And be quiet, Zinah. Don't bother me with the gossip you pick up in Nantes."

The weeks came and went. Every day Marie-Anne postponed our return to Nantes. Endless shopping and fittings filled our days. In June a heat wave swept over Paris. The house was so stifling that one night, after dinner, Marie-Anne suggested we go out for a stroll. She wanted to see the Palais-Royal gardens at least once before leaving Paris. These gardens, which belonged to the Duke of Orleans, were open to the public, and it was said they were the meeting place of the most fashionable society.

We had to reconsider this opinion as soon as we stepped through the gates to the Palais-Royal. It was indeed a meeting place—but the fauna was somewhat strange and unexpected, and even rather alarming. It seemed to be not the most elegant but the loosest society, corrupt noblemen, great ladies in search of young flesh, dandies avid for gold, foreigners on flings, idlers looking for adventure, and streetwalkers whose names and rates were available at the entrance. Every shaded corner sheltered brief encounters which were then pursued in neighboring rooms. Everywhere there were whispers, laughter, silhouettes entwined beneath the trees. As if drawn out by the heat, the crowd milled around the cafés, the shops, the restaurants. Just as we began to realize that we didn't belong here at all, I was jostled in the crush, separated from Marie-Anne, drawn on by the current. Luckily Zinah could still see me, and she elbowed her way through the throng, coming to my rescue just as three men encircled me. The crowd was so thick that we couldn't get away from them, and suddenly they began to assault us. One was a huge blond man who grabbed me by the waist and drew me against him, while his companion, a bearded man with a turban, stuck his huge hands on Zinah's breasts. The third one, a shadow dressed in black, watched disapprovingly but without intervening. I was all the more horrified by the fact that our aggressors were laughing loudly and exchanging obscene comments. I shrieked, scratched, and struggled, and at the very moment when I felt my strength giving way, Marie-Anne appeared, her face twisted with rage, her voice scathing.

"Cousin! Your behavior is appalling! Would you let go of that young lady at once and disappear! Get out of my sight, Monsieur de Beauharnais!"

And, while speaking, she dragged me out of the arms of my assailant. Alexandre de Beauharnais, Josephine's notorious husband, was too drunk to realize what a scandal he was creating. A troop of mirthful bystanders had collected around us. A clear, firm voice rose from the crowd.

"I think it would be wiser to move on, Viscount Beauharnais."

The new arrival was an extremely elegant young man with a haughty smile and expressionless blue eyes. Poised delicately on his arm was the most marvelous-looking creature I had ever seen, a very young woman whose angelic face seemed to float above a cloud of pale muslin. Our three aggressors, led by Beauharnais, gave up and vanished into the throng. The gentleman who had rescued us bowed gracefully and introduced himself. "Mesdames, I am the Abbot of Périgord. Allow me to introduce Mademoiselle Lange, the incomparable ingenue of the stage. I am most upset that your stroll at the Palais-Royal should have been ruined by those characters. . . ."

We learned that the bearded man who had assaulted Zinah was none other than Ishak Bey, the Turkish ambassador in France. The man in clerical garb was called Pierre Ruffin. He served as guide to the ambassador and spy to the French government. "The Turkish ambassador a companion to Beauharnais's debauchery? Is it possible?" asked Marie-Anne.

The Abbot of Périgord explained: "Ishak Bey has long been a favorite of Crown Prince Selim. He is in disgrace now, and has been sent away as ambassador. But diplomacy, as I'm sure you've noticed, interests him less than other activities. . . . And now, Mesdames, allow me to escort you from this place to a safer one."

The unpleasant incident at the Palais-Royal marked the end of our stay in Paris. After that Marie-Anne had only one thought—to go back to Nantes and her fiancé.

On our way there we stopped at Chissay, near Amboise, at the country estate of our uncle Jean Dubuc de Ramville. We were received into a large and comfortable house by a man who, if he had indeed retired from the world, was nonetheless welcoming. Immediately upon meeting him I was impressed by his physical and moral stature, and by the wisdom of his words. He was a sort of Epicurean philosopher who observed the world from afar with the advantages of perspective and a keen analytic mind. Never, in Paris or in Nantes, had I heard such lucid, perceptive, and courageous opinions as those he voiced during that dinner which we ate in the company of his son, Louis François, and his daughter, Desirée. They were for the most part the opinions of a pessimist, for my uncle Jean Dubuc deplored the insouciance of the French aristocracy, which was then enjoying life to the full, unable to recognize the dangers looming over them. "We are headed for troubled times. Great upheavals, unpredictable phenomena, are about to take place, and meanwhile the ruling nobility thinks of nothing but pleasure and intrigue."

"Do you think, Uncle, that troubles could erupt at Versailles, or in Paris?" asked Marie-Anne.

"Not only in Versailles or Paris—in all of France, dear child. And believe me, the best thing you can do as far as Aimée is concerned is send her back to her parents in Martinique. . . ."

At the mention of Martinique, young Louis François piped up to say that if need be he would escort me there. The adults smiled, and while I blushed to the roots of my hair, Louis François smothered me with an eloquent gaze.

In response to Marie-Anne's curiosity, my uncle drew up a severe portrait of the young man who had rescued us at the Palais-Royal. "The Abbot of Périgord! A rascal, as corrupt and depraved as they come. But one has to admit he is highly intelligent and remarkably able. With his cynical wit and his passion for politics, he'll go far. And I must say that the times we are living in seem to favor the ambitions of that sort of man. . . ."

But political considerations would not hold sway over more private concerns for very long in an adolescent mind. That evening I noticed that my thoughts fluttered around the handsome face of my cousin Louis Francois. No doubt the vehemence with which I protested Zinah's teasing remarks at bedtime indicated the turmoil in my mind.

"Well, Aimée, how do you like your fiancé?" she asked, while helping me to undress. To this annoying question I answered flatly—and quite stupidly—that since he was obviously not destined to rule any empire he held no interest for me.

And yet no matter what I told Zinah, my young cousin's homage had shaken me. No sooner was she asleep than I rose from my bed to question the mirror. Perpetually startled and lively blue eyes, a tiny round mouth, pale gold hair—were the character and sensuality evident in those features really mine? And this body, which the last three years had shaped into womanly form . . . It was Narcissus's delight, or that of any other young girl discovering, for the first time, her reflection, and the seductiveness of that reflection.

Where is he now, Louis François, after all these years? Is he alive? Is he dead? And what would my fate have been had I married him?

Enough of this. I have lived the way I planned to, and nostalgia is not something I like to wallow in.

The wedding of Marie-Anne de Bellefonds and the Chevalier de Laurencin was celebrated at Saint-Clément de Nantes on July 8, 1788. I was not a little proud to be asked to sign the parish register along with the other witnesses.

About a hundred guests had been invited to Marie-Anne's house after the blessing. It was an exceptionally clear and sunny day, and it was decided to walk to Hotel Montfraboeuf in procession rather than pile up in the coaches. We were a real country wedding party as we meandered through the narrow shaded streets, talking and laughing gaily. Led by the bride and groom, we emerged onto the sun-flooded promenade, to find it crowded with people. Workers, artisans, shopkeepers, tradesmen, costermongers had gathered there to listen to a skinny man perched on the statue of Jacques de Bourgues, Nantes's famous mayor. The orator was exhorting the populace to revolt:

"My friends, I repeat: Let us follow the example of the people of North America, who have rid themselves of tyranny. They have overthrown the British, who oppressed and exploited them. It is now our turn to rid ourselves of the princes who oppress us, and let us rid ourselves of their henchmen, the aristocrats. . . ."

Despite their surprise, Marie-Anne and her husband continued on their way without flinching, the wedding party in their wake. The crowd, curious but not hostile, drew back to let the procession pass—a peculiar sight, which lasted no more than a minute. Then, just as the crossing was about to end without incident, several coaches with emblazoned doors appeared at the other end of the promenade, surrounded by mounted guards. This was the Intendant of Brittany, Monsieur de Moleville, driving home with the Bishop of Nantes, Monseigneur de la Lorencie. The coaches, clattering down the promenade at high speed, headed straight toward the crowd, which suddenly abandoned the orator to throw itself before the horses, shouting slogans:

"Down with the Intendant! We want bread! Down with the ministers! Bread and justice! Death to the Intendant!"

The coaches slowed down; the guards, waving their sabers with one hand and trying to control their frightened mounts with the other, attempted to make way for them. Still we had to walk on through the enraged crowd without showing any fear. Several times the Intendant's coach was brought to a standstill. The Bishop then poked his head through the door and uttered a few words in an attempt to appease the crowd. First a tomato, and then an egg, burst on the prelate's lacework rochet, and his head withdrew hastily into the coach. Now the crowd grew even fiercer; shouts of rage burst forth from every mouth.

"Down with the Intendant! We want bread! Down with the Bishop!"

A guard, wrenched from his saddle, fell and slipped under his horse's hooves, sparking panic among his companions. There was a sudden flash of steel under the clear sky. One of the demonstrators, his face bloodied, fell to the ground with an endless, abominable shriek.

I was petrified with horror, unable even to run. A strong hand gripped my elbow, and a voice said, "Don't run—walk. If we look afraid, they'll tear us to pieces. You have to impress them. Stay calm."

The voice belonged to François de Laurencin. Having already led his young wife to safety, he had dived back into the throng to fetch me. Still gripping my arm firmly, he brought me to the porch of Hotel Montfraboeuf—in other words, to salvation.

A few moments later the entire wedding party was safely within the mansion. We crowded at the windows to watch the final debacle. A second demonstrator had been felled, and now the crowd dispersed in terror, dashing off the square and up the side streets and alleys, while the Intendant's train regrouped and rattled off toward the bishopric.

A deathly silence and stillness settled over the square. Had it not been for that terrible smear of blood blackening the stone, for that single saber and those three hats on the ground, one would have thought it had been a bad dream. Besides, everything within Hotel Montfraboeuf conspired to make one forget the incident. The reception was going full swing, and everyone made a point of displaying spirit and gaiety to fit the occasion. Only the service suffered somewhat from the recent drama: Some orders were misunderstood, and a few trays shook as they glided through the drawing room.

It was not until late at night that Hotel Montfraboeuf recovered its normal aspect. The guests had left; the rich scent of the lindens wafted in through opened windows. I was preparing for bed, utterly drained by emotion and fatigue, when Marie-Anne sent for me. I found her in her bedroom, wearing her wedding dress. She had discarded only her veil of Brussels lace; long diamond pendants still sparkled at her ears. She invited me to sit on the edge of her bed, gently drew me close to her, and after a moment's hesitation, she said:

"My little Aimée, I don't want to wait any longer to tell you of the decision I made a few days ago. I am going to send you back to your parents in Martinique. Our uncle Dubuc's advice alone already shook me, and what we saw today shows quite clearly that if such a demonstration is really called for, his suggestion is indeed the wisest."

Often had I dreamed of the moment when I would begin my return to Martinique. Now the moment had come and I no longer wanted to leave. I had grown attached to the gray streets of Nantes, to Marie-Anne. I had experienced moments of great fear during the riot, and yet I was ready to face any danger if it was one I could share with Marie-Anne.

She swept all my objections aside. "If you want to show me your affection and your gratitude, Aimée, obey me."

"Keep me just a little longer, then."

"No, Aimée, there is little time. I have booked passage for you on *La Belle Mouette*, which is to sail next month."

The emotion of the day had been too much for me. I began to cry.

"Don't be sad, Aimée. We'll be together again soon." But I knew that she herself did not believe it.

". . . together again soon." Mother Marie-Agnès, when I went to bid her goodbye, did not even attempt to make me believe any such thing. She approved of Marie-Anne's decision, but she made me understand that we would be apart for a long time, if not forever.

"Promise you will write us, Aimée. I have grown fonder of you than I expected to—more than I should have. Thinking of you distracts me from the service of God. Write me to send news of yourself, and also, if need be, to lean on my advice. You have always had my best wishes, and you shall have my attentive ear."

One month later to the day, I said goodbye to my family at the port of Nantes. Besides Marie-Anne and her husband, my aunt Elizabeth de Bellefonds had insisted on coming to see me off at the docks. I could have been one of the Three Kings, I was so laden with parcels, with gifts for those I was to rejoin in Martinique; and of course I was deluged with instructions:

"Don't forget to tell your mother that I've looked and looked for that silk she had asked for. I've sent her some moiré instead, I hope she likes it."

"When you come back next year, you must bring your little sister Alexandrine!"

How painfully they ring in my memory, those trivial, affectionate phrases, so absorbed in mundane cares. In retrospect, they show clearly the extent of our blindness, our incapacity to recognize the seriousness of our situation, to face the imminence of tragedy. Thus we laughed, and spoke of rags and returns and reunions, while I took leave of my loved ones forever.

And yet there was a lump in my throat, and I had to fight back tears. Was there within me, despite the general euphoria, an obscure premonition telling me that ties of love were being broken forever, that a certain part of my life had irremediably ended? I cannot honestly say that it was so; but I remember that despite Zinah's familiar and comforting presence beside me on the deck of *La Belle Mouette*, my heart grew heavy as I saw the coast of France draw away and disappear.

CHAPTER 3

THE THOUGHTS of passengers on a long sea voyage tend to center on the natural elements, the effects of which are so much more important to their lives than on dry land. Perhaps I was even more interested in the conditions of our crossing than the other passengers, since that old threat of a shipwreck still weighed upon me. I had questioned the crew as soon as we set sail: they predicted a smooth crossing of the Bay of Biscay, which was considered dangerous only at the equinox. There would be more to fear once we entered the Caribbean, which at that time of the year was prey to tornadoes and typhoons.

As predicted, it was very calm, and I waited. But this day, as we drifted down the coast of Spain, had been particularly stifling. We were facing La Coruña when the day began to wane; the air was heavy and still. I had gone out on deck, seeking a little respite from the mugginess below, and there I found the other passengers lost in admiration before a magnificent sky set ablaze by the setting sun. And then night fell all at once. In a few moments, without warning, the sky had filled with huge dark clouds. A brutal wind rose

41

over the water, and pelting rain bore down on *La Belle Mouette's* deck. Captain Dudeffand requested that the passengers regain their cabins; Zinah complied eagerly, livid with terror, pushing me before her.

There was no question of sleeping, because of the ship's incessant pitch and roll, because of the groans of the hull and the rigging, the crew's shouts, the thud of the waves throwing themselves at *La Belle Mouette* like battering rams. Any sort of rest was impossible.

I put out my lamp, fearing that burning oil might spill over and start a fire. It was pitch dark in the cabin, and I could see nothing except at moments when a bolt of lightning at the porthole lent an eerie flash of existence to our cramped quarters. All my faculties of perception seemed to have taken refuge in my hearing; I could hear the drumming of the rain, the harsh roar of the storm, the violent exchanges between sea and ship. I was terribly afraid. For years I had awaited the fulfillment of Euphemia's predictions eagerly; now I dreaded it. There was no comfort to be had from Zinah, who tossed back and forth on her bunk, moaning, reduced to total wretchedness by nausea.

Then the din of the furious elements was pierced by a hubbub of human voices, of shouts and anxious orders, of hurried steps in the passageways. I slid off my bunk and, balancing precariously on my feet, threw a cloak over the humid clothes I had lacked the strength to change. Thrown from wall to wall, pulling myself along by means of any handle or rope I could grasp in the dark, I left the cabin and headed down the passageway. I must have lost my footing a dozen times; but, guided by the voices of the sailors, I eventually found my way onto the deck. There I faced a staggering sight. Monstrous waves emerged from the darkness into the circle of the ship's lights a split second before bearing down on us with an infernal, terrifying roar, tossing *La Belle Mouette* about as if it were a nutshell. The ocean seemed an uproar of demoniacal rage, relentless in its efforts to destroy us.

The sailors rushed back and forth between the decks and the hold, but there seemed to be more panic than efficiency in their activity. Captain Dudeffand himself had lost the last traces of his geniality; noting my presence on deck, he barked at me to return to my cabin, then stalked off to his task, fierce and tense. Yet I remained where I was, gripping the guardrail, at once horrified and fascinated. I did not move until an old sailor dropped a few words in my ear as he rushed by: "There's a breach in the hold. We're sinking!"

He was right; in fact, the ship was already riding lower. I rushed headlong to my cabin, back to Zinah. I had no desire to see that last wall of water ride in, rear up, and swallow us—I preferred to die lying on my bunk, eyes closed, fists clenched. As *La Belle Mouette* slowly and inexorably opened herself to the sea, I began to say a prayer.

"Deliver me, O Lord, on the day of judgment, forgive me for my sins. . . ."

"Everybody on deck!" Someone pounded violently on the cabin door, forcing me to collect the last of my strength to shake Zinah, who was still moaning, awash in nauseous torpor. I pushed and pulled and dragged her up to the deck, where our unfortunate companions had already gathered—a pitiful little flock huddling together in utter horror and misery.

The depthless darkness of the night had given way to a dull, drab dawn, khaki in color. The gigantic waves, whipped and frothing in the wind, were the same unhealthy sulfurous shade as the sky. The shivering passengers, disfigured by terror, were gathered at the prow, all eyes turned to the same sight: a large ship dancing a few cables' lengths away. But we weren't at all sure she could save us. The swell was so strong there was no question of her coming alongside, and the only course open to us was the use of grapnels. The crews of both ships set to work on their respective decks. They were butted by the waves, knocked over, thrown against the bulwarks; crawling on all fours when they couldn't stand, they bled, sweated, and swore. At last, after numerous attempts, they managed to link the ships and began to draw them closer together.

The transfer of the passengers was a nightmare of disorder. Delivered from the terror of death into the panic of hope, they simply lost control. Men straddled the bulwarks at the risk of their lives; women, half paralyzed by their sogged petticoats, shrieked with terror. Nevertheless the rescue worked. Following the custom, Captain Dudeffand was the last to leave the ship, after the sailors. The lines linking the two ships were then severed with axes—just in time. *La Belle Mouette* was sinking fast; her deck was already submerged, and soon the poop disappeared. There was then a heartrending moment while *La Belle Mouette* seemed to hesitate between two waters, defying death with a last surge of will, her masts pointing straight to the sky. Finally she gave up the ghost; the masts toppled and the ship sank in a swirl, the waves carrying over to rock our new vessel.

La Belle Mouette's passengers—a helpless, dazed horde, still reeling from the experience—were taken in hand by the rescuers, who improvised comforts and bedding from the ship's limited resources. Finding my way down to the wardroom, I collapsed on a bench; I was so exhausted I was to sleep fourteen hours.

I awoke to find a haggard, rumpled Zinah watching over me, her features altered by fear and suffering. Hiccuping and heaving pitiably, she explained that we had been rescued by the *Aliaga*, a Spanish ship, about forty miles south of La Coruña. We were now bound for Palma de Mallorca, the capital of the Balearic Isles.

We were heading, then, in a direction exactly opposite to Martinique. But at least we were saved. For the next few days the *Aliaga* sailed under radiant skies, while the ports of the coast proceeded to starboard. I saw Cape Saint Vincent, Cádiz, and Gibraltar, the sight of which elicited long strings of disgusted oaths from the Spanish sailors. Questioned about this reaction, Captain Dudeffand explained that our hosts had still not resigned themselves to the British takeover of the rock seventy-five years before; Gibraltar remained a bone of contention between England and Spain. A quick glance over sleepy Cartagena, more or less abandoned since trade with the Americas had forsaken it for Cádiz, and again we sailed out into the open sea.

At last one morning we spotted Barbary Cape jutting out of Formentera, the smallest of the Balearic Isles. I learned, again from

Captain Dudeffand, that its peculiar name was justified by its position facing Africa's Barbary Coast, the lair of the Barbary corsairs.

Yet there seemed little danger of falling in with bad company, for we were almost home. Gathered together on deck, passengers and officers alike rejoiced at the prospect of reaching dry land. For us it was the conclusion of a trying adventure; for the Spaniards, the end of their voyage. Already the islet of Cabrera and Mallorca's Cape White and Cape Salinas had come into sight; Palma would appear within a half hour. But the wind, alas, was dying. The sails drooped, and the *Aliaga* now barely drifted over still waters. My impatience only increased, and I stalked up and down the deck, elaborating plans to get back to Martinique as quickly as possible: the first thing to do in Palma was to find a ship bound for Marseilles; there I could stay with our Saint-Aurins cousins while waiting to leave for Bordeaux; and at Bordeaux, I would have no trouble finding a ship setting sail for Martinique. . . .

"Sails astern!"

This shout from the topsail drained the entirety of the *Aliaga*'s population toward the stern. On the horizon one could make out three light ships. A second shout rose from the sailors' group, this one a strident cry from a knotted throat:

"They're Barbary corsairs!"

Once again a nightmare descended on the deck where I stood: anxious questions, orders, calls to action, a mad scramble from one end of the deck to the other and from the deck to the cabins. Contrasting cruelly with the frenzy aboard her, the *Aliaga* rested serenely on the calm water, rocking gently in the swell; the wind had completely subsided. Meanwhile the pirates' lighter frigates continued to draw up behind us, slowly but gaining nonetheless. One of them separated from the other two and began to describe a wide arc obviously designed to cut off the *Aliaga* from any possibility of escape.

Aboard the *Aliaga* there was nothing to do but await the inevitable. There were some, however, who refused, with all the energy of desperation, to admit it. Everyone was tensed to the breaking point. Total confusion reigned in our spirits, and each had a suggestion:

"We must fire the cannon to alert Mallorca!" "There is no cannon on the *Aliaga*, sir." "But we must organize a defense!" "Let's swim to the coast!" "What about sharks?" "Hide the women and children!" "Everybody in the dinghies while there's still time!"

But there was no time. We had to face the fact that nothing could save us any longer. When this was understood, the excitement abated. The rage of refusal gave way to tears and lamentations. In the midst of these unhappy souls I felt nothing but the numbness of fear. Everything conspired to rob the moment of all reality. The stillness of the sea, the welcoming coast so close by, the sweet glow of evening, the frigates' lazy, almost protective maneuvers—all these seemed the elements of a dream.

Suddenly a cannon volley, and then a second, rent the air—not simply a measure of intimidation, but also a kind of salute, a greeting of the hunter to its prey. Soon the frigates drew up alongside, one on either of the *Aliaga*'s flanks. The pirates leaped over the gunwales with simian agility, their sabers drawn, hollering savagely. This, like the cannon volleys, was designed to impress us, to render us powerless in the hands of fear. There was to be no resistance, not a drop of blood shed. The pirates seized the *Aliaga* with swiftness and ease, and immediately moved on to the next stage of the operation, which was conducted just as smoothly as the attack and was obviously quite as well rehearsed. The pirates' officers demanded and received the keys to our trunks and the ship's stores. A column of turbaned ants swarmed down belowdecks, to reappear, laden with assorted loot, a few minutes later. I recognized my traveling bag, my dresses, Zinah's calicoes. All this was carried out in calm and orderly fashion, without eliciting a single word of protest from the passengers. These last were then invited to come aboard the frigates riding alongside the *Aliaga*. During this transfer, directed by the pirates with broad operatic mimicry, I noticed a selection being made: the passengers, financially the better morsels, were gathered onto the pirate commander's frigate; the *Aliaga*'s crew, mere small fry, were herded onto the other.

We were immediately led before the commander of the pirate flotilla. A tall, gaunt man with a pointed goatee and liverish skin, he was enthroned on the forecastle, wearing a haughty and disdainful expression. A secretary-interpreter at his side translated his questions into an approximation of French, and then transcribed our answers in a thick ledger: name, age, place of birth, family, fortune. After the interrogation we were requested to place our money and valuables on the table, in exchange for which we were each given a receipt.

The organization and the precision of this ceremonial was most impressive. Piratry, as I discovered it here, seemed a sort of mobile administration as efficient as it was tried.

The wind rose—that treacherous wind which, three hours before, might have saved the *Aliaga* and her passengers. Naturally the pirates welcomed the sight of their billowing sails with shouts of joy. Left to our own devices, we watched the corsairs set to manning the ship, yelling encouragement to each other with two words which were taken up in echo by the crews of the four ships.

"El Djezair! El Djezair!"

"Algiers! They're taking us to Algiers," whispered Captain Dudeffand.

A few moments later the three frigates and the *Aliaga* turned about and, wind astern, sailed away from the coast of Mallorca, where the lights were coming on one by one. Those beacons were the last we saw of freedom.

To this day I shiver at the mere memory of that crossing and the conditions in which we made it. Each night we were crammed together in discomfort and promiscuity at the bottom of the hold and made to endure each other's snores and groans and lamentations, the smell of the piled-up bodies, the quarrels that broke out sporadically among the prisoners, the endless speculations as to what fate held in store for us in Algiers. Were we going to be sold as slaves, sent to the galleys, or merely thrown in prison to await payment of a ransom?

Huddled on the coils of rope I used for bedding, sick with anxiety and disgust, I would throw off Zinah's protective arm and stop up my ears so as not to hear the morbid refrains with which my companions distracted themselves from their misfortune. Captivity irritates the imagination, and especially that of prisoners grouped together under harsh conditions. It was like a never ending verbal delirium, a sort of contest of spirits bent on making the wildest predictions, on remembering terrifying accounts of captivity, on making pessimistic assertions.

"If only we could be lucky enough to cross another ship! We'd be saved!"

"God forbid! The pirates would drown us sooner than return us. Believe me, they wouldn't hesitate for a second if our rescuers were getting the better of them."

"There is nothing to hope for but lifelong slavery."

"But is there no ransom, no escape, no rescue?"

"Very rare . . . One never leaves the prisons of Algiers."

"And what about that Italian woman? They say she was so beautiful and so able that she seduced the Dey and even managed to go above his head and that of his ministers. After two years of captivity she was sent home with pomp and circumstance. . . ."

"Legends! Old wives' tales! Don't believe a word of it. The King of France wants to keep his privileged relationship with Algeria far too much to intervene. He'll make all the right noises, mind you; the consul at Algiers will very diplomatically lodge a protest with the Dey. But the Dey will turn a deaf ear, knowing very well that France will not compromise her political relations for a handful of her subjects. . . ."

"But who is this Dey, after all? Is he really so powerful that he can allow himself every whim with impunity?"

"I hear he's an old man, over eighty. Algeria is a Turkish province, and the Dey is nominally a vassal of the Sultan. Nevertheless he does as he pleases. He extorts from European states an annual payment, in exchange for which he promises not to kidnap their subjects. And woe to those who, like France, refuse to pay—heads fall easily in Algiers. Over there history is written with blood rather than rose water. . . ."

"Oh, enough! Enough, enough, for God's sake!"

It always ended that way. Someone's nerves would snap, and he would start screaming, and collective hysteria ensued. After which silence returned for a few instants. But silence, in that stuffy hold, among those bodies, seemed the hardest thing to endure. It soon became unbearable, so someone would say something—anything—and delirium would set in again.

In spite of my pitiful attempts to abstract myself from my surroundings and to resist despair, a few words returned again and again to harass my thoughts, bearing down on me like the blows of a hammer: slavery . . . to become a slave. Born and raised among slaves without ever truly reflecting on their state, I now seemed fated to know it as intimately as they. I saw Zinah with altered eyes: her existence had always been bonded to mine; she had left her native Martinique to follow me, she had lived all the events of my life, she had always been there behind me, with my shadow. To become a shadow—was that slavery? Not being able to claim ownership of one's own life?

"Tell me, Zinah, is one unhappy as a slave?"

I can still see poor Zinah when I asked her, point-blank, that unexpected question. She hesitated a moment, then answered softly: "It depends on the master, Aimée."

"Can a slave have slaves?"

"No, my pretty one; then she wouldn't be a slave."

"Then I'm going to lose you. They're going to separate us."

Zinah's hand traveled through the stinking, sweaty darkness of our cubbyhole and came to rest tenderly on my cheek, which was bathed in tears.

One morning pandemonium broke out on board our frigate. We had just emerged into the morning light, stiff and aching from another night in the hold, when a sail stood up on the horizon, dead ahead. Drawing closer, it proved to be a merchant ship flying United States colors. We were herded back to the hold, while the pirates prepared for battle in a frenzy of anticipation. Captain Dudeffand, who had taken me under his wing since the beginning of our troubles, had a few lugubrious comments to make:

"Those poor Americans are the Barbary corsairs' favorite prey.

They're new to these seas, they're not cautious enough, and they're easily caught. Furthermore, the corsairs are prodigiously annoyed by the way the country's leaders ignore them. Every time they try to force payment of a tribute they get a contemptuous silence for an answer. They don't take to it kindly."

Huddled in our jail belowdecks, tense and silent, we followed the course of the battle raging above our heads between pirates and Americans: savage yells, stampedes, cannon salvos which deafened us and shook the hull violently; then more shouts—of anger and disappointment this time—and then silence. That day the pirates were so furious at having missed their prey that they forgot to let us out of the hold, and we went twenty-four hours without food.

Our captors' mood allowing, we were normally fed twice a day. But our diet was hardly varied, and each meal was a pretext for the same invariable comic routine. Once the eternal couscous had been served, we would be offered various tasty side dishes at the highest imaginable price—mutton, vegetables, shrimp, spicy sauces; all had to be refused, for the simple reason that our money had been confiscated when the *Aliaga* was seized. Yet the scene would be repeated, inexplicably, at the next meal.

One can get used to almost anything; even in the most desperate situations one can always draw upon some inner resource to soften the blows of fate. And after a few days of this existence, I had found a way of stealing a few moments each evening from the horror of the hold, where my companions wallowed in misery. At nightfall I would slip, sight unseen, to the foredeck to enjoy a little peace. We prisoners were normally not allowed there, but I knew how to make myself tiny and almost invisible. There were always a few sailors there, sitting in a circle on the boards, smoking their hookahs. Almost every night the same sailor, an enormous black man, would begin a song, soon to be joined by the others. I understood none of the words, but felt all too acutely the nostalgia of the melody. It would seem to me then that these brutal men, throwing their joint voices toward the evening sky, were gripped by a sort of melancholy, a universal feeling; their song recalled memories of home and hearth and tenderness, and tears would come to my eyes as I imagined the plantation on Martinique, my room, my parents, all that I knew I would never see again.

There were a few other exceptional moments, which happened at the pirate commander's initiative. His mood mellowed as we approached Algiers, and he adopted a curiously amiable attitude toward us. Nothing could surprise us anymore, not even the social graces of a pirate chieftain entertaining aboard his ship the captives he was about to sell into slavery.

Thus one afternoon I was invited, with a few others, to his cabin. He served us tiny cups of piping hot green coffee from Yemen. With the aid of his interpreter, he launched into interminable stories of his adventures and exploits in war. But his narrow cabin was infernally hot, and boredom and sleepiness had already begun to make us nod, when a sudden shout snapped us out of our lethargy.

"El Djezair! El Djezair!"

Algiers was in sight. The pirate commander leaped to his feet, followed by the interpreter, and headed for the deck. We stayed close behind them, delighted to be freed of his hospitality and avid for fresh air. Over the water lay a sight of indescribable beauty. Dropped in the center of the graceful arc of its bay, Algiers rose in immaculate white tiers to the Kasbah, the fortified city, itself crowned by a fort over which flew the green standards of Allah. Beyond the walls one could see other whitewashed cities of lesser importance scattered among the deep green of the orchards. The hills, sloping gently to the sea, were planted with vineyards; ocher fields studded with prickly pear trees shimmered under the sun.

There was a tremendous bustle in the port toward which we raced. Feluccas, cutters, small craft of all sorts, slipped between three-masted merchantmen and long, flat galleys gliding over the water. From a distance it looked like a marvelous nautical ballet designed simply for the pleasure of the eye.

We were met with the triumphal greeting which the population of Algiers reserves for its corsairs, its purveyors of slaves and income. A noisy crowd had converged from all quarters of the city to the docks along which the three frigates and the *Aliaga* moored. They cheered the captain and his officers at length, and seemed already to be weighing us with their eyes.

Aboard the frigates the time for kindness and courtesy had passed. The commander barked orders right and left. As for the crew, they did not conceal their joy to be home, and I noticed with astonishment that even the prisoners seemed pleased to reach port.

I was to have learned much about the complexities of human nature in these exceptional circumstances, among people who had just lived through shipwreck and capture in rapid succession and yet regained dry land—even enemy land, where nothing but outrage and ill use awaited them—with relief. That day, standing by the white cheek of Algiers, I told myself that each and every moment of life was worth living.

CHAPTER 4

Night was just falling as our procession started on its way, walking between two hedges formed by the mob of Algiers. Guided by our guards' torches, which illuminated laughing faces and groups of spectators gathered on their balconies, our passage sparked cheers and shouts of joy as we climbed the steep and narrow streets of the town. Had we not known the reason for their curiosity and their elation, we might have been taken in by the Algerians' greeting, and forgotten that in their eyes we were no more than merchandise.

It was pitch dark when we reached our destination, a tall building topped with numerous cupolas, like a Byzantine church. It was in fact a former hammam, a Turkish bathhouse, now transformed into a slave jail. We were immediately taken in hand by the head warden, a tall, gangling black man, who led us through a maze of rooms and courtyards to the place where we were to sleep. It was a large marble-walled room, bare except for a derelict fountain and its basin. Ratty straw pallets were thrown on the ground for us, and we had no sooner sat down than our first meal arrived—yet again the eternal couscous, which I eyed sadly while the warden loudly encouraged us to feed ourselves. "Come on, come on, eat! You have to recover your strength!"

Our jailer's rough solicitude must not be attributed to any goodwill on his part; his interest lay in keeping us as healthy and well-looking as possible, so that he would get a good price for us.

Tomorrow ... My harassed companions, their hunger sated, collapsed on their pallets and, for the most part, fell asleep. I myself could find no rest. The meal over, the warden had taken his guards and his pots and his torches, leaving us to the unsettling shadows of this sepulchral room, lit only by a filigreed lamp. Its aqueous light disturbed me, kept me tense and awake. It was then they appeared, those nightmarish visions, more larvae-like than human, ragged, emaciated, sightless creatures who drifted in among us, contemplated us wordlessly for a moment, and drifted away into darkness again, a phantom horde. When they vanished I was seized by uncontrollable tremors. Once this fit of nerves passed, however, I felt only curiosity: I had to make sure, I had to find out whether that pitiable herd belonged to the world of the living or to that of spirits.

I rose to my feet, walked cautiously to the porch where I had seen them disappear, and traveled for a moment through darkness before reaching the main room of the hammam; and there they were, crouched in silence on the steps and benches where the bathers had once taken their ease.

"Come for a visit, little one?"

I gave a start. The words had been spoken in perfect, accentless French. The man was old and wizened; he sat quietly on a nearby bench. I noticed his smooth white hands, which he held flat on his bony knees.

"Yes, I'm French—does that surprise you? Or perhaps I had better say that I *was* French. You lose everything here, down to your very identity, your nationality. I was also a nobleman. A nobleman! Would you believe it?"

A horrible wretched laugh tore at his throat. It made me shiver.

"But now I've been the valet of one of the Dey's secretaries for forty years. In your opinion . . . would you still call me a nobleman? You know, when I was taken by the pirates I had a daughter about your age—a little younger, perhaps."

"Your family didn't ransom you?"

"How would I know? Perhaps they never found out what had happened to me."

"If my family doesn't ransom me, what do you think they'll make of me? A cook? A maid?"

He laughed his horrible bitter laugh again. It seemed that his laughter sullied me, spattered me with mud.

"Oh, don't worry about that. With that pretty little face of yours, that lovely skin . . . they wouldn't dream of making you a cook. It's off to the harem for you."

"The harem?"

"Yes, the harem—where every pious Muslim keeps his wives and his concubines."

I didn't dare ask any more questions. Annoyed by my silence, the hateful old man went on:

"Oh, yes, my little one, you're going to become an object of pleasure. And don't delude yourself: when a woman enters the harem, she never leaves it again, not until she dies. But with a little luck, you shall fall to a lord who is neither too old nor too ugly. That is what I wish for you, dear child."

I stepped back, wanting only to escape this hideous wretch and his abominable laughter, to run back to the others. I searched frantically for Zinah in the dark, threw myself in her arms, and, sobbing and shaking, told her of my encounter with the old man.

"Oh, come, my lovely, have you forgotten that old witch Euphemia David's predictions? She foresaw all this, and now I say it too: You shall be the wife of a great ruler who shall love you."

Marvelous Zinah! Now it was she who recalled that prediction, in order to console me. But that night, not even the promise of a fabulous destiny could have lightened my grief. Trapped in that sinister hole, with only the living dead for companions, I would have given anything to take refuge in my mother's arms.

Dawn found us standing nervously around the warden, who told us we were to be taken to the administration building, to be submitted to the Dey's judgment.

Again we walked through the city, again escorted by large crowds. Halfway there, we crossed a group of slaves on their way to building sites, and I noticed that they were chained together. But that was nothing to the sight that awaited us in front of the administration building: six freshly cut heads, buzzing with flies, neatly lined up on the ground.

"Bad ones! Rebels!" explained the warden.

I had to lean on Zinah as we stepped over them, unable to avoid walking in the dried blood; my legs had gone completely limp.

We were then left outside the building, abandoned to the curiosity of the bystanders. Shouting and gesticulating, they walked right up to us, touched us, felt our limbs, exchanged comments and opinions and argued about our worth. We were examined and discussed like animals on their way to the slaughterhouse, and it was an animal fear that took hold of us. We remained there for six hours, parked under the scorching sun, delivered to the moods and speculations of the Algerian crowds.

At noon we were brought into the administration building's first courtyard, a vast sandy esplanade bordered on three sides by whitewashed arcades. Here we were awaited by a different throng, composed of notables, merchants, and pirate officers. The colorful clothes of the seamen clashed with the drab brown and gray djellabas of the local burghers. One heard all sorts of tongues spoken—the administration's Turkish, religion's Arabic, the natives' Berber and Kabyle, and Spanish, Italian, Maltese. The Keznadar, the minister of finance, took his place on the dais with the naval minister and a swarm of scribes leaning over thick ledgers. A small red-faced man gesticulated before this assembly, protesting vehemently; he was the British consul, trying to obtain freedom for a group of British prisoners. Eventually he seemed to get his way, for his compatriots were pushed off in his direction. This sight sparked a brief surge of hope in us, soon to be disappointed: No representative of our government came to plead for us when the French captives from the *Aliaga* were paraded before the notables. A first selection was made immediately: all the *Aliaga*'s sailors were grouped together and packed off to the slave galleys. The rest of us were taken to be seen by the Dey. Once more our miserable column shuffled off, to yet another courtyard, this one a little smaller, where again we waited with no respite from sun or anxiety.

We were no longer in any state to react when the Dey arrived with the Keznadar, surrounded by armed guards and eunuchs in resplendent uniforms. The procession of automatons started all over again: Each prisoner was called forward in turn; a secretary tersely muttered the information recorded in his lists; the Dey pronounced his sentence—slave market, ransom, and so on. Then the next one was shoved forward. I grew afraid as my turn approached; but I had promised myself to cling to my dignity no matter what happened.

Therefore I stared the Dey right in the eye when I took my three steps forward. Baba Mohammed had piercing eyes, set so deeply in his face that I could only guess at their color. His long wispy beard and all his clothes, from his turban to his slippers, were white. Despite his great age, a feeling of authority and power emanated from the slightest of his movements.

As I stood before the Dey, the pirate commander walked up to him and whispered at some length into his ear, bowing and scraping all the while. Baba Mohammed still gazed at me pensively, and it was only with great effort that I returned his stare. At last the Dey emerged from his meditation and answered the pirate commander briefly without even looking at him. The pirate commander bowed a last time and withdrew. The Keznadar stepped down from the dais and motioned to the guards, who surrounded me and led me away. At that point I lost all resolve—I was being separated from the others, separated from Zinah. Zinah! I called to her in spite of myself; and when I turned around, it was to see her standing before the Dey, to hear his laconic order: "Slave market," translated for me by the Keznadar. I called her again. She tried to run after me, but the guards restrained her and brutally pushed her back. I was led inside the palace. It was over.

So Euphemia David had been right.

The old French slave had been right.

Fate had got the better of me: I had just been given as a present to a man—to a ruler, to the Dey of Algiers, as the Keznadar proudly told me.

How could I ever have felt any joy at the prediction of such a fate? Was it true that for years I had hoped for what I now faced? They had all been right when they told me I was mad.

I was taken away, having abandoned all thoughts of resistance. We walked along wide corridors giving onto tiny rooms, up and down stairs, through courtyards, through suites of deserted rooms, to arrive at last in a long and narrow patio. There, before an imposing portal, I was delivered to an old black man who weakly waved an ivory-handled flyswatter before his wrinkled features, his eyes sad under drooping lids. With a single gesture, he motioned me to follow him, and guided me through another maze of corridors and stairways and courtyards, until we reached a ridiculously low doorway which led into a large, high-ceilinged, whitewashed room. Heavy carpets covered the floor in loud colors, and the only furniture consisted of a few cushions and some copper trays resting on three-legged tables. A leaded-glass door opened on a tiny terrace. Leaning over, I could see only blinding whitewashed walls reflecting the sun, and roofs of varnished tiles.

This, I thought, must be the harem the old Frenchman had threatened me with, the prison I would not leave until my death.

The old black man left me after giving the key several turns in the lock. For the first time I was imprisoned alone. Never had I felt so destitute, so miserable, so lonely. I even found myself longing for those difficult hours spent in the frigate's hold. There at least I had shared a common fate with my companions, desperate though they were. Why had I been taken from them? Why had Zinah been taken from me?

Little by little the shadows of evening spread through the room, and fatigue at last dulled my thoughts. At the end of this exhausting day, in the midst of an endless wait, I rose to my feet and walked to the terrace. The setting sun splashed the immaculate walls with orange and mauve, and seemed to set fire to the varnished tiles of the roofs.

I awoke surrounded by three or four whispering Algerian women. They were apparently amused by my stupor. Their skins were dark, the palms of their hands were stained with henna, and each had a blue tattoo between her eyebrows. They had brought various flasks and toiletries and silk robes with which to dress me, and they began to busy themselves around me as soon as I stood up.

It was with great relief that I doffed the soiled clothes I had been wearing since the attack on the *Aliaga*. I abandoned myself with delight to these women's expert hands. They washed and massaged and rubbed my body with fragrant oils. I suddenly felt revived, light, and I shall always remember my shiver of pleasure when I slipped on the first silk dress they handed me. My costume, in fact, consisted of several superimposed dresses. The last one, wider than the others, cut of some vaporous gauze, had a long train and a belt of gold filigree studded with small emeralds.

Finally one of the women lifted my hair and imprisoned it under a pink muslin scarf embroidered with gold sequins.

I was ready to receive the Dey.

His visit was the first event I recorded in my diary. At the time, I spent entire days in my small room without any company, and it was then I decided to fill a portion of my interminable idleness by relating the events of my life, as I had seen my mother and my cousins do. In pantomime I requested writing materials, which were brought to me a day later. The effort of writing in my maternal tongue, of assembling sentences with the care I had learned at the convent, anchored me to reality; a reality that was slipping away into adventure and disorientation aggravated by my solitude, and the uncertainty in which I lived.

The Dey of Algiers appeared one morning and stared at me in silence. Several minutes passed before he uttered a sharp order. Half a dozen secretaries appeared, to receive various instructions spoken in a low monotone. The Dey then resumed his silent contemplation of my person. I had the painful feeling that a multitude of thoughts were jostling each other behind his forehead, that my fate was being settled there and then. Then, wordlessly, he left.

The following morning a slave brought me the travel bag the pirates had taken from me on the *Aliaga*. The recovery of my personal effects, including the coral necklace my aunt Elizabeth gave me so long ago, lent me a feeling of security, and some of my confidence returned.

Another surprise: The Algerian women in charge of serving me—whose manner had been so jolly and familiar at first—began to treat me with deference. Furthermore, an honor guard replaced the usual jailer at my door.

The following days confirmed the impression that I was now being treated as a prisoner of high rank. Although I was not allowed to leave my room, the Algerian women came and went all the time, bringing me delicious meals, sweetmeats, flowers, perfume, dresses. I sometimes wondered about the pleasant change in my status, but rather than lose my mind in useless conjectures, I busied myself with frivolity, changing my dress ten times a day. The Dey did not reappear, leaving me in uncertainty for more than a week.

One morning, my servant girls awoke me at dawn and began to pack my belongings as soon as they had dressed me. I was then led to the palace courtyard and hoisted into a purple-and-gold palanquin on a camel's back. The camel bore me through the palace grounds and then through the city, on our way to the port. Once we reached the pier the palanquin, in which I still sat, was removed from the camel and transported onto a ship. I was freed from my brocaded prison only when the anchors were raised and we had sailed out of the Bay of Algiers.

It was to my great surprise that I recognized, pacing the deck, the Keznadar—the Dey of Algiers' minister of finance. He addressed me without much amiability:

"Look at that admirable bay—look at it closely, for you shall never see it again. . . . Oh, yes, I speak French. Greeks can muddle along in any language, and I am Greek. You look surprised. Yes, I am a Greek, and I am a renegade, like many Barbary corsairs. Most of us are Europeans who have forsaken their religion to embrace the Muslim faith."

Noticing my indignation, the Keznadar explained that, all things being equal, he preferred to take slaves and have slaves than be one. This first conversation with the Keznadar, held while Algiers disappeared on the horizon, left me dreamy and somewhat confused. I was not able to draw any information from him as to the purpose and destination of our voyage, and we left each other on a rather cool note. I had no idea of where we were going or what was to become of me.

After several days at sea, the boredom of the crossing and the Cyprus wine he consumed in quantity loosened his tongue.

"The Dey is at present indebted to his suzerain, the Sultan of Turkey, who came to his aid when the Spaniards threatened to invade Algeria. The tribute which he sends him annually under my custody had to be particularly well stocked this year. That is why he is sending you to the Sultan. You will note that Baba Mohammed's notoriously tight fist, and his indisputable taste in matters of feminine beauty, are happily married in his choice of a gift. You are indeed, miss, a priceless treasure, far more precious than all the gold amassed in the Dey's chests. . . . I can only agree with him: You are worthy of the great sovereign you are destined for."

I could have been dreaming. Those words I had heard ringing in Euphemia David's throat: sovereign, great empire . . . No, I wasn't dreaming at all: I was aboard a ship on the wing between the Barbary Coast and Turkey, and the Keznadar was grinning at me smugly. . . .

We sailed by Carthage—a mass of ruins, stone blocks and fallen columns, on a flat and arid coast. We had to make a detour to avoid the island of Malta and its masters, the Christian knights, who never hesitated to give chase to pirate ships.

Then we sailed along the Libyan coast and caught a glimpse of

Tripoli before heading off toward Greece. The Keznadar, who had finally revealed himself to be extremely garrulous and never left my side anymore, was unable to resist another monologue as we drew close to Crete, his native island. Paradoxically, he began to extol the merits of Turkey:

"The Turks have built one of the greatest empires in history. The starving tribes they arise from came down from their godforsaken mountains in Central Asia and within three centuries became master of territories stretching from India to Austria. On the way they adopted the Muslim faith, the first real religion those pagans ran into. However, the empire isn't what it used to be. Division, civil war, palace revolutions, have weakened its extraordinary hegemony. Still it controls lands all the way from the Atlantic to Persia, from Belgrade to the Sudan. The coasts along which we sail, North Africa, Greece, Asia Minor, all belong to it—as well as the Balkans, Armenia, the Caucasus, Egypt, and all the Levant as far as distant and mysterious Arabia. Yet this is an old, ailing empire. The tables have turned, and now it is we who tremble before Europe."

I put my well-learned history lessons to use. "Will Europe, which was once invaded by the Turks, respond in kind and invade the empire?" I asked, filled with hope.

"Not so fast, pretty one. The European powers are weakened and divided. Spain and Portugal, who used to attack us so often, are in a state of decadence. Italy is no more than a patchwork of minor states. Sweden and Denmark, in the Middle Ages, sent their piratical sailors throughout the Mediterranean and all the way to our coasts, but now they've been reduced to insignificance."

"But France is still powerful and fierce!"

"That is true, and her fleet ranks among the finest in the world. But her rival, England, is about to take her place. You who come from the West Indies should be well aware of that. . . . And then the French monarchy is a rotting structure. One day it will crumble—with the help of the English, who are at this moment distributing gold among French agitators."

"In that case, it is England that the Turkish Empire will have to fight."

"England is much too busy extending its colonies around the globe and gaining control of distant seas. And Austria, our neighbor and thus our hereditary enemy, is busy with Germany. Besides, she is completely absorbed in the task of shoring up an ever more contested hegemony in the face of the rise of a new power, Prussia."

"So no one threatens the Turkish Empire?"

The Keznadar answered with irony. "Don't worry, there's always Russia. The Russian Empire is younger than ours; it emerged from barbarism and from under the Tartar yoke only two or three centuries ago. Russia is determined to make up for lost time, however. She fights war upon war with us, and nibbles at our northern provinces. . . . Oh, yes," he added quietly, "Russia is a constant threat. . . . "

Taking advantage of the fact that he seemed in a confiding mood, I asked him about the Sultan himself—this unknown man to whom I was promised, and whose very image filled me with apprehension.

"Sultan Abdul Hamid, twenty-ninth ruler of the Ottoman dynasty, twentieth successor to Mohammed II, the conqueror of Constantinople, is as sweet as he is erudite. He's a poet who has never done anyone any harm. Like his empire, he's old, quite old, but"—and here the Greek chuckled salaciously—"he is very fond of women."

We sailed through the Dardanelles, and drew near to Constantinople. I had slept little and badly. I was obsessed by the thought of that harem where a lifetime of imprisonment awaited me; and what the Keznadar told me about it, as we sailed into the Golden Horn, left me little to look forward to.

"It is a palace within a palace, a state within a state. It is a city which its inhabitants never leave. It has its own laws, its own intrigues, its own dramas. No information, no rumors, filter through its walls. It is best not to go too near to them; best not to try and find out what happens within them."

PART 2

SULTAN ABDUL HAMID

CHAPTER 5

It is a fact I have had many an opportunity to verify: Ignorance of the future spares us certain unbearable states of mind. How often could one not say with all certainty: "What I am living now will never recur; this is the one and only time."

It is in that very state of clairvoyance, which added a painfully sharp edge to each of my perceptions, that I discovered Constantinople from the deck of our ship in the Golden Horn on that day of August 1788. The sight of the city etched itself in my mind with such implacable clarity that neither time nor the imprint of new images and new memories has been able to dull it.

The Dey's Greek Keznadar, who took his role of guide very seriously, was standing at my side. I can still hear the strange satisfaction in his voice as he described the spectacle of Constantinople unfolding its splendors across the water.

To our right were the Christian quarters of Pera and Galata, dominated by the tall, pointed tower of Galata, where large European houses and embassies rose in tiers from the gardens. On the left stood the old town of Constantinople, a prodigiously intricate tangle of wooden houses pierced, here and there, by the long facade of a palace or the elegant silhouette of a kiosk. A multitude of pink cupolas emerged from this confusing mass, the remains of the old Byzantine churches; a sprinkling of mosques and minarets leaped straight to the sky, like the cypress trees that inspired their design. At the far end of the old town we could see the gardens, the pavilions, and the domes of the Seraglio—the imperial palace, the Sultan's residence—with the tangle of the harem jutting out to one side.

"That, my child, is where you shall live from now on," said the Keznadar.

No sooner had the ship been moored to the pier than the first crates containing the "ordinary" tribute of the Dey to the Sultan were lowered, without eliciting any particular enthusiasm. The bystanders massed at the docks had come to see something else, and they were not disappointed. There soon appeared a solemn procession consisting of guards and eunuchs from the Seraglio. Some of these men wore baggy breeches and vividly colored waistcoats and red-and-gold turbans. The Negroes wore white-and-red-striped skirts under dark-blue caftans, and a peculiar sort of headgear, rather like a conical felt hat. They were the eunuchs of the imperial harem and their presence on the pier unleashed in the crowd a passionate curiosity, which was to remain unsated: Stepping forward, the eunuchs unfurled two lengths of white cloth from wooden sticks, thus improvising a sort of cloth corridor between the ship and the pier. The rule here was the same as in Algiers: No one was to set eyes on me.

At the other end of the cloth tunnel, on the pier, I was literally stuffed into a tahtarvan, a brocaded litter borne by two sumptuously harnessed mules. Then the procession set off. The Greek rode his horse beside my litter and named the monuments I could glimpse through the curtains veiling me from the world. The offices of the prime minister—the Grand Vizier—were sheltered inside that modest wooden building, he said, known to the entire world as the

Sublime Porte. Farther on, that pyramid of domes and cupolas turned out to be Saint Sophia, one of the most famous cathedrals in Christendom before it was transformed into a mosque. "And here is the entrance to the Seraglio, the Imperial Gate, which a woman may cross only once in her life," said my mentor. "Here we are, my child."

The Greek spared me nothing, not even the severed heads that stood like a dreadful sign announcing the Imperial Gate. The heads were piled up in stone niches on either side of the gate, and their blood trickled down to the ground. The Greek explained that only the heads of the lowliest of criminals were exhibited in this fashion. And his facetiousness was not yet exhausted: After traversing the First Court, bordered on both sides by barracks and arsenals, we stopped before the Middle Gate, flanked by two towers pierced with narrow slots, and the Greek informed me with malicious pleasure that we were standing on the very spot where executions took place. "Here, the hangman is an artist: Traditionally he is also the head gardener. His functions consist of growing flowers and cutting heads. Here are his most recent works. . . . "

I almost fainted. He was pointing at shapeless blackish objects stuck on metal spikes, each one carefully labeled.

"Please note that in order to have one's head so well exhibited one must hold at least the rank of pasha. On the labels are written the former owner's rank and his crimes. After the heads are cut, they are left here to dry before being returned to the families."

I had a difficult time overcoming the horror and disgust which the sight of these barbarous customs inspired in me. The Greek snickered.

The Second Court was a rose garden and an aviary, studded with gigantic antique capitals and century-old cypress trees. At the other end were the gates to the harem, where the Greek was to take leave of me, his mission accomplished. He delivered me to the head eunuch, the Kizlar Aga, one of the most important personages of the empire.

"His Black Highness," as Europeans called him, was a gigantic Negro with hands as wide as carpet beaters. He wore a white caftan trimmed with black fur, left open over a long red shirt.

He was expecting me. He looked me over; I saw surprise in his somber gaze. Then he bowed to me with a sort of deference, to the Keznadar's astonishment. Suddenly nervous, the latter cut short our leavetaking and quickly rode off while the heavy oak and bronze doors shut mysteriously behind me; I had crossed the threshold of the imperial harem.

Following the Kizlar Aga, I walked through a series of narrow courts, of high-ceilinged, windowless anterooms and gloomy corridors. At last we entered a dark and rather cluttered room where I could make out the silhouette of a woman sitting on a low couch. She was smoking a long pipe, the bowl of which rested on a small glowing brazier. She spoke to me at once in impeccable French:

"I am Vartui, the Khaya Kadin, which means superintendent of the imperial harem."

At first sight Lady Vartui was an ageless woman, very short, and so stout that she moved with some difficulty. Above the shapeless body her face remained smooth and firm, lit up by very round blue eyes which lent her features a childish character. Her mass of dark hair was pinned up in an opulent chignon, and I found her rather majestic-looking in her gold-embroidered bonnet and bolero. Her direct greeting in my mother tongue reassured me somewhat. "You are entering my service because I have been entrusted with the responsibility of your training. Follow me; I will show you to your dormitory."

That particular room gave onto a desolate sunken court known as the Court of the Slavewomen. Its vaulted ceiling was divided by a row of low columns, and its narrow windows of multicolored glass were reinforced with thick grating. I felt ill at ease the moment I set foot there, oppressed by its sinister cell-like atmosphere.

I had been alone for only a few moments when a swarm of women, all of them equally young and pretty, burst into the room. Laughing, mocking me lightly with their curiosity, they swirled around me, examining me without shame. My skin, my clothes, my hair, every detail of my person, drew incomprehensible chatter and laughter from them.

After this curious introduction, as if to show they were adopting me, my companions led me off to the hammam, a series of tiny rooms lit by glass lenses embedded in the domes. There they immediately stripped me of my European clothes, which had been returned to me at Algiers and which I had insisted on wearing for my arrival. These were thrown into the stove without a moment's hesitation. Worn and stained though they were, I had not wanted to lose those clothes; they were all I owned, all I had to remind me of my former existence. Watching them burn brought tears to my eyes.

I was then initiated into the various rites of the Turkish baths, in a confusion of laughter and exclamations. I was successively subjected to the steambath, in which I almost suffocated; to jets of freezing water, which made me wince and jerk about as if I were being whipped, then to jets of hot water to stimulate the blood; and finally to a massage with scented oils, administered by women who beat my flesh and pounded at my body until I thought they would break my bones.

But in the end I had to recognize the effectiveness of the treatment. I left the hammam invigorated in spirit as well as in body. My only thought, and a rather peculiar one, was that after such a scouring there could not remain a single speck of French dust on my skin.

My new companions did not leave me for a moment until curfew. Then they unfolded their mattresses, which were kept rolled up in a corner, and helped me with mine. Not until I was surrounded by darkness and the others' slumber was I left alone with myself, with my thoughts. I had reached the end of my travels, the end of that insane odyssey—Nantes, the shipwreck, the pirates, Algiers, the weeks on the Mediterranean, Constantinople—and now the last link in the chain, and I was bound forever to this palace. . . . This certainty, as well as fatigue, soon got the better of me; I sank into a despair filled with images of my family, of my house, of France, of Zinah. Zinah! If only you were here with me now!

I was given a daily session at the hammam, and soon found myself looking forward to it. People here care for the cleanliness of their bodies—a happy contrast with the hygiene of the French. In France we washed sparingly and without conviction, smothering bodily odors under great dollops of perfume. Bathrooms were so scarce that in the King's palace at Versailles courtiers relieved themselves on the stairs and in hallways. Here, for the first time, I discovered hot and cold running water, marble bathrooms, and flushing mechanisms.

My companions took it upon themselves to instruct me in the thousand secrets of stylishness. Most of their leisure was spent adorning themselves, indulging in orgies of kohl—an ointment kept in tiny worked phials, which they smeared on their eyelids— of lipstick, which the Turks had learned to use from the Greeks, and of henna, which they used to condition their hair. Women here plaster their faces to an extent matched, in France, only by the streetwalkers I had seen in the gardens of the Palais-Royal. I was more impressed by the tremendous variety and refinement of the perfumes we were generously provided with: musk oil, tuberosa, sandalwood, bitter orange, geranium, jasmine, all distilled within the Seraglio, in the laboratories of the imperial apothecary.

It did not take me long to learn to dress and apply makeup myself; at the beginning I had felt rather like a doll abandoned to the whim of her companions. I dressed after the Turkish fashion: plain baggy silk pants in different colors, held up by a sort of shawl tied around the hips; a blouse of gold-embroidered white muslin, over which we slipped the dualma, a very tight-fitting velvet overblouse which might be embroidered with gold, silver, or even small pearls; and a light veil or an ornamental cap, the talposh, cocked at an angle to hold the hair in place.

It sometimes occurred to me that by wearing this costume and adopting Turkish habits I was losing my real identity. Curiously, this did not cause any bitterness in me. Partly because of my youth, the discovery of a new universe, so different from my own, intrigued me. Nevertheless the shock had been very sudden, and sometimes I lapsed into despondency, and cried over everything I had loved, everything I had lost, over the mercilessness of fate.

We lived in absolute confinement, unable to go beyond the strict limits of the buildings reserved for the slavewomen. We were very cramped, and lived one on top of the other, by night as well as by day. In the evening we unfolded our mattresses and laid them out anywhere we pleased. The density of human bodies in the palace of this powerful ruler was prodigious; the Negroes on our plantation in Martinique had been far better housed, or at least they had enjoyed more space. This promiscuity, which at first I had enjoyed, soon began to wear on me. Our singular community functioned in such a way that it was impossible to isolate oneself for a moment of solitude or intimacy. Deprived of all freedom, even that of spending a few moments alone with myself, if only to think awhile or record a few impressions in my notebook, I began to suffocate.

It was a feeling only reinforced by the configuration of the harem. "It is a palace within a palace," the Keznadar had said. The harem contains the Sultan's apartments, those of the Valideh Sultana, his mother, and those of the imperial princes and princesses; the living quarters of the women who are highly placed in the harem—the six kadins, who are the Sultan's "official" favorites, and the forty "unofficial" favorites—for the Sultan does not marry and therefore has no wives; and those of the four hundred slavewomen and the three hundred black eunuchs. The harem has its own mosques, its own kitchens, its laundry rooms and hammams, its treasure chambers and hospital. Ariadne herself could have unraveled all her skeins in that oppressive labyrinth without finding her way, and even after all these years, it still happens that I lose mine.

One travels through an incoherent series of minute gleaming rooms, dark courtyards, secret stairways, vast and sumptuous halls, sinuous corridors, windowless apartments which follow each other or rise in different levels in a chaotic tangle. The topography of the entire harem mocks every law of architecture. It was built without any plan, at the whim of successive sovereigns. It is true that for centuries the Turks were a nomadic people, and now that they are settled, their conception of lodgings retains an air of improvisation and precariousness.

Living exclusively in the company of women—and eunuchs— was something which, at my beginnings in the harem, I had to accept as best I could. The radical segregation of the sexes in this place seemed to me anomalous, if not monstrous. Besides the Sultan and the imperial princes, the only men allowed in the harem were the baticalars, halberdiers who served as porters. But the rules forbade them to see us, and they had to go about their business with lowered eyes. Workers and gardeners were occasionally admitted; the eunuchs would shout, "Helvet!" at the approach of a woman, and the unfortunates would scamper off in all directions for fear of being beheaded.

I was given the duties of Superintendent Vartui's chambermaid. I got along well with that impetuous, garrulous woman—an Armenian, as she did not hesitate to inform me. Although she was sometimes a little brusque, she seemed to take singular interest in me.

At the beginning her primary concern was extracting information from me about the latest fashions in Paris. I noticed with sacrilegious satisfaction that despite Turkish national pride, the French style had overthrown local custom. The decoration of the new apartments in the harem naively imitated that which I had admired in the mansions of Nantes and Paris. From France they imported china, knickknacks, cloth—in short, the indispensable trivialities through which my country rules the universe. While Lady Vartui applied her makeup, I held before her a looking glass, backed with ornate silver, and she interrogated me endlessly on what Frenchwomen were wearing.

In return she instructed me—zealously—in Turkishness. Gradually she initiated me into the unbelievable complexity of the rules and customs of my new society.

Various ceremonies punctuate the Turkish day. The preparation of pipes and coffee requires concentration and industry difficult to imagine. I learned that the Sultan had his own designated coffee-preparer, a post that was one of the most coveted at court. The coffee, served piping hot, flavored with a grain of cardamom or a drop of orange blossom, is poured with its dregs into tiny cups of porcelain mounted on bases of precious metal. Vartui's coffee cups were made of gold and enamel, and she assured me that those of the imperial family were encrusted with diamonds and precious stones.

Besides the preparation of the pipes—Vartui was intransigent on the dosage and berated me loudly if it wasn't to her taste—I learned to manipulate the scent-burners, to set out the cushions, to present sweetmeats to guests. My apprenticeship continued during the "recreation" hours in the slavewomen's kitchen. There my companions made all sorts of confections and delicacies I loved: dry cakes powdered with sugar, syrup or honey cakes, baklavas, kadaifis, galactobouzikos, not to mention the so aptly named rahat loukhoums, literally "throat soothers," in varied pastel colors. We also prepared the national sherbets in many different flavors, conserved in ice brought from Mount Olympus in Bithynia, and the "spoon sweets" made from fruit—lemons, Chinese oranges, kumquats, nuts, figs— half candied and half stewed, served in a spoon with a glass of water. Need I say I could not always resist such temptation?

Besides these delicacies, which we nibbled all day long, two meals were served each day, at ten in the morning and around five in the afternoon. Just as there are no real bedrooms here—mattresses are unrolled on the floor of living rooms—dining rooms are non-existent. We gather anywhere to eat from copper trays which are brought covered from the imperial kitchens, and removed as soon as the meal is over.

The Seraglio's cooks, who have their own hierarchy and their own guild, feed five thousand people each day, including the harem. The frugality of the dishes surprised me after France's complicated and interminable menus: herb soups and vegetable soups, much fresh fruit, and, around the eternal pilaf—the national rice— dishes of pigeon, chicken, or mutton; only the eunuchs, who are passionately fond of it, eat veal. I was especially delighted with pastourma, camel meat marinated in vinegar and garlic, the thought of which would horrify the elegant Parisians.

Eating while seated tailor-fashion demands certain gymnastics, which I soon grew accustomed to. In the beginning I had some trouble doing without silverware, but then I learned to eat with my hands like everybody else here, except of course the imperial family, who use spoons of gold, agate, jade. . . .

At Vartui's orders I began my private lessons. I was taken to the harem's little mosque, a dark room decorated with tiles representing the Holy Cities of Islam. The mufti, the serving priest, was an old man whose toothless mouth was always open in laughter, and who continually tapped his fingers on a fat leather-bound book, croaking, "Al-Koran, Al-Koran," the Koran. Like a parrot, I repeated its verses after him hour upon hour. In point of fact, none of this was particularly important, for Turkish tolerance in matters of religion is remarkable. No conversion is required of the girls who enter the harem, none of whom are Turkish or Muslim. Allah forbids the capture and sale of his faithful, and since the harem is stocked only through piracy and slavery, it is necessary to make do with non-Muslim foreigners. They convert to Islam if they wish or else keep their religion, provided they do so discreetly and are capable of droning out verses of the Koran when necessary.

Vartui also sent for a man of letters to teach me the court language. Ristoglou was a black eunuch, paunchy in spite of his thinness, with a head tilted to one side and a pathetic mien. His real name was Heliotrope—all eunuchs are named after flowers—while his nickname, given to him by his companions, who thought him a sage, was a perversion of Aristotle. He was nastiness and culture incarnate, and prided himself on being an expert in the subtleties of the official literature. He taught me that mixture of Arabic, Persian, and Turkish in use at court, a tongue very different from the popular Turkish, for which he had nothing but contempt.

In spite of obvious differences and its exotic backdrop, my life in the harem reminded me of that which I led at the Convent of the Visitation in Nantes. Once again I was forced to rise at dawn, which I hated; but here at least I awoke to music. The Sultan's military orchestra plays martial tunes to draw the Seraglio out of sleep two hours before daybreak. Then, throughout the day, the hours alternate the constraints of service with the rigorous discipline of classes. For the harem is also a school for music, dancing, singing, painting, embroidery, bookbinding. The authorities strive to discover a particular talent in each young woman and encourage her to develop it. It was an ironic destiny which, after so many unexpected detours, led me back to the rules and imprisonment of the convent. Try as they might, the nuns had not succeeded in keeping me among them; the harem, on the other hand, would never let me go. It was as if I had taken religious vows. Nevertheless I did not suffer the boredom of the convent.

First of all, there was even less free time. The harem's schedule was designed to keep the uprooted girls busy at all hours, to level them under iron discipline, to leave them no time for nostalgia or melancholy. And then the curiosity I felt toward this novel universe, my fear of the unknown, my will to adapt through the instinct of survival, maintained a state of tension which kept boredom at bay.

To remind me of Nantes there was also the protocol of hierarchy, for which the Turks are as keen as the nuns were. Depending on the rank and position of the person one approaches, one must kiss either his hand or the hem of his robes. Vartui, who was extremely involved with the prerogatives of her position, never tired of describing everyone's attributions, while insisting on her own with satisfaction.

The Valideh Sultana, the Sultan's mother, was in theory the ruler of the harem, but she had died. The Kizlar Aga, the tall black eunuch who had met me at my arrival, was therefore the supreme master of the harem; but he was also the Sultan's confidant, and his many responsibilities did not leave him time to govern the harem in its details. In fact, Vartui was regent, presiding over a sort of cabinet consisting of the Mistress of the Robes, the Guardian of the Baths, the Guardian of the Jewels, the Guardian of the Underclothes, the Reader of the Koran, the Guardian of the Warehouses. Although she refused to admit it, she had a rival in the Hazinadar Usta, the Grand Treasurer, whom, according to perfidious Ristoglou, she cordially detested.

Dismissing, with a wave of her flyswatter, the painful topic of the Hazinadar Usta, Vartui proudly reminded me that she was responsible for all four hundred and twenty women of the harem. Each of these enjoyed a different status, depending on seniority, beauty, docility, talent. And what would mine be? Would I, like so many others, spend my life as a chambermaid, or was I promised to the higher ranks? Would I reach the summit of all my companions' ambition—to be the concubine, even briefly, of a fickle old man? For in fact this crowded convent school had only one purpose, which I forgot or tried to forget: the Sultan's pleasure. Vartui refused to answer my questions, and left me torn between curiosity and anxiety.

Soon I was able to read the Arabic characters of the court language, less through Ristoglou's lessons than thanks to the walls of the harem; like those of the convent, they were covered in graffiti: "I did not steal Leila's mirror—besides, it's worthless"; "The eunuch Rahim is cross-eyed"; "Hatifa keeps three boxes of loukhoums under her mattress"; "The Khaya Kadin [Vartui] is too fat." Those who saw me, convulsed with laughter, deciphering these childish scribblings with the care of an archaeologist thought I was quite mad.

Deciding that I had made rapid progress in a few weeks, Vartui made me move out of the slavewomen's dormitory and installed me in a corner of her apartment in order that she herself might put the finishing touches on my education. I had the feeling I had been put on the honor roll; but I was vaguely disturbed and confused by all the hopes and ambitions she was obviously investing in me.

I constantly touched my good luck charm, a present from one of my companions, a marble of blue glass with a white circle and a black dot simulating the iris, which was supposed to ward off the evil eye. This is the most popular and widely used amulet in the Orient. It completed the sorceress's kit I was already laden with— hands of Fatma, fake Egyptian scarabs, medallions engraved with Allah's name.

When I took leave of the dormitory, the women joyfully made a circle around me, chanting "Nakshidil, Nakshidil," in every imaginable tone of voice. It took me a moment to understand they had chosen a new name for me. Nakshidil means "imprint of the heart" or "most beautiful among the beautiful." At Vartui's decree, it was the name I would bear from then on. I felt as if the last shred of my past, of my identity, were being torn from me, and I reacted violently. An impassive Vartui, seated on the low couch, puffing at her pipe, tried to reason with me. "Calm down. Revolt is always vain here: It is better to bend and to adapt. You are an intelligent girl; you would do better to accept your fate, make the best of your life here, and derive from it as much advantage as you can. Don't make yourself suffer. I shall help you, but first you must renounce your past, you must forget who you were. No more Aimée, no more France, no more family. You are Nakshidil."

Khaya Kadin Vartui's twin affections for me and for Cyprus wines, in which she indulged in secret, launched her into long, lyrical tirades:

"You see, my child, the road to honors is long and arduous. Many are called, few are chosen. The gediklis, as I have told you, are those who have the privilege of serving His Highness. They dress him, soap him in his bath, arrange his pillows—all the while hoping, of course, to attract his attention. The next echelon is that of gözde: The gözde has been noticed by the Sultan and awaits his pleasure. If it happens, if she has the honor of sharing the imperial bed—even only once—she becomes an ikbal, a concubine. An ikbal who gives birth to a child who is not certain to enter the imperial family is called a haseki. Above the haseki are the kadins, six in number, the mothers of the imperial princes and princesses. But you mustn't think that His Highness can dispose of any woman in the harem as he pleases. It isn't so. In fact, his choice is more or less directed by the harem government, which weighs the qualities of each candidate and decides which one will be put in the Sultan's path and, later, led to his bed."

"But what about love?" I cried. "What part does love play in all this?"

This question seemed to confuse her. I had the feeling it was one

Vartui had never thought of, that it was completely out of place here. I immediately took advantage of her silence:

"Without love, without freedom, without choice . . . those poor women! You rear them so carefully to make dumb animals of them, objects of depravity. That is what you plan to do with me, with all your billing and cooing—to make me a courtesan."

"You forget power," she answered, not in the least disconcerted by my insolence.

"Yes, and power must be gained, and the Sultan seduced," answered Ristoglou when I told him of my conversation with Vartui. "As for the unfortunates who haven't the luck to attract the Sultan's attention, they might be given to an old potbellied pasha, or become some cruel kadin's scapegoat, or be exiled from paradise—proximity to the Sultan—and be sent to the Old Seraglio." I had already heard of that crumbling and dusty palace, where favorites in disgrace and the kadins of late sultans were sent to end their miserable existence in darkness and decrepitude. It was known, quite aptly, as the Palace of Lamentations, and young ambitious girls as well as old women sagging under honors shivered with horror at its mention.

Thus, while Vartui strove to paint a flattering image of the harem for me, Ristoglou described it through its most terrible aspects, as if he wished to discourage me. But discourage me from what? And for what purpose? Both their tales were equally strange and distressing to me, though the universe in which I lived seemed more frivolous and petty than frightening. I loathed the smell which floated about Vartui's apartment, that smell of stale tobacco, old perfume, cheap wine. All I wanted, most of the time, was to escape from this place, to recover my lost freedom, to be in the open air, if only for a moment. . . .

CHAPTER 6

My taste for solitary wanderings about the harem and my incorrigible need to explore led me to an unsettling discovery: I was not the only Frenchwoman imprisoned in this place. The second kadin, Humasah, came from Provence.

She lived at the far end of a hideous apartment composed of three narrow rooms bathed in a stingy, dusty light. An enormous Norman sideboard virtually filled one of these rooms, testimony to her pathetic efforts to retain some shreds of her past.

Humasah had a very broad face with a heavy jaw, a flattish nose, and a graceless mouth. But she had presence, and beneath the brocade and the silk, one could guess at a superb body. She lost no time in beginning a litany of bitter thoughts. "Here you lose your nationality, your rank, your language, your religion, and your education"—almost word for word the complaints of the old French slave I had met that first night in the prisons of Algiers.

"The entire system of the harem," she continued, "is meant to annihilate the will and the personality of the new arrivals, before pitting them against each other in a struggle for the illusion of power."

The French kadin seemed obsessed by the fear of being supplanted by a younger rival and ending her days in the Old Seraglio. I understood that this was the only cause of her hostility toward me. She was a strange mixture of lucidity, bitterness, and aggressiveness. She retained her disenchanted manner and that tense, almost ferocious attitude even when she spoke of her son Mahmud. The three-year-old child was at that moment with his father, the Sultan.

"He keeps him in his apartment all day, playing with him as if he were a toy, then gives him back to me in the evening, like a pup to his bitch. Besides, the child will be taken from me in a few years to be handed over to the men, and I shall hardly ever see him."

She worried about his future. Mahmud had an older half-brother—and, she added darkly, this was not a healthy place for younger brothers, who often came to a bad end, and before their time.

Suddenly she returned to Turkish to dismiss me. "Go away now," she said. "You upset me. You and your language make me nostalgic, a nostalgia I thought was dead, which can only poison me. In you I see the pink walls of our town, the cedars around it, the mottled olive groves, the morning sunlight in my childhood bedroom under the eaves. Go away, I tell you!"

Humasah's unexpected evocation of her childhood unleashed in me a storm of painful memories. I took refuge, crying, at Vartui's. But she did not, and could not, understand.

My encounter with the French kadin left me in deep distress. Listening to that broken, disenchanted woman, who nevertheless still kept a rebellious spirit, I understood that I could never endure such a life, even in a gilded cage, even if my destiny was to be, by the harem's criteria, a glorious one.

My conversation with her inspired in me a number of peculiar ideas I could not get rid of, all of which led me to the same conclusion: I had to get out of here. I thought I had found a way to do it. Every week some peddlers were admitted to the harem to sell their merchandise. The transactions took place near the harem's gates, by means of a turnstile. The merchants placed their wares on a platform which was then swiveled in such a way that it became exposed to the sight of the women gathered on the other side. My plan was to write a note to the French ambassador, slip it among the returned merchandise, and pray that one of the merchants would find the note and bring it to the addressee. I awaited "market" day feverishly, and when it came, followed the women to the turnstile, clutching the note.

My companions threw themselves like madwomen on the turnstile, which poured out a sea of fabrics: thick Chinese silks, Persian brocade with small designs, embroidered muslin from India, Genoa and Brusa velvet, flowered silks from Lyons, multicolored muslins from Iraq. . . . The women fingered the fabrics and fought over them with shrieks of delight. I stood aside, faint with anxiety. So as not to alert Vartui, who was surprised by my lack of enthusiasm, I joined the throng. At last I managed to approach the turnstile and thrust my message between the folds of the fabrics. This is what I scribbled in my diary that evening:

I am relieved. So far everything has gone according to plan. I have entrusted my "bottle" to the sea and the grace of God. Now it remains to be seen whether the man who finds it will take it to the Maison de France in Pera. My fate rests in the hands of a total stranger. I have begun to wait, in uncertainty and fear; will I be freed?

Three days later my evening lessons were interrupted by a summons from Vartui.

Her welcome seemed just as suspicious as the moment she had chosen for our interview. She sat me down next to her and began a trivial conversation, showing me unusual kindness and consideration. She spoke to me of the fabrics she had acquired three days before, and asked my advice as to the use she might make of them. I had a feeling she was doing her utmost to mislead me with her drawing room chatter, and I was sitting on burning coals.

Then, suddenly, she showed her hand. Without a word, she placed before me the note I had written to the French ambassador.

No doubt the merchant who had found it, too cowardly to risk punishment, had returned it to the palace immediately.

Then came a litany of reproof, delivered without anger, in a quiet monotone. I had betrayed Vartui's trust, I was an ungrateful girl who did not even recognize the devotion and kindness she had shown me, after she had invested so much hope in my future. She could not understand how, while I enjoyed a privileged status, I could have thought of leaving the harem. No, really, she did not understand. I saw in her eyes the shadow of genuine sadness; at that moment Vartui must have felt the disappointment and the sorrow of a mother before a child who had let her down badly.

Such a fault deserved a punishment, she continued. And so I was whipped. Two black eunuchs in charge of such matters were brought into Vartui's apartment. They sneered while they whipped me, apparently enjoying the suffering they inflicted. Vartui watched my flagellation without uttering a word.

Strangely enough, the whipping did not mark or break my skin. It is true that it was administered by specialists anxious not to spoil the merchandise.

The physical pain I forgot moments after feeling it; the humiliation I have never forgotten.

As I lay heaving on the ground, Vartui made me rise, without brutality but firmly. Crushing my hand in hers, she dragged me through the harem to a narrow stairway descending underground. She pulled me down, stumbling from step to step. The stairway gave onto a sort of vast hangar with bare stone walls and a very high vaulted ceiling, lacking even a small window. Wooden scaffolding formed three separate stories, linked by ladders, between the ceiling and the floor. On each of these levels women of all ages were preparing for the night. How many were they, these underground shadows? A hundred? Two hundred? All of them had been found unsuitable for the Sultan's bed, and were therefore condemned to perpetual slavery. They fell silent as we entered, and turned frightened gazes on Vartui.

"Do you want to live here," she asked me, "and share these

women's fate? Or would you rather be reasonable and follow my instructions? Do not forget that in either case you shall never leave the harem."

Those women were neither mistreated nor desperate; they were simply resigned. The horror I experienced at the sight of them penned up like cattle in that cellar haunted me for a long time. And I reflected on it—more deeply than Vartui would have wished. She had wanted to frighten me. But she herself was afraid—I had felt it—far more afraid for herself than for me, afraid of what would happen to her if I slipped through her hands; afraid to the point of sparing me.

Normally, any attempt to escape or to communicate with the outside world is punishable by death. I had not been sewn into a sack and thrown into the Bosporus, and I wondered what this singular leniency could mean.

Soon after this incident I was introduced to Kadin Mirizshah, the late Sultan Mustafa III's favorite and mother of Crown Prince Selim. Although she lived retired in the Old Seraglio, the Palace of Lamentations, she was far from lamenting. She remained important, for she would become Valideh when her son ascended the throne. She was on good terms with the reigning Sultan, Abdul Hamid, and often came to the New Seraglio to see her daughter, Princess Hadidgeh. One evening, the Kizlar Aga came to fetch me, and took me to the first floor of the harem, to the wing of the imperial princesses, which gave onto the Valideh's vast court. The apartment was composed of two light rooms. Bright-colored bouquets painted on the paneling were echoed in the Persian carpets. Low divans covered in purple Brusa velvet embroidered with large gold carnations ran along the walls. Otherwise there was no furniture except Koran boxes, pedestal tables or tortoise shell inlaid with mother-of-pearl, and large ornate braziers of golden brass.

Standing by the window was Princess Hadidgeh. She was a tall girl with liquid dark eyes and a heavy, sensuous mouth. Uninterested in what was going on around her, wearing a vague, distant expression, she affected a deep melancholy. In the harem she was famous for her passionate and unhappy love affairs. All the time we were there she kept her tragic, stubborn mask, and did not condescend to take part in our conversation.

Contrary to Hadidgeh, her mother, Mirizshah, welcomed me warmly. This Circassian woman was still strikingly beautiful and seductive for her age. Her bearing was tall and imposing, her skin very white. Her eyes slanted up toward the temples, and her very hooked nose, far from making her ugly, lent a strong character to her beauty. She wore an unbelievable array of jewels with the most perfect and unaffected ease—several strings of pearls and emeralds, huge diamond earrings and buttons, a cap encrusted with pearls and studded with emerald pins, and diamond-and-emerald bracelets. When addressing me she was careful to speak very slowly so as to be understood. From time to time she attempted, in hesitant French, a sentence which ended in a coy little laugh.

She questioned me with much solicitude about my first impressions of the harem, about my progress, and about the difficulties I experienced in adapting myself to my new life. Then she asked sharp, intelligent questions about France, a topic which seemed to fascinate her. I was surprised to find, hidden in this isolated palace, a woman so cultured and informed about distant events. She spoke of every subject with the greatest of ease—French politics, the European situation, the philosophers, the British constitution, reforms. . . . More than once I was incapable of answering her. She did not take offense at my ignorance, but I felt that under all her kindness she was in fact sizing me up. Behind half-closed lids her green eyes observed me without rest. Mirizshah knew everything about me, and I understood that it was she, and not Vartui, who held the strings of the puppet I was. But why did I interest her so? What did she expect of me?

After this audience I understood, from Vartui's radiant expression, that I had passed the examination with flying colors: I had met with the future Sultana's approval.

When the Kizlar Aga returned me to our apartment, Vartui hurried toward the ivory-inlaid wooden casket where she kept her jewels. Rummaging frantically, she drew from it a lovely pair of Persian earrings, corollas of gold and enamel of decreasing sizes, ending in small emeralds and baroque pearls. She gave them to me solemnly, saying: "Keep them in remembrance of me. When you wear them, remember that Vartui has been good to you and will always love you."

Did Vartui want to make sure of my gratitude in the event of my reaching an enviable position?

My status became so ambiguous that I could not even call myself Vartui's chambermaid anymore. A newcomer, Nur, replaced me in that post, and I no longer had any obligations save that of my lessons. Nur was a lively, impulsive blond girl, her face dotted with freckles, and the least one could say was that she was plucky.

Under the barrage of Mirizshah's questions I had admitted my fondness for the harp, knowing very well there was no such instrument in the harem, that no girl played it. As if by miracle, a brand-new golden harp appeared, and was put at my disposal. I practiced in the music school, which was reserved for the more talented "pupils" of the harem, who perfected their skills there before being admitted to the Seraglio's private orchestra. The school was situated on the ground floor of the Sultana's apartment. The tiny rooms opened onto a meager garden enclosed by very high walls, and thus had little light. The perpetual gloom, the Valideh's overhanging balcony, the narrow casements, the heavy brocade curtain which hid a staircase leading to the upper floors—all this caused me vague uneasiness. In fact I could not shield myself from feeling that the place was haunted. But I was happy to be playing my favorite instrument again. It was as if I had regained a little part of myself which had been lost in the harem's training.

One afternoon while I practiced, I felt I was being watched through a gap in the curtains which hid the staircase. Several times I was tempted to get up and check, but I restrained myself: The fear of discovering something that should remain hidden, or of infringing some rule of the harem, kept me back. Yet I was so tense and so nervous that despite my efforts to concentrate I played quite a number of false notes. Evening fell; I stopped playing and remained immobile, listening to the melancholy wails of the muezzins calling to prayer.

"O illah kibiz . . . Allah salah"—God is great . . . come to prayer. Their cries echoed from minaret to minaret. Suddenly the curtains parted forcefully, letting forth a sort of fury who began to hurl violent invective at me. The woman—quite pretty, a redhead with green eyes—took me to task about her religion, which, according to her, I had insulted. How could I disregard the hour of prayer to go on playing the harp! She heaped abuse on me, and threatened me with decapitation for my alleged sacrilege. Seeing that I was left speechless by this brusque, outrageous display, she shouted:

"On your knees! On your knees before the daughter of your Sultan!"

Apparently I was in the presence of Princess Esmee, Abdul Hamid's favorite offspring. She was beginning to annoy me.

"If I had known who you were," I answered, "I would have greeted you appropriately."

These words seemed to soothe the harpy. "Be careful—be very careful. Being a pretty girl is not exactly a restful occupation here. You have to know whom to respect and whom to obey. Otherwise you might well end up with a eunuch pulling a silk bowstring tight around your little neck."

Then she gave my harp a violent kick, and disappeared up the staircase in a burst of laughter.

The scene had been so unexpected that I might have thought I was hallucinating. I could have sworn that someone else was standing behind that curtain—that person whose hateful gaze I had felt on my neck.

I immediately told Vartui what had happened. She tried to minimize the incident. "Princess Esmee, like her father the Sultan, likes to play jokes on people. Sometimes they can be cruel without realizing it. Esmee is not really nasty—merely scatterbrained. Unfortunately she is under the influence of her mother, Sineperver, the first kadin. And Sineperver really is an evil woman."

So that piercing gaze I had felt throughout my practice session must have been that of the first kadin, Sineperver.

I was beginning to feel the effects of the ferocious rivalries which underlie this society; on one hand Vartui's kindness and Mirizshah's consideration; on the other, Ristoglou's dark warnings and that intangible but powerful hostility emanating from Sineperver.

The cold weather arrived. Vartui had her furs taken out of the chest where she kept them, stored, as is the custom here, in pepper. After slipping into her sable, she went to the Sultan's drawing room, where a ballet was being staged. No sooner had she left than Nur, the new chambermaid, appeared in our apartment, as merry and impudent as ever. As I wondered what she was doing here at this hour, instead of being in the slavewomen's dormitory, she held out to me a little jade box inlaid with rubies and gold arabesques.

"A present from the French kadin," she said.

The box was filled with little pastilles which seemed to be made of pure gold.

"These are sweets made exclusively for the kadins. The imperial confectioner coats them with several layers of gold. Take one. They're absolute marvels!"

I bit into one, and then another. They had the flavor of chocolate, but with a strange bitter aftertaste. Nur, watching me with her usual mischievous air, had settled without further ado on the couch, where she invited me to join her.

While we chatted, I suddenly felt myself invaded by a strange well-being, by new and delicious sensations. It seemed that I was miraculously relieved of my fears, of my cares and worries, and I could have stayed where I was for hours, for days, without sleeping. I felt that all my faculties had been sharpened; all the objects around me—the furniture, the carpets, the fabrics—seemed more brightly colored.

Nur had begun to sing an enthralling melody in a low voice, a song which bathed my body in delicious sounds. It was at that moment, I think, that Nur began to caress my breasts, to cover my face and my throat with kisses, against which I did not think of defending myself. I was concentrating wholly on recording each one of these new sensations, immersed in total euphoria.

I did not react, either, when Vartui burst in upon us; and it is only with difficulty that I recall the rest of the scene, which I lived through in a sort of trance. I remember Vartui's howl of rage at the sight of our embrace; I remember Nur leaping off the couch, rearing up like a snake. I was then pummeled with blows, which I resisted no more than I had resisted Nur's kisses; Vartui, to my total unconcern, continued to shout. There was a new upsurge in her rage, this time directed solely at Nur, when she found the pillbox and understood that Nur had tried to drug me and rape me.

There followed a few moments of utmost confusion in Vartui's apartment, a storm of shouts, orders, calls, furious explanations. The Kizlar Aga appeared in his nightclothes, followed by his servants. Undaunted, utterly serene and detached, I watched the eunuchs seize Nur and drag her away; I saw her resist, and heard her bestial cries with total indifference.

I spent the next day in bed, in the clutches of the most frightful nausea. Toward evening the migraine, the shivers, the need to vomit, subsided. Vartui had not left my bedside all day.

"Those pastilles contained opium," she explained. "The 'corrosive sublime,' as we call it here. Opium is the plague of the empire in general and the harem in particular. Many Turks take it to justify their laziness, and the idiot harem girls dizzy themselves with it to help themselves bear an existence which they see as one of bitterness and ennui. Even some of the kadins use it—which explains the layers of gold on those wretched pastilles."

Then, after hedging awhile, Vartui explained—very cautiously, and in the most delicate and roundabout words she could find—that lesbianism was another prevalent practice in the harem, a practice almost inevitable in a society of cloistered women, and one to which a blind eye was turned. This tolerance could of course not be extended to cover Nur's actions, for she had tried to ruin me: a deflowered and drugged girl was no longer good enough for the

Sultan, who was presented only with untouched and unadulterated products.

"Of course it isn't that criminal idiot Nur who thought out this diabolical plan. I knew that as soon as I saw the pillbox. She could have stolen the opium pills, but not the box."

It was Sineperver, then, who had entrusted it to Nur, and who lay at the bottom of this plot! The first kadin, jealous of her hold over the Sultan, would stop at nothing to prevent others from weakening it. At last I fully understood what I had always refused to admit: I was no more than a fruit being carefully ripened for the Sultan. Concubine to the Master of the Empire, and who knows, his favorite . . . It was enough to dazzle anyone's ambition, including mine. But I could not resign myself to being a lamb pampered and fattened for the slaughter. I could not allow anyone to decide for me, without consulting me. If I chose to pursue an exceptional destiny, I wanted to do it freely, on my own terms.

"And Nur?" I asked.

"Thrown into the Bosporus this morning," Vartui answered calmly.

I envisioned Nur, pretty, young, laughing Nur, sewn into a rough sack, thrown from the ramparts with a weight attached to her feet, falling into icy water, drowning in her burlap prison. I would never accept these barbarous customs. I was overwhelmed by a wave of revulsion. I remember dashing out of the room and running headlong, not knowing where I was going, my heart on fire. When I stopped I was in a long, deserted gallery from the walls of which emanated, at this hour of twilight, a deep melancholy. After a moment I realized this was the Djinns' Council, a place my companions spoke of with quasi-religious terror and which they refused to approach after sundown. They claimed that the djinns, those dangerous spirits, held their reunions there and did their ablutions in the pool below.

I stayed there a long time, letting darkness enfold me, resting in that mysterious and slightly threatening atmosphere. At that moment, with my spirit torn by the knowledge of Nur's fate, I feared meeting those clownish djinns less than I feared living beings, who seemed to me by far the more cruel.

Rereading these notebooks, I realize that I have not told of the unexpected encounter I had that night. Could it be that our meeting was so sharply engraved in my memory that to evoke it was pointless? I suppose it is so; for each moment and each detail of that evening come back to me as clearly as if I had lived them yesterday. And yet it happened almost thirty years ago. . . .

At the far end of the Djinns' Council there was a door, which I found ajar. Still under the effect of shock, I slipped through this opening without quite knowing why, and found myself in the loveliest room imaginable. The evening light filtered in through immaculate marble lattices and stained glass, played lightly on the sumptuous ceramics on the walls—big bouquets of tulips and carnations mingled with blue and green geometric patterns, quotations from the Koran painted in white against a sea-blue background, interlacings of vines and stylized artichokes. In the middle of this porcelain garden gleamed a conical bronze fireplace.

There were books everywhere—in niches, on the sofas, on the ground. To my great surprise, I noticed French volumes among them, including some very recent ones—*Young Anacharsis' Travels in Greece,* by Abbé Barthélémy, and even *Paul et Virginie,* by Bernardin de Saint-Pierre—the margins of which, I noticed, were crowded with notes in Turkish.

A voice behind me said, "By what miracle did you get in here? Do you know you're risking your neck?"

I turned around. The man was young, tall, slightly stooped. A thinker's brow, an aquiline nose, a long and very black beard. A few pockmarks scarred the face without detracting from its austere beauty. He wore a green turban and a modest beige abaya, a light and ample mantle.

Gently, he repeated the question. "What are you doing here? You're not allowed—"

That hated word kindled my anger. "Not allowed! Not allowed! That's all you know how to say around here, all of you! I go where

I please, and especially where I think I can be alone. And what about you? Are you sure you're allowed to question me? Look it up in the rules—can a white eunuch question a slavegirl?"

He then burst into laughter—frank, young laughter—and before he could speak again I realized my mistake. "You must be new here, if you don't know that eunuchs have no beard."

His large, dark, almond-shaped eyes did not leave my face. There was something unfathomable in his gaze, which was warm and intelligent.

"You read French," he said, noticing *Paul et Virginie* in my hands. "You must be the new girl, the French one. Aren't you? My mother, Mirizshah, told me about you."

It was Prince Selim, heir to the Turkish Empire, destined to become the thirtieth Sultan of the Ottoman dynasty.

"How is it that you read French?" I answered. "Is it necessary, for a sultan? I thought a sultan needed words only to order executions and massacres."

My insolence merely brought a smile to his lips. "I read French—alas, far too poorly for my taste—because I like your novels, and because that language is the vehicle of liberalism and progress."

I mumbled some biting remark about the incompatibility of savage Turkish customs with the liberalism and progress he claimed to admire, but still he did not take offense. He spoke to me at length of his mother, Mirizshah. He literally venerated that intelligent and liberal woman. "My mother opened me to the world. She forced me to read, she placed men of worth around me. Despite the virtual impossibility of bringing them into the Seraglio, she put me in touch with foreigners, who taught me about their lands and customs. There was a French gardener, a Polish painter, and there was an Italian doctor, Doctor Lorenzo, who was supposed to look after my health but in fact brought me books on politics, law, economics."

My own purveyor of forbidden literature sprang to my mind. "It's just like Monsieur Jolibois," I said.

"Who is Monsieur Zolivova?" asked Prince Selim.

Naturally I had to tell him the whole story of Monsieur Zolivova. I described the convent, Nantes, my life in France. Prince Selim listened and questioned me with grave attention. Encouraged by his curiosity, I gave free rein to my own.

"Why is it that we haven't met before, my lord, if you live in the harem?"

"Because I am kept prisoner in my apartment, which is known as the Cage."

"What crime can the crown prince of the empire have committed to deserve imprisonment?"

"The crime of being born." The prince seemed delighted by my astonishment. He continued: "Besides, I am but the latest in a long series of imperial princes to occupy that prison. All this is bound up with the order of succession to the throne of the empire."

I understood less and less. A true Oriental, Selim drew me by his words into a labyrinth, to enlighten me only once I was thoroughly lost. "Succession in the Ottoman Empire is a complicated matter. It is based on seniority: the sultanate is transmitted not from father to son, but from eldest to eldest. Thus Abdul Hamid, my uncle, succeeded my father, Mustafa III, because he was the oldest member of the dynasty. This order of succession has always created an abundance of murderous intrigues between uncles and cousins and nephews. Everyone did the utmost to eliminate his elders. In order to ensure that their sons would inherit the throne, the reigning sultans had no other means but the assassination of all their male relatives—brothers, nephews, cousins. This blood-soaked custom subsisted until one of my ancestors, Ahmed I, decided to put an end to it: He built apartments in which he locked up his relatives, rather than have them massacred. Since then the princes are no longer strangled, but merely imprisoned in the Cage. A considerable improvement."

"But since when have you been in the Cage?"

"For the last fifteen years, ever since the death of my father, Mustafa III. I was thirteen years old then, and I haven't left the Cage since. But my uncle Abdul Hamid is very kind. He allows me to communicate with the outside, to receive letters, messages, and books, as you see. And then I have my slaves, my teachers, and my kadins. . . ."

Suddenly he looked perturbed, and I felt he would not say more. He called Billal Aga, his tutor, an old bespectacled black eunuch with the air of a shy intellectual, and asked him to escort me back to my apartment. I turned around as I crossed the threshold, and saw Selim sitting tailor-fashion on the carpet, pretending to be absorbed in reading—but I noticed his hands were shaking.

It was the first time, in this place where everyone was formed and deformed and conditioned by the rules of the Seraglio, that I found myself face to face with someone who, though a prisoner himself, seemed free and open. For the first time here I had had the feeling of talking to an equal; and the mixture of tenderness and virility emanating from the man had touched me.

Very early one morning I was taken to the music school by Vartui herself, whom I found unusually nervous. Once we were there, she had me sit down, then stand up, and made me change places a dozen times, moving the stool and the heavy harp herself. When at last she thought she had found the proper place and the proper lighting she said, "Now sit down and don't move," and set about putting my hair in order and rearranging the folds of my dress, so much so that I began to wonder whether she wasn't preparing me to sit for a painter. I understood nothing of this game.

"Choose the most beautiful piece you know and whatever happens, go on playing until I come to fetch you."

And she left without further explanation. I thought this was some sort of whim of Vartui's, and that I would only have to wait to find out what it was all about. I started to play a song supposedly composed by Marie-Antoinette, which my cousin Marie-Anne had taught me.

Little by little I let the melancholy words and melody absorb me; then a slight rustle made me turn my head. A man appeared between the curtains, an old man with a kindly face softened by sadness and fatigue. I was struck by the almost sickly pallor of his skin, and noticed that his beard was dyed. Perhaps because of his majestic bearing, or because of the richness of his dress, I knew immediately that it must be Sultan Abdul Hamid. He wore a caftan of black silk embroidered with large golden leaves and red-gold flowers spotted with turquoise, and a white turban topped by an aigrette held in place with a spray of diamonds.

For a moment we stared at each other in silence. His long hands fingered a precious chespi, the worry beads of every self-respecting Oriental, and in the silence around us I heard the pearls knocking against each other. His eyes were no more than black slits under strongly arched eyebrows which lent him a doubting gaze. I was not intimidated; I simply wondered what one was supposed to do when put in the Presence—Vartui having omitted, perhaps deliberately, to tell me.

At last, with an effort, he smiled and said, "It's cold today."

With these words he drew from his wide sleeve a muslin handkerchief, which he dropped to the ground; then he turned around slowly and left as silently as he had come.

No sooner had he disappeared than Vartui poked her head through the doorway, looked right and left, and rushed toward me as quickly as her respectable girth allowed. She was followed by her foremost ally, the Mistress of the Robes, and the Kizlar Aga. All three threw themselves on my neck, hugging and kissing one another and me. They laughed and cried at the same time. When they found the handkerchief left by the Sultan they went as far as to kneel without daring to touch it. At last Vartui picked it up, so solemnly that one might have thought it one of the Holy Relics of Islam. And in their frenzy, they could not stop squealing, "Nakshidil gözde, Nakshidil gözde."

When at last she calmed down, after she had brought me back to her apartment and lit her dear pipe, Vartui explained: "Now you are a gözde, one of the women who have caught the Sultan's eye. He's noticed you. He finds you attractive. He desires you."

I thought these conclusions a little hasty. "But he didn't say anything, or do anything."

"He spoke to you."

"Yes, he spoke about the weather. . . . "

She interrupted me curtly. "He spoke to you, and that's the sign. He marked you by that. And what about the handkerchief? Think—the handkerchief!"

"He dropped it by accident," I said sullenly.

"By accident! You little barbarian! The handkerchief is *the* sign of the Interest. It is reserved for those who truly please him. And you had both a word and the handkerchief. Allah be praised!"

Vartui also told me that she was happily surprised by what had just happened, for she hadn't thought me quite full enough for the Sultan, who normally liked buxom, generous women rather than unripe fruit. But, she added, the Master's eye was infallible, and there was no better judge of feminine beauty than he.

CHAPTER 7

———◆•◆———

I WAS MADE to move to the second floor in the gözdes' wing, above the court which bears their name. The lightness and spareness of my new apartment contrasted sharply with the gloomy clutter of Vartui's. The ornamented brass bed, of European inspiration, took up half the room, but I preferred it to the narrow mattress I had unrolled in a corner of Vartui's room. There were no more lessons, no more hours of service, no more exploratory expeditions through the harem. I had been chosen, and now I passed without transition from the state of slave to that of potential odalisque. I was kept in enforced idleness, a regimen usually reserved for the fattening of geese. Mountains of cakes and sweets were brought to me every day, so much so that to this day the sight of them nauseates me.

The presents normally given to a gözde never stopped streaming in: rows of pearls, sable-lined pelisses, Brusa velvet caftans, dozens of striped silk robes; in addition, several slaves and eunuchs were attached to my service. I was no longer allowed to do anything myself, not even carry a tray. Each of my steps, each of my gestures, was watched anxiously, as if I were made of glass and threatened to break at any moment.

From Vartui, who spent her days "hatching" me and keeping me company, I learned that my encounter with Abdul Hamid had not been fortuitous, as I had so naively believed, but was the result of long premeditation and a number of ruses. Having heard that the Sultan had reopened the apartments of his mother, and that he often went there to evoke her memory, Vartui had organized my harp practice, knowing full well that one day, attracted by that unusual sound and his taste for music, the Sultan would walk in on me.

I also learned that immediately upon my arrival at the harem I had been "typed." According to the experts I was a product of great rarity, from which one might derive considerable advantage: I was French, I was blond, I was spirited. The fact of my having been chosen at once had been carefully kept from me so as not to spoil my spontaneity, which, I was told, added to my charms.

I inquired as to who my sponsors were. The Kizlar Aga had noticed me immediately, but Vartui proudly told me that it was she who had brought me to Mirizshah's attention.

This name awoke an absurd fear in me, and I asked, "Does Prince Selim know about all this?"

"Certainly not. He would disapprove of this sort of . . . action."

I was relieved. As for Vartui, she swam in happiness, seeing her months of care and effort rewarded at last. From now on the sky was open to her . . . and to me.

"Gözde? Not bad," murmured Ristoglou, who had come to see me in Vartui's absence. "But the Sultan can forget you as he has forgotten so many others," he added. "And then, from one day to the next, no more jewels, no more dresses, no more slaves. They take everything from you, you become a slave yourself, and to punish you for your fall from grace they keep the dirtiest work for you."

Ristoglou's venom was the last straw. I had had enough of my idleness, Vartui's chatter, the waiting. In order to live here I had accepted many constraints which offended my nature and my personality. For better or for worse I had resigned myself to being cut off from my past, to imprisonment, to isolation in a stifling atmosphere. I had played the game of docility and had bent myself to the rules. I had adopted their customs with all the goodwill of which I was capable. But now my whole being rebelled against the fate that had been chosen for me. I refused to be thrown like a white goose into the bed of a stranger, sultan or not, to be deflowered. I had no wish to be sacrificed to an old man's lust.

I was then an adolescent, barely emerging from childhood; therefore I was excessive in my reactions. I chose to simply let myself die.

I came very close to succeeding. Having decided not to feed myself and to die of hunger, I accepted only water. Vartui paced around me like a caged animal, trying every trick she knew, from entreaty to blackmail, to bring me to my senses. I responded to her questions and exhortations with absolute silence and indifference.

After a week's hunger strike I had lost a good deal of weight, my skin had acquired an ugly yellow tinge, and I was too weak to stand on my feet.

I spent all day lying on my pillows, lost in vagueness, my lips sealed. Vartui wailed and beat her breast at my bedside. I think she herself had begun to waste away. She seemed to have given up questioning me and trying to convince me to feed myself, and was now content with staying beside me, holding my hand, shaking her head once in a while and crying silently. My condition became so serious that I was taken to the harem's hospital, below the slavewomen's wing. There I received the visit of Veli Zadeh, Mirizshah's adviser, a learned theologian with the reputation of a sage. He was a man, but in the hospital, which was considered death's antechamber, the barrier between the sexes was lowered. Was there not, in the courtyard, the Corpse Gate, its name a clear indication of its function? Although I was on the verge of coma, I can still remember Veli Zadeh leaning over me, his long pale face, his gray mustache, his kindly air, his eyes fixed on mine; those blue eyes were piercing, luminous, and had great hypnotic power. Veli Zadeh was, besides, a crafty politician and a fearsome wielder of psychology.

He began by telling me that he understood my position very well, that he had no intention of forcing my hand, that I could let myself starve to death if that was my wish. Nevertheless he wanted one favor from me, a single one: he wanted me to discuss it with him.

I did not react to his proposal—I was quite unable. He then suggested that I eat a little, just enough to give me the strength to explain my point of view and, if necessary, defend it. It was less my weakness than Veli Zadeh's eyes that made me nod assent. A light snack appeared immediately, an artfully dosed concoction of hulled rice, fruit juices, and sweetened stimulants.

When I had regained a little strength I whispered that I did not wish to be stuffed, pampered, and decked in ribbons in order to be served up as a slave to a man—worse, as a slave to a man's desire. Everyone was extremely concerned about my health and my physical state, but no one thought of worrying about my soul.

Veli Zadeh, who had listened to me patiently until then, interrupted me. "You are wrong, my dear child. It is precisely because we recognize the qualities of your soul and your mind that we chose you for the Mission."

I was in no state to listen. The effort of speaking had exhausted me. Veli Zadeh returned on the following days to check on the rapid progress of my youthful constitution. He kept up his indoctrination, diving into long tirades on Turkish politics. I followed with interest, my body weak but my mind alert.

The Ottoman Empire was still a great power. In order to remain one, however, it would have to leave the ruts of tradition and the past. The empire needed to wake up, to adapt to the changes of the era. It urgently needed radical reforms, without which the neighboring powers would get the better of it. Sultan Abdul Hamid was an intelligent, open-minded man, but he was old and tired, and a powerful party built on fanatical conservatism worked hard at maintaining the status quo. This party included the clergy, with its ulemas and its muftis, and a part of the army, with its fearsome janissaries—the terror of the empire—that praetorian guard which made, or rather unmade, sultans. Thanks to Sineperver's influence, they controlled the affairs of state.

I understood what was expected of me. I was supposed to seduce Abdul Hamid and dominate him in order to neutralize Sineperver's role, and thereby cut the trail for the reformers, for Mirizshah and her advisers, for Prince Selim. . . . Veli Zadeh reached my heart by treating me as an adult, by speaking to me directly and without affectation.

Soon I regained my gözde's apartment, Vartui's babble, and Ristoglou's semi-clandestine visits. "Mission! Reforms! Progress!" he would cry indignantly. "But they couldn't care less, you poor child! All they want is to have a girl at the Sultan's side who is entirely devoted to their cause, who will be the instrument of their power, and who can stifle the Sultan's suspicions toward them—for there is quite a little plotting around Prince Selim. They even say that some have thought of overthrowing our Sultan. And there has been conspiracy, contacts with foreign powers. . . . If we lived under a ruler slightly less kind than His Highness, your Prince Selim would have felt that silk bowstring around his neck long ago. Please understand that they need you only to protect him!"

Perhaps the hateful Ristoglou was right and they wanted to make use of me in a bitter struggle for power—but the party I was to represent was that of the future, that of Prince Selim.

How exalted I was! Did she really know what she was heading for in order to "protect Selim," that fifteen-year-old child I was? I still wonder. In any case, there is no trace in her notebooks of that night she was dragged, trembling, to old Abdul Hamid's bed.

The terse order was brought one November night by the Kizlar Aga. He appeared at Vartui's apartment and dropped a single word, my name: Nakshidil. There was an explosion of joy from Vartui, who immediately assembled the harem's female authorities—the Mistress of the Robes, the Guardian of the Jewels, and even her detested rival, the Grand Treasurer. For hour upon hour they busied themselves around me in turn, each of them directing the operations within her scope.

First I was taken to the hammam, where I was washed, scrubbed, and massaged with scented oils. Then they brushed my long hair, which they decided to leave loose down my back. The Guardian of the Baths, wielding her collection of Bohemian crystal flasks, scented each part of my body with a different essence. After that the Guardian of the Underclothes slipped me into a chemisette of almost transparent white Dacca muslin, lightly embroidered with gold. The Mistress of the Robes then brought long baggy trousers of red satin and a robe of silk decorated with silver flowers, and Vartui knotted a wide belt of purple Persian brocade on my hips.

The last phase of my adornment was left to the Guardian of the Jewels, who had sent for all her many-drawered little chests. She chose a very long necklace of pearls entwined with rings of gold set with rubies. An enormous pearl was hung from either ear, and twists of rubies and diamonds were pinned in my hair to fasten a veil of pink muslin. At last I was ready; in other words, I was petrified with terror.

Then Vartui gave me her last instructions: "In half an hour His Highness will retire to his apartment. You will be led to him. Remember that you are to approach the bed on your knees, kiss the counterpane, and wait."

Up to that moment, throughout those interminable preparations, I had not flinched. Now, facing the imminence of the event, I panicked. "I won't go! Do what you want to me! Whip me, kill me, but I won't go to the Sultan! You can't make me go! I don't want to!"

Vartui began to heap threats and abuse on me. She cried, she huffed and stuttered, she ran right and left, rounding up the ladies of the council, who all insulted and pleaded with me at once, vying with each other in demonstrations of despair. The Kizlar Aga appeared in the full splendor of his white silks, of his sable, of his train of eunuchs. It was time; he had come to fetch me. His entrance and the order he gave cut through the collective hysteria reigning in the apartment. All the wailing and rushing about ceased at once.

The Kizlar Aga, drawing his gold-handled dagger, walked up to me, grabbed me firmly, and pressed his blade against my neck. "You will go, woman, or I shall cut your throat here and now."

"I won't go!" I yelled. "Cut my throat, but I won't go!"

As I tried to squirm out of his grasp, the blade pricked my skin and a drop of blood beaded on my neck; the women resumed their shrieking.

The Kizlar Aga let me go. He sheathed his dagger carefully, and turning to Vartui, said, "Fetch Mirizshah—she's with Princess Hadidgeh."

Hiking up her skirts and her fur, her makeup running in her tears, Vartui obeyed with astonishing speed. Soon afterward she reappeared, red-faced and panting; in her wake came Kadin Mirizshah, as elegant, as collected, as gracious and smiling as always.

"Leave me alone with Nakshidil," she said.

When all the others had withdrawn, she spoke to me in the same friendly, even tone of voice she used in trivial conversation. "You have a difficult choice to make, and you have to make it quickly, for we have little time. On the one hand, there is nothingness—I'm not speaking about punishment or death; I know you and I know you're ready to face them. No, I'm speaking about an obscure, meaningless, joyless life. On the other hand, there is the possibility of glory, with its train of difficulties, of suffering and self-denial, but, in the end, success. Look at me; believe me, I knew a similar moment: I too felt that surge of horror and refusal, though I didn't show it, for I wasn't as brave as you. . . . And look at me now. I have known the love of a man, indeed a Sultan. I have a son, I have rank, I have power. Believe me, little Nakshidil, submit today and tomorrow you'll go further than all the rest of us. . . ."

She spoke these last words with a fervor which reminded me strangely of Euphemia David's prophecy: "You will earn the love of an unhappy ruler. . . . You will command a great empire. . . ."

So, speaking in a voice as assured as I could muster, I said, "I am ready."

All the lights in the hallways and the courts had been dimmed, and the harem was preparing for sleep, when I left Vartui's apartment on the heels of the Kizlar Aga. We crossed the Valideh's apartment and the long, dark, empty hallways of the imperial hammam. Reaching the last door, the Kizlar Aga bowed deeply before me, kissed the hem of my sleeve, and made way for me to pass.

I entered the room of Padishah Abdul Hamid I, which was in deep darkness. The room seemed very narrow and high-ceilinged, overloaded with decorations and gilded furniture. For a moment I stood frozen at the door, looking at the shiny, ornate canopy which sheltered the bed. Two old women in dark clothes, no doubt entrusted with keeping the torches lit, sat silently, without stirring, on the ground.

"Come here, my child, come here, and don't be afraid."

I could not yet see the man who gently called me. I took a step forward, and then another, and despite Vartui's orders, approached the imperial bed walking, holding myself very straight. With a sign, the Sultan bade me sit down on the edge of the bed, which was covered with embroidered cushions. He watched me serenely, and I did not flinch under his gaze.

Close up, wearing only a navy-blue robe without his turban and his diamonds, the Padishah did not look particularly impressive. He was just a rather bald man on whom the years had left their mark. Suddenly a wave of harmonious words spilled from his mouth as he watched me with a tender, amused expression:

"My capricious one, how did you grow so bold?
And how did you grow so straight, to defy the cypress tree?

That scented color which drains the rose,
Did you steal it, my love, from that flower's embrace?

That robe, scarlet with roses—does it not wound your fine skin,
My lovely, for a rose is never without thorns.

When you come to me, holding the rose and the cup,
My heart gives in. . . . "

It took me a moment to understand that Abdul Hamid was reciting poetry to me. Then, without taking his eyes off me, he drew me near to him, and slowly began to caress my hair, my shoulders, my arms, and then, through the light cloth which covered them, my breasts. He whispered disconnected words in my ear; they were only trivial compliments, but their sound and the rhythm of his intonations stirred me strangely. Little by little I was invaded by an irresistible torpor, a sort of warmth, and when he began to undress me, I let him kiss each part of my body as he uncovered it, with a slow science which exasperated my senses. When I was completely naked, pink and blond against the dark velvet, I felt a surge of shame at the thought of the two old women crouched in the room. But already Abdul Hamid's soft and skillful hands were parting my thighs, and I forgot all modesty; a new and violent desire drew me to that man. I gave myself up to him, wanting only the weight and the warmth of his body on mine.

Later, while we rested side by side, sated and relaxed, I shuddered and my hand clutched the coverlet. Abdul Hamid sensed my tension and again began to caress my hands and face tenderly. In a warm, hoarse voice, already heavy with sleep, he murmured:

"Thank you, child, for what you have just given me. Your youth and your innocence are the most beautiful gifts an old man like me can receive. May you be as happy as you have made me."

"But I am happy, my lord. Thanks to you I have become a woman in joy and in tenderness."

"So you don't regret not having starved yourself to death, or letting yourself be stabbed by the dagger of my Kizlar Aga?"

I started. How did Abdul Hamid know? Later on I was to learn that Abdul Hamid always knew everything. Now I even dared tease the Sultan: "I expected to be devoured by an ogre."

Abdul Hamid smiled. "It is more Kadin Mirizshah than chance who led you to my bed. But her choice was inspired—by your beauty and your spirit. You are a gift from Allah."

In the morning I awoke alone. A dirty light seeped in through the tall casements, shining coldly on the excessive gilding of the bed and the paneling. The clothes I had worn the night before were strewn on the floor, mixed in with Abdul Hamid's. Well in evidence at the foot of the bed was a new pelisse, of silver-frogged cobalt-blue cloth lined with chinchilla. On a cushion next to me lay a fat purse and an enormous round ruby of an extraordinary deep red, set in diamonds—presents left for me by Abdul Hamid.

The door opened as soon as I stirred, admitting the Kizlar Aga and his eunuchs, who had been waiting for me to waken. Bustling about me with much deference, they wrapped me in my new pelisse and led me to Vartui, who went into raptures at the sight of the Padishah's gifts, carefully counted the gold pieces, and smothered me in kisses.

I turned on her bitterly, saying that I had been rewarded like the most common courtesan, and again she scolded my ignorance. "How can you say such stupid things? The importance of the gifts shows the Sultan's gratitude and appreciation. And believe me, the harem has never seen such a sum and such a jewel given after a first night. The ruby given to Abdul Hamid by the Mogul—just imagine!"

After one night in the Sultan's bed I had become an ikbal, one of the favorites, the twelfth in rank. Once again I had to change apartments; I moved into the favorites' wing. My new lodgings consisted of two small rooms under the eaves, badly lit through the fanlights which overlooked acres of lead, bronze, and sheet metal—the harem's rooftops. Although to have such an apartment was the dream and ambition of every harem girl, I was unable to repress a disappointed pout as I took note of the worn drapes, the peeling frescoes, the cramped surroundings. In an effort to console me, Vartui pointed out the new carpet, which I thought too loud, and the mahogany clock, made in London, which had Arab numerals on its face.

I might have been only the twelfth ikbal, but the Sultan neglected the first eleven.

Every evening when the harem's curfew had sounded, the Kizlar Aga led me to his master's stifling and disgraceful room. I hated its tall windows, the heavy baroque of the gray volutes on their yellow background, the naive imitations of French landscapes on the paneling.

I was quite inexperienced in the games of love, and yet I felt that what that master voluptuary liked in me was precisely a natural, frank, instinctive sensuality. As prodigal in love as he was with gifts, Abdul Hamid delicately taught me the secrets of sensual delight and rejoiced at my progress. With him, thanks to him, I learned the joys and also the power of pleasure and possession. I surprised myself by forgetting Abdul Hamid's age at such moments, forgetting his wrinkles, his baldness, his dyed beard, his narrow shoulders and weak belly—all those things which might have repelled me.

Not once did I wonder about the question of good and evil according to the moral code of my former environment, of my family and my upbringing. I reacted solely by instinct, and my instinct told me that the intimacy, the tenderness, the pleasure I shared with my lover could not possibly be sinful. Our relationship fulfilled us both; he gave me, after love, the affection and protection of a father, while in exchange I had a feeling of restoring self-confidence to an old man nearing the end of his troubles. His experience and wisdom were precious to me; I had nothing but respect for him, and sometimes it occurred to me that I loved him.

We would spend long hours in each other's arms, gradually discovering the happiness of being together. Within a few weeks Abdul Hamid was no longer content with my nights, and demanded my days as well. One morning the Kizlar Aga came for me and we took an unfamiliar itinerary to the Sultan. We followed the gözdes' corridor on the second floor and then climbed down a very dark and narrow staircase, a sort of tunnel which seemed to penetrate into the very bowels of the Seraglio. The Kizlar Aga swiveled a secret door concealed in the paneling. It opened upon a drawing room with a sculpted fireplace and light, flowery paintings. I found Abdul Hamid in a connecting room, large but low-ceilinged, each wall of which was covered with mirrors fitted into gilded strips of wood.

Abdul Hamid immediately relinquished his hookah and, flattered by my surprise and curiosity, conducted me around what he modestly called his "lair." One by one he showed me the primitive paintings of the principal cities of the empire: Adrianople, Belgrade, Bucharest, Athens, Baghdad, Jerusalem, Damascus, Cairo, Tripoli, Algiers. . . .

While the Sultan lives and sleeps in the harem, among women, his days are spent in the selamlik, which is the men's domain. Served by pages and white eunuchs who are not allowed in the harem, he works and gives audiences in the kiosks and pavilions which he builds, at whim, among the terraces and gardens. Abdul Hamid had installed himself at the border between the harem and the selamlik; the pavilion he had built there bore the name Mabeyn, which means "in between," and there he could receive members of either sex.

"Especially the weaker sex," I said, interrupting him in the midst of his explanations.

Slightly embarrassed, he began to talk to me in verse, as was his charming habit.

> "The call of your dimple, upon my word, is clear enough;
> Verve perhaps we lack, but not reason.
> Between the cup of love you hold and us,
> There is more than one secret understanding: Give it . . .
> My pretty one, in the old quarter of Besiktas
> My old shack awaits you; come and be its mistress."

I didn't know whether I would be the mistress of that luxurious pavilion which he called his "old shack," but I certainly was his mistress inside it. My incongruous presence in that place which was usually reserved for work, or perhaps a sudden desire to see my naked body multiplied and reflected to infinity by the mirrors, had aroused him.

"Take off your clothes, Nakshidil," he asked tenderly.

Later he told me that never until then had he made love there during the day. And I told him I had some trouble believing him.

If love trysts were new to the Mabeyn, they soon became a habit. I wondered why Abdul Hamid had covered all the windows of the "old shack" with mirrors; he explained that in order to achieve perfect concentration in his workroom he had to protect himself from distracting views.

"He doesn't want to be seen because he's afraid of assassins," whispered Ristoglou when I mentioned this.

At any rate, the Sultan opened up in the Mabeyn. Little by little he consented to speak of himself, to tell me of his memories:

"My father, Ahmed III, died when I was five. Throughout their reigns, my cousins Mahmud I and Osman III forgot me in the Cage. The only comforting presence which helped me endure my fate was that of my mother. I spent all those years devouring ancient chronicles, and often it was only my conviction of our greatness which kept me from despair. Imagine, Nakshidil: I spent forty-three years in the Cage. And then one day my brother Mustafa III, the father of my heir, Selim, died; and I found myself Sultan, with no transition between the Cage and supreme power."

"Of all the women you have known, my lord," I asked suddenly, "did you love many?"

"Only one. Her name was Rusah. She was stubborn and rebellious and she wouldn't give in to either my threats or my entreaties. The letters I wrote her! Pure delirium! And I wasn't eighteen years old anymore. I'm still ashamed of it. She was literally untameable. Perhaps that is what attracted me to her. You remind me of her a bit."

"And what became of her?"

"She went on a pilgrimage to Mecca a few years ago, and there she was touched by grace. She decided to retire from the world and live as a hermit. I never saw her again."

Abdul Hamid gave me three presents: first, Ali Effendi, a very small and fat black eunuch, with a round face topped with a tousled mop. Abdul Hamid assured me that he had chosen Ali Effendi because of his equally remarkable intelligence and skill. He was wily, funny, full of tricks, and he made me laugh constantly.

The second present was named Cevri, and was a gigantic Georgian woman built like a wrestler, with a pug nose and tiny searching eyes. "She's fidelity personified," Abdul Hamid assured me. "Besides, she's so strong that she'll be able to protect you and, if necessary, defend you."

As for Abdul Hamid's third gift ... I was dressing in my apartment one night, getting ready to join him, when a strangely muffled voice made me jump. "Good evening, beautiful Nakshidil!"

I was alone in the room, and I thought I had been dreaming. But the voice repeated: "Good evening, beautiful Nakshidil!"

These mysterious greetings seemed to emanate from a small wicker chest I had never seen before. I rushed over, opened it, and found a parrot. I named it Monsieur Jolibois, for his voice reminded me of that of my old harp teacher.

Vartui went wild with joy at the sight of these presents. She could already see me surpassing in fame those former favorites whose destinies were all the talk of the harem. She launched into an enumeration of every long since dead kadin who had left her mark on history. The most famous of all was the legendary Roxelana, a jovial Russian woman highly skilled at ridding herself of rivals and unaccommodating viziers. She enslaved Suleiman the Magnificent, before whom all Europe trembled; and she was also the only one to have managed the unthinkable—marrying the Sultan. And then Kussem! Kussem was Greek; besides beauty, charm, and exquisite manners, she was endowed with skill to match her limitless ambition. She had been Ahmed I's favorite, and her wish was his command. She became an all-powerful Valideh when her son Murad IV came to the throne, and remained in power throughout the reign of her second son, Ibrahim, and her grandson Mohammed IV.

"Yes, and the old hag was strangled when her daughter-in-law decided to become Sultana herself," added Ristoglou when, during one of his visits—which had grown brief and rare—I mentioned Kussem's prodigious destiny. To hear him was to know that intrigues, plots, and assassinations had always been practiced in the harem. His favorite sultan was cruel Ibrahim, the mad ruler who, on suspicion, on a eunuch's denunciation, had two hundred and sixty women of the harem sewn into burlap sacks and thrown into the Bosporus. According to Ristoglou, the three pillars of the harem were jealousy, slander, and concealed violence. The favorites were their most obvious victims, and few were the kadins who reached an advanced age or died a natural death. I slept badly that night, with nightmares of blood and violence that would have delighted Ristoglou, who inspired them.

One morning in December I found a very nervous Abdul Hamid pacing up and down in the Mabeyn. He was preoccupied by the war with Russia. With unusual vehemence he painted his old enemy Empress Catherine II as a sort of ogress with exorbitant ambitions. "Now that she's had herself proclaimed Empress of all the Russias after assassinating her husband, she wants to restore the old Byzantine Empire and be crowned Basilissa of the Greeks, here in Constantinople, at the Basilica of Saint Sophia. She never stops harassing my empire, and when she isn't waging war on me she foments plots and stirs up the provinces against us. All this has been going on for too long, and so I have decided to attack. One hundred and fifty thousand of my troops have crossed into Russia and are already on the Dnieper. Today I shall send my fleet to lend them support. Come with me; I'm going to review it."

Carried away with enthusiasm or absentmindedness, Abdul Hamid had asked me to accompany him without realizing that he ran the risk of causing a state scandal. How could an ikbal leave the harem for a few yards to reach the terrace of the selamlik with the Sultan?

Vartui and the Kizlar Aga were summoned. Both suggested complicated and unacceptable solutions. Finally crafty Ali Effendi proposed a satisfactory compromise. Perhaps one of the imperial princesses might decide to attend the review and, claiming fatigue, go to the selamlik in a litter? In that case, who could object to my presence, hidden from all eyes, at the side of the princess?

Princess Esmee then had to be convinced to interrupt her work distilling scent; and at last I found myself lying next to a hostile Esmee, rocked by the movement of the eunuch litter-bearers. We traveled the entire length of the corridor called the Golden Road, passed in front of the Mabeyn, and arrived at a small arched door made of bronze. Behind it stretched the selamlik, the Fourth Court, the men's domain, the Sultan's private quarters—a checkerboard of terraces and pools, of gardens studded with cypresses and century-old plane trees and the graceful kiosks of Erivan, of Baghdad, of the Circumcision, of the Tent, of Mustafa the Black. . . . The procession came to a halt in a forest of columns between the pavilions of Erivan and the Circumcision, facing a large marble pool. Abdul Hamid sat down on his silver sofa-throne and had the litter placed next to him. Two colorful processions of eunuchs and courtiers emerged from the pavilions, surrounding the ten-year-old Prince Mustafa, son of Sineperver, and little Prince Mahmud. I was curious to see the French kadin's son; the little boy, wearing a brocaded caftan, moved toward us with a grave dignity unusual for his age.

The opening in the litter's curtains suddenly revealed an enormous lion, held on a leash by a eunuch, and walking slowly in our direction. A start of terror threw me into Esmee's arms.

"My best friend, Karayoz," said Abdul Hamid. "He's tame and as meek as a lamb."

Whether the beast was tame or not, I noticed that the dignitaries maintained a respectful distance.

The Capitan Pasha arrived at last, surrounded by his staff of officers wearing baggy breeches and fringed turbans. Hassan Pasha, the hero and defender of the empire, was then the talk of all the harem. A solemn, steady old man, he did not at all fit the image I held of a powerful war chieftain.

"An adventurer risen from nothing," said Esmee, who despised him. "He had to run from Algiers after having robbed the Dey."

"And I fished him out of prison to make him my Capitan Pasha," finished Abdul Hamid.

Everyone took his place according to rank, and soon everything was ready—except for one detail: How were we to review a fleet from this place where neither the port nor the sea could be seen? I was busy contemplating this mystery when, on a sign from the Sultan, there appeared a flock of eunuchs, each one carrying a model ship which was then placed in a marble pool.

"These models are exact reproductions of my ships," Abdul Hamid whispered proudly. "Look, Nakshidil—twenty-five convoy ships, fifteen frigates, and forty-five bombardiers."

Water spouts in the pool were turned on, and the turbulence they created on the surface pushed this strange fleet along. Abdul Hamid told me the name of each ship as it bobbed past us. They all bore the names of late sultans: Osman, Orkhan, Murad I, Bajazet I, Suleiman I, Selim I, Ibrahim. . . .

Waving at his ridiculous toys, Abdul Hamid told Hassan Pasha, "With all of that we can beat them, those damned Russians!"

The Capitan Pasha, while respectfully agreeing, tried to moderate his master's enthusiasm. The Russian troops were well trained, their one-eyed leader, Potemkin, Empress Catherine's most recent lover, was an experienced general, and his aide Suvarov a worrisome devil. But nothing could diminish Abdul Hamid's enthusiasm, which began to irritate me.

When we were alone again I asked, "My lord, wouldn't you prefer to inspect your ships rather than that make-believe fleet?"

"Those models, what you call my make-believe fleet, are quite enough."

"Don't you fear that people might say that the make-believe fleet belongs to a make-believe sultan?"

"The winter wind on the Bosporus is too sharp for the Sultan to face."

"Is that because it is the wind of reality? How can you defend your empire, my lord, if you never leave this palace, which is hermetically sealed to truth and the times?"

"The Seraglio, it is true, begets illusion. But what is not illusion? The power of the empire—an illusion. The greatness of my reign— an illusion which lives only in the verses of the court poets. Everything is illusion here, and it's all for the better."

"And you, my lord, you who know the truth—are you satisfied with the illusion?"

"At my age, Nakshidil, illusion is my only comfort. Even you, even your love for me is but an illusion."

I was about to protest, but Abdul Hamid did not give me time enough. "Look, Nakshidil—Hassan Pasha's present."

Hassan Pasha had given Abdul Hamid a dwarf for his collection of jesters. He was, I must say, quite a rarity: a one-eyed, one-armed, club-footed, mute eunuch. Enthused at the sight of this arrival, Abdul Hamid named him Fateh—the Conqueror—hoping the dwarf would bring him luck in war.

A very strange and upsetting incident took place. The protocol of my visits to the Sultan had been growing somewhat more lax. I had been going to the Mabeyn accompanied not by the Kizlar Aga and the eunuchs, but only by Cevri, my Georgian giantess.

The day had been rainy, and night fell early from a cloudy, sullen sky. I walked ahead with the lantern, hurrying because the darkness and solitude of the corridors and stairways only added to their sinister character.

We climbed down the favorites' staircase, crossed the Djinns' Council, and were heading for the Golden Road when suddenly I detected a presence, a movement, in a recess on my left. Almost simultaneously a violent blow to my hand made me drop the lantern, which crashed to the ground and went out. Instinctively I leaped back, and then everything happened very fast. I heard Cevri behind me; I felt, rather than saw, her enormous arm rise and crash down on some indistinct form. There was a groan of pain, and then silence. Cevri lifted me in her arms and carried me off at a run. She put me back on my feet only once we had reached the lighted part of the Golden Road. She was barely out of breath from her race, and only her little prying eyes darting around showed any signs of anxiety. I was trembling; but once I overcame my fear, curiosity led me back to the spot where we had been attacked. We took two torches from the Golden Road and retraced our steps; although we explored every corner, every recess, the place was deserted. Not a trace of our aggressor. But we did find an object on the ground, a curved dagger. . . .

I was preparing to report everything to Abdul Hamid when Ali Effendi stopped me. "First have the goodness to examine the matter with your servant."

I protested, "But someone tried to kill me!"

"Perhaps someone only wanted to frighten you. The dagger is not the harem's favorite tool for elimination."

"But who? I cannot swear it, but I think I recognized the voice that groaned under Cevri's blow—it was Ristoglou's. I know he hates me, but I can't see why he should want to kill me—or even frighten me, as you put it."

"Gold lurks behind many an indelicacy."

"Who would have paid him? A jealous kadin?"

"I can think of only one who would dare attack the Sultan's favorite—the most ambitious and dangerous of the kadins: the first kadin."

"Sineperver! I shall report her to the Sultan."

"You will achieve nothing by that, except embarrassing His Highness. Besides, he won't take action against the first kadin."

"I'll have Ristoglou arrested and questioned."

"He'll deny everything, and if that isn't enough, he'll lay the blame on some innocent eunuch, who will lose his life."

"So there is no way of confronting Sineperver?"

"She's too powerful for that."

"How then can we put a stop to her machinations?"

"By becoming more powerful than she is."

Suddenly Ristoglou's terrible stories of the harem's past returned to my memory, and his pleasure in telling them. Had he wanted to warn me against an overly swift climb? An Oriental court, a harem, I discovered, were forever the scene of a constant struggle for power, a struggle all the fiercer for the fact that it remained underground. In any case, Ali Effendi had convinced me. I decided to keep the affair a secret, and not mention it to Abdul Hamid, nor even to Vartui. What point was there in stirring up sterile agitation, when the harem shelters its mysteries so well?

Christmas came, my first Christmas away from my people. I was overcome by the sadness and nostalgia borne by memories of former Christmases—especially the happy ones of my childhood in Martinique, where, despite the heat, we made every effort to uphold tradition: the family celebration, midnight mass at the Robert church, the exchange of presents in front of the crèche. . . . I also thought of Christmas in France, in the fairyland of winter, with my cousin Marie-Anne: the return from the cathedral through the snowy streets of Nantes, supper by the heat of the fireplace, the first glass of champagne I was given. . . .

To top it all, Abdul Hamid could not receive me that night. He was busy with his advisers and the war with Russia. Finally I yielded to Vartui's invitation, since she was always so happy to prattle about the latest harem gossip over a glass of Cyprus wine and a box of loukhoums.

The evening was quiet, and I was only half listening to the dear chatterbox when explosions rent the air. We rushed to the window, to see fabulous fireworks gradually lighting up the harem and the entire city. Rockets flared up from everywhere, to burst into multi-colored compositions in the sky. Of course we were not celebrating Christmas; the big event was the birth of Princess Hibetula, daughter of Abdul Hamid and his fourth kadin, Cebicefa.

This news, which Vartui gave me with perfect calm, unleashed in me a violent, unfamiliar, overpowering emotion. No matter how hard I tried to reason, telling myself that the child had been conceived before I entered Abdul Hamid's life, I suffered; and for the first time, I suffered because of a man. Vartui, unaware of the effect of her gossip, babbled on:

"By order of the Sultan, the Princess's dowry has already been established: twenty-eight shops have been bought, thirty-one offices in Argos, two important vineyards in Anatolia; and she has also been given a palace at Kurusene."

I burst into tears in the midst of this terrible enumeration. Vartui looked at me with stupefaction, her blue eyes rounder than ever. How could I explain the emotions which stirred in me, which continued to stir in me for days afterward? Suddenly I felt a foreigner again, despite all my efforts to adapt to my situation and bend to the rules and customs of this universe. What I wrote in my diary that evening clearly shows the turmoil that reigned within me.

December 25, 1788: Loving and generous though he is, I remain an object of Abdul Hamid's pleasure, spending long hours doing nothing other than wait for his call. I am nothing but a slave—and a slave among others. Though he hides it, and no one dares speak of it to me, I feel that he has not renounced his kadins. Am I jealous, then? But if I am jealous, then I must be in love. Could I be in love with that fickle old man? No—I simply refuse to share a man who I thought belonged to me. But where does possessiveness stop and love begin?

I avoided answering that question in my diary. I completed the entry by simply promising myself that Abdul Hamid had something coming to him.

One night before joining him in the mirrored drawing room, I devoted particular care to my apparel. I deliberately put on all my jewels—emeralds, pearls, and diamonds—omitting only one: the big ruby Abdul Hamid had given me after our first night together. Never had I appeared before the Sultan in such magnificent attire. He gaped with admiration.

I looked like a queen, and played the part of a slave. I took upon myself all the tasks of the humblest of gediklis, the "privileged" girls who served him as chambermaids. While I prepared his hookah, arranged his pillows, and adjusted his lamp, he watched me in silence, fingering his worry beads and the diamond setting of his ring.

Unlike poor Vartui, he was quite a connoisseur of feminine psychology. While adjusting the emerald-encrusted bowl of his hookah, he began to talk to me. He loved me, he said. He preferred me to all his other women; but he could not keep himself exclusively for me. He was too old to change the habits of a lifetime, to change the ancestral customs. Besides, he added, I had to admit that monogamy was not a sign of love. Over the centuries even the best-loved and most domineering kadins had never demanded physical exclusivity from their lords. Kussem and even Roxelana—who had governed the harem, the Sultan, and the empire—had never taken offense at the fact that their lords sometimes slept with other women.

At the end of this speech Abdul Hamid fell silent and waited. I too remained stubbornly mute. Dinner was brought, and I continued to follow protocol to the letter. I served him the white bread—

the Sultan's exclusive privilege—made of white maize from Bithynia and goat's milk. I gave him the soup bowl of antique china, the sherbet cup of gold and diamonds. I lifted the covers of the dishes of boiled mutton, grilled lamb on a pyramid of rice, roast pigeon—the Sultan's delights. Abdul Hamid did not break the silence, conforming to the Oriental custom of courtesy and hygiene by which one does not speak while eating. His meal over, a glass of raki in his hand—the Turks drink after their meal, not during—he leaned toward me and, smiling, began:

> "One day you shall be the slave
> Of this love you disdain,
> And you shall see how hard it is;
> I know that time will come."

Unfortunately, for him, I knew the rest of the poem—the erudite Ristoglou's lessons had borne their fruit; I continued it for him:

> "Unfaithful? You were so a thousand times,
> And you took your pleasure elsewhere.
> The pain you caused your lover
> Will be returned to you a hundredfold."

The aptness of the quotation brought tears to my lover's eyes. Enthused, he continued the joust, knowing already that I was surrendering.

> "One day, without requital,
> You shall love; it will hurt.
>
> Throw me not that perfidious glance,
> And give me not that smile. . . .
> Pay no heed to my lovelorn words.
> You shall see—I speak the truth!"

My fit of jealousy had various repercussions. Although the Sultan told me nothing, I learned through the harem grapevine that he no longer spent even a single night with any of his kadins, and that he had mended his mischievous ways with the gediklis. Those who counted on his unfaithfulness to me had earned their disappointment. In apology, but without saying as much, he decided to have a fountain built in my name in the city. He let me choose the spot; and I said I wanted it built in front of Constantinople's big prison, in order that it might be seen by the inmates, my companions in misfortune. Abdul Hamid seemed not to notice my perfidy and ordered the work to begin. It stands to this day, facing the prison, the fountain of Nakshidil Kadin.

My parrot, Monsieur Jolibois, was also to retain some memory of my jealousy, in the form of insults I hurled at my lover in his absence. "The old pig! The lubricious satyr!" he would croak, usually in the presence of my servants, while I shivered at the idea that one of them might understand French. It was impossible to shut him up. One cannot gag a parrot—nor the human heart.

One morning Abdul Hamid burst into the music school while I was practicing the harp. His eyes sparkled with mischief. It was a day of Divan, the council of ministers. The Sultan does not preside over the Divan, but attends it hidden in a latticed gallery above the Grand Vizier's seat, so that the ministers cannot be sure he is present. He takes no part in the deliberations, but after the session he is free to approve, to criticize, or to summon the executioner.

"I've just come from the Divan," he told me, "where I was doing my job, spying. My Grand Vizier is at the front, where, I might add, he is scoring victory after victory over the Russians. His aide, the Caimacam, replaced him. He's so old, and he speaks so slowly, all the heads in the room were nodding, and I too began to fall asleep in my box. So I went out into the eunuchs' courtyard to stretch my legs, and there I ran into your Ali Effendi. He gave me an idea. . . . Come with me!"

I followed him down the spiral staircase that leads to the box in the Divan. Through the gilded lattice I could see, below me, the government of the Turkish Empire at work. The green robes of the kasaskeris, the high magistrates, clashed with the viziers'—the ministers'—caftans: white and gold, pink and gold, yellow and gold. The respectable turban of the Rais Effendi, minister of foreign affairs, seemed very modest next to the yellow-and-white scaffolding on the head of the Kehaya Bey, minister of the interior, and the red-and-white version of the Jeniseri Agassi, head janissary. More than half the dignitaries had fallen asleep on their sofas. In a corner, trying to stay awake, the Tchaouch Batchey, minister of justice, gossiped with the Stambul Effendes, governor of Constantinople.

Suddenly we heard a prodigious roar. The sleeping assembly leaped up; the viziers, aghast, looked at each other in terror. Then, prodded by Ali Effendi, the lion Karayoz trotted into the Divan, spreading indescribable panic among the notables of the empire. Ministers and scribes rushed for the exits, jumped out the windows, buried themselves in their sofas. The old Caimacam found himself hanging from the lattice of the imperial loge, while the Kehaya Bey, who had been slumbering so peacefully moments before, was trampled by fleeing scribes. The sight was irresistibly funny, and watching those usually solemn and pompous officials tripping over their robes and shrieking like old women, I laughed to tears, next to a convulsed Abdul Hamid. I was deeply touched by this need to laugh, by this fondness for practical jokes. It was moving to think that I brought out the child in that powerful sultan, that man smothered in years, in women, in misfortune.

Although I could not truly speak of happiness, my existence did not lack elements to compensate for it. Sometimes I grew nostalgic at the thought of the past I had been torn from, of the future that might have been mine. Nevertheless, family, love, freedom—those are words which seemed so much out of context here, so distant. I had a growing feeling of unreality, as if I were living someone else's life, as if I were sleepwalking. When I arrived in the harem I had been too tense, too insistent on not adapting myself to my new surroundings, to succeed. At the same time, everything that happened to me seemed perfectly natural. I almost loved an old man who worshiped me. I had at my feet the all-powerful master of an immense empire. The unbelievable seemed to me perfectly believable. In lesser words, I was quite conscious of the advantages and privileges I enjoyed. Sometimes I thought of the poor girls who spent their lives washing floors and serving the kadins while awaiting the Sultan's whim, and I shuddered at the thought that their fate could have been mine.

It was at this time that I received Mother Marie-Agnès's first letter.

My child, I was both surprised and unsurprised to get your letter. Surprised, as you may imagine, to learn that you are still alive. Unsurprised to find that your character has enabled you to overcome your trials. Surprised that the favorite of a heathen ruler should take up her pen to correspond with a servant of God. Unsurprised that you should write to me before writing to anyone else. In that I recognize your instincts, and I bless them. You may well conceive our despair at the thought that you had perished in the wreck of *La Belle Mouette*. I have heard that your father still does not master his grief, and that your cousin Marie-Anne cannot forgive herself for having unwittingly sent you to your death. Nevertheless I strongly advise you not to write them, if you are planning to do so. Your "resurrection"—may God forgive my use of the word—could only be, of course, the happiest of news. Of course your family would rejoice at your having escaped a terrible death, just as they would have only compassion for the terrible state of slavery you endured. But your present state, and moreover the fact that you seem resigned to it, would cause them shame and horror. The consenting concubine of a heathen would be a stain on the escutcheon of a Christian and an aristocratic family. Your fate is one they would think worse than death. They would find themselves torn between their love for you and the intransigent principles of our religion. It is only because my state brings me to closer to God that I can better understand and tolerate. Believe me, it is best to let them mourn you and think of you as an angel in Heaven than to cause them suffering and perhaps force them to rebuff your advances.

Our convent, your former school, has not changed since you left; but outside its walls France seethes in silence. King Louis XVI, our sovereign, sees his good intentions rent asunder and his power paralyzed by various pressures. The people grumble, and the mighty dizzy themselves with reckless amusements; an order in place for a thousand years cannot, in their opinion, possibly change. I put myself among those who claim to be clairvoyant, and I feel a coming storm. Therefore it is a source of relief to me that you are far away from here.

You ask me for guidance, my child. What advice can I give a person in your position? Keep your faith, even if you are unable to practice your religion, even if you are presently living in sin. Pray. . . . God forgives more readily than human beings. Try to make yourself useful to others. Distress hides in every corner of life. Track it down and do your utmost to alleviate it. It is thus you will please God, whose favorite children are the unfortunate, no matter what their religion. It is thus you shall erase what the world would see as the scandal of your life. The Sultan, a heathen, the all-powerful master of an empire, is only a man and might need your help more than you imagine. If he has allowed you to write me, he must be a kindly man, if it is true, as you tell me, that such a thing breaks the immemorial rules of the harem.

I shall continue to write you under the fictitious name you wish me to use, in the hope that your able eunuch will manage to collect my messages. Please believe, my child, in my devotion to and my religious affection for you.

Mother Marie-Agnès's letter was worthy of her, and nothing less than I expected. It clarified points I could face only in confusion. I could not renew ties with my family. But did I really wish to? Mother Marie-Agnès had answered my call. Her support and her advice were enough for me.

In February of 1789, the roofs of the harem were covered in white cotton wool. Bad news came with the first snow: The Capitan Pasha, who had attempted to land his troops in southern Russia, had been repulsed. There remained almost nothing of the fleet whose illusion Abdul Hamid had so proudly reviewed. I was given this information, as I awoke one morning, by Ali Effendi, who was always the first to know anything.

I hurried along the interior corridors to the Mabeyn. I was about to open the panel concealing the secret stairway when I heard a man's voice, which I recognized as Hassan Pasha's. I stayed hidden, but pushed the panel slightly so as to hear without being seen.

"We fell into a trap," Hassan Pasha was saying. "Suvarov had hidden his artillery behind the dunes on the banks of the Dniester. He let our fleet sail up into the river before unleashing a hail of cannon fire. Six of our ships sank; seven, including mine, ran aground. Crushed under the Russian cannonballs, our sailors jumped overboard to try to swim ashore. I found myself sitting on the sand, crying as I watched the disaster, utterly powerless. I managed to assemble the shreds of the fleet and sail out of the trap, only to find that retreat was impossible. An American pirate in the pay of the Russians, George Wainscott, who had hidden in a creek until then, attacked us from behind. We were caught in a pincer. Nevertheless I succeeded in slipping through and gaining the high seas, but we lost fifteen convoy ships and eighteen frigates. Five thousand of our men died, and another six thousand were taken prisoner. Alas, my lord, fate decreed that I must lose this battle, and I have come to give you my head. The hand of fate is against me."

Abdul Hamid dismissed Hassan Pasha's offer of his life with a wave of the hand. "No, Hassan Pasha, it is I who am dogged by fate, and your head will not appease her. Retire, rest, and pray for your Sultan."

I joined Abdul Hamid later on, only to learn that the situation on all fronts was nothing short of catastrophic. Crushed, he told me that he could not understand why the truth had been hidden from him for so long; it was not the right moment to point out that it was he who had hidden it from himself. In Serbia and in Bosnia the armies of the Grand Vizier had been forced to retreat. Moldavia was lost, and the Turkish lines of communication cut. There was no longer any barrier protecting the Balkans from enemy invasion.

In the midst of this litany of disasters I saw Abdul Hamid suddenly bring his hand to his chest and open his mouth as if he were fighting for breath. I rushed over to him and helped him lie down. His face had grown waxen. I begged the Kizlar Aga to fetch the doctors, but Abdul Hamid, in a barely audible voice, stopped him. "That isn't necessary; I've already had this sort of seizure. Just bring me a glass of raki. Don't be afraid, my child; it's nothing. Only let me rest a little."

Later in the evening I joined him in the mirrored room. I found him recovered, but deeply depressed. "There is a prophecy which foresaw a woman come from the North entering Constantinople in triumph and being crowned Byzantine Basilissa at Saint Sophia. I used to make fun of it, but my subjects knew. . . . In the end, Catherine will take my capital."

"And what will you do then, my lord?"

"I'll cross the Bosporus. The Asiatic shore has always been our refuge."

That afternoon he had begun to prepare the transport of his court and his treasury to Asia. Several loads had already crossed the Bosporus, and he had ordered the restoration of an old unused palace at Bostanci, on the Asiatic shore of the Sea of Marmara.

"And I've reserved the most beautiful apartments facing the sea for you. I hope you'll like them, Nakshidil."

"Is it not true, my lord, that when your ancestor laid siege to Constantinople, the Byzantine emperor decided to stay, to fight and die among his people, even though he could have fled?"

"Yes, but he had weapons," objected Abdul Hamid. "Our arsenals are empty. We wouldn't hold twenty-four hours under siege."

"But what will your subjects think if you leave?"

"It is their example I am following, Nakshidil. They've already prepared their retreat. My faithful collaborator, the Kizlar Aga, has emptied his harem apartment as well as his houses in town. The Grand Vizier has sent orders from the front to remove the capital he has accumulated during his years in my service. Sineperver, my first kadin, left a few hours ago for my most distant palace."

I was discovering, for the first time, the old man's total solitude. Yet I insisted that he stay. He listened to me thoughtfully, and then explained that he was fighting not Catherine but kismet, fate—"far more powerful than the Czarina," he added.

"My reign has always been one of disasters. I have known only defeats. I have seen my empire eroded and weakened. One cannot struggle with kismet, Nakshidil. When you're young, at least you can still hope. When you're as tired as I am, there is nothing to do but give up."

"Is everything lost, then?"

"There is still a single dim hope. Our troops still hold the fortress of Ochakov on the Dniester. The Russians are laying siege to it, and our garrison is prepared to die rather than surrender. But Potemkin, with his one hundred and twenty thousand men, will make short shrift of our garrison of twenty-five thousand soldiers!"

"You can send a fleet to their rescue."

"You know the facts. Hassan Pasha is beaten, and his fleet smashed to pieces."

"Exactly! He'll only fight harder for revenge!"

"Certainly, but with whose ships? All we have left are those needed to defend our ports."

"Send them, my lord! Don't let Ochakov fall!"

He glanced at me with surprise. Caressing my cheek, he whispered, "You are so passionate, Nakshidil!"

The surprising thing was that Abdul Hamid gave in to my arguments. He assembled a new fleet in record time. It was entrusted to Hassan Pasha, who returned to the fray.

The news astounded the world, which already wagered on a quick Russian victory, which thought Hassan Pasha beaten once and for all and his fleet destroyed.

Yesterday, fate (or kismet) had decreed that Empress Catherine would enter Constantinople in triumph. Today, fate (who had assumed the name of Nakshidil) ordered restance. The Turks interpret kismet, which dominates their life, any way they choose to . . . and Abdul Hamid swung from the blackest pessimism to foolhardy optimism with disconcerting ease. Under the layers of lassitude the years had wrapped around Abdul Hamid, there remained a noble pride for his position and his country, a protective instinct far stronger than his will to defend them. Had I known him in his youth, we might have achieved great things together.

Thereupon Mirizshah called, as if by chance, on her daughter Princess Hadidgeh. She summoned me to the latter's apartment and immediately made it clear that she was entirely aware of my intervention. "Well, my child, you seem to have discovered the power that a pretty face, a little character, and straightforward talk can have on men!"

"I did not seek such power, but now that it has been bestowed on me I shall use it as I see fit, for the greater glory of our Sultan."

"Allah bless you, Nakshidil. But above all use your influence to prepare the way for the reign of his successor!"

The mere mention of Prince Selim made me blush, to my great embarrassment. I tried to turn the conversation to other topics. "The Sultan has recovered his spirits. He thinks he might still triumph, and I have encouraged him in this belief. But now it happens that I am less confident than he."

"Above all you must lend confidence to men," said Mirizshah. "Only then do you acquire the right to lack it yourself."

CHAPTER 8

SOON AFTERWARD the French kadin, Humasah, died of some sudden disease; I cannot remember which.

One morning I found Prince Mahmud, Humasah's son, with his father the Sultan in the mirrored room. Dressed in white—the color of mourning among Muslims—the boy sat quietly on the sofa, very straight, seeming even more collected than the first time I had seen him, on the day of the "naval review." His natural dignity, so impressive in a four-year-old child, almost intimidated me. He would not take his black eyes off me. There was no hostility in his gaze, just curiosity battling with a deep reserve and a touch of mistrust.

His father cleared his throat. "I was thinking, Nakshidil, that you might take over as mother to Mahmud."

The suggestion was so unexpected and so peculiar that I laughed nervously. Abdul Hamid must have been mad to think of entrusting a four-year-old boy to a girl of sixteen!

Yet neither Abdul Hamid nor the child laughed. They continued to watch me patiently. Armored with gravity, Mahmud seemed walled up within himself. A loveless child, I thought. Hating herself, the French kadin had been incapable of loving anyone, even her son.

"And what about him, my lord—does he want me for his mother?"

Abdul Hamid turned to the child with an inquisitive look. The child did not answer, did not budge. He merely stared at me. Then, in French, I said very gently, "Come, little one, come into my arms."

No doubt his mother had taught him some French; upon hearing these words, the child dropped his inscrutable expression. His eyes widened, his mouth opened without making a sound, and big tears ran down his cheeks. I sat down next to him, and as I embraced him, he threw his little arms around my neck and continued to cry on my shoulder. A gleeful Abdul Hamid watched us silently.

I replaced the French kadin, then, which meant yet again another move into a new apartment. These descendants of nomads truly relish moving about. I begged Abdul Hamid not to give me the dead woman's apartment; I was therefore assigned the only available lodgings, which gave onto the same courtyard as the dormitory of my early days. There was a vestibule, a well-lighted room large enough for Mahmud and myself, and a little cubbyhole for my slaves.

From my windows, decorated with colored glass, I could see the harem's narrow garden, the ramparts of the Seraglio, and the exotic chaos of the old town, with the minarets of the Mosque of the Valideh and the cupolas of the Egyptian bazaar. My apartment had not been redecorated in the French style. It had kept its earthenware tiles bursting with the colors of flowers and fruit, its traditional paneling of red, green, and gold, its golden stars adorning the ceiling. This sort of decor was considered completely out of fashion in the harem, but I preferred it to the heavy imitations of Europe.

My slaves brought my chests of tortoiseshell and mother-of-pearl and my many-drawered ivory boxes; I distributed my flasks of Bohemian crystal in the niches. I liked my new rooms, although I still spent most of my days and nights in the Mabeyn or in Abdul Hamid's room.

I was then, at sixteen, second kadin and mother to a four-year-old imperial prince who was not my son. This did not seem to surprise anyone. At first sight the Orient bristles with laws and interdictions; nothing seems possible. But that is only an appearance to deceive intrusive foreigners and fools. Behind this facade, insistence, ingenuity, and power elicit the most extravagant solutions, and everything becomes possible, even and especially the impossible.

"Make yourself useful to others," Mother Marie-Agnès had said. Now was my chance, and my chance was named Mahmud. Already I had in my care an old man, my lover. All the more reason to take on a child, in whom I could find a purpose for my life. He had not said a word when his father had entrusted him to me. The fact that he was so withdrawn intimidated me. I could not give Mahmud the tenderness of a mother—I was still at an age where a mother's tenderness was what I needed myself. Besides, he had received precious little of it from his real mother, and it was difficult to make him accept love from anyone. I could see how annoyed he became when Vartui smothered him in kisses and caresses. Like him I was proud, and like him I refused pity; he soon sensed that common trait in us, and this did much to draw us together. Our similarities, considering the role I had been assigned, could well have made a barrier between us. On the contrary, they bound us in complicity. I took great pleasure, for instance, in playing with him. His miniature cannons and rifles, his janissary dolls, all his warlike toys, looked incongruous in the hands of an odalisque, but who cared! Within my family in Nantes I had learned to play backgammon, and now I came upon the game again in Turkey, where it is popular among all social classes. I taught Mahmud the rules, and from that moment on we spent hour upon hour at the board. He was a reflective child and had no difficulty concentrating. I decided to improve the little French his mother had taught him. I had some grammars brought from the Fathers of the Christian Schools of Constantinople. The French kadin had never given her son a book. His joy upon receiving the first of many to come was to me very sweet gratitude. He learned to read French before Turkish. To the rudiments of grammar and arithmetic I added historical tales, which he loved, and some geography. Very early Mahmud showed a fierce penchant for learning. To teach him was to win him.

Perhaps to celebrate my "promotion," Abdul Hamid gave a party, the first I attended in the Seraglio. I was to appear before the entire harem, and decided I would look my best. I dressed in a robe of white satin with sleeves so long they swept the floor, and over that wore a sleeveless black caftan trimmed with sable. Knowing the harem's outrageous taste for accessories and jewels, I opted for simplicity—no jewels except rows of very big pearls around my neck and in my hair; no embroidery, no makeup.

Followed by my entire household—Cevri, Ali Effendi, my chambermaids and eunuchs—I made my way to the Sultan's drawing room. From a distance we heard the confused rumor of the large crowd assembled there, and my stomach was knotted and my throat dry when the heavy doors swung open to admit us. The guests fell silent when I walked in, and all stared at me with interest and curiosity. I felt myself being sized up by a single collective stare.

I remained frozen at the door, dazzled by the sparkling, multicolored spectacle. The Kizlar Aga, breaking the tension, walked up to me and led me to my place.

The favorites were installed on a sort of raised platform of gilded wood, and seated according to the strict order of protocol. The sofas were reserved for the imperial princesses, while comfortable cushions had been laid out for the kadins. Hasekis and ikbals sat on slightly less sumptuous cushions, and all the other women stood.

Following the Kizlar Aga, I parted the silent crowd and walked to the gallery, where I sat down quickly—too quickly—on an unoccupied cushion. A shocked murmur rose from the crowd. I had chosen the first kadin's seat. The Kizlar Aga, rolling horrified eyes, leaned over and whispered in my ear an order to stand up. I obeyed, with as much dignity as my confusion allowed, and sat down on the next cushion, my own.

Beside me, the cushion of the first kadin, Sineperver, remained unoccupied throughout the evening, an absence clearly expressing some no doubt unpleasant intention.

Soon after me came Mirizshah, who smiled at me in greeting, and the melancholy Hadidgeh, the eternal romantic, the eternal unhappy lover. Behind them walked Princess Esmee, who turned her head away from me ostentatiously.

The Sultan's drawing room was the largest in the harem. Against the walls, in negligent disorder, were lined up the gifts of foreign rulers: dozens of English and French clocks—which the sultans collected furiously—colossal Russian vases, Chinese pots, Venetian armchairs.

The costumes were a spectacle in themselves, for their richness, their beauty and variety. In this dazzling scene, among a thousand candles illuminating the enormous room, the women's jewels sparkled and reflected in the gold-framed mirrors. Each had donned her most beautiful assets, and my strict black-and-white attire stood out elegantly against the extravagant bouquets of women dripping with brocade, diamonds, and emeralds.

The crowd near the door began to stir, and everyone stood up as the Sultan made his entrance. Abdul Hamid wore a black-frogged red caftan trimmed with fur. The aigrette of his turban was held in place by a brooch made of two rubies and a truly monstrous emerald, disposed like a cloverleaf. Majestically parting the standing crowd, he came to take his seat under the gilded canopy next to the favorites. His amber pipe with the diamond-encrusted handle was placed before him with his cup of coffee and his pillbox, which was carved out of a single emerald. The throng of eunuchs who had accompanied him to his throne settled down. The show could begin with the Dance of the Hare, known as the Tavsan. The harem's orchestra, composed of the most talented and beautiful musicians, took its place in the gallery above our dais. Guitars, sitars, bouzoukis, and violins struck up a shrill tune, at once catchy and nostalgic. The dancers, all of them equally young and beautiful, leaped onto the stage and pursued each other around and around, imitating the hare, light and graceful in their multicolored muslins. The dance seemed so bizarre to me that I let out a guffaw, which echoed strangely under the cavernous domes. The music and dance stopped immediately, and every gaze turned to me. Scarlet with embarrassment, I saw Abdul Hamid lean over slightly, look for the source of that shocking laughter, discover my contorted face.

Then he smiled thinly into his beard, straightened himself, and resumed his impassive pose, thereby signaling that the festivities could continue.

The dancing was followed by the Karayoz, the famous shadow theater, whose origins are lost in the mists of time, and whose traditional characters are intimate friends to every Turk. The main hero, Karayoz in person, a poor, hunchbacked character laden with children, incarnates the people with his misery, his grumbling, and his contentiousness. He comes out of his hovel to complain to Hatziavandi, his inseparable companion, about the hardships of life and the severity of the authorities. He goes on to describe to him in detail his amorous exploits.

From the start I was disturbed by the crudeness of the dialogue and the incredible obscenity of its allusions. Apparently I was alone, for the women around me showed their enthusiasm with all sorts of little laughs, excited exclamations, and chuckles.

A different orchestra was in the gallery above us, this one composed of the palace's pages. These effeminate young boys played blindfolded, for they were not allowed to see the women of the harem. With a lilting and highly suggestive melody, they accompanied the evolutions of three dancing girls whose supple bodies swayed elusively as they offered themselves with extraordinary sensuality. Their clothing was more indecent than nakedness, their arms and legs were quite visible through the muslin, while velvet emphasized breasts and waists. One of them in particular contorted herself in front of Abdul Hamid with all the science of lasciviousness. She was very beautiful, wrapped in that evocative music, and every movement of her body seemed a provocation. I could see my lover's eyes follow her and undress her, while his fingers beat time nervously on his emerald pillbox. Again, stupidly, I felt the sting of jealousy, mingled with exasperation at my own absurdity.

I felt someone's gaze resting on me. I turned around suddenly and met Prince Selim's black eyes. I had not seen him in the bustle preceding the show, and it hadn't occurred to me that he would be allowed to attend. Yet there he was, leaning against the wall not far from the Sultan's throne; he was watching me, watching me alone. And his stare burned through me with such intensity that, afraid of understanding, afraid of answering, I looked away. A wave of heat, the flush of an imaginary blaze, welled up in me. I was breathing rapidly as, motionless, I watched the show without seeing it, my eyes bulging. The temptation to seek out Selim's gaze, to meet it again, was irresistible. Twenty times I held myself from turning my head in the direction of those eyes, which I still felt glued to me. That night I gave myself to Abdul Hamid with a new fervor, verging on wildness. Later, while he lay asleep, I remained awake beside him, letting images of the celebration run through my mind. In that kaleidoscope of faces, diamonds, lights, colored silhouettes, two eyes returned again and again, two luminous dark eyes I could not get out of my mind.

One night when I had already dressed and was preparing to join Abdul Hamid, Mahmud returned from his father's apartment, where he had spent the afternoon. He complained of pains in his head and stomach, and as I was readying him for bed, he vomited on my dress. I assumed that he had simply fallen ill from stuffing himself with loukhoums all afternoon, and I was furious with him: My dress was soiled, I was late, and, more irritated than alarmed, I put the child to bed rather briskly and went to the imperial room without even waiting for him to fall asleep.

I told Abdul Hamid what I thought of his educational methods, and upbraided him in general for spoiling his son to the point of making him sick. The Sultan himself assumed the sheepish look of a scolded child, so much so that I ended up laughing.

Nevertheless I was vaguely worried about Mahmud and, contrary to habit, I returned to my room in the middle of the night to see how he was. I found him in a terrible state, groaning and shivering with fever. He seemed to have violent stomach cramps, and was breathing with difficulty.

Panic-stricken, I woke Cevri and sent her to fetch Vartui.

Vartui's arrival with the imperial apothecary only increased my anxiety, for while the child writhed in pain the two of them could think only of arguing over protocol. The apothecary was not allowed to see a kadin, a rule which could not be broken no matter what the circumstances. Since I was stamping my feet with exasperation and refused to leave the room, we had to agree on a compromise. I went to cover myself with a veil and an abaya, and only when I was hidden under these garments did the doctor consent to come into the sickroom.

He seemed blessed with an all-pervasive optimism, and would not stop joking for a moment. After giving Mahmud a cursory examination he diagnosed indigestion and prescribed an emetic, which, he said, would relieve the child immediately.

The potion, of course, did nothing for Mahmud, and I began to panic. Still I tried to reassure him, to reassure myself, by uttering soothing phrases: "You'll get better soon. Tomorrow it will all be over."

Mahmud then began to ask me strange questions: "Am I going to see Allah soon? How shall I recognize him? What does he wear?"

The signs were becoming more and more alarming, and I sent Ali Effendi to warn the Sultan, feeling the need for his presence and support.

After an unbearable half hour of waiting I saw Ali Effendi return alone. Abdul Hamid would not come; he could not face the sight of his child's suffering. He wanted to be kept informed of the development of the illness minute by minute.

I felt hurt and completely abandoned. Wanting to change the boy's soiled sheets, I called Cevri, but there was no reply. Even the faithful Cevri had left me at the critical moment.

Sitting at Mahmud's bedside, crushed, I started to sob, mechanically repeating: "Cevri . . . Cevri . . . Cevri . . ."

And suddenly she was there in the recess of the door, with Mirizshah on her heels. Cevri had gone to fetch the headwoman on her own initiative. Woken from her sleep, Mirizshah had slipped a pelisse over her nightclothes. Now she walked quietly and serenely toward me, her long black hair loose down her back. Only the sparkle of her green eyes showed any tension.

She leaned over Mahmud and made her diagnosis immediately: "This child has been poisoned."

"But how?"

"In his food—in his last meal, in the pastries his father gave him. Anything is possible. Poison is everywhere in the harem."

"But who? Who?"

Mirizzshah sighed, and tilted her beautiful head. "Whoever would profit doubly by Mahmud's death—first by eliminating a younger rival, and then by blaming and discrediting you, who have responsibility for the child."

"Sineperver."

"Yes, Sineperver." Then, turning to Cevri, Mirizzshah said, "Fetch Rashah, quick!"

A few moments later I saw a completely toothless old woman arrive; I knew she had been one of the harem's floorwashers for sixty years. What could that senile woman do for a dying child?

Mirizzshah beamed her luminous smile. "Trust me, Nakshidil, trust Rashah—she's the best healer in the Seraglio. She knows every spell and every antidote. Rashah has Allah's gift: She can heal."

The old woman tied a copper hand of Fatma to the child's neck, knelt by his bed, and started to drone a long litany of prayers— incomprehensible formulas in an unknown language, mingled with verses from the Koran. I had to admit that Mahmud was less tense, that his contractions were diminishing. Old Rashah produced from inside her rags a flask filled with a nauseating black liquid and poured a few drops between the child's lips. Then she whispered a few words into Mirizzshah's ear.

Mirizzshah stood up and said, "The child is saved."

Thereupon she returned to her apartment, leaving me alone with the old witch, who had resumed her prayers. Suddenly the child's moans and contortions returned, stronger than ever. I thought the end had come. The old woman remained unaffected. I buried my head in the sheets, and, holding Mahmud's hand, I repeated under my breath the prayers I had learned in my other life. I do not know how long I remained there, paralyzed by anguish, waiting for Mahmud to die; but when at last I looked up I saw the child sleeping peacefully, a light blush on his cheeks. Only Cevri's gigantic shadow remained in the room. Broken, I fell asleep against the child.

All night Ali Effendi had rushed back and forth between my apartment and the Mabeyn, where Abdul Hamid, undone by fatigue and anxiety, followed the situation. When he knew that his son was saved, and only then, he came to see him.

"He slipped on a fur pelisse and came here without even putting on his turban," said Ali Effendi. "He watched you and the child for a long time, and I think I saw tears rolling down his face. While you slept, kneeling by the bed, he picked you up in his arms, placed you next to the child, and covered you both with the blanket."

I was ready to turn the harem inside out in order to reveal the person behind that odious attempt on Mahmud's life. Once again Ali Effendi restrained me:

"That time when someone tried to kill you or frighten you, you had proof—the dagger, and the fact that you thought you had heard Ristoglou's voice—but you were not powerful enough to exact vengeance. Now you have the power, Kadin, but you have no proof."

"Mirizshah herself denounced Sineperver."

"Of course it's Sineperver. The entire harem knows that. But you can be sure she's taken precautions. This is no longer a case of trying to eliminate a rival, as when she attacked you. Now she is trying to preserve the future for her son by killing yours. There can be no doubt that she organized her crime with care, in such a way as to be unassailable even if she is suspected."

"But there has to be a guilty party."

"In the Orient, Kadin, it is difficult to tell to whom belongs the fist that strikes. It can belong to many people. Everyone whispers, everyone has suspicions, everyone has an opinion, but no one knows with certainty. And even when it is obvious whom the crime profits, the path back to him is too tortuous to follow."

"So according to you and the Orient, Ali Effendi, I can do nothing but fold my arms and wait for someone to assassinate Mahmud and me."

"The science of the Orient, Kadin, teaches one to predict the blow and, if possible, return it before it has been struck."

"The Sultan loves his son. He cannot, he will not, allow such a crime to go unpunished."

"The Sultan knows better than anyone the dangers which threaten Prince Mahmud. It is for that reason that Mahmud has been put in your care. The Sultan is counting on you to protect him. But that is as far as he will go. If you ask for the punishment of Sineperver, you ask for her head. The Sultan will resent your putting him in that difficult position—and you shall lose face if he refuses."

"Is there nothing I can do to stop that evil woman?"

"Yes, Kadin. You can have her poisoned. Just give me the order."

"I will not stoop to using her methods."

"Then double your watchfulness and guard over Mahmud as we, your faithful retainers, guard over you."

The anguish of that night when I thought he would die virtually chained me to Mahmud. Formerly he had been a responsibility; now he became my flesh and blood. Everything about the child moved me: his curiosity, his intelligence, his orphan's loneliness, his pride, the sensitivity hiding behind his swagger. I wanted not only to take care of him but also to make him laugh, to make him happy. I finally understood Abdul Hamid's crafty stratagem, which I had thought simply a convenient whim. He had entrusted Mahmud to me knowing that a child's fragility would bind me more securely than an old man's love. My imprisonment in the harem had become voluntary.

I was gradually recovering from the incident when, one afternoon, Ali Effendi invited me to play the harp for the Princess Hadidgeh in her apartment. I felt little friendship for Hadidgeh, and no desire to play. I justified my refusal by saying that I still felt vulnerable. Ali Effendi became mysteriously insistent. He had the gift of persuasion, and I gave in.

I did not understand until I entered the princess's apartment. Not only had my harp been brought—Selim was there as well. His sister's apartment was the only place in the harem for which he could leave the Cage.

Hadidgeh greeted me like a third-rate actress: "My brother Selim, like you, Nakshidil, loves music. I thought I might bring you together to discuss your common passion."

Her task accomplished, Hadidgeh disappeared into her room, apparently exhausted by the effort.

Selim looked at me mutely, with an expression both grave and tender. We filled an uneasy silence by sipping our coffee and nibbling at pastries. Then, like a man diving into deep water, Selim began to bombard me with questions, showing the same insatiable curiosity I had noticed at the time of our first accidental meeting. He questioned me avidly on the works of contemporary composers. I must have disappointed him, for although I had played music from a very early age I was quite ignorant of the glories and fashions of the era. He knew Mozart, Gluck, Haydn, Piccinni, much better than I, and showed me some scores he had somehow managed to acquire and which he read with ease. As I commented with surprise on his erudition, he explained sadly that only such a passionate interest could mitigate the rigors of the Cage. A great number of his predecessors had developed similar pursuits to help them endure their fate: Selim I had been a master goldsmith; Ahmed III a great calligrapher. . . .

"And one day they shall speak of the musical talent of Sultan Selim III," I added.

Smiling that beautiful sad smile of his, he asked me to play a Mozart fantasy on my harp. Little by little I let the delicate music enfold me, feeling more deeply than ever its profound but contained romanticism. It was then, I think, that Selim began to recite to the music.

> "Do you know the wish of the poet?
> He wishes to take you in his arms,
> And whisper, 'Accept me
> For your servant and your slave.'
> Come to me, my love,
> Try to understand.
> Give me one of your braids
> That I might breathe it
> As one breathes the rose."

I continued to play despite the turmoil his transparent words awoke in me. When I had finished, Selim grabbed his wooden flute, his ney, and began to play. At first the shrill notes struck me unpleasantly. I know now they belonged to the strange, magical music which accompanies the dance of the whirling dervishes. Selim played it admirably, and despite myself I was seized by the spellbinding tune, torn from my body, taken out of my own control. Instinctively, almost against my will, I stood up and began to move to the music, swirling slowly inside my veils, inventing the fascinated dance it suggested. I was in such a trance that I did not know the flute player had stopped, that he was standing next to me; I did not know whether it was a movement of my dance or a gesture of his which brought me into his arms. . . .

Suddenly Hadidgeh appeared on the threshold of her room, with her usual expression of supreme boredom and indifference, coldly witnessing our embrace. She did not seem shocked that her brother, the Crown Prince, should lay his hand on the Sultan's second kadin. She contented herself with remarking, in a mundane tone of voice, that it was time for me to return to my apartment.

Without saying a word, my heart, my soul, my face afire, I turned and left the room. Back in my apartment, I felt as if crushed by an avalanche. The wonder had been worked: for the first time, I loved and was loved—a love which could hope for nothing. I was the Sultan's kadin, and in the harem only a horrible death rewarded adultery. This love could not be; and yet it was. I had betrayed my respect and affection for Abdul Hamid; I had insulted the love and the trust he had given me. Contradictory emotions raged and crashed within me, while, above the storm, shone the terrible light of my love.

Mirizshah sent for me in the harem's little garden. I found her as affable and pleasant as always, walking along the garden paths, wrapped in a pelisse against the chilly weather. In that season the garden was lugubrious, its flower beds bare, its rosebushes thorny and fleshless. Dark green, almost black, ivy covered the surrounding walls. Everything, including the fountains, seemed suspended, frozen in the disgrace of winter. Nevertheless Mirizshah liked fresh air and exercise, did not fear the cold, and insisted that confinement was bad for one's looks. What friendliness in her monologue, what praise for my beauty, my elegance, my behavior, my devotion to Mahmud! What flowers—and what thorns! The Orient is expert in the art of allusion. She had wrapped a very clear message inside her compliments, reminding me that it was she who had put me beside Abdul Hamid and that she was powerful enough to tear me away from him and cast me into the void: Had she not managed to curb Sineperver's influence? If I had become the Sultan's favorite, it was in order to accomplish a mission, and not to lark about with his heir. She knew very well of our feelings for each other. She consented to ignore our love—for there was no question of abiding it—as long as I found in it the energy and the courage to remind the Sultan of his heir as often as possible, to make him get to know him better, to praise his qualities and ideas—in other words, to further my beloved's cause with my lover.

"But you must be careful; Abdul Hamid is a very clear-sighted, shrewd man. If you feel strongly for my son, you will no longer act naturally and he will notice it in no time at all."

I remained silent, shivering with cold, while Mirizshah concluded: "My dear child, always remember that I am here to help if you need me. Come to me if ever you feel a need to talk, to unburden yourself. I shall always lend you a friendly and devoted ear. We are equals, Nakshidil, we are allies in a noble cause."

On these words she turned away gracefully, dismissing me, and continued her stroll.

All that day I was in a frightful mood. I rebuffed Vartui, who was panting with curiosity about my conversation with Mirizshah, I insulted Monsieur Jolibois, my parrot, and I barked at Ali Effendi; and the miserable expressions they assumed when I treated them harshly were not enough to make me laugh. Mirizshah knew of my love for her son and thought only of exploiting it! The shame of being discovered, my rage at the feeling that the intimacy of my emotions had been violated, my revolt against the oppression that victimized even the last secret of my heart—all these things fought within me against a hateful and envious admiration for Mirizshah, who would stop at nothing to serve her son's interests, and who held me in her velvet claws. I remained sullen even with Abdul Hamid.

"What is wrong, my child? What trouble draws down the corners of your mouth? What worry wrinkles your forehead?"

I had to dissimulate, but I lacked the courage. I could no longer bear Abdul Hamid's caresses, his endearments, the sham love I was forced to show him. Every day I was tempted to tell him the truth, and every day I held myself back, torn between the necessity of continuing to pretend and the terrible risks involved in admitting the truth.

All sorts of arguments raged in my mind day after day. Sometimes, judging by my knowledge of the country's morals and mentality, I would tell myself that no matter how kind and open-minded he might be, Abdul Hamid—as man, as Turk, as Sultan—could never even conceive that one of his women should love another man; and at other times I would think that a full confession was the only possible course.

The hours and days ran by, while I remained silent.

It was Abdul Hamid who spoke first, during one of our lonely evenings in the Mabeyn.

That night I was more sensitive than ever to the intimacy and enchantment of the Mabeyn—the candlelight flickering in the mirrors, the rich vapors rising from the scent-burners to mingle with the smell of the cedar logs burning in the fireplace. Night had fallen and I knew it was cold and windy outside as we ate peacefully in the warmth of our shelter. I felt so well that after the meal I was unable to resist my greedy curiosity: Under Abdul Hamid's indulgent gaze I took a pastry I had never tasted before, made of sesame vermicelli and sugar syrup. While he was served his cardamom-flavored coffee, I licked my syrupy fingers.

Abdul Hamid . . . that smell of cardamom, mixed with the smoke of Macedonian tobacco, will always remind me of Abdul Hamid.

Throughout dinner he told me stories of his ancestors. He had an extraordinary knowledge of the history of Turkey and his family, acquired during his long years in the Cage.

Suddenly he addressed me directly: "Of course, if you had known me when I was young, you could have truly loved me. But I am old, you are still young, you haven't lived. It isn't right that you should devote your life to loving, or pretending to love, an old man. You were made to love a man much younger than I—a man who has a future to give you, whereas I have only a past."

It was obvious that Abdul Hamid knew, that he knew everything. Then there was a pause, an unbearable silence, after which he continued, in the same tired, quiet voice: "I am old, Nakshidil; I know I don't have much longer to live. I am not ill, but I am exhausted. Even the love I feel for you cannot restore my youth, or give me back the life ebbing from me. I shall die soon—I feel it, I know it. I am grateful for all you have done for me. You have lit up my existence in the past few months, you have given me more than any other woman. . . . I don't ask for your love—I ask only for your friendship, for your presence. I wish only that you should remain at my side for a few more months, until my death. When I am gone, my successor shall have a backbreaking task: He will have to save the empire I could not save, enact the reforms I could not enact. In order to succeed where I failed, in order to accomplish that enormous labor, he will need the help of a woman—he will need a woman's love. I wish him everything that I lacked—the energy and the courage necessary to save the empire, and the love of a woman. You see, Nakshidil, I wish him that with all my heart. I hope he shall have it, I want him to have it."

I almost fell at the feet of that pathetic and magnanimous old man, who not only forgave my guilty love, but even wished it well. I threw myself into his arms, but he gently pushed me away.

"No, you're tired, Nakshidil. Go away."

I insisted.

"No, no, Nakshidil, please go away," he repeated. "I want to be alone, I need to be alone, believe me. . . . And you too must be weary. One tires easily, walking up and down those paths in the harem garden."

I smiled; yes, he knew everything. The allusion to my recent conversation with Mirizshah was unmistakable. He took advantage of this momentary relaxation to speak of Mirizshah with gentle irony.

"Mirizshah is a very intelligent woman, for whom I have the deepest admiration. Nevertheless she is a little overzealous as far as her son is concerned. She has nothing to fear—I get along very well with her son. I might even say that we understand each other perfectly well independently of her."

He laughed a very short laugh and once again urged me to go to bed. I obeyed.

At once relieved and crushed, I wanted to cry. In the last few days I had imagined every possibility except this reaction from Abdul Hamid. Failure had not embittered him: he wished others the happiness he had not known—he even abetted it. How I had misunderstood that man, his generosity, his nobility—and how poorly I had rewarded him. I could have done so much more to support him, to assist him; and now I felt unworthy of him and ashamed. But after all, injecting me with the poison of remorse—was that not the most subtle revenge?

During one of our daily lessons, I had planned to teach Mahmud a new French song. But he was morose and apathetic, and simply refused to sing with me. Thinking it was merely a childish whim, I did not insist, and instead began to tell him the stories he loved. At the end of the first story, however, contrary to his habit, he did not ask for more.

"What's wrong, Mahmud? Don't you feel well?"

Silence. And then, point-blank, he shot a question: "Do you love my father?"

I tried to answer naturally. "But of course, Mahmud. I love him for himself, and also because he's your father."

As if considering my answer, Mahmud remained silent for a moment. Then, apparently unsatisfied with his thoughts, he ventured to voice them: "You wouldn't want my father to die, would you?"

I stood up, grabbed the child's arm, and shaking him roughly, asked him who had put such notions in his head.

Mahmud did not try to free himself from my grasp, but his expression remained stubborn. Finally he said, "My brother Mustafa told me that you wanted to poison my father so that Selim could take his place and become Sultan. He says you love my cousin Selim."

I let go of the child. I could not fight such baseness. This time Sineperver had gone so far as to set two children against each other, to corrupt their spirits. I began to cry, from disgust, rage, despair, weariness.

Then, suddenly, I felt little arms around my neck. Mahmud had stolen into my embrace in silence. "Don't cry, please don't cry. . . . Mustafa is mean, I know. He tells lies to hurt people. He's insulted me too; he calls me a giaour."

A giaour! A Christian, an infidel—a subhuman—the worst insult in the mouth of a Turk. Disgrace had reunited the giaour prince and the poisoning kadin. Sineperver had omitted to take Mahmud's intelligence into account. Far from estranging us, she had only deepened his understanding and strengthened our bond.

Abdul Hamid fell sick soon afterward. It was April, but winter still held us in its grip. The old man felt very weak; he had caught a chill, and suffered a chronic cough and a slight but tenacious fever. Although he made light of my alarm, I persuaded him to call the apothecary for a consultation. The latter, whose casualness I had already had the opportunity to admire at Mahmud's bedside, examined his master and concluded with great joviality, "It's nothing but a little seasonal cold. Our Sultan is strong, his organism resistant. He'll be on his feet again in a few days."

But the Sultan's fever and his difficulty in breathing persisted. Abdul Hamid was not recovering, and still he insisted on fulfilling his duties as usual.

One morning, in the Mabeyn, he showed me the most extraordinary jewel I had ever seen: a pendant more than two feet long, a gold plate set with gigantic hexagonal and round emeralds, pearshaped pearls, and monstrous diamonds. I pointed out that its weight made it impossible to wear.

"It was not made for a woman, but for the Prophet's tomb," explained an amused Abdul Hamid. "It's part of the Surey, the annual tribute the Sultan sends to the Holy Cities, Mecca the Revered and Medina the Illuminated."

The departure of the Surey traditionally included a procession which the Sultan had to attend. I protested, exclaiming that he was still too weak to go out in the cold, but neither my supplications nor my exhortations could sway him.

"All the court dignitaries await me to load the Surey onto the camel which will carry it. The mullahs and the muftis will pray, and after that I shall hand the sacred trust to the guards who are to escort it across Asia Minor and the Middle East to the Holy Cities."

One last glance and he set off, followed by his eunuchs, leaving me alone in the Mabeyn.

Outside, a bitter wind blew in from the Black Sea. I could not make up my mind to return to my apartment or do anything in particular, and stayed idly where I was.

It seemed to me that the ceremony had long since ended, but Abdul Hamid did not return. My vigil weighed on me, heavy with vague threats, with loneliness and forebodings.

The afternoon was already waning when at last a shivering Abdul Hamid reappeared. After the ceremony he had been to the Hall of Circumcision, at the other end of the Seraglio, to see his son Mustafa.

I put him on a sofa by the fire and brought him some very hot green tea; but he would not warm up. He wanted to work, but he was unable to concentrate and soon had to abandon his reports. I suggested sending for Mahmud to amuse him. Then, leaving father and son together, I returned to my apartment.

Monsieur Jolibois watched me from the heights of his perch and tried to make me smile with his clowning. At first I ignored him, but eventually I succumbed to a series of his more perverse imitations: Ristoglou's squeaky voice, Vartui's squeals of joy, and so on. He even managed to make me burst into laughter when he reproduced Vartui's curious clicking of the tongue as she brought a loukhoum to her lips.

I cannot say how many hours or minutes had passed when Ali Effendi entered the room. Hassan Pasha had suffered a new defeat; he had failed to save Ochakov.

When I joined Abdul Hamid in the mirrored room I found the

Kizlar Aga reading Hassan Pasha's report aloud: "The Russians managed to open a breach, and thirty thousand of our people, military and civilians, perished while trying to save the city. After his victory, Potemkin ordered looting and massacre—the Russians massacred not only the five thousand survivors of the garrison, but also twenty thousand women, children, and old people."

I saw the blood flowing down the streets of Ochakov, I saw the fires, the rapes; I heard the victims' cries.

Then Abdul Hamid's voice, beyond the grave, dragged me from my nightmare.

"Ochakov has fallen. There is no hope left."

All the color had drained from his face; his features sagged. He ordered that his writing case be brought. He dipped his pen, waved it over the paper, and suddenly toppled backward, dropping the pen and dragging writing case, papers, and inkwell with him in his fall. I saw the ink spread on the floor; it seemed as if it were Abdul Hamid's very blood flowing out of him.

I rushed to my old friend's side; he was curled up on the floor, panting horribly, one hand on his heart. I tried to sit him up, but I wasn't strong enough. The Kizlar Aga helped me, and then ran off to find the apothecary. I waited what seemed like an eternity for his return.

Despite Abdul Hamid's extreme weakness, the apothecary decided to bleed him and roughly ordered me to assist in the operation whether I wanted to or not. I brought the basin and held it under Abdul Hamid's elbow during the bleeding, after which, satisfied, the apothecary retired with his usual assurance: "A few days, and everything will be all right!"

Abdul Hamid regained consciousness little by little, and slowly his breathing grew easier.

I repeated the apothecary's words, which I did not believe myself. Abdul Hamid patted my cheek and did his best to smile, but he was not deceived.

"No, Nakshidil, my heart is failing me; I am condemned. I know it. I have only a few hours left. But I want to live them. I won't lie down, I don't want to risk dying in my sleep. All I desire now is that you stay here, next to me, tonight. I wish only one thing—to spend my last hours chatting with you, watching you, listening to you."

He sent for some Mavrodaphnè, a sweet wine from Samos, thanks to which we gradually came to forget that we were living our last moments together. More than ever, that last night, we were close and in collusion, almost happy.

With the help of the wine to dissipate the gathering shadows of death, Abdul Hamid began to speak of his past, of his earliest memories. For the first time he told me about his father:

"Sultan Ahmed III had many women, and he loved them all; he never knew which one to choose. Therefore he left the matter to chance; he instituted a sort of contest to determine each day's choice. Each of his women owned a tortoise. They were placed in a line at one end of a bed of tulips and made to race, and the first to cross the finish line earned the honors of the imperial bed for its owner."

He also spoke to me of his own women: that Rusah who had so mistreated him and who had finally passed away; Humasah, the kadin from Provence, who had been unable to break with her past; and even Sineperver, so evil and yet so beautiful.

He spoke for a long time, and he weakened; yet his interest in life, in me, remained. He asked me to tell him my story as well.

For him, then, I passed in review the memories of my childhood in Martinique. I described our house and our customs, the fauna and the vegetation of the island, the spectacular storms at the equinox. I evoked all the figures of my past—my parents, Josephine, Zinah, even Pierre Dubuc, my famous ancestor, the Norman adventurer who had made my family's fame and fortune. I told him of my sojourn in France, my occupations and my schoolgirl's pranks at the convent in Nantes, my audience with Queen Marie-Antoinette, Marie-Anne's wedding.

Abdul Hamid shut his eyes; his breathing was almost imperceptible. He still found the strength to whisper, "I wish to die to music."

The Kizlar Aga and his eunuchs were keeping their silent vigil in the Mabeyn's antechamber. On my order they rushed off noise-lessly to bring my harp. While placing it in the Mabeyn, one of the eunuchs accidentally brushed the strings, which moaned. I played—though I cannot remember what, or for how long. But my ear still remembers the soft and melodious chords of the harp an-swering the wind that buffeted the invisible windows and cried in the chimney. Beside me the old man remained motionless. Only a fragment of life still moved his chest.

I knew the end was near, but I remained calm; Abdul Hamid's very expression, the consciousness that he was dying as he had wished to, now made the event acceptable. I left the harp and took one of his hands in mine. Suddenly a strange memory sprang to my mind. It was that of my uncle's death at Montauban five years before. On that occasion there had been resignation. Here was more . . . serenity. After drinking a glass of his favorite wine and listening to music, Abdul Hamid was taking his leave with the tranquil elegance that is the stamp of deep souls. Never did I love him more than in those last hours, when he robbed our imminent separation of much pain by transforming it into something natural. But that made it all the more difficult—Abdul Hamid would have been aghast had I cried. I did not need to cry. My heart was at half mast.

Time passed; I think I even drifted into a light sleep until a con-traction of his fingers alerted me. I bent over him; it was finished.

I gently kissed his face and walked into the Mabeyn's antecham-ber. From a window I saw a pink glow rising very far away on the horizon, in Asia. It was the dawn of April 22, 1789.

PART 3

———◦◦◦———

SELIM

CHAPTER 9

─────◦•◦─────

SELIM WAS proclaimed Sultan on the very morning of Abdul Hamid's death. The Kizlar Aga, escorted by the highest civil and religious authorities of the empire, the Grand Vizier and the Sheikh-Ul-Islam, went to the Cage to inform Selim that he was the new Master of the Empire. After kissing the hem of his robe, the Sheikh-Ul-Islam gave him the sword of his ancestor Osman, the founder of the dynasty, which is transmitted from sultan to sultan. The weapon, a simple steel blade with an iron pommel, was presented with the traditional formula: "Receive it with confidence, for it is sent from God."

Then Selim went to meditate in the Chamber of the Sacred Cloak, where jewel-studded chests under a canopy of gold contain the Holy Relics of Islam: the Prophet's black cloak, his sword, and his banner, the Sanjak-i-Sherif, the Standard of the Prophet.

I spent the following days entrenched in my apartment, taking care of Mahmud. I never saw the child cry, but his grief was evident in his silence and mulish demeanor. Abdul Hamid had spoiled that favorite son, surrounding him with the warm, impulsive kind-

153

ness that was so particular to him. I knew that nothing could replace his father, and for the moment I tried to keep Mahmud busy at all times, playing or reciting his lessons.

I forced myself to fulfill my daily chores, but my heart was not in it. I missed Abdul Hamid. That gentleman of another era, that noble poet of refined sensibilities, had enchanted me. He had made me discover the satisfactions of love, while shielding me from its anxieties. In my grateful affection for him I also pitied that luckless man, whose life and reign had ended in defeat and disaster. A pleasure seeker—and a selfish one, it is true—he had loved comfort in all its guises, including the highest, happiness, which he had tried to instill in all those around him, in me. All his kindliness and his experienced sensitivity had been devoted to guiding my first steps as a woman and an adult, as if he had been my father rather than my lover.

Mahmud and I played backgammon halfheartedly one day, both of us lost in our thoughts. Suddenly I said, "Your father leaves two orphans behind, Mahmud—you and me."

"He was my father, not yours," he answered fiercely. "You have another one in your own country."

"Sultan Abdul Hamid was a second father to me, and I loved him as much as the first."

"He was happy with you," the child admitted.

"In losing him I lost my protector. Now it is you, Mahmud, who must protect me."

"When I grow up. In the meantime my cousin Selim will protect you."

Had he said that through affection, or did he have something else in mind?

"Sultan Selim will protect you too," I said, "because he loves you."

"I love him too. Much more than I love my brother Mustafa."

Selim! No matter how unpleasant the thought, I had to admit that the death of the man to whom I owed so much freed me, so to speak, for the man I loved. But the latter was now the Padishah, the Caliph of Islam, the Shadow of Allah on Earth, Sultan and Master of millions of souls and territories stretching over three continents. We had never been close; and now the aura around him threw a new barrier between us.

Selim was crowned on the date set by the court's chief astrologer.

Naturally it was unthinkable that a woman might attend the ceremonies, but thanks to Ali Effendi, I had the best seat. He led me through a series of passages, corridors, and narrow stairways to the top of the Tower of Justice, a former lookout post which dominates the entire Seraglio.

Like children excited by the risks of a forbidden escapade, we had fits of giggles as we climbed the narrow spiral staircase, dark as an oven, leading to the uppermost chamber. There we stood over the Second Court, with the Divan and the imperial kitchens. Farther on we could see the First Court, where, in their dress uniforms, stood the janissaries, the halberdiers, the bodyguards with their bonnets crowned with fans of white feathers, the equerries with their golden pointed helmets, and the Sultan's messengers, wearing yellow robes and conical brown hats.

Ali Effendi, thoughtful fellow that he was, had equipped himself with a box of loukhoums. His lips powdered with sugar, laughing and pointing down through the crenels, he ran an uninterrupted commentary on the ceremonies unfolding below us.

Spring was late that year, and only tulips lighted the flower beds of the Second Court. Lined up along the walls and the alleys, as straight as the cypress trees around them, the janissaries stood at arms in their purple uniforms. The Bayran Throne, a sort of enormous chest covered in gold encrusted with thousands of pale-green tourmalines, had been placed on a multicolored carpet under a canopy of gilded wood by the Gates of Felicity.

The High Officers of the Court had already taken their places: the Grand Equerry and the Lesser Equerry; the Bostandgy baj, head of the Seraglio's soldier-servants, the only dignitary wearing orange slippers; the masters of ceremonies, in red-and-gold caftans, and the chamberlains. Then the Kapu Agassi, the chief white eunuch, the white equivalent of the Kizlar Aga; and the Bearer of the Cloak, the Bearer of the Stirrup, the Bearer of the Ewer, the Folder of the Turban, the Master of the Wardrobe, the Chief Headwaiter, the Master of the Hounds, His Highness's Chief Barber, the Head Falconer, the Steward of the Baths. I staggered under this avalanche of titles pouring forth from the protocol-drunk Ali Effendi. To the right I saw a plantation of black pointed caps—the bostandjis, the Seraglio's domestic soldiers; to the left, a flowery mass of gold, pink, and blue—the pageboys in their different liveries. In a corner, clothed in somber caftans, stood the mutes, formerly responsible for bearing the Sultan's death sentences, and the dwarf jesters in pink-and-yellow robes.

At the hour prescribed by the astrologer, the majestic Gates of Felicity opened to reveal Selim, supported, according to custom, by the Kizlar Aga and the Bearer of the Sword. He wore a long silk robe under a sleeveless ceremonial caftan of pink-and-gold brocade, trimmed with fur. On his head was the largest turban I had ever seen. I could make out three very large rubies, like three drops of blood, on the brooch holding the white heron feathers to the headdress.

Sitting down on his throne, Selim took the traditional pose—also prescribed, from time immemorial, by protocol; then began the procession of dignitaries who had been waiting in the Divan: functionaries, viziers, judges, agas, mullahs, generals and admirals, the tall silhouette of Hassan Pasha among them. One by one they walked down the alley bordered by janissaries and cypress trees, knelt before Selim, kissed the hem of his robe as a pledge of submission and allegiance, and lined up next to the throne.

Everything in the ceremony followed protocol to the letter: each person's place, the color of his robe, the shape and the height of his turban. From my lookout I could see the moving wall of brocade caftans, the field of multicolored turbans, the forest of plumes swaying gently around the gold block of the throne.

Selim rose from the throne to greet the Grand Vizier, holder of civilian power, and the Sheikh-Ul-Islam, the supreme head of the clergy, who closed the procession. He did not sit down again. To Ali Effendi's stupefaction—to the stupefaction of all—he began a speech. He spoke in an unconstrained tone of voice, as if he were conversing with two or three people in the intimacy of a room. He was obviously not a trained orator used to addressing a large crowd, but his words were borne clearly by his grave and moderate voice, to be greeted by his listeners with silent surprise. He exhorted the janissaries, the officers, and the functionaries, and through them the entire population of the empire, to keep up the fight against Russia. He himself would return his sword to its scabbard only when all the territories of the empire had been recaptured from the infidels.

At last he moved on to his plans for reform. Wisely he stuck to generalities, but determined to make his point, he announced that he would fight injustice and restore the empire's prosperity.

The crowd, which until then had been all ears, let out an enormous cry, repeated three times: "May you live a thousand years, O Padishah!"

This traditional formula was to conclude the ceremony, but a murmur, a rumble of approval, prolonged it. Selim's speech had found its mark. From my perch atop the tower I could feel the waves of excitement carrying from court to court, to reach the crowd massed at the gates of the Seraglio.

Selim mounted a white horse, harnessed with studded gold, to travel in pomp to the Mosque of the Conqueror. He was surrounded by the dignitaries of his house, who protected him from the mild sunlight with a large green-and-gold parasol. Behind him came the two imperial princes, Mustafa and Mahmud. The procession crossed the courts, cheered by the soldiers' hurrahs; and long after it had crossed the Gate of Glory and disappeared from my sight, I still heard the clamor of the population of Constantinople acclaiming the new Sultan.

The people had heard Selim's appeal, and they answered it with enthusiasm. A hundred and twenty thousand volunteers, come from all provinces of the empire, set off to halt the Russians, whose advance had killed Abdul Hamid.

Selim's accession was followed by a tremendous commotion in the harem. Abdul Hamid's women now had to make way for Selim's. They packed up all their affairs and took their slaves and eunuchs off to the Old Seraglio, where they were to vegetate until their deaths. The lamentations of these fallen queens were answered with insolence; the irremovable eunuchs, after years of serving them, took their revenge with open contempt.

I was happy at the departure of Sineperver, whose removal would lessen the danger around me. Unfortunately she would still be allowed to return to the palace to see her son Mustafa, who was to stay on in the Hall of Circumcision: Selim, in an act of inconceivable novelty, had very simply abolished the practice of the Cage.

As I took my walk one afternoon, I saw that the Mabeyn was being closed for good. The shutters had been boarded up, the doors sealed; from now on that apartment, where I had spent so many happy moments with Abdul Hamid, would be left to dust and mice.

The approach to the Valideh's apartments was guarded by eunuchs who prevented me from entering. Workers—men—were readying it for the arrival of Mirizshah, who was now the mother of the reigning Sultan.

During the transition period a gale of madness shook the harem. Vartui, already accustomed to giving orders right and left, assumed the airs of a commander in chief. Sweating, scarlet-cheeked, her big blue eyes aflame, she was everywhere at once, with an order on her lips; sometimes in the evenings I would find her utterly exhausted, panting, complaining, as always, that no one respected her authority. My eunuch Ali Effendi was in a permanent state of hysteria, driven mad by the sheer volume of the gossip he had to relay. He stammered and stumbled, and his voice slid up into registers so high that I could barely understand his words. Even the unshakable Cevri, usually so discreet, abandoned her muteness to feed us her own little tidbits.

Everyone—myself included—awaited the arrival of the triumphant new queens with curiosity. Selim's women, who until then had been shut away in rabbit hutches above the Cage, were about to invade the departing kadins' apartments. Husnumah, Nurusem, Tabirafa, Zibifer, Safizar, Refet. This last, I knew, had been Selim's favorite. Did he love her still? I experienced a confused irritation every time I imagined Refet settled in the first kadin's apartment.

The "intruders" were slightly at a loss in their new situation, and the eunuchs took advantage of this to inflict on them every little mortification, contributing to their newcomers' discomfort. These were days of total confusion, a swirl of orders and counterorders, comings and goings, shouts and stampedes in the corridors, scenes and minor tragedies. It was that perfectly organized commotion, the highly orchestrated confusion particular to the Orient. Acting from experience, I locked myself away in my apartment, but the rumbles and the tremors of the earthquake shaking the harem reached me nonetheless.

I was then, at sixteen years of age, the unwed "widow" of a sultan, and the mother of an imperial prince who was not my son. What did fate hold for me? I asked Vartui: "Why have I not been given orders to clear out my apartment and leave with the other kadins?"

"Sultan Selim has decided to settle your case once order has returned to the harem."

"Why this exception?"

"I don't know, Nakshidil. And now leave me. I'm so tired." I had tackled Vartui at the end of a particularly exhausting day, and the Cyprus wine with which she tried to unwind made her tongue a bit heavy. I attempted another question: "Would Sultan Selim send me to the Old Seraglio with Mahmud?"

"I'd be surprised if he sent Prince Mahmud away. He's very attached to the child."

"Then might he keep me here until Mahmud is of age to be put in the care of tutors?"

"That's impossible. No late sultan's kadin has ever remained in the Grand Seraglio. Even Kadin Mirizshah, whom Sultan Abdul Hamid held in great esteem, had to move to the Old Seraglio on the death of her sultan."

The idea of the Old Seraglio haunted me. I could imagine myself separated from Mahmud, kept away from Selim, condemned to live out my days exiled from the present in an outmoded palace with crippled old eunuchs and embittered kadins who had nothing left to expect from life. I shuddered at the thought of Cebicefa, that kadin who had inspired such jealousy in me, in my weakness, when she bore Abdul Hamid's child. Only slightly older than I, she was already locked up among the living dead in the Palace of Lamentations.

Compared to that universe of decrepitude and ennui, the Seraglio, in which I was spending perhaps my last weeks, and which so often had seemed an unbearable prison, now seemed a paradise—a paradise I did not want to leave. I had given up asking vain questions of anyone. I was becoming irritable, and one thing I could no longer tolerate was Vartui's habit of bursting into my apartment several times a day on the flimsiest of pretexts. Often I would chase her away angrily.

I had been left—or rather I had kept—the privileges of Abdul Hamid's chamber. I took refuge there when I wanted to get away from the harem's lack of privacy, from Vartui's visits, from Ali Effendi's gossip.

After all the years, I can still see that chamber, which I had come to hate by dint of pacing there idly for hour upon hour. I can still see the primitive frescoes painted on the walls, depicting pseudo-European landscapes. I loathed those walls, of that drab gray meant to evoke the Louis XVI style. The casements, their lower edge ten feet above the floor, only deepened one's feelings of oppression.

Then one evening, as the light waned and I paced up and down in that horrible chamber, the door opened without warning to admit Selim. He was still wearing his ceremonial clothes, for the official celebrations followed one another without respite in those first days of his reign. Three brooches sparkled on his turban—a privilege strictly reserved for the Padishah. He bowed to me ceremoniously. I felt that he hesitated to speak, that he was searching for the proper words. At last, in a low voice in which I discerned a slight tremor, he said:

"Nakshidil, I have come to tell you that if you wish, you may leave here and return to your country and your family. I am willing to send you back to your people."

Had I really heard those words? Never before had such a suggestion been made in the harem. Thoughts and images swirled within me: the house at Robert, Chateau Dubuc, my father, my mother, my sister, the slave children, Nantes and its docks, its ships, the streets of Paris.... My entire past, which Selim had offered to restore to me!

And yet I did not answer yes.

Even today, after all this time, I wonder what prevented me from accepting. Was it Mahmud's affection, and the awareness of my responsibility toward him? Was it awareness of my destiny, or rather my instinctive knowledge of it, which stifled that "yes" on my lips? Or was it perhaps Selim's gaze, the tremor in his voice as he forced himself to speak his suggestion? To this day—I swear it—I don't know, and still wonder.

But if I hadn't said yes, I hadn't said no either. I am a Norman, and therefore somewhat underhanded. I like to take my time.

I answered, "Not right now."

This sentence effectively toppled the surprise back from me to Selim. His face expressed astonishment, incredulity, and happiness in turn. Yes, I could see both surprise and joy in his eyes. But it was joy which dominated, which lit up his features and brought to his lips a smile of a sweetness I have never seen on any other face.

After that smile, he could only say, "But why?"

"Because," I said, "Mahmud will be five a year from now. Only then, when he is handed over to the men, will I be free. Then I can go . . . if I wish to."

Selim was no longer looking at me; he had dropped his gaze to the floor. He muttered an inaudible sentence, the gist of which, I think, was "We have a year before us" or "I have a year before me." I wasn't certain I had understood correctly.

He bowed even more ceremoniously to take leave of me. "Let it be as you wish, Nakshidil."

Mirizshah, now the Valideh, the ruler of the harem, took solemn possession of her new apartment. Selim awaited his mother by the Middle Gate, at the entrance to the Second Court. Following the custom, he took Mirizshah's hand, kissed it, and helped her step down from her coach. Beside him stood Mirizshah's adviser, Veli Zadeh, the theologian who had made me stop my hunger strike, whom Selim had just named Sheikh-Ul-Islam, the religious leader of the empire.

The entire population of the harem—slaves, eunuchs, and new kadins, under the direction of Billal Aga, Selim's former tutor, who was now Kizlar Aga—stood in the Valideh's courtyard, waiting to pay homage to Mirizshah on her arrival. Because of my singular and ambiguous position, I stood aside in the corridor which leads to the Valideh's apartment in the company of the steward of my household—Ali Effendi, whose recent promotion to that honorary post had made him a happy man. With his yellow pelisse and the imposing turban he was now entitled to, he looked like a tiny obese wasp.

I saw the two tall silhouettes of mother and son moving toward me. Mirizshah, majestic and gracious, laughed and chatted on Selim's arm. She saw me only at the very last moment, and I thought I noticed a fleeting glimpse of disapproval in her eyes—just a flash. She immediately composed herself and when I leaned over to kiss the hem of her robe she quickly made me rise and embraced me.

"You here, Nakshidil! I imagined you had already left to return to your country."

Stupidly, I answered, "I postponed my departure, venerable Sultana."

"I'd have thought you were anxious to see your family again."

"I don't know anymore," I murmured.

"You seem in no hurry to seize the opportunity—the unprecedented opportunity—that my son has granted you."

At that moment she caught sight of Mahmud, who had been lurking behind me.

"Come here, my child. We'll take good care of you. We love you. You'll be another son to us."

"I already have Mama Nakshidil. One mother is enough," he said.

"Then keep her, my child. No one wants to take her from you," answered Mirizshah lightly but without conviction. And smiling at us both, she continued on her way with Selim.

Despite her self-control, it was obvious that Mirizshah was disconcerted and annoyed at finding me there. While Abdul Hamid was alive, I had been useful to her plans. But now that Selim ruled, I had become a burden. What was more, I threatened to come between her and her son, between her and power.

I continued to devote myself exclusively to the care of Mahmud, and felt my love for the child grow with him.

My status was vague enough to slip through the net of the harem's protocol. It was convenient for everyone to "forget" me in the second kadin's apartment and it hardly mattered that the new arrivals were a little cramped because of me. The rumors which reached me claimed that their lord and master neither visited nor received any of his kadins, news from which I derived a secret satisfaction. I myself saw Selim only when I brought Mahmud to visit him. He had installed himself in two rooms, one above the other, near Abdul Hamid's lodgings, which had now been shut. A staircase connected his half-Oriental, half-European drawing room on the ground floor to his yellow-and-silver chamber above, which he had redecorated in the most abandoned rococo.

Selim made every effort to replace the child's father, both in his responsibilities and in Mahmud's heart. Mahmud understood this and became attached, with all the exclusivity and possessiveness of his age, to this cousin who had suddenly become an elder brother. It seemed that Selim was determined never to be alone with me, and I could not understand why. Was he avoiding me? I lost my way in various conjectures, for the child I was refused to see the obvious. At any rate I missed Selim, and dreamed of being alone with him. My intentions remained as nebulous as my future; yet a heady expectancy had replaced the anxiousness of uncertainty. It was no longer something unpleasant which I awaited, it was something extraordinary.

My first outing from the Seraglio since my arrival took place one morning when the court went on a picnic. It made me think of those of my childhood, when on the hottest days of summer my parents and my sisters and I would set off in a charabanc to spend the day in the shade of the forest. I could see my mother, dressed in a simple cloth petticoat and a caraco, my father in shirtsleeves, the children running about under Zinah's vigilant eye and her exhortations to remain close by and watch out for insects.

Like everything else here, the excursion required a formidable amount of organization and mobilized hundreds of eunuchs and slaves.

Walls of cloth had been strung up all along our path to the Seraglio's private pier, in order to protect the women from the sight of onlookers. The oarsmen were taken aside for long enough to install us in the small curtained cabins aboard the barges. I piled into mine with two new kadins and Cevri.

The oarsmen then resumed their positions and the barges glided out onto the water. There were about forty of them, long thin craft with twelve pairs of oars, their rowers dressed in scarlet-and-gold livery. In the center of the flotilla was the larger imperial barge of gilded wood, with twenty-six rowers. Selim sat on the aftercastle, sheltered by a canopy of red velvet.

On the Asiatic shore of the Bosporus we were awaited by curtained coaches, the kotchis, drawn by dolled-up mules.

The spot chosen for the picnic, the Grand Signor's Ladder, is a sort of valley veined with many streams, overgrown with a profusion of laurel, wild jasmine, and strawberry trees which shelter the songs of nightingales and turtledoves. Tents had been pitched for us in a charming clearing; they were lined with Brusa velvet and furnished with Persian carpets and embroidered pillows.

We ate to music. The women chattered; Refet minced about shamelessly to attract Selim's attention; I admired the sights nature had spread out before us. At siesta time all retired to their tents for sleep, for dreams, for the hookah or hashish.

Wishing to take advantage of the exceptional freedom of that afternoon and explore the surroundings, I slipped into an abaya, put on a veil, and, well wrapped and hidden, tricked the sleepy eunuchs' vigilance and ventured onto the paths winding through the forest.

I came out into a clearing filled with wild flowers. I had bent over and begun to pick some—a gesture which came back to me from my childhood—when I was interrupted by Selim's voice behind me.

"Is it for me that you pick those flowers, Nakshidil?"

"Oh, no, my lord. They're far too modest to rival those in your gardens."

He must have seen me leave and followed me, escaping his swarms of guards and eunuchs.

He began to pick flowers with me, as if he had done nothing else all his life. When we joined our bouquets—mere pretexts—we sat down in the grass to chat. That was all Selim wished—to speak of his empire, his responsibility, his obsession. "I want to fight those habits which have hardened into law, those absurd traditions which exclude the possibility of progress. In the past century the empire has done nothing but weaken. The pashas in the provinces are free to indulge their every whim, and foreign powers stand watch, biding their time, over our slow agony. Corruption, misery, and injustice triumph everywhere. I shall fight them to my last breath."

"My lord," I interrupted, "if your empire is anything like your Seraglio, it definitely needs to be dusted and aired out."

Selim smiled. "I want to redeem our decadent empire and make of it a contemporary power," he continued. "Of course I know there are obstacles—mentalities to change, minds to open." Indeed there were the janissaries, that fiercely conservative army elite, jealous enough of its privileges to oppose reform by any means at their disposal—especially the worst. There were the ulemas, those obtuse and intransigent religious elements, who clung tightly to the fanaticism which justified their supremacy. There were the provincial notables, who were hostile to any reforms which might deprive them of their opportunities for plunder. There were the various factions at court, busy tearing each other to pieces in intrigues to gain power. "Will I be able to convince them or force them to do my will? Sometimes I wonder. . . ."

"You are young, my lord, and you have faith in your mission."

"For years I did my best to prepare myself for the time when I would have to act. I learned from anyone who could teach me. I read everything I could find. I thought. But all that is not enough. The Cage kept me isolated from the world. I know nothing of our times."

"Question those who do."

"Beginning with you, Nakshidil. You have known France."

His faith in everything that issued from faraway and fabulous Europe was such that he asked for advice without taking my age into account. But what use could I be to a ruling sovereign when I was so ignorant? Selim, carried away by his own words, insisted. "You have had the luck to live in the land of liberty and progress. Tell me what you saw there, what you learned, what you understood." His ardor galvanized me, sweeping away all my hesitations. Selim's sincerity gave him irresistible powers of persuasion. I ransacked my memory for the opinions of my uncle Jean Dubuc de Ramville and the sayings of the philosophers whose forbidden works Monsieur Jolibois had lent me. Mostly I attempted to express remembered impressions in words:

"At home, unlike here, the people don't live in constant abject fear of their sovereign. They speak freely, and if need be they complain freely. The laws protect them against oppression, and if the laws aren't good enough, then new ones are made. In some of our countries there are parliaments which control and limit the monarch's power. Those kings who continue to refuse them will soon have to submit. The people must have their say in affairs of state."

"And by what means, Nakshidil?"

"By means of the States-General."

I explained to Selim that mechanism of European monarchies by which representatives of the various estates of the nation were summoned to give the monarch their opinions and suggestions. The strangeness of the situation struck me all at once: There we were, sitting in a clearing, discussing grave topics like two ignorant children. I was young, and had no experience of politics; and he, a sultan beginning his reign, was no more equipped for it than I. Though Selim was anything but a child, his faith and idealism lent him the purity of childhood. He had enthusiasm, and I had love.

The ardor with which I immediately embraced his cause made me understand—or rather made me admit to myself—that I loved him with all my strength, with all my soul.

The shadows of evening were gaining in the woods around us. It was time to go back. We took a wrong turn on one of the paths and came to a road which cut through the forest. It was the hour at which the peasants bring their cattle back from pasture. Those we met, seeing us walk peacefully side by side, mistook us for husband and wife and honored us with the traditional greeting: "Peace be with you, Effendi, and with your hanun."

Selim answered them each in the same fashion, blessing the man and his wives, his children, his cattle.

I shall never forget that return along the farm road, in the mauve twilight, where the Lord of the Ottoman Empire spoke to me of the future of the large segment of the world he commanded. . . .

Soon afterward Selim summoned a States-General, or an approximation thereof: representatives chosen from all classes and all provinces of the empire. I believed myself to be the instigator of this sensational innovation, and perhaps I was. It caused general stupefaction in the Seraglio, for until then the almighty Padishah had always disposed of everything and everyone without answering to a soul. The first session was opened on May 14, 1789, in the Pavilion of Baghdad in the gardens of the selamlik, formerly devoted to pleasure and celebration, where Selim liked to work. It was the largest of the kiosks, but still I wondered how it could fit two hundred judges, administrators, scribes, professors, officers, and soldiers.

Selim opened the debate himself, inviting the participants to describe the ills besetting the empire and the courses of action which might solve them. This preamble was welcomed by stunned silence. The assembly was completely disconcerted; none of its members were used to expressing their ideas frankly, and especially in the presence of the Master of the Empire. Then Veli Zadeh, the new Sheikh-Ul-Islam, as agreed beforehand, played the devil's advocate. He stood up to describe the constant sufferings and vexations visited upon the people; the injustice, the inequality, the disorders of the army. The strategy worked; when Veli Zadeh sat down, others rose to take his place.

There followed a litany of condemnation: the corruption of the judges; the misfortunes of the peasants who were driven from their lands when they couldn't meet the heavy taxes; the nepotism which crippled the country's administration; the abuses, the incompetence, found on every level.

Throughout the following sessions Selim discovered, in the torrent of grievances, facts which horrified him. The state of the empire was even more desperate than he had imagined. Selim had all the notables' complaints written down in a fat ledger. This book, he told me, the lament of the whole empire, would henceforth be his Koran.

I began to see Selim more often. When Mahmud and I went to visit him, he would find a pretext to send the child away and remain alone with me.

Without any exterior change, my existence had acquired a new dimension. Our conversations soon became a daily occurrence, and I always awaited them eagerly. Selim spoke to me of all his thoughts and asked for my opinions and my advice; sharing his concerns thrilled me.

He was in the process of reuniting his friends and sympathizers into a sort of council to help him prepare the reforms he planned to enact. He called to his side his childhood friends, slaves who had shared his years in the Cage, people who had been exposed to Europe and its institutions while working in embassies abroad. His supporters, who had remained in the shadows or in exile during Abdul Hamid's reign, were now rallying to his banner. One name among them gave me a start: Ishak Bey. Was he not that character who had assaulted Zinah and me one night in the gardens of the Palais-Royal?

On the strength of his old friendship with Selim, Ishak Bey had returned to Turkey, ready to take his place at his master's side. No sooner had he set foot in Constantinople than he was arrested, thrown aboard a ship, and taken to the island of Lemnos, where he was to be beheaded at Selim's orders. This news, relayed by Ali Effendi, was all the talk of the Seraglio.

It was the first time I had heard mention of an execution since the accession of the Reforming Sultan—as Selim had resolved to be remembered by History—and immediately I became plagued with insidious questions. Why would Selim execute a friend of long standing, a supporter of reforms who might have been a valuable collaborator? Could it be because under the fire of his questions, I had told him what had happened at the Palais-Royal? Was he jealous? Was he capable of a jealousy which might bring out in him an unusual act of cruelty?

I hesitated several days before questioning him. When I risked it, Selim's answer was uncharacteristically dry: "Ishak Bey betrayed me."

Whereupon Selim launched into an enumeration of the most urgent reforms he had already decided on: He would enact laws encouraging the peasants to return to the cultivation of their lands. He would make deep-seated changes in the judiciary system and in the administration of the provinces, which he wanted to free of the capricious pashas. He would reorganize the army, which needed new order and discipline. He would ban the alcohol brought in by foreigners, and put curbs on the utilization of gold, silver, and precious cloths.

The gaze of reformers—like Selim's, like mine—turned toward France. We had learned of the storming of the Bastille on July 14, and like so many of my contemporaries, I saw only a trivial incident in what was really the official beginning of the revolution my uncle Jean Dubuc de Ramville had predicted. At the time, our liberals were enthused. The end of absolute monarchy, the rise of an assembly, the elaboration of a constitution—all these changes were like a wind of liberty and progress, the breath of which we hoped to feel even as far away as the Turkish Empire.

During one of my daily visits to Selim, Cevri came to tell me that someone was waiting to see me. In my anteroom I found a woman completely wrapped in veils, through which I could not distinguish her features. "Who are you and what do you want?" I asked.

Very slowly the woman turned around and removed her veils. For several moments I remained unable to move, afraid that a simple word would make the apparition vanish. It was Zinah who walked to me slowly, opened her arms, drew me close to her. I burst into tears and cried in her arms as I had cried so often before. Zinah let me cry myself out, gently stroking my hair in silence. Then came a flood of questions. No, she had not suffered too much. She had been bought by a rich Algerian merchant whose principal vice was avarice; but he was not a cruel man, and had not mistreated her.

"But how did you come all the way here?"

One morning the guards of the Dey of Algiers had come to knock at the door of her master's house. After long negotiations they took her away and brought her before the Dey himself, who told her that she had been bought by none other than the Padishah. She was then put aboard a ship, sent especially to fetch her, which streaked toward Turkey. She was taken to the Seraglio and to the Sultan, who questioned her about me at length. Zinah admitted to me that she had understood nothing of his curiosity. He had kept her for hours, prying from her the most detailed information about my past, my childhood, my life in France, my character, my tastes. . . .

But how on earth had he known, how had he found her? Then I remembered that I had told him of our separation, and how he had wanted to know all the details of Zinah's disappearance. Despite all the worries laying siege to his attention, he had decided to organize this greatest of surprises. His solicitude and the admirable tidiness of the slave registers of Algiers had accomplished a miracle.

Selim had offered me a chance to leave. I had put off making a decision. He had suggested that I reestablish contact with my family. I had refused. In her letter, Mother Marie-Agnès had delineated a choice, and I had chosen. Had I decided to leave, I knew, my family would have welcomed me with open arms, and soon I would have been absolved of the scandal of my Turkish life. If I stayed, on the other hand, I could not allow myself any contact with them. My "state," as Mother Marie-Agnès called it, forbade that—for it was not my shame that I feared, but that of my family. Only Zinah . . . but Zinah, I thought, was gone forever. Not for a moment could I hope to see her ever again. Not for a moment did I think of asking Selim, who would have done anything for me, to order a search for her; I knew that was impossible. But Selim had guessed, and Selim had done the impossible.

More than anyone else, it was Zinah I had missed in my new life. She had shared the beginning of my adventure, and she alone of all the people in my past could have found a place for herself in my new life—and in the Seraglio. Like so many others here, she was black and a slave. Thus she belonged in the world that had become my world. Now Selim had fulfilled my dream, and she was here at my side. She was the only link I could have had between my past and my present, between the person I had been and the person I now was. It was as if my own self had been returned to me. She knew and understood me; she was my friend, my elder, and I had mourned her ever since our separation. Never again would I know the abyss of solitude that sometimes opened at my feet in that overpopulated palace. Now I was protected by Zinah. Armed with her solidity and her common sense, I could once again firmly face the dangerous mirages of the future.

Out of thoughtfulness, in order to leave us to the joy of our reunion, Selim did not call for me in the next few days. Zinah and I needed entire days—weeks, in fact—to tell each other all we had to say. When I saw Selim again I was tongue-tied with emotion and gratitude, and could only thank him over and over again. He did not like to have me in his debt, and soon he sent me away, claiming he had to attend an audience.

Zinah's reappearance was not without repercussions. Cevri remained aloof and only barely tolerated Zinah's presence. Ali Effendi felt supplanted and, at first, showed me some irritation and jealousy; but soon the high spirits they shared brought together these two beings who were always game for jokes and derision. One could hear their giggles and guffaws throughout the harem.

Mahmud resisted somewhat longer. Obeying her nature, Zinah treated him more as a little boy than as an imperial prince, just as she had once treated me as a little girl rather than as her master's daughter. This lack of deference hurt Mahmud, who had been accustomed to servility from the crib. He ran from her because she frightened him. But she soon found the key to that reserved, secretive child; she alone could make him laugh—as much by her jokes and her stories as by her informal ways and her daring cockiness, which Mahmud came to think of as a most exciting sacrilege. In short, Mahmud, who at first had refused her presence, could no longer do without it, and would not leave us to each other for a moment.

One morning in October, Selim took me to the Asiatic shore of the Bosporus, to a derelict palace which he planned to restore.

Our outing was kept secret, and therefore failed to cause the usual stir. A closed litter bore me to the pier, where the inevitable cloth corridor had been strung. Two barges awaited us, one for Selim and one for me, both discreetly painted black, with only eight pairs of oarsmen.

One of Selim's predecessors had erected a palace at Beylerbey some seventy years before. An attractive sadness emanated from this place, which had since been relinquished to nature and the bareness of winter. At Selim's orders the guards and eunuchs stayed on the pier in order to let us enjoy its discovery in solitude.

The marble terraces, invaded by yellow weeds, had caved in; the balustrades were shattered. The beautiful garden, well tended in its time, had returned to wilderness. Disorderly lianas hung between the black tree trunks, and parasitic bushes blocked the paths.

The palace, built of wood, had once been pale green, but years of weather had stripped the paint, which flaked dirtily off the wood.

We discovered a loose door, through which we slipped into the palace. It was terribly cold and dark inside, for all the shutters were closed.

The melancholy inside this place abandoned to the work of time and the voracity of insects was even stronger than outside. Shredded draperies hung miserably from the walls; the mildewed carpets had lost their color, and the crystal of the chandeliers had dulled.

The main drawing room on the first floor must once have been delightful. Selim struggled with the shutters, which were swollen and warped with humidity, and after exhausting efforts he managed to pry them open. Pale winter sunlight flowed into the room. The walls were lined with sofas covered in mauve brocade. Immense Venetian mirrors, all tarnished, framed a fireplace of yellow Alep stone which, according to Selim, exuded a delicious scent as soon as a fire was lit.

"Stay here," he said. "I'll fetch some wood."

Waiting for him to return, I leaned against a window and beheld the dark and dense vegetation, the caved-in terraces, and farther on the waters of the Bosporus, bathed in gray-gold light, and the European shore, rising in deserted parks.

Meanwhile Selim, the Grand Signor, the Shadow of Allah on Earth, was off looking for his wood.

He returned out of breath, his arms loaded with logs. As soon as the fire began to sputter, the Alep stone let off a musky scent.

We were like two marauding children who might have broken into a stranger's abandoned house, standing next to each other in front of the fire. Without looking at me, Selim began to speak.

"I love you. I have loved you ever since the day you wandered by accident into the Cage. You will never know how I have suffered the knowledge that my love is forbidden, that you belong, even beyond his death, to another. You will never know how I fought it, and what torment I endured before offering to send you back to your family."

It seemed to me that his words burned as hot as the flames at which I stared, reddening my cheeks, my forehead, my hands.

Selim would not stop talking. "I cannot do without your presence. I need you at my side in order to live. You are the only one I can speak to—because you are free, free of spirit and character, and because you are the only one who shares my adventure without ulterior motives. I hope I shall be able to forget you when, a few months from now, Mahmud is old enough to go over to his tutors and you leave."

This last sentence was meant to be a question; but I did not answer. Even if I had been awaiting it, this avowal upset me. Never had a man opened himself to me in that way, asking nothing in return. Even Abdul Hamid, though he treated me with great consideration, had taken me against my will. Suddenly I felt gauche and ill at ease, more muddled than happy. The spell of the afternoon, of the deserted palace, had been broken. I wanted only to leave. Selim did not protest. Soon we started on our way back, and separated at the pier where the barges awaited us.

I shivered as the barge glided on the gloomy water. Staying, to accept Selim's love, would not make it any less forbidden. By now I was too familiar with the customs of the Turkish court not to know that the kadins of a late sultan—and, furthermore, the mother of one of his sons—could not become the kadin of his successor. Although it was not expressly forbidden by religious law, the harem, which had laws of its own, would have thought such a thing a monstrosity. The sultans come and go; the traditions of the harem endure. Already they had been shaken by the fact that I had not followed my companions to the Old Seraglio. Becoming Selim's kadin would have unleashed a scandal big enough to shake the harem to its foundation and even threaten Selim's throne. Our love remained sacrilegious adultery even after Abdul Hamid's death. I was not afraid of scandal; defying scandal, especially for love, seems an act of heroism to a sixteen-year-old girl. One must reach my age to think of scandal as something useless and destructive. And then, in my youth, I was almost amused by the idea of shocking the harem's old fogies. Still, I was afraid—unconsciously afraid of Selim's love, of his power, of my responsibility; unknowingly afraid, also, of my own love for Selim, of that fever which already left me no peace, of that commitment which sealed my whole being and my entire life. Today it is easy for me to dissect the emotions that tore at me that afternoon. At the time I understood only that I was prey to obscure, imprecise forebodings.

"I'm afraid, Zinah," I said when I told her what had happened. She only laughed at me. "If you both love each other there's no reason to split hairs."

"But this love—it's impossible!"

"No love which is pure and sincere is impossible."

"No—it can't be! I tell you it can't be! I'm going to leave. . . ."

"It's a sin to resist love."

The solemnity Zinah put into that statement made me smile. "A sin. May I ask before which God it's a sin?"

"Before the universal God—the God of Love," she answered.

Zinah did not convince me on the spot—that is clear from the confusion and reticence of an entry I made in my diary shortly after that conversation.

October 25, 1789: I feel as if I were falling into an abyss—I resist, I cling to the walls, I slip. . . . He told me he could not live without me. Is it true? Is it only a ploy of seduction? Does he only know himself? And I know not whether I long for his visits or dread them. . . .

Luckily for me, the state of the empire suddenly took a turn for the worse and monopolized Selim's time and attention. Led by Hassan Pasha, the new Grand Vizier, the one hundred and twenty thousand volunteers who had answered Selim's call on the day of his coronation had succeeded in stopping the Russian advance in the Balkans. They were resting on their laurels when the enemy, whom they thought in retreat, swept down on them and cut them to pieces.

There was nothing left of that army but twenty-seven thousand wounded, ten thousand prisoners, and sixty thousand fugitives who had abandoned tents, kits, and cannon in their flight. That formidable rout completely demoralized the troops, and, blow by blow, we lost Walachia, Belgrade, and Serbia. The imperial council begged Selim to make peace with the Russians. He refused, and instead sent his gold cutlery to the mint, to be melted and transformed into coins to feed the war treasury.

Tireless, Hassan Pasha returned to the fray. But the janissaries rebelled against his authoritarian measures and paralyzed his attack.

Hassan Pasha came back to Constantinople exhausted and desperate. Three days later he was dead. His disappearance cleared the political stage of the only man who had dominated it by the weight of his authority. A fierce competition for his succession ensued.

Mirizshah had her own candidate for the grand viziership. Hussein Pasha, Selim's best friend, and the leader among his secret advisers, wanted a reformer in the post. The conservatives, resting on the power of the janissaries and the ulemas, reared their head; they were being stirred up from the shadows of the Old Seraglio by Sineperver. All these different parties harassed Selim simultaneously and tore him in opposite directions.

I followed these events from afar, bathed in a sort of fog. Not seeing Selim both relieved me and made me miserable. Yet he did return, one afternoon during my nap time. He walked into my room and asked me to come with him. I followed him through the labyrinth, deserted at that hour, to the Kiosk of Osman III.

That miniature palace, which had been shut for the past fifty years, was situated in the most isolated part of the harem, from which it was separated by a marble courtyard. Suspended over the gardens, it was a sort of windowed nacelle from which one had an incomparable view of the old town, the Golden Horn, the Christian quarters. We crossed the central drawing room, filled with mirrors and crystal, and several rooms which had obviously been redone and regilded recently.

We arrived at the door to the last room, and I gasped with surprise when Selim opened it for me. Inside was an almost perfect facsimile of my room in Nantes, at my cousin Marie-Anne's. Its decoration had been reproduced with unbelievable attention to detail. I recognized the blue-and-white paneling, the curtains of toile de Jouy printed with pastoral scenes, the bedcover of white percaline. It was virtually identical, down to the white wooden furniture, the last word in simplicity, which had undoubtedly been brought from France, and on which porcelain and knickknacks had been placed. My harp was there too, enthroned in the middle of the room on an Aubusson carpet. Selim opened the closets one by one, revealing a complete wardrobe in the latest French fashion. Nothing was missing—dresses, skirts, lawn fichus, lace, stockings, shoes, hats. Not only had Selim questioned Zinah at length about my tastes and the surroundings in which I had lived, but he had even found out my measurements to order this trousseau from Paris.

"This way you can reaccustom yourself to the clothes of your country before you return there," he said with a thin smile.

What could I do with these creations of Mademoiselle Bertin? How could I wear them in the harem now that I had adopted all the refinements of Turkish dress? And that Louis XVI room, the acme of luxury in the Seraglio, which only the Padishah could afford—how poor it seemed in the midst of this palace bursting with that most extraordinary decor I had learned to cherish. Selim's naiveté moved me as much as his thoughtfulness.

When I fell into his arms he held me so tight that I felt he would never open them again. I felt his light kisses cover my face. We remained still for a long time, giving ourselves one to the other in that embrace. Then, without letting go, he began to undress me. Outside, the wind whistled in the trees, and the constant agitation of the branches made light and shadows dance on the walls.

Selim put me down on the bed, and he took me with the tenderness and the consideration of a young lover. Later we lay long in each other's arms, lost in our happiness, motionless, as if we feared to shatter the miracle.

"I would have wanted to be the first," murmured Selim. "Imagine—even now I am jealous of my poor uncle Abdul Hamid."

"But you are the first, my lord—the first to give me the joy of giving and of sharing love and sensuality."

"I would have imagined my uncle a greater expert than I."

"That he was—an expert, a sort of artist. He knew how to draw the ultimate in physical pleasure from the instrument of a woman. But with you I discover the instinct, the need to join myself to the other, to fuse with the other—with you."

Night was falling on our cocoon, so happily forgotten to the world, and it was time to part. Selim disappeared noiselessly. I remember how I was struck, that evening after our hours of lovemaking, by Selim's ability to move about in silence, like a cat.

My new room drew gales of laughter from Mahmud. He leaped from sofa to sofa, shouting loudly enough to wake the entire harem. Finally he began to swing from the curtains, until the mass of drapery fell down upon him and he found himself buried under mountains of cloth. Then he insisted on showing me his own apartment. It consisted of two rooms separated from mine by the central drawing room. He was especially delighted by the fact that all his toys and his books had already been brought there.

My servants explored the place together, sparing me neither their opinions nor their comments. Ali Effendi did not hide the fact that he thought my room hideous; he much preferred Turkish gilding and brocade. Zinah was amused by the others' surprise, and Cevri actually smiled, something she almost never did.

CHAPTER 10

————◦•◦————

OUR LOVE, sealed in the Kiosk of Osman III, was to last many long years. But to tell the truth, we were perfectly happy for only a few weeks—the very first.

We were discovering love, discovering each other. Every day, every hour, brought us new joy. The harmony of our bodies sealed the harmony of our souls.

We told each other everything about ourselves. He delivered himself of his long years of solitude, and I of my past and recent trials. I could tell Selim anything, and in his company the most trivial aspect of daily life became important.

Ever since our first day of love, Selim called me Aimée. He pronounced my name with a terrible accent. He said—I can still hear it—"Aamé."

Prudence and necessary discretion kept us locked up in the Kiosk of Osman III, and for this we blessed our fate. Our days and nights were never long enough for us to be together, to talk, to make love. We were waited on only by Zinah and Ali Effendi, who erected a wall of silence around us and protected us from the gossip of the harem. In the glow of love every detail of my existence took on an extraordinary depth. I awaited each meal with hungry impatience, whereas before I had hardly noticed them. Each loukhoum, each baklava I bit into seemed the most delicious on earth, each lick of sherbet fresher and sweeter than the last. The rise of dawn on the walls of my room was more beautiful while Selim lay at my side, and the sunset on the city moved me that much more if we watched it together, leaning on my windowsill. I took extraordinary pains in my dress, or rather in my disguise as a fashionable Frenchwoman, as if I were about to be reunited with my lover after years of separation, when in fact he had left me only minutes before. Everything was an excuse to talk, and every talk was a pretext for our kisses and caresses.

It is true we were somewhat guilty of neglecting Mahmud. He obviously felt this, but kept his counsel. I continued his lessons, but there was less time to devote to stories or backgammon. But what the child missed most of all were his daily hours of outdoor exercise with Selim. On open ground in the lower gardens of the Seraglio the two used to train in the traditional men's game of mace-throwing. Selim, who was a remarkable shot, taught the child to use his miniature rifle, damascened with gold. And both were passionate players of polo, that Indian game that enjoys such popularity with the Turks. Selim had made two teams among his pages, and tiny Mahmud on a galloping Arab was a wonderful sight, for already he showed great talent with horses.

Now Mahmud missed all these things, and Selim and I knew it. But we knew also there was little time ahead for our happiness, and although we did not speak of it, we had agreed, it seemed, to live our happiness as intensely, as exclusively, as we could. Besides, our intimacy pleased Mahmud, if only because Selim and I were the two beings he felt closest to. I was at once mother and older sister to him, while Selim became, from now on, a father figure as well as an older brother.

From this period of happiness came the following entry in my diary:

This morning, with the utmost seriousness, Selim said:

"Aamé, you should think of beginning to prepare for your departure."

"Where are we going?" I asked, delighted at the prospect of a trip.

"It only concerns you. Mahmud will be five years old in a few days, and you shall be able to leave, as you wished to."

I pummeled him with my fists, laughing, and called him a wily Turk. He confessed that he had been haunted by the appproach of the fateful date of Mahmud's birthday.

Then he handed me a jewel, a tear-shaped pearl, one of a kind, half black, half white, and said: "I give you this pearl as a symbol and a pledge of fidelity. I chose it in the shape of a tear so that you will never forget the tears I shed in secret at the idea that you would leave me."

The political crisis sparked by Hassan Pasha's death came to knock at the walls of our refuge. In order to ensure our tranquillity and justify Selim's long absences, Billal Aga, our Kizlar Aga, would tell the adherents of one party that his master was conferring with their opponents, and vice versa. So they left us alone, and kept to their calculations and the elaboration of their strategies.

Yet the party struggles reached such heights of furor that in the end Selim was forced to make a decision and name someone to the grand viz=iership. He chose the drabbest and most insignificant of his subjects, a certain Chelebi, formerly the governor of a distant province. He was so obviously an incompetent puppet that his nomination satisfied everyone, for it left the race to power open; thus our intimacy was granted a reprieve. Selim's decision, designed to protect our love for each other, was the only one he ever made without examining his conscience and his duty.

Selim had the Ottoman sultans' hereditary passion for flowers. On his own initiative he redesigned the flower beds of the terrace courtyard that bordered my new lodgings, and had them planted with my favorite country flowers. Around the central basin grew cornflowers, carnations, sweet peas, and campanulas.

One night, in secret, he had an enormous aviary installed in the garden, filled with birds of different plumage and different songs, whose twittering blended with the familiar gurgle of the fountain and welcomed me on the following morning when I awoke.

Monsieur Jolibois alone disapproved of the introduction of his cousins into the neighborhood. He displayed his contempt for them with all sorts of rumblings and scrapings, and went so far as to bite Ali Effendi in his anger.

Selim also sent to Paris for a famous gardener—who claimed to have worked at Versailles—to entrust him with the Seraglio's hothouses and vegetable garden. Selim dragged me there, duly wrapped and veiled, along lonely hidden paths. There was a profusion of carnations and tulips, the sultans' pet loves, which one found reproduced in glazed earthenware on all the panels and embroidered in gold on all the velvets of the harem. Selim had also had plants brought from the most distant regions—forbidding giant cacti bursting with brilliant yellow and red flowers on their crests, orchids from Ceylon, and an extraordinary variety of mountain flowers transplanted from Greece. But the gardener, Monsieur Quinteux, ached to show Selim the extraordinary fruit he had managed to produce after months of effort and research. It was a peach of perfect size and downiness, just ripe, but it left Selim indifferent. What he was waiting for, I knew, was a cucumber. The cucumber! The Turks' primordial passion! Selim wanted one fatter and greener than any other; a cucumber head and shoulders above all other cucumbers in the empire. His position forbade Selim to take any chances with French, and the gardener's dignity prohibited his understanding Turkish. There followed an astonishing pantomime between the two men: Selim sketched the shape of a cucumber in the air, reinforcing his gestures with demands in the court language. Monsieur Quinteux, appalled at the indifferent reception of his masterpiece, still holding his peach, grumbled disgustedly in the dry French of a Norman peasant. Certain that he would not be understood, he became downright insulting, and finally called Selim a savage incapable of appreciating the finer things of life.

Losing patience, I intervened in French: "Monsieur Quinteux, there is no point in shouting. His Highness is trying to make you understand that he wants cucumbers."

Thereupon I turned on my heels and left, leaving the gardener frozen to stone and Selim somewhat shaken.

Eventually our intimacy was shattered by the pressure of foreign affairs, and Selim was compelled to leave the happiness of our retreat. The Russians had been quiet for several months, when suddenly they swarmed down on the Balkans. Very soon they reached the Danube and snapped up, one by one, the Turkish forts that controlled the river. Every day brought a fresh batch of alarming news as the Russians advanced toward the last of our protective ramparts, the fortress of Izmail. Potemkin's orders to his aide Suvarov were to take it "at any cost." Suvarov relayed them to his troops as a simple, terse command: "Izmail or death."

Our Grand Vizier, the incompetent Chelebi, whom Selim had appointed in order to remain at my side, managed to inject forty thousand men into the besieged fortress. Confident but also cautious, he himself maintained his distance. "We shall see," he wrote Selim, "the firmament fall to earth before Izmail falls to the Russians."

Waiting for news made us nervous—especially me. I cursed the Russians and the war that had torn us from our happiness. I cursed politics, which prevented me from spending the time I wanted to spend with Selim, whose councils and audiences kept him away from me in the selamlik.

One night I found him with Mahmud, poring over a very large map, which I mistook for a map of the front. In fact, it was one of the Seraglio's strangest treasures, the map of Piri Reis. That Turkish captain had, in the sixteenth century, drawn in great detail not only continents that were completely unknown at the time, but also underwater lands. No one knew by what miracle Piri Reis had obtained his information, and he was suspected of having flirted with the occult.

Selim was explaining the map's history to a fascinated Mahmud.

His calm demeanor annoyed me, and I interrupted him:

"Does the Sultan have nothing better to do right now than examine magical maps?"

Selim looked up, and answered, "There is nothing to do but wait."

"Wait! Wait! Is that how you're going to save Izmail? You're like your uncle Abdul Hamid. He too was satisfied with just waiting. Perhaps you too are marked by fate? This is not the way to save the garrison at Izmail," I protested.

"Allah verah," he said. "God has ordained what must happen."

This was not kismet, the fatality so dear to Abdul Hamid. It was the sincere submission of a believer to the impenetrable designs of the Almighty. Selim's God was too different from mine for my understanding. My own God, more than a figure to whom I continued to address the prayers of my childhood, had become a being quite different from that of my former priests and nuns, and perhaps closer to truth than they might have wished. Solitude had taught me to speak with Him, for lack of any other company. I spoke to Him aloud, confessed to Him, asked favors of Him, and reproached Him when He did not comply. I was young then, and as impetuous with God as I was with Selim.

"Allah verah. . . . No, my lord, God will not give orders if the Sultan does not. You discourage Allah just as you discourage your subjects with your lingering."

Selim folded his map and looked at me pensively. Mahmud too stared at me with reproachful eyes.

Yet under his impassiveness Selim was tense. An irritating incident made us quarrel. The black-and-white pearl which he had given me disappeared from the many-drawered Goa chest where I kept my jewels, and was found under Cevri's mattress in the slavewomen's dormitory. It was either an intrigue against my bodyguard or, more likely, a jealous slave's practical joke: the pilfering within the harem went as far as serious thefts. Selim had Cevri arrested immediately. I protested her innocence. Selim, letting loose his anxiety in a blind rage, had nothing but torture and execution on his lips. I called him a cruel and stupid tyrant. He yielded with bad grace, and Cevri was brought back. She showed no relief at being saved, just as she had made no effort to defend herself against the charges.

Christmas arrived and, for a present, I was given a particularly unpleasant memory.

Following the law of the Orient by which the impossible becomes possible, Kadin Nakshidil often made her way to the selamlik along a path laden with dignitaries and guards, to the Pavilion of Baghdad, where the Sultan liked to work. Kadin Nakshidil was present, duly veiled, when the Sultan received men, and she even attended certain audiences.

On December 25, 1789, I found Selim with Grand Vizier Chelebi, who had just returned from the front, and a simple sergeant who had been wounded in the fighting. Haggard with exhaustion, the man told his tale with difficulty.

The double assault had swept down on Izmail in the dark. Daylight had not yet touched the domes of the mosque when the ramparts, climbed under heavy fire, overflowed with Russian soldiers standing on mountains of corpses. The fort's commander died in the breach. Suvarov threw his battalions into the city. Each house struck by cannon fire crumbled onto both attackers and defenders. Both races kept their oath with the same fury and heroism—the Russians to win, the Turks to prevent their victory. Sixty thousand of Suvarov's troops walked slowly in eight columns along the burning avenues to the center of Izmail. Turks, Tartars, women, children, let themselves be ripped apart by grapeshot, burned by fire, crushed under toppling minarets. Young girls, yataghan in hand, embraced the Russian soldiers and stabbed them to death on the corpses of their parents. The sixty thousand inhabitants and defenders of Izmail, of all nations, all ages and sexes, resisted the Russians and prolonged the agony for ten hours. The massacre of the wounded and the looting lasted three days and three nights. Suvarov, as savage in victory as he was fearless in assault, gave the Turks up to his soldiers the way the quarry is given to the hounds. Fifty thousand Turks died in that slow and bloody nightmare. The earth, frozen by winter, was too hard to accept the dead. A week was barely enough for Suvarov's army to drag to the Danube and throw to its water thirty-three thousand soldiers killed in the breach or in the streets; ten thousand horses who died by the cannon; and fifteen thousand women and children who perished in the flames. A single Turk had escaped by throwing himself in the Danube and swimming to the Grand Vizier's camp; this was the sergeant who had just given us his account of the disaster.

We remained alone, Selim and I, silent, crushed. We knew very well that the loss of Izmail was to be blamed on Chelebi's cowardice and incompetence. And who, after all, had appointed him?

The news of the fall of Izmail threw the people of Constantinople into a stupor, from which they emerged enraged; there followed an explosive rebellion. The crowds took to the streets, stoning the guards, setting fires, looting, and mauling.

I witnessed their fury and the collective madness myself from the windows of the Kiosk of Osman III. Little Mahmud, at my side, showed no fear. "When I grow up," he said, "they won't behave like that."

One night of rioting, Ali Effendi burst breathless into my room and announced that the Grand Vizier had just been executed on Selim's order. And executed in the traditional and most cruel manner, which made of his death a sporting event which the Seraglio followed with passionate interest. According to custom, the Grand Vizier was merely condemned to exile; thereupon he had to rush to a certain gate in the ramparts, known as the Gate of Fishermen, which opened onto the sea. The head gardener, whose other function was that of executioner, also hurried to the Gate of Fishermen. If the Grand Vizier arrived first, his life was spared. If the head gardener won the race, he waited for his victim and beheaded him at the finish line.

So a breathless race for life or death was held between the fallen Grand Vizier and the gardener-executioner. I could envision the luckless Chelebi, weighted down by his caftan, running as hard as his advanced age allowed, egged on by an insane hope, and arriving at the Gate of Fishermen, to find his executioner already there; his head was cut off on the spot, and his body thrown to the sea.

Selim had sacrificed the minister he had chosen himself, had served him up to the crowd. It was more the weakness the gesture revealed than its futile cruelty which upset me. I felt as if something were breaking inside me.

Ali Effendi, seeing my obvious confusion, tried to console me: "That is the custom here. Every time there is a disaster the Grand Vizier is sacrificed, and everything falls back into place."

But I had thought Selim was firm in his decision to put an end to such antediluvian and barbarous customs. Was he a modern ruler determined to pull his empire from the rut of the centuries, or was he a prisoner of the past and its cruel traditions? Was he really different from his ancestors? Did he have the courage to dismiss public opinion and forge ahead, or would he give in to the clamor of the crowds?

Selim was careful not to show up that night. He did not come until the following day, and then only at the hour when he knew Mahmud would be present.

The expression on my face spoke for me. Unable to contain himself, Selim murmured, "I had to do it."

"No, my lord," I replied, "you didn't have to. If today you sacrifice your ministers to the crowd, tomorrow the crowd will ask for your own sacrifice."

Clumsily, he argued that at last the riots had ceased. Mahmud, cautiously, had left. Selim stepped toward me; I pushed him away.

"Come, Aamé," he begged. "Don't forsake me. Today I need you more than ever. Only you can help me."

I did not love him less for what he had just done. I opened my arms, and he took refuge in them. But he was too sensitive and too sharp to fail to understand that doubt had just opened a rift between us.

That doubt was one I was unable to hide from Zinah. "Have I made a mistake?" I asked her. "Has Selim deceived me with his promises of reforms?"

"Sultan Selim is the most remarkable man I have ever met, and you ought to bless your luck every day."

"He doesn't confide in you as he confides in me. He hasn't told you of his goals, his principles, his hopes."

"I do know that he will keep his promises."

"He's a weak man."

"He's anything but weak."

"He certainly acts in weakness."

"You're mistaken, Aimée. Sultan Selim is a thinker, a thinker with an ideal. When politics and the mundane force him back into reality, he loses his powers and becomes a different man."

"And what can I do for him, up in his clouds?"

"You can help him stay there. . . . By the way, my girl, swallow this for me, will you?" Zinah handed me a glass half-filled with a brown concoction—a contraceptive. She had never given it to me before.

I knew it was out of the question for me to hope to bear Selim's child. Our affair had to remain a secret—even if the entire harem gossiped about it. The "widow" of a sultan, pregnant by his successor . . . we could not have avoided the eruption of the scandal which already was brewing. Besides, I did not really want a child. Yet the knowledge that I was being denied the very possibility by an authority other than my own was intolerable to me. Once again I had to submit, even in this most private of matters. Zinah, who bore the brunt of my temper, tried in vain to convince me of the wisdom of prevention over abortion; my anger did not subside. Formerly, the children born by accident to princes in the Cage were smothered in their cribs. Therefore generations of apothecaries had devoted themselves to perfecting effective contraceptives in order to prevent any untimely birth which might threaten the dynasty.

The most expedient and most scientific means were used to conserve the customs of the harem in all their inhumanity. It seemed that everything was geared to keeping me in the shadows. I should have been pleased. But love, pure, exclusive love, was—alas—so rare in the harem that I rebelled against the necessity of keeping it hidden.

Not long afterward Selim told me that he meant to sue for peace with the Russians. A new catastrophic defeat had forced his hand, and the viziers, those eternal defeatists, morosely encouraged him

to negotiate. I did not understand this sudden change in his determination, and told him as much. Until then I had always loved and
respected his tenacity, his need to win at any cost.

"We must save what can still be saved," he told me. How could
we hope to win with an army neither trained nor disciplined,
whose supply lines were falling apart, whose weapons were both
insufficient and obsolete?

I insisted. Twenty times I had been told of the latest defeat as the
final one; twenty times I had heard of armies completely destroyed,
and yet there always remained fresh troops to continue the fight.

Selim's calm inflamed me. I reproached him with having deceived me, with having made me love him by convincing me of his
firmness when in fact he was weak. But his usual gentleness did
not leave him.

"Give me time," he asked. "I need time more than anything
else—to put my program into effect, to continue my struggle. To
regain your confidence. Just give me time, Aamé."

Our conversation took place at sunset in the Kiosk of the Pearl,
hidden at the bottom of the gardens, at the far end of the Seraglio.
Of all the pavilions which rose from the external ramparts, this was
my favorite. A narrow path led to it, circling among the bushes in
bloom. The women did not risk themselves in such faraway and
deserted places, so that Selim and I could often meet in all tranquillity on that balcony suspended over the sea, where we usually did
nothing more than listen to the waves lapping at the ramparts. The
poetic splendor of the surroundings contrasted sharply this day
with my mood. The lively bouquets of flowers painted on the
glazed panels echoed the multicolored marble of a Byzantine
church on the foundations of which rose the aptly named Kiosk of
the Pearl. I looked at the rivers of pearls hanging from the golden
dome, from which were also suspended spheres of gold and diamonds. I followed the paths of the pearl motifs drawn on the gold-
en brocade of the sofas, mulling over my frustration, no longer
worried about whether I was in the right. I then buried myself in
the French gazettes which Selim had taken to ordering for me. The
news I read that evening, already several weeks old, did nothing to

improve my temper. One evening in June, the King and Queen of France had left the Tuileries Palace with their children, and, disguised as burghers, traveling under assumed names in a simple berlin, they had attempted to flee the revolution into foreign lands. Recognized at Varennes, they were arrested and brought back to Paris in shame. Their attempted desertion shocked me. Like the French people, I had lost all respect for sovereigns, for all sovereigns. I read the article to Selim, spicing it with venomous comparisons; in the end they were all the same, those rulers who shirked their duty and betrayed their countries.

Selim decided to hold a feast.

"Are we celebrating our victory over the Russians?" I asked. No. We were to honor the wedding of Hussein Pasha and Princess Esmee. Their union combined one tradition, by which the imperial princesses choose their husbands themselves, with another, by which the sultans offer their sisters and cousins to the most deserving servants of the state, regardless of the obscurity of their origins. In order to escape the boredom of the Old Seraglio, where she had lived, with Sineperver, her mother, since Abdul Hamid's death, Princess Esmee—that madwoman who had once burst into the music school while I practiced the harp, to hurl abuse at me—cast her wishes upon Hussein Pasha, and Selim was delighted to marry his closest collaborator and best friend to one of his relatives.

After the very simple marriage ceremony, which only the imperial family attended, there was *grand couvert*, as they would have said at Versailles.

The reception was held in the gardens of the selamlik, and no men—guards, dignitaries, or even the husband, Hussein Pasha— were included. Gold and silver tapestries bordered a vast area piled with several thicknesses of rugs. The alleys were lined with red night lights, and garlands of flowers and filigreed lamps hung from the trees. Large Chinese vases, overflowing with rare flowers, were placed here and there on the grass, and several canopies of embroidered silk had been strung over the embroidered cushions on which we settled. The harem's musicians and singers gave the best of themselves, but still the entertainment was somewhat drab. We were far removed from the follies conceived by sultans in the past, or even from the naughty shows produced under Abdul Hamid. Our present Master was a lover of music, and he wanted to impose his tastes on the frivolous company, which had little appreciation for the excellent music played by the harem's orchestra. The whispers and chatter of the ladies could be heard throughout the concert. They rivaled each other in the refinement and extravagance of their costumes, and although I had already grown accustomed to the luxury of Oriental finery and ornament, I had never before seen such a display of splendor.

Sineperver had come out of the Old Seraglio to attend her daughter's wedding. I had never seen her before. Dressed in black, gold, and diamonds, her features frozen under white lead makeup, her gaze brighter than her jewels, she seemed a queen of the night, a superb and somber magician. One could not deny she had beauty, character, and sparkle. Yet I noticed that age and a sweet tooth had thickened a body which must once have been flawless. Of course I was very careful not to stare at her or even notice her, and kept myself from turning my eyes in her direction. But she was more skilled than I at that game: more than once she turned toward me, and her gaze went right through me to rest on someone behind, as if I had been transparent, or simply nonexistent.

But the woman who outshone us all was Kadin Refet, whom Selim had once favored. She was extraordinarily beautiful and sensual, her long black hair free on her back, her thin and supple body at once veiled and unveiled in gold and white muslins. She had a fragile, androgynous grace, and that night her black eyes sparkled with a singular intensity. No doubt the diamond and emerald necklace Selim had recently given her was partly responsible for her happiness. Selim owed his kadins at least some compensation for neglecting them in my favor.

That night his former love behaved as if she were still his favorite, with all her ruses and the assurance of her power. She knelt before him like a supplicant to give him his pipe or serve his coffee, and then threw her head back in throaty laughter, in response to a word he had whispered in her ear.

Selim sometimes rolled back the emerald which concealed a minute watch on the handle of his dagger, but he also ran caressing looks over Refet. I guessed he was not unresponsive to her kittenish ways.

I had no heart to appreciate the Oriental melodies that wafted, warm and evocative, into the scented moonlight. I would not have suffered more had Selim and Refet made love before my eyes. I knew that Selim had to throw the harem gossip off my scent and pretend to cultivate his kadins. But how could he accept to play the part? And for whom, after all, was he playing that night? Yes, Abdul Hamid told me there was no such thing as sensual fealty in the harem. The Sultan, even if he was called Selim, would not renounce the most beautiful women of the empire, who awaited his pleasure, to devote himself to one in particular.

I stood up and slipped away as discreetly as possible, and I ran more than I walked through the corridors of the harem. I wanted solitude, the shelter of my room. I stopped on the terrace of the Kiosk of Osman III, its marble floor blue in the moonlight. The birds were asleep in the aviary, small, motionless silhouettes; only the murmur of the fountain disturbed the silence.

Zinah found me leaning on the balustrade, sobbing. Selim, worried by my sudden disappearance, had sent her to look for me.

"Let him worry!" I shouted, between sobs.

"You're nothing but a spoiled child and you've become infernal recently," said Zinah.

According to her I was mad to doubt Selim, and I certainly did not deserve the love of such a man.

"Why didn't I leave the harem? Why didn't I leave Turkey when he told me I could? Tell me, Zinah, why?"

"Don't be silly. Come to bed. After a night's rest you might come to your senses."

Zinah gently took my arm and began to lead me back to my apartment; in the milky darkness we saw a vague shape which seemed to be stuck to my door. Zinah lifted her lantern; my parrot, Monsieur Jolibois, had been nailed to the door.

Zinah began to moan in front of the bloody sacrifice, rocking on her feet as if she were possessed, stuttering incantations in the dialect of Martinique as she tried to ward off the spell. Her hysteria only steeled my nerves. "You see I was right, Zinah. The harem is not the right place for us. We can still leave, you and I. We'll leave tomorrow and go home."

Unlike Zinah, I did not believe that the murder of my parrot was an act of witchcraft. On the other hand, it was clear that I had enemies in the shadows of the palace who wished to intimidate me. Refet? Sineperver? It hardly mattered. My position as a favorite, even concealed by every possible discretion, could not be to everybody's liking. The underground machinations, the muffled violence, the childish or sinister pranks, the low blows from undetectable parties, were not as frightening to me as they were exasperating. Especially at the very moment when I was no longer certain of Selim's love, or at least of his faithfulness.

Curiously enough, it was Cevri who showed the most grief at the death of Monsieur Jolibois. Perhaps in her reticence she had been susceptible to the parrot's volubility. I saw her cry for the first time.

This time, far from holding me back, Ali Effendi encouraged me to take revenge. "The plots of Kadin Sineperver were one thing; those of Kadin Refet are another. You must react."

"And what if it is still Sineperver?"

"Although she's been relegated to the Old Seraglio, the former first kadin is still powerful and active. But she wouldn't stoop to something as infantile as this. It can't be anyone but Refet."

"But do you think she acted alone? You don't think Sultana Mirizshah might have encouraged her, even if it was only by dropping a hint?"

"All the more reason to take action." And Ali Effendi launched with delight into an enumeration of the various treatments to which he might submit Refet: poisoned coffee, a near-fatal dagger thrust, the silk bowstring. . . .

"Leave it alone, Ali Effendi. I don't care about Refet. If Sultan Selim wants vengeance he can take it himself."

"Sultan Selim is not as aware of goings-on in the harem as Sultan

Abdul Hamid was. He won't suspect Kadin Refet. He doesn't understand these things."

"Well, it's not my place to point her out to him. If Sultan Selim has returned to Refet, I'll only alienate him more if I demand that he punish her. If he still has any feeling for me, my desire for vengeance would disappoint him."

Ali Effendi bent his head thoughtfully and said, "How you love him, Nakshidil Kadin!"

"I don't know anymore, Ali Effendi. I simply don't know."

Selim was soon informed—not by me, but by harem gossip. He promised that punishment would be harsh. People had been thrown to the Bosporus for much less than a parrot. He was ready to arrest, to torture, to execute. No sooner had he pronounced these words than he stopped guiltily. Cruelty seemed to be a universal panacea in this country.

I told him that I wanted neither his consolation, nor his suggestions, nor his vengeance. Then, following Abdul Hamid's charming habit, he answered me in verse.

> "My beauty of the honeyed eye,
> Do not treat me as a stranger.
> Let me be your belt of gold,
> That I might wrap around your waist.
> My heart, do not draw away for so little.
> Mingle me into your hair,
> That I might shine at least on your head."

His poetic remedy did not produce the desired effect. I had had my fill of everything. I told him as much.

"I have decided to accept the offer you made; I want to leave here with Zinah and return home, to my family. Will you let me go, my lord, or do you intend to keep me prisoner?"

I was free to leave, he said, and I always would be. Nevertheless he feared my return to a France torn by revolution. I reassured him with further cruelty, declaring that I would return immediately to Martinique, where I could live in peace and happiness among my people.

There were no protestations, no supplications. I added, "Mahmud no longer needs me, and my presence here has become useless."

"It shall be as you wish, Aamé."

Then he picked up his flute, sat down, and began to play. I shall never forget that afternoon, the fog sticking to the windowpanes, the poignant notes he drew from his flute while I struggled to resign myself to the insane project I had just announced.

"All right, let's leave," said Zinah that evening. "But let's leave tomorrow. As you say, we have no reason to stay here another day."

Tomorrow! To leave, to leave Selim forever! Tomorrow! Zinah's common sense and her ruse gave me a salutary shock. But I too was cunning, and the Orient had taught me not to lose face.

"A sudden departure would upset Mahmud. We must give him time to get used to the idea."

I have never found out who informed the child of my intentions. He came to see me, wearing an expression of the utmost loftiness. "You're leaving. You're abandoning us, Nakshidil." He called me Nakshidil and not, as was his habit, Mama Nakshidil.

"I have nothing left to do here, Mahmud."

"My cousin Selim will be sad."

"He'll get over it."

"I'll be sad."

"Soon you'll have your tutors. You'll be at the Seraglio's school. We'd hardly ever see each other."

"I'm very happy to be going over to the men. I prefer their company. Women are all idiots." Thereupon he wrapped himself in his dignity and withdrew, while I dissolved in tears. I did not understand then that Mahmud felt I was betraying him. His character forbade him to beg me to stay, and in his sadness at letting me go he forgot himself. He was just a child—like me; and I was more than ever a child in the pain his rejection caused me. My diary of those days clearly shows the hurt:

I'm leaving. "Be useful," Mother Marie-Agnès told me.
Well—I tried. But no one here has any use for me. They
wouldn't let me. So I'm going back to my own people. My

leaving the harem voluntarily will absolve me, in their eyes, of the scandal of ever having been here. Within the warmth of my family I shall forget my present torment. I no longer know the man I love. I don't know that I love him. I don't know that he loves me.

The crisis we were going through, Selim and I, was perhaps the result of a spell, as Zinah claimed. But I could find more rational causes for it. We were irresistibly drawn to each other while a thousand years of civilization stood between us. He was ignorant of the West, and I still knew so little of the Orient; we grew out of ethical traditions so different that inevitably we clashed and tore at each other.

One morning Selim appeared and asked me to follow him. Crossing the Black Eunuchs' Court, we reached a sort of stone tunnel which sloped down toward the harem gardens. Selim opened a little iron gate. It gave out onto one of the halberdiers' courtyards, in which two or three hundred men were engaged in military exercises. To my surprise, I saw that they were not wearing the resplendent finery of Turkish soldiery, but modern uniforms of European inspiration. They maneuvered in impeccable Prussian order unknown to the imperial army, and carried light weapons entirely different from the usual Turkish soldier's armament. Selim let my surprise and my curiosity wait a long moment before he explained. These men, these weapons, abandoned by the Russian enemy, had been picked up from the battlefields. The prisoners of war, supplied with modern weapons, were trained intensively in the European manner by European instructors.

"What you see here, Aamé, is the nucleus of my new army, which I call the Nizam-i-Jedid. I have been building it in secret for months."

"Why didn't you tell me about it before, my lord?"

"Recently you haven't been particularly inclined to listen to me, Aamé."

I was mortified by that well-deserved answer. I still have a clear memory of the scene—the aged, rounded cobblestones, the high walls of dirty stone ending in a sort of tunnel. We were alone, I wearing my chinchilla-trimmed pink pelisse, Selim in his old-fashioned red satin caftan embroidered with blue-and-gold arabesques which stood out against the drab gray of the surroundings. "I asked you to give me time, Aamé. Did you really think I would accept a Russian victory? The most important thing I had to do was reorganize the army—or rather create a new fighting force, a modern, European one. And without attracting attention, so as not to scare up conservative opposition. With my new army we shall beat the Russians, liberate the empire. We shall replace, we shall eliminate the janissaries."

"The janissaries! I thought they were the elite of the army."

"They were once, but they have degenerated. Originally the janissaries were Christian children who were taken from their parents at an early age and educated in the barracks. Over the centuries they acquired considerable power, partly because they were both a military and a religious caste, which made them a natural ally of the ulemas, the doctors of law."

Bitterly, Selim added, "They make and unmake governments and even sultans. For obvious reasons, the privileges they enjoy have made them fiercely conservative. Furthermore they have lost their fighting spirit in the wars of the last decades, but they still 'hold' the empire—in fact, they terrorize it.

"The janissaries were once the guardians of the empire; now they have become the empire's enemies, and therefore my enemies as well. But I must act cautiously and patiently. I can't do anything until I have built my new army. I am sorry you won't be here to see their success, in a few months, a few years. . . . "

I bowed my head and remained silent. It was the first time Selim had mentioned my plan of departure. Mahmud, Zinah—no one around me ever alluded to it. It was a conspiracy of silence.

In January 1792 the Turko-Russian negotiations opened by Selim gave birth to the Treaty of Jassy. On Selim's instructions, the Turkish commander in chief had fiercely defended our interests, refusing to give sway to the Russians. In the end, he had obtained a return to the prewar situation.

This was quite different from the total surrender I had reproached Selim with. I was ashamed by the way I had misunderstood his intentions and his firmness. Peace with the Russians was declared "perpetual and solid," and at the time, we believed it. Meanwhile peace returned also to Selim and me.

It still happened that I thought of my departure; but every day I told myself the time was not right. Selim mentioned it in a roundabout way by giving me a present—a fairy tale coach built on a European pattern, but with an Oriental sense of luxury. The outside was embellished with glass diamonds; the inside had a mother-of-pearl lining, and cushions and curtains of white-and-silver silk.

"This coach, Aamé, will take you to the port on the day you embark for France."

I answered that I would not fail to use it as soon as possible; but in fact, I was never to climb into that coach to leave Turkey.

CHAPTER 11

ONE DAY I was alone in my room when the rousing strains of a strange martial concert drew me to the window. There I beheld a surprising sight: Behind the Seraglio's walls, in the little square below me, a group of men—obviously foreigners—waved tricolor flags and, with the help of an orchestra, sang: *"Allons, enfants de la patrie, / Le jour de gloire est arrivé."* I learned only later that this song was the *Marseillaise*, the new French anthem.

Then they solemnly planted a tree of liberty in that very square, quite visible from the Seraglio. Thereupon one of them climbed onto an improvised podium and began an incendiary harangue denouncing the arbitrary power and the cruelty of the Sultan. He invited the Turkish people to follow the example of the French and overthrow their tyrant. He described the delights of a paradise under the rule of liberty, equality, and fraternity. The "Turkish people"—the usual crowd of bystanders—had assembled around him. They could not understand a single word of the speech, which was delivered in French. They simply stood there, curious, amused, as if watching a troupe of wandering entertainers.

199

The grotesque incident made me laugh, but the French Revolution itself caused no laughter. The news that reached us grew more astonishing day by day.

The French monarchy had been overthrown. Selim and I, uncomprehending, expatiated endlessly on that strange convulsion. How could so powerful and respected a monarchy, an order in place for centuries, topple so easily? Nothing, then, was ever stable: the strongest edifice might crumble without warning.

A few months later I received a letter from Mother Marie-Agnès, addressed "To Master Constantine Hatzipetrop, Doctor to His Highness," and snatched up for me by Ali Effendi.

In your letter, received some time ago already, you told me, my child, that we came close to meeting again when you decided to return to Martinique by way of France. I am sad that this is not to be, for you dwell often in my thoughts and my memories; yet I approve of your decision to remain at Constantinople. Do not reproach yourself for the impulse which caused you temporarily to neglect your duties to Prince Mahmud, a child whose age ought to make you his sister rather than his adoptive mother. An error is permissible if one repents and repairs. And now it seems that you have become indispensable to another man—another sultan! Will your life never cease to amaze me! It is difficult for me not to smile when I contemplate the image our revolutionary propaganda paints of Sultan Selim—a bloodthirsty tyrant whose existence is devoted exclusively to the satisfaction of hideous vices and monstrous whims. I prefer to believe your portrait—that of a well-intentioned, dedicated man preoccupied with progress and the welfare of his subjects. There is no doubt you can be useful to him.

I can only be thankful that you shall not see what has become of France. As you know, the predicted storm has come; it is only that the violence of that storm could not be foreseen. No doubt you have heard that the impossible, the unthinkable, has become reality—the trial of the King, a vulgar farce, and his murder. In this case it is absurd to speak of "execution." It was no more and no less than a ritual murder reminiscent of murky prehistoric ages. Louis XVI died like a saint. You have also heard that France has been at war since last year against a powerful European coalition. It is with great surprise that we have seen her undisciplined hordes of ruffians—for the revolution has decapitated the military as well, depriving it of its elite—victoriously resisting the onslaught of the allied powers, but no one knows how long this can last. The threat of invasion hangs heavy over us. And that is not all, for we have also been in the throes of civil war since Brittany and her neighboring provinces refused the sacrileges of the revolution and rose up in the name of God and King. The whole country is in flames.

Furthermore, terror reigns everywhere in what was once "the most beautiful kingdom after God's." The nobility and the clergy are the designated victims of the revolutionaries' fury. Hundreds of men and women have been massacred in their prisons by mobs drunk with vengeance and blood. Most of the names of the victims would be familiar to you, for you surely heard them mentioned during your sojourn in France, or even at your parents' in Martinique. Everywhere the innocent are hounded, arrested, beheaded. I have no news of your parents, but I am told that Martinique is less affected by revolutionary madness than France. I have heard nothing about your cousin Madame de Beauharnais except that she has returned to live in Paris. I see your other cousin, Marie-Anne, as often as the circumstances allow. Your kin in Nantes are safe, but all of us here live in fear of the future, knowing not whether tomorrow will find us still alive and free. I could not imagine, when I entered this convent, that there would come a day when I would wonder whether I have a vocation for martyrdom. Unfortunately that is a possibility for which I must prepare. Pray for us all, my child. Pray that we find the strength to bear the trials ahead with courage and resignation.

It was remarkable that despite the warnings of the French Revolution, Selim did not stray an inch from his projects for reform. I admired him for persisting in the liberal path and preparing a program derived from the current of French ideas when he knew what disasters and excesses that position could lead to. Freed from other concerns by the end of the war with Russia, he had returned to his program for modernizing the empire and worked at it relentlessly, with his friends of the secret council—and with me. I had practically become his private secretary. Like the Turks, I arose early and set to work immediately. I spent the entire day sitting on a sofa, chained to my gold-and-agate writing chest—a present from Selim—reading and condensing files. I copied documents, drew up reports from minutes, translated diplomatic texts, which were all written in French. A man of letters, Selim lived in his papers. He was always surrounded by scribes, but since he did not have absolute trust in anyone but me, I was completely submerged in work. I did not even have time for music. But did I really wish to play? I had put my harp away after Abdul Hamid's death, after plucking from it the melancholy chords that had soothed his last moments on earth.

I did not take any exercise, which upset me. I did not want to become a fat hanun like most of the harem women, whose beauty sagged under the weight of idleness and pastries. I wanted to stay desirable for Selim, and therefore it was necessary to beware of the loukhoums, sherbets, cakes, and especially the baklavas, for which I had a particular weakness. Ah! Those baklavas, that crisp pastry dripping with syrup . . . I spent such efforts keeping myself from swallowing, after the first, a second and a third. . . . Today I could eat them to my heart's content, but I have no desire for them. I have lost even my gluttony.

I also had Mahmud's education to supervise. Now that he had passed the age of five, he had "gone over to the men"—in other words, he had been placed under the benign rule of his hocca, his tutor. Every day he walked to the Princes' School, a rather sinister apartment situated in the Black Eunuchs' Court, where a learned ulema came to give him lessons. He would appear in my room at the most unexpected hours. Without interrupting my work, he would sit down next to me and do his homework, which I would then correct.

Usually I worked in my apartment, in the Kiosk of Osman III. I liked those bright, airy rooms, so different from the other harem apartments. I shall never understand why powerful kadins and almighty sultans had preferred to pile up in those dark chicken coops. Furthermore, in that isolated wing I was sheltered from the harem's tempting indiscretions.

The creator of that little marvel, Osman III, had the reputation of a madman. He had spent fifty years in the Cage, and had emerged from it sick with bitterness and hatred. He had no interests other than gluttony, and it is said that he often disguised himself in order to buy sweets in the bazaar without being recognized. Yet the eccentric misanthrope had created for himself a perpetually festive decor of windows, mirrors, and gilded paneling.

Selim often dropped by to ask for a favor or advice. Or else he would call me to the selamlik, to the Pavilion of Baghdad, where he had installed his cabinet. There I would meet his closest advisers, who were busy elaborating, in feverish secrecy, the reforms that were to transfigure the empire. I felt particularly warm toward Selim's closest friend, the husband of Princess Esmee, Hussein Pasha. A Circassian by birth, he was one of those former slaves so commonly found among the most important men of the empire, elevated from their humble positions by the favor of a sultan and launched into fabulous careers. He was fond of reminding us, not without affectation, that he was not yet enfranchised, that he had refused Selim's offer of his freedom, and would not accept it until he had regained for Selim the provinces we had lost to the Russians. He was the same age as Selim, and had shared the latter's life ever since the distant day when he was bought and placed in the future sultan's service. Tall, bony, with curly fair hair and slanting blue eyes sparkling with intelligence and wit, Hussein Pasha exuded loyalty and energy. He was a charmer with the gift of persuasion, the life and soul of the reformers. It was under his flag that I fought; he often enlisted my help, which he claimed he could not do without. While Selim was an idealist, Hussein Pasha remained pragmatic in all circumstances. He often prevailed upon me to curb Selim's impulses to carry the reforms too far too soon, insisting that all the science of men was not worth an ounce of a woman's ability. It is true that Selim never understood why we should want to moderate his enthusiasm with practical considerations.

Hussein Pasha made of me a bridge between Selim's dreams and reality. That was the extent of my role in the reforms. I was then too young and too innocent to provide Selim with any support other than my love for him. Later I was to read pamphlets which insinuated that "a Creole favorite had a disastrous influence on the Sultan." Excluded from the political alchemy of the Pavilion of Baghdad, the harem attributed to me powers far wider than those I had—especially Mirizshah. She herself had guided Selim into the path of reform from his earliest childhood, but she nevertheless remained a woman of the past. The scope of the changes Selim proposed threw her into a panic. She tried to stop him, but he wouldn't listen. She then tried to find the influence, the woman, behind her son's stubbornness. Thereupon Hussein Pasha convinced Selim to dismiss those creatures of hers for whom she had managed to secure vizierships, and whose conservatism and dullness made them unsuited to the task of enacting the reforms.

Mirizshah came to see me. She made an impromptu visit to the Kiosk of Osman, and I could well imagine what it cost her pride to seek me out. She admired without reservation—though perhaps with some envy—the French decor of my room. Then without transition, she attacked: "I am worried, Nakshidil. The people are not ready for the reforms the Sultan is planning. They will cause only disorder and confusion. Conservative opposition—the ulemas, the janissaries—will step in, and will threaten the Sultan's throne. I know and respect your feelings for the Sultan. Help me deflect the danger he is bringing upon himself. Counsel him to stop these reforms."

I noticed that, like Selim, Mirizshah had the nervous habit of rubbing her hands together as she spoke. I took my time to answer.

"Even if I wanted what you ask of me, Princess, I couldn't do it. The Sultan decides alone."

"Yes, but not without consulting others. The Sultan used to listen to me. Now he is deaf to my opinions. That means he listens to others'—yours, Nakshidil."

"He listens only to his conscience."

"I am his mother and I know him better than you. The Sultan has always needed guidance."

"He is not an adolescent anymore. He has become a responsible man, Princess, a ruler imbued with his duty."

"Surely thanks to you," she said ironically.

She turned around so abruptly that the strings of her pearls and emeralds around her neck knocked together. "Have you forgotten our alliance, Nakshidil? Why are you trying to supplant me? Why did you have the Sultan dismiss the wise advisers I placed at his side?"

I tried to defend myself against this accusation, but Mirizshah would not listen. She would not understand that her brave, her admirable work as Selim's educator was now over, and she insisted on attributing her loss of influence to a rival. I tried to make her believe that I had only respect and gratitude for her.

"My only desire, Princess, is to serve the Sultan."

"It is also mine, Nakshidil, and it has been mine for much longer than it has been yours. I was already serving my son long before you were born. And I shall continue to serve him with all my strength, even if I have to crush those who endanger him."

"Which means, Princess, that you will crush all those who you think stand between you and him—at the risk of hurting him, even breaking him. Do you love your son, Princess, or do you love power?"

My insolence did not faze her. But her bearing became more haughty, her eyes flashed, and contained rage trembled in her voice. "My son can love a woman, but not for very long. You can ask Kadin Refet, for example. He is romantic, like the age, but also fickle, like his ancestors. He will change favorites, but he will keep his veneration for me. When he has replaced you he will return to me, and when that happens, you might be in need of a friend. And I am ready to remain your friend if you help me now."

Mirizshah had succeeded in shaking me. The thought of being abandoned by Selim brought tears to my eyes. I murmured, "If the Sultan leaves me, I will have no use for friends—I will no longer have use for anyone or anything."

Mirizshah's gaze softened a little. She looked at me thoughtfully. "Perhaps you are right, Nakshidil. Perhaps you are not as powerful as people think."

With these words, which might well have been meant unkindly, she strode away with a quiet dignity, as if a tide of silks, of jewels and scent, had flowed out.

The eternal conflict between mother and "wife" had made enemies of us. I took Hussein Pasha into my confidence and told him in detail of our conversation. I regretted having unwittingly incited a remarkable woman against me, a woman I admired and who could still be useful to her son. I also wished to spare Selim from getting caught between us.

Hussein Pasha made light of my worries, soothed my conscience, and even joked. "The Valideh thinks you're not powerful!" he cried, bursting into laughter.

"Those are the words she used, Hussein Pasha."

"Not powerful! You! Well, I'm going to give you proof to the contrary. You are now going to resuscitate the dead."

I stared at him. His stentorian voice fell to a mutter: "Ishak Bey."

"That satyr who tried to rape us in the gardens of the Palais-Royal in Paris! But Selim had him executed!"

"That is not a fact, Nakshidil Kadin."

That fanatic whom everyone thought dead had been saved by two Jews who had taken pity on him, and since then he had been vegetating dejectedly under the wing of the French consul at Smyrna. Hussein Pasha begged me to forgive Ishak Bey, claiming that his knowledge and his competence were indispensable to the work of the reformers.

I defended myself. "It is up to the Sultan to grant him a pardon."

"The Sultan will grant it with your consent. He told me so emphatically."

So we resurrected Ishak Bey. I made only one condition: I did not want to lay eyes on him, ever. Thus Ishak Bey, disgraced, condemned, executed, returned to the Seraglio, his head held high.

Meanwhile France wallowed in blood. Now Queen Marie-Antoinette had been beheaded, and perhaps because I had had a chance to meet her, or perhaps because she was a woman, I was haunted by her terrible end.

I received no letters from Mother Marie-Agnès, and thus feared the worst for her, even though her name appeared nowhere in the grisly lists published in the French newspapers. On the other hand, those same papers informed me that "the former Marie-Anne Bellefonds-Laurencin and her husband, François Laurencin," had been arrested and incarcerated to await their trial. Citizen Carrier, who ruled—or rather terrorized—the city of Nantes, had evolved an original system to rid himself of his prisoners: He crammed them onto barges, which were then towed to the middle of the Loire River and sunk. This monster apparently was aided by a general prosecutor who showed himself a zealous recruiter for the death barges; his name was Citizen Jolibois! So my harp teacher at the Convent of the Visitation had found, in the revolutionary courts, an outlet for his bitterness and his hatred of the aristocracy. Did he still have time, between the reading of death sentences, to play the harp?

In Paris, the guillotine did not take a moment's rest, thanks to the laws enacted by Robespierre, France's pitiless dictator. "Enemies of the people," defined in the vaguest and broadest of terms, were sent to their deaths without trial. The prisons of Paris alone contained eight thousand prisoners; within seven weeks, one thousand three hundred and sixty-six of these were sent to the guillotine. I read that "The Committee for Public Safety has concluded that the former General Beauharnais is to be arrested and imprisoned in Paris." The same committee ordered the arrest of "the woman of the same name, wife of the former general."

Thus poor Josephine, who had suffered such ill use at the hands of her husband, was now imprisoned for the crime of bearing his name. In the last year I had thought of her only intermittently, but now the concern I felt brought my memory of her back to life. I feared deeply for her; as I feared for Mother Marie-Agnès, for my cousin Marie-Anne, for all those I had known and loved.

A few weeks later I learned that Alexandre de Beauharnais had been condemned to death by the revolutionary courts and executed along with fifty other prisoners. From that day on, reading the French papers became a torture. Every time I opened one I expected to find my cousin Josephine among the victims.

To take my mind off my anxiety, Selim offered one morning to take me for a walk through Constantinople's big bazaar, incognito.

"The power of the Sultan is such that his subjects cannot recognize him," he explained, smiling. A colorful, inaccessible icon, the Sultan in fact appears before his subjects only at a distance. There are no portraits of him, for Moslem law forbids the representation of human features. Therefore Selim could easily blend into any crowd.

At his prompting I dressed in the fashion of the women of Kurdistan, with an enormous black veil which covered me entirely; he himself chose the disguise of a holy man of the Syrian desert, hiding under a brown hooded burnoose. We followed Ali Effendi to a hidden gate cut in the Seraglio's wall.

On the way my "holy man" explained that it was a sort of tradition for the rulers of the empire to take an occasional stroll through Constantinople's bazaar. It was, in fact, their most effective means of feeling the pulse of public opinion. With its traditions, its laws, its hierarchies, the bazaar served as a cauldron for events and the Sultan's political barometer.

No sooner had we left the Seraglio's walls than I was completely overwhelmed by the noise, the agitation, the light. It was the first time in four years that I found myself in the streets. To see people walking in the open, going about their business, hailing each other and hawking their wares—all this perfectly usual animation made me dizzy. We walked slowly, jostled by the crowd; Selim had to support me, because I stumbled frequently, like a convalescent walking her first steps after a long time in bed.

Everything was new and enchanting to me: the treetops peeking over high garden walls, the facades of the pashas' palaces, the charming alleys, so narrow that the corbeled balconies seemed to touch above our heads; the lattices throwing their cool shadows on the uneven cobblestones polished by the years, the little cafés in which men sat quietly and smoked their hookahs or played backgammon. All this was the Constantinople I had never known, a town I now discovered with delight.

Guards came running down the street in our direction, shouting for us to make way: we were standing in the path of a dignitary's cortege. Selim and I slipped into a doorway. Between lackeys and pages came a horseman in whose sly features I recognized Ishak Bey. Did he notice me staring at him, did he know Selim under his cowl? Several times he turned around as he rode off, looking at us quizzically.

We then crossed the charming garden of the Nuruosmanye Mosque—built by that same Osman responsible for the kiosk where I lived—before reaching the grand entrance to the bazaar.

Once inside, one feels a part of an admirably orchestrated spectacle. The bazaar is a deafening labyrinth, which is nevertheless impeccably laid out in wide alleys and small streets bordered by shops. With its cafés, its restaurants, its infirmaries, its public parks, its mosques, and its caravansaries, the bazaar, like the Seraglio, is a city within a city. Each quarter is devoted to a particular guild and has its very own atmosphere, its own sounds and smells. It is difficult, watching the merchants sitting behind their stalls or hiding in their minute shops, to imagine their prodigious wealth. Yet Selim assured me that most of them are great landowners and possessors of many villas and palaces. The old jeweler to whom Selim led me was the uncrowned king of the bazaar, the sage consulted in case of disputes or litigation, the arbiter in political matters who could spark a riot with a mere word. We found him standing modestly behind his stall, waiting, like his neighbors, for customers. We chose a pair of earrings made of little gold chains from which hung minute coins stamped with the monogram of Selim, the reigning Sultan. Following the custom, the jeweler quoted a high price and Selim began to bargain. It was the ritual game, the codified play, both comical and indispensable, which presides over each and every transaction in the bazaar, and indeed in the Orient. But the Sultan, of course, was not acquainted with all its finer points; and when the old merchant grew angry, complaining that we were trying to ruin him, Selim burst into laughter. Each ritual protestation only doubled his hilarity, and I could tell the old man was greatly offended that Selim should corrupt a sacred game and deprive him of the pleasure of bargaining. I therefore pushed Selim aside.

"Four gold piasters, you say! You're trying to rob poor provincials like us!"

"They cost me five piasters, and I'm giving them to you for four."

"Two piasters, dealer."

"You must be joking, Hanun. Another hanun has seen them and is going to take them at six piasters; she's on her way back here at this moment."

"Keep them for her, then. Farewell, dealer!"

"Don't go, Hanun. You're young and pretty. It's to you I want to sell them."

"Two piasters."

"You're robbing me, Hanun. I'm poor. I have a large family. Three piasters."

Finally I got them for two and a half piasters. Everyone was highly satisfied, and the jeweler even went so far as to congratulate Selim on having a wife so skilled at defending his savings.

Later we sat down on a bench in front of a café at the intersection of two alleys. We ate "harem delights," ices which are also called dondourmas, while watching the crowds go by. All bustled about their business or dawdled in the shops, with a sort of century-old rhythm which excluded all hurry and agitation. The Turks rubbed elbows with blacks, Arabs, Rumanians, Yemenites, Armenians, Caucasians, Jews, Greeks, all of them recognizable by their distinctive national costumes.

"Look, Aamé, look at the mosaic of our empire. All nationalities, all races, fused into one. And they shall remain that way as long as

the empire rests on the twin pillars of authority and tolerance—
tolerance because authority, and authority because tolerance."

I was so fascinated by the sights around me that I barely listened
to Selim. I drank in the scene as if I wanted to store it all inside me.
For the first time in five years I felt free. And yet I was afraid. Five
years in the harem had accustomed me to its familiar rites and familiar faces, to its confined, muffled atmosphere. In order to feel at
ease in the open air, in a crowd of unknowns, in the reality of the
mundane, I would have had to change completely. Was that something I really wanted? Formerly I would have thrown everything
away for the sake of a single escapade, a single whiff of freedom.
Now love had chained me voluntarily to the gilded prison of the
imperial harem.

The coffee seller stood on the threshold of his shop, not far from
us, and soon Selim fell into conversation with him. One thing led
to another, and Selim brought up political matters. The man shook
his head sadly and explained that the reigning Sultan was a good
man, who wanted to unburden the people by generous reforms,
but that he was doomed to failure.

"They won't let him. Too many people have too much at stake,
and he is surrounded by men who will do anything to prevent
those reforms. He's helpless."

Already the coffee seller had left us, to answer the call of other
customers. We finished our dondourmas in total silence and then
walked home quietly, our shopping finished, like two burghers of
Constantinople. And while Ali Effendi opened the little secret gate
for us, Selim turned to me with a strange smile and said, "So! He's
helpless, a prisoner at his own court. Well, we shall see. . . ."

The very next morning Selim's reforms were heralded all over
the city.

A restructuring of state finances was planned, along with the
total reorganization of the administration in order to provide it
with greater speed and efficiency, and the elimination of superflu-
ous posts and fairer recruitment through contests. The practice of

the "presents" given by administrators to their staff was eliminated and replaced by a salary. Taxes levied by administrators in the provinces were lightened, while rigorous controls attempted to stem the tide of corruption, that eternal scourge of the Orient. A plan of organization of grain reserves and their rapid transport to the cities was to reduce chronic famines. Protectionist measures against foreign imports guarded the empire's economic balance. Finally Selim proposed the founding of a newspaper published in French and Turkish—Turkey's first newspaper.

"That sclerotic, rotten old empire is dead now," I told Selim. "In its place you laid the basis of a modern state. You have done it."

"Thanks to you, Aamé."

"Me, my lord? It's you who took the decisions, you who did it all."

"I could never have done it without your love, without the support of your love—without the confidence you have given me."

Everyone was affected, to some degree, by this series of measures. All of Selim's efforts tended toward the minimization of inequality and social injustice.

Of course the population warmly welcomed the prospect of a more comfortable life. As for the rich, those who were to suffer from Selim's measures, they were dumbfounded. Selim's most ferocious adversaries were so stunned that they failed to react immediately. No one in the ranks of the janissaries or the ulemas, or among Sineperver's or even Mirizshah's parties, dared move a muscle.

Zinah seemed to listen with only one ear when I would speak to her of the modernization shaking the Turkish Empire from top to bottom. For some time already she had seemed indifferent to everything around her. Curious, and even somewhat offended, I questioned her about her behavior. As always when she had something to hide, she put on a great show of coy reluctance; finally she admitted that she was in love. I expected anything but that, and could not understand how, locked up in the harem, she had managed to meet a man, let alone become enamored of him. Without losing any of her countenance, she calmly announced that she had set her heart on a eunuch. For a moment I was speechless, and then I was seized by a terrible fit of the giggles which brought me to tears and prevented me from saying a single word.

Her arms crossed on her voluminous chest, Zinah waited for me to regain my wits before taking her revenge. In a few dry sentences she informed me of something I did not know—namely, that the emasculation of certain eunuchs is not entirely successful; while incapable of procreation, they are nevertheless able to enjoy sexual relations with a woman. Highly satisfied at having shut me up, Zinah then allowed herself to tell me the entire love story, which had begun on the boat taking her to Constantinople. Idriss, for that was his name, was a black slave who had been given to Selim as a present by the Dey of Algiers. Fate had placed him on the same boat as Zinah, and thus it was during the crossing between Algiers and Constantinople that their idyll was born.

I told Zinah to bring me her fiancé. Instead of the fat and wrinkled man I expected (for most eunuchs share these traits), there soon appeared a tall young fellow of rare beauty. He had great velvet eyes in a face marked by high cheekbones and a sensual mouth, and his general appearance seemed to indicate kindliness. Idriss seduced me completely, and I promised the lovers that they would marry with my blessings as well as Selim's.

I saw a look of dread cross Zinah's features, which I always read so easily. Questioned, she finally admitted her fear that once wedded, they would be sent away to serve in some palace far away from me, for such is the custom in the rare cases when two slaves marry.

But of course there was no question of my losing her, and I assured them that both would remain in my household. Zinah threw herself in my arms, and I think that only respect and a sense of propriety prevented Idriss from doing the same.

In January 1795, Selim's pet project had become a reality. The new army, that Nizam-i-Jedid whose secret training I had witnessed, had been officially created, and since then Selim had recruited, trained, and armed twelve regiments independent of the regular army.

Simultaneously Selim reorganized the latter. He introduced the cavalry, the artillery, and the infantry to European methods. He opened a naval academy and a school for military engineers. He created shipyards in order to build a modern war fleet. Will, energy, and funds were not lacking for these projects, but there was a pressing need for foreign instructors. There were never enough to fill new posts as they opened up.

"Send for Frenchmen," I told Selim.

I often thought of my former compatriots now that France was weathering the horrors of revolution. I felt a confused sort of solidarity with them, a mixture of pride and pity. For three years now they had been at war with the whole of Europe. To everyone's astonishment, their undisciplined troops had successfully resisted the armies of the great powers.

"If they are such good fighters they are bound to be useful to you," I would say.

But Selim vacillated. A coup had overthrown the bloodthirsty Robespierre, who had been tried and sent to the guillotine. Other notorious extremists had met the same fate—Carrier, Nantes's executioner, and his public prosecutor, Jolibois, among them. But the revolution continued to run its course, and all monarchs feared that it would spread. By introducing French instructors into his army, Selim might well be setting loose in his empire a legion of relentless propagandists determined to overthrow him.

"Not all Frenchmen have a knife in their teeth. Am I not proof enough?" I asked him. That specious argument and his desire to hurry the modernization of his army brought him to take the risk. But that did not solve the problem of finding the Frenchmen. Turkey had broken all diplomatic relations with France since the beginning of the revolution, and there was no contact, no channel through which to send for instructors.

It was then that we received the unexpected help of a Frenchman who had lived his whole life in Constantinople. Pierre Ruffin was that clergyman-like diplomat I had seen in the company of

Ishak Bey in the gardens of the Palais-Royal in Paris. He had managed to make himself almost invisible in order to remain here after the departure of the French ambassador and the closure of the embassy. But he had kept his contacts in the Seraglio, and eventually he heard that Selim wished to reestablish relations with France. Long a lover of Turkey, he stepped in discreetly and took up my cause with enthusiasm. Soon afterward the Sultan officially recognized the revolutionary government of France; he was the first sovereign to do so. In gratitude she sent us not worshipers of the guillotine or ardent propagandists for revolution, but instead serious, capable military men who set to running our army and navy through the mill of modernization. I had won my wager, and for my reward I secured Selim's gratitude.

Applications began to pour in from France. Selim would review them himself and have me examine the files. That is how I came to read one application from a French officer who wished to enlist in the Grand Signor's artillery. The letter he had written his superiors contained one remarkable sentence: "I shall be of good use to my country if I can make of the Turkish forces a threat within Europe." The file was accompanied by an unfavorable recommendation by the French authorities, who thought the petitioner unreliable on the basis of friendships in Robespierre's entourage. This officer who requested the honor of serving the Ottoman army—and whose request was denied—was named Napoleon Bonaparte.

At last came a letter from Mother Marie-Agnès:

God has not asked for my martyrdom. I was imprisoned with
my sisters in religion and I waited, day after day, for
execution. One by one I saw them go to the guillotine—my
companions, your former teachers. My turn had not yet come
when the tyrant Robespierre was overthrown and sent where
he himself had sent so many. His death opened prison gates
everywhere and set me free. It seems at last the Terror is
over. But disorder, anarchy, violence, foreign war, and civil
war continue to torture our unhappy country. I survived, as
did others, your family among them. Blessed be the Lord.
Your cousin Marie-Anne, her husband François de Laurencin,

and her mother, your aunt Elizabeth, are all safe and sound.
So is your uncle Jean Dubuc de Ramville. All were spared
and now lead quiet lives.

We have no news of Martinique or of your cousin Madame
de Beauharnais.

Mother Marie-Agnès's letter stood in sharp contrast to those we
received from Ali Essaid, whom we had sent to Paris as ambassador
upon recognizing the revolutionary government. He had turned
out to be a lusty correspondent, who sent us countless pleasing
reports filled with indiscretions about the Directoire, as the new
regime in France was called. Ali Essaid wrote of an astonishing,
frenetically licentious Paris. The relief of having survived the Terror had thrown the entire capital into cynicism, dance, and debauchery. Only the Constantinople Jacobins, always a little behind
the times, continued to feast on speeches and subversive pamphlets. One mark of the Parisians' extravagance was the extent to
which they were taken with the Turkish ambassador. His costume
was an enormous success, he wrote, and all the society "lionesses"
had copied it; the fashion now demanded nothing but turbans, tu-
nics, and baggy breeches.

And who was the queen of the Paris salons, a fashionable tyrant
who dressed as an odalisque and imposed her tastes on all others?
Citizen Josephine de Beauharnais!

The last time I had heard of Josephine, she had been rotting in a
cell, awaiting her turn at the guillotine. And now it seemed she was
queen of all Paris and the official mistress of Barras, head of the
Directoire and of France! She was as light as a feather—or as a
kitten which always falls on its feet.

During those months, every letter from Ali Essaid brought a new
surprise. Now we heard that Josephine had hastily married a young
and promising general, six years her junior, Napoleon Bonaparte.
That name seemed familiar; wasn't he the officer who two years
before had petitioned for the honor of serving in the Turkish army
and been refused?

The groom, after a period of disgrace, had earned the Directoire government's favor by restoring order to the streets of Paris after crushing a popular rebellion under his guns. He had become a companion to Barras, and the latter, tiring of his mistress, Citizen de Beauharnais, had relinquished her to Bonaparte.

Selim suggested that I write to Josephine to congratulate her and let her know that I was alive and well. Once again he offered me a chance to take up with my family, and once again I refused. There was a new reason for that decision. The first time, it was my "state" in the harem which made me give up the idea of writing home; now it was love that forbade it. A single letter to dear indiscreet Josephine would have been enough to let all Europe know of my presence in the harem. Rumors would naturally filter back to Constantinople, where my existence and the role I played at Selim's side must not be suspected outside the harem's walls. The knowledge that a French kadin ruled Constantinople, or ruled, at least, the Sultan's heart, would be a powerful weapon in the hands of Selim's enemies. Threatened on all sides as it was, our love could be preserved only at the cost of absolute secrecy.

Selim was too sensitive not to guess the pain this sacrifice caused me. Even though I had long ago renounced my country and my family, I was spared neither nostalgia nor regret.

In order to escape the overpowering heat of summer, Selim and I had adopted the custom of spending our evenings in the courtyard of the Kiosk of Osman III, which was slightly cooler than the rest of the harem.

One night the wind brought us echoes of irresistibly joyful music. It seemed to emanate from the slaves' quarters, but at this late hour the harem was supposed to be sleeping. It was only after several minutes that I understood what it was: They were celebrating the wedding of Zinah and Idriss, and I had completely forgotten about it.

Despite my entreaties, Selim refused to come, claiming that he didn't belong in the slaves' quarters and that his presence would spoil the party. So I went alone, taking only Cevri with me.

The celebration was being held in that part of the harem where I had spent my first nights, in the slavewomen's kitchen where my companions and I had once made so many pastries. The hubbub of laughter and shouts, mingled with the sounds of tomtoms and flutes, grew louder as we approached. I looked in at the window without showing myself; it was an authentic celebration of African joy, like those I had seen in my childhood in Martinique, in the outbuildings of our slaves. The eunuchs, normally so grave and so awkward, had recovered for one evening the genius of their race: they worked their instruments like devils, laughed, danced, twirled about. I saw there something which was lacking in all the most sumptuous occasions in the harem—spontaneity, instinct, and a spirit of fun. All of them, men and women, feasted to their heart's content. Enthroned in the midst of the jubilant crowd, the newly-weds sparkled in their finest attire. Zinah especially looked superb in the diamonds and emeralds lent to her by the Guardian of the Jewels—a tradition at the harem's infrequent slave weddings.

Drawn by the gaiety and music, I stepped inside. Everything came to a stop. The slaves smiled at me with deference; but as Selim had warned me, my presence was clearly an embarrassment. Then Zinah came to the door; she took me by the hand, signaled for the music to start again, and drew me into the dance. That night it was she who was queen, and only she could grant me a place among the slaves, the right to participate in their joy. The others understood, and gradually returned to their dances. These were not the lascivious, symbolic, skillful dances of the Orient, but sheer physical exuberance, the unleashing of primitive forces through a savage, obsessive music. The rhythm began to accelerate, I forgot the harem and my imprisonment, and all my shackles fell away from me as I let the beat of the drums invade my body. Nakshidil Kadin must have been quite a sight that evening—sweating, her necklaces and veils flying as she twirled about like a madwoman. The other kadins would doubtless faint with horror when they heard of it, and Mirizshah drop a few acerbic comments, but I didn't care. That night I danced tirelessly, drunk with that barbarous music, drunk with my own freedom, and the slaves accepted me as one of their own. I stopped only because I felt a sudden surge of nausea. Filled with regret, I had to leave the party. For several days already I had not been feeling well.

My ill health persisted through the following days. My discomfort was such that I thought I was pregnant. That was not the case. Nevertheless I continued to feel nauseated and, as I was unable to hold any food, I began to weaken.

The harem astrologer told me that I was going through a difficult period, which would eventually pass.

Meanwhile my condition was growing worse, and I could no longer even stand on my feet.

In a panic, Selim called Mirizshah, who had the reputation of an infallible diagnostician. I will never forget the expression on her face while she examined me. My fate was being settled behind that smooth forehead, and despite my extreme weakness, I understood very well that my life was in Mirizshah's hands. Would she save me, a Frenchwoman who stood in her way to power, who had pushed her son down that insane course of reforms? Or would she abandon me to disease? She glanced at Selim, prostrate by my bed, beside himself with love and grief. Then she leaned over me, examined me attentively, and, rising, said:

"Poison. Probably arsenic."

For days I was fed every known counterpoison, and gallons of milk. But there were no results; I continued to waste away, and my hair started falling out in patches.

It was then that I learned, through Zinah, of something that was being kept from me: Vartui was dying. I begged to be taken to her, but I was quite incapable of walking; so I was carried to that apartment where I had spent my first months in the harem. I was so weak that I had to be placed next to her, lying down. The enormous lady was in agony; every breath was a terrible effort. Still she was able to whisper that I had been her greatest joy, her best try. Yet she wanted even more for me. Yes, she said, she wanted to know in Allah's paradise that I would become the Valideh when Mahmud came to the throne. I lacked the courage to contradict her, and told her that if I reached that highest of ranks I would do my utmost to show myself worthy of her teachings.

Then I lapsed into a sort of coma, through which I saw my loved ones despair over their inability to save me. Sitting tailor-fashion, as immobile as a statue, Selim prayed in whispers. He tried to keep his eyes closed, but could not stop from opening them to cast upon me a gaze heavy with anguish and love. Zinah set herself to the rites and incantations I had often seen her use to ward off evil, wherein African witchcraft made common cause with Christianity. Mahmud, a fierce eye on my bed, moved his lips in silence.

"What are you saying, Mahmud?" I managed to utter.

"I'm speaking to Allah. I'm telling him I don't want him to take you."

The news of Vartui's death, late one evening, barely pierced through to my consciousness.

I felt myself slowly dying in a whirlwind of faces and images from my past. My escapade with Josephine, one hot summer afternoon in Martinique; Ristoglou teaching me Turkish; my trembling approach to Abdul Hamid's bed that first night. In rare flashes of lucidity I thought of my mother and imagined how sad she would be if she knew the state I was in, the despair she would feel at the idea that her daughter was dying out of the Church.

Selim asked his mother to come back and see me. She came with the floorwasher-healer who had saved Mahmud. The old black witch examined me at length, and then, standing up, shook her head sadly. She didn't understand; there was nothing she could do. Nevertheless she began to pace about the room, staring at the furniture, the objects, and even the walls and the moldings of the ceiling. Suddenly the old woman turned to Mirizshah and launched into a vehement tirade, in a garbled jargon which only Mirizshah appeared to understand. The latter immediately gave an order: I was to be taken to another room that very minute. Selim himself picked me up in his arms and carried me, moaning and inert, to the farthest room.

They had to pry my teeth open with a spoon in order to feed me the old witch's antidotes, which were even fouler than those of the imperial apothecary. The first reaction was violent; my insides seemed to rebel, and I thought that now, at last, I really would die.

The very next morning I emerged from that fog in which I had been sinking ever more deeply for days.

A jubilant Mahmud displayed his happiness in unprecedented fashion.

"When I was small and someone tried to poison me, you saved my life, Mama Nakshidil. This time I saved you."

"Of course you saved me, Mahmud—but how?"

"I promised Allah that if he let you live I would never again be impatient or impolite."

"Never again, Mahmud?"

"Not for a year. I don't know if I could manage any more."

It was already a considerable sacrifice. Sorrow, and the thought of losing me, had allowed Mahmud to be the child that, in many respects, he no longer was.

Little by little, life—and with it curiosity—returned to me. First of all, why was I lying in this strange room? Very gently, Selim revealed the old witch's discovery: the paint on my walls contained staggering amounts of arsenic. It was then that I remembered an incident which had taken place several weeks before. I had been asked to leave my room in order that it might be repainted. I thought that Selim, who knew I was not particularly fond of the color of the walls, had given the order to change it. But it turned out that he had never given any such order. Both Billal Aga—the Kizlar Aga—and Vartui had been called, but neither could shed any light on the matter. One heard so many orders and counterorders in the harem that finally we had come to believe that the workers had simply made a mistake and painted the wrong room. In fact, the workers, who had since disappeared, had deliberately coated my walls with arsenic, and I had gradually poisoned myself by breathing its noxious fumes. This practice, Selim explained, came from ancient Egypt, where the priests coated the walls of the tombs with poison in order that grave robbers might be punished at the very scene of their crime. The science had been passed down to us through the ages, and those who had mastered it could thus cause a slow and inevitable death in all impunity.

My first outing as a convalescent took me to the Valideh's apartment to thank Mirizshah for having saved me. With a wave of the hand she interrupted the flow of my gratitude.

"I did no more than my duty, Nakshidil. Anyone would have done as much."

"You saved my life, venerable Sultana."

"I saved the life of my son. He would have died if you had."

Mirizshah had spoken the last words with icy irony. I decided to tease her a little.

"You stop at no sacrifice where your son the Sultan is concerned, if you even consent to keeping me alive."

She smiled, a sparkle of understanding and pleasure in her eye. Then she stifled it before continuing: "May you learn from the trial you have just been through. May it make you think things over and decide to help my son not as you want but as you should. Hold him back, instead of enticing him down the dangerous path he has chosen. He is making enemies, and thereby making enemies for you too. That is something you ought to know. I won't always be around. Protect him, and protect yourself."

Her warning, I felt, was more an expression of concern than a threat. When I returned to my own apartment I sent for Billal Aga, who I knew had a long-standing devotion to Selim and an even longer experience of the Seraglio.

"My life doesn't count, Aga. But the life of the Sultan is precious. If people can make attempts on my life in all impunity, it means that tomorrow others will be plotting against the Sultan. This time again it was, as always, Sineperver."

"Either Sineperver or her henchmen, Kadin. She wanted to kill you, probably, because she is convinced that without you the reforms of our Sultan cannot meet with success, that without you he would be disarmed, vulnerable, perhaps in danger of losing his throne—which might allow her son, Mustafa, to begin his reign earlier than expected. She thinks of you as the Sultan's talisman as well as the mainspring of his program. And she isn't the only one," he added, bowing.

"I suppose an investigation, as usual, would yield nothing?"

"Alas, Kadin! Now that Kadin Sineperver lives in the obscurity of the Old Seraglio, her actions are difficult to spy on. Furthermore, she has supporters, often unsuspected, among all classes in all places. The immense fortune she accumulated during the reign of the late Sultan allows her to purchase widespread devotion."

"Couldn't one take advantage of her present obscurity to get rid of her discreetly?"

"That is precisely what I begged the Sultan to do, Kadin. As you can imagine, he refused. He cannot, he says, push reforms with one hand and perpetuate the tradition of cruelty with the other." I knew as well as Billal Aga the hatred Selim bore for any crime, his shame for those his ancestors had committed. I myself was anything but a criminal, and yet I knew that as long as she lived, Sineperver would remain a danger for Selim as well as for me. Billal Aga concentrated. "Perhaps," he continued, "the Sultan's leniency is also a form of wisdom. Even if Kadin Sineperver were eliminated, there would still be enemies, plots, and other dangers to threaten the Sultan and his loved one. It is neither he nor you they want to destroy; it is the progress you want to bring to the empire."

"So, once again, nothing can be done."

"There is something, Kadin—you must push the Sultan to accelerate his reforms. They will change not only the empire but also its mores. They will cause the old habits of conspiracy and poisoning to become obsolete."

"In the meantime, if I understand correctly, my task is to watch out for the Sultan."

Soon I was able to resume the normal course of my existence. I emerged from my sickness inoculated against naiveté and indulgence—stricter, tougher, firmly decided to defend myself and fight the enemies hiding in the shadows. Through me they had also tried to destroy Selim by depriving him of my support, and that I could not abide.

My sickness had also changed me physically. At twenty-four, I was no longer the full-cheeked adolescent who had seduced Abdul Hamid. I had become thinner, my features had sharpened, and Selim's eyes told me that the change was not to my disadvantage.

CHAPTER 12

We were soon to need my youth and firmness, for something we had long dreaded finally came to pass: The janissaries, displeased by the reforms, rebelled.

In order to tame them a little, Selim had begun by adopting measures in their favor, thanks to which they had accepted civilian reforms without grumbling. However, the creation of the Nizam-i-Jedid, the new army, upset them, and the arrival of foreign instructors to teach them modern warfare finally stirred them up. They denied the instructors access to their barracks. Selim shut his eyes and let it pass.

It was then that violent demonstrations, secretly organized by the conservatives, broke out in the streets of Constantinople. The chaos was such that Selim had to call for the intervention of the troops of the Nizam-i-Jedid. The janissaries joined in the fun, and suddenly we found street battles raging between the army of yesterday and the army of tomorrow.

To top it all, Mirizshah had been intriguing with the janissaries and the ulemas, and she now openly joined the ranks of the opponents of reform. Mirizshah's turnabout astonished me, and crushed Selim. How could the woman become an ally to the enemies of her son, whom she sincerely wanted to defend?

Every Friday Selim attended the solemn weekly distribution of rice to the janissaries in the Seraglio's Second Court. This ceremony served as a barometer for their mood. Each regiment's caldron-bearers brought their pots to the imperial kitchens. These caldrons were the immemorial symbols of the janissaries, and far more sacred than a standard. In battle the soldiers marched behind the caldron-bearers, who were high up in the military hierarchy, and the loss of a caldron in battle meant disgrace and dishonor for the regiment.

If, during the weekly ceremony, the janissaries tipped over their caldrons, they were officially declaring their discontent. The gesture was a signal for revolt.

One Friday, then, Selim walked as usual to the little kiosk where he presided over the distribution of the rice. He was worried; certain rumblings and his Oriental sense of premonition told him something was brewing. I was awaiting his return in my room when suddenly I heard a terrible racket in the distance. I needed only to see Ali Effendi's terrified look in order to understand: The janissaries had overturned their caldrons. Livid with fear, stammering, Ali Effendi began to shriek:

"They're beating on their caldrons! They're going to kill the Padishah!"

Selim! Already I had lunged for the door when Ali Effendi leaped forward, locked it, and thrust the key in his pocket.

"Give me that key immediately."

"It's useless, Nakshidil Kadin. You cannot leave the harem."

"I want to see Selim."

"The Sultan has entrusted you to my care. I cannot let you go."

I cried, I screamed, I slapped and pummeled Ali Effendi. He did not budge.

"Give me that key. Or defend yourself!"

"A slave has no right to lift a hand against a kadin."

His meekness shamed me into silence.

The din of the caldrons had ceased. Selim did not return. Each second stretched into a century. . . .

I paced up and down, wringing my hands, tugging at my robe, tearing up my muslins. Mahmud too was afraid—for Selim, for me, for himself. He remained seated, in silence, perfectly motionless, his back very straight, his face very pale. Ali Effendi was as immobile as Mahmud, a pillow among pillows on the couch, one eye on the door and the other on me.

At last Selim returned. Had I not known him so well, I might have thought nothing had happened. Finally he consented to describe the event.

"When the janissaries overturned their caldrons I thought I would be attacked. What could I do? I had no weapon other than my ceremonial dagger. I stepped forward to face the massed regiments and ordered them to stop their racket. They obeyed, and then I spoke to them. I upbraided them for their ineptitude in battle and for the lack of discipline which has caused us to lose wars. I reminded them that the empire has been diminished and weakened by their fault. I made it clear that a number of things will have to be corrected in order to restore their past glory as well as that of the empire. They'll have to accept certain reforms, and therefore they'll have to obey my orders. I could feel their excitement gradually subsiding, then the caldron-bearers picked up their utensils. It was over."

What Selim's humility restrained him from telling us was that the janissaries had been completely bewildered by the daring of their Sultan, who would stand up to them alone and unarmed. The curt, unexpected speech he addressed to them had the effect of a cold shower. Thanks to Selim alone, the coup had failed.

"When I grow up I will avenge you," declared Mahmud. I knew instinctively that it was not the child that had spoken but the budding man. Selim flashed that irresistible smile of his, at once dazzling and contained.

"There won't be any need to avenge me," he told Mahmud. "The janissaries have already returned to order."

"They rebelled against the Sultan."

"It isn't the first time, and this time they recognized their error."

"If I were Sultan in your place, cousin, I wouldn't allow them to commit errors."

Mahmud's determination pushed me to intervene. "How do you intend to punish them, my lord?"

"Punish them? But they submitted!"

"Harsh words will never have the effect of exemplary punishment. You have the upper hand, but you won't keep it long unless you execute the leaders of the revolt."

"Is it you, Aamé, who speaks that way? The liberal, the friend of revolutions, who insulted me when I talked of executions?"

"I have learned my Turkish politics since then, and besides, a few beheadings won't shock anyone here."

"I want—just as you wanted—my reign to be one of clemency."

"There will be neither reign nor clemency if there is no authority. And authority must be paid for...."

And Selim paid. On the following morning the heads of the rebel caldron-bearers and a few of their companions among the mutineers' officers were placed in the niches of the Seraglio's Imperial Gate. I well remembered the horror and the revulsion I had felt at the sight of other heads there, ten years before, on my arrival at the Seraglio. Now it was I who demanded executions—as long as they denoted firmness and not whim, intimidation but not cruelty. The example was salutary. Everything returned to order, and from then on the janissaries toed the line.

I convinced Billal Aga to spread through the harem the rumor that I was responsible for the executions. I wanted my enemies to know that I was determined to answer them blow for blow.

Now that the janissaries were muzzled, it was time to deal with the rebellions in the provinces. The central government was always threatened by seditious pashas and rebel chieftains. When it wasn't the Levant in the south, it was the Balkans which stirred in the north, so much so that the empire seemed to be built on quicksand. The warlords made their own law everywhere.

Of all these colorful and amoral personalities, it was Ali of Tepeleni, the Pasha of Iannina, who intrigued me most. His fantastic life had gained him fame throughout the empire, and like everyone else, I had heard quite a bit about his adventures. After his father's death, young Ali followed his mother, the fierce and beautiful Chamco, who, at the head of a band of brigands, held the mountains of Albania. Vanquished, raped, and imprisoned with her children, she seduced her guards and resumed her adventurous existence, bent on turning her son into a true bandit. She had succeeded admirably. Ali of Tepeleni became the most fearsome rascal of the empire. In horror and sheer numbers his crimes surpassed any other's, and the treasures he had plundered were even greater than the Sultan's.

He was an elusive, unpredictable man, who could simultaneously call himself a Muslim and drink to the Virgin with the Greeks, who could just as easily intrigue against the Sultan as lend him his support.

The kingdom he had carved for himself with his sword stretched from the mountains of Albania to the Gulf of Corinth. And he continued to enlarge it, now snapping up another piece, now inciting his neighbors to revolt. Somehow we had to interrupt the development of this hostile state within the state.

"Send troops to keep him in line," I told Selim, who shrugged.

"One army has already been sent to Bulgaria to put down a warlord who has been fighting us for years. Another one is on its way to help the Greek princes who rule Rumania, the hospodars, whose territories are being bled white by bandits. A third has been dispatched to Syria to deal with the Pasha of Damascus, who has rebelled."

"Why don't you send Ali of Tepeleni a messenger with the order to execute him?"

"The days when the pashas received the sultans' death messengers on their knees are long gone. Now they tear up the order of execution—when they don't send the messenger's head back to Constantinople in place of their own."

Selim could tell that our impotence hurt me, enraged me. He continued: "Why do you think I am in such a hurry to enact my reforms, Aamé? Only the modernization of the army and the state will restore the Sultan's authority."

"And in the meantime, my lord?"

"In the meantime, we must rely on deception. In its weakness, the empire has made ruse its favorite weapon."

"And with what ruse shall we deceive Ali of Tepeleni, the Pasha of Iannina, the uncrowned king of Greece?"

"Flattery, Aamé! Ali of Tepeleni has always hated his neighbor Kara Mohammed, another bandit of his kind, who 'reigns' in Montenegro. All I have to do is order him to disarm Kara Mohammed. He'll be delighted to destroy his rival, and flattered by my trust."

"And what if Kara Mohammed gets the upper hand?"

"Then I shall unleash Kara Mohammed on Ali of Tepeleni."

"And what happens if Ali of Tepeleni and Kara Mohammed join forces against you? What will you do then, my lord?"

"In that case I shall bestow on both of them the most sought-after honor of the empire. I shall make three-horsetail pashas of them both. Giving them the same rank will make rivals of them and destroy their alliance."

"Selim III, the Reformer, can sometimes be cynical."

"I am not cynical, Aamé. I simply know human weaknesses. It is the duty of the ruler of a weakened empire to study them. Their use is the only substitute for might," he concluded with a bitter smile.

But Selim never had to stoop to conferring the title of three-horsetail pasha on the rival bandits. Enthused by his mission, Ali of Tepeleni crushed Kara Mohammed. In doing so he extended his territories, but he also returned to the fold of the empire.

It was at this time that we celebrated the inauguration of the Palace of Joy. Selim had just finished building it for his mother, not only to honor her but also to console her for the fact that he no longer listened to her advice.

It was announced that we would feast to European dances and European music. With a revolutionary stroke, Selim had brought a dancemaster into the harem to teach the minuet, but only to as yet unconverted odalisques in order not to shock the traditionalists. Of course I could not resist the urge to witness the rehearsals in the slavewomen's quarters. The balletmaster was an old powdered fop reeking of sweet violet, dressed, in the fashion of the days of Louis XV, in apple green. His affected aristocratic manners and voice were utterly grotesque. Every false note or false step of his lovely pupils drew high-pitched moans from him, as if teaching his art to such boors was unmitigated torture.

I was present when Yusuf Aga, Mirizshah's adviser, came to discuss the festivities with Selim. It was the first time I met him. He was a sort of dwarf, bent by the years, with a large head and a hooked nose. Originally from Crete, a former slave, he had risen through the Seraglio with prodigious skill to become Mirizshah's most trusted aide. His hunger for power was such that he did everything he could to feed her resentment toward Selim and push her in her ambition. Although he ignored me during the interview, it was clear that he detested me. He had come to suggest that Selim take advantage of the celebration to flatter Ali of Tepeleni by inviting his mother, Chamco. The latter was soon to arrive in Constantinople with presents for Selim from her dangerous but grateful son. Among them was a real pearl: Vassiliki, a young Greek virgin kidnapped by Ali during one of his frequent raids. She was not an unusual present; had I not been offered to Abdul Hamid in precisely the same way? Vassiliki, the Pasha of Iannina's gift, was a godsend to my enemies, and they lost no time in putting her to use as a weapon.

Yusuf Aga let Selim understand that it was necessary to "honor" Vassiliki, lest he offend Ali of Tepeleni and turn him against us. Moreover, the consummation had to take place before Chamco's departure, in order that she might tell her son how well his present had been received. In short, Mirizshah was doing her best to inject a rival into Selim's heart. She had never been able to admit that her son really loved me; later I found out that she thought I had bewitched him with spells. Wishing to break them, she did not fail to seize the opportunity presented by Vassiliki.

My life in the harem had taught me to dissemble. I appeared to be in full agreement with Yusuf Aga and, in his presence, advised Selim to comply, both for the good of the empire and for his own enjoyment.

I do not think Mirizshah realized that in trying to harm me she was also harming her son. She had chosen her moment well: There were already rumors circulating at court, caused by his faithfulness to me, which had to be denied. Launched by my enemies and spread by the ignorant, they insinuated that Selim had a taste for boys—he would not have been the first sultan with such a penchant, and the rumors did not shock anyone. The accusation which followed, however, was far more serious; it was said that Selim did not wish to or could not sire children. It is true that until then he had never had any.

Young Vassiliki was therefore prepared for her night with the Sultan, in accordance with tradition, in Mirizshah's apartments. I had decided to attend these preparations—it was within my rights to do so—and Mirizshah showed no surprise when I came. She greeted me with her usual courtesy and introduced me to the doll who was being primped and pampered in the midst of a swarm of women. I had to admit that Vassiliki's reputation for beauty was well deserved. She was tall, with extremely fair skin, and her body was generous but without excess. Her face assembled all the features of classical beauty: a perfect little nose, fleshy and well-rimmed lips, green eyes slanting up toward her temples, and straight black hair falling down to her waist—in other words, perfection made woman. When I arrived she was being dressed, after having been subjected to the usual treatment—washing, brushing, massage—and she stood superbly in the midst of the slaves, quite conscious of her beauty and perhaps already dreaming of a glorious destiny. Although she was born in a hovel she behaved as if she were quite accustomed to such luxury, as if she expected nothing less.

Returning to my apartment to dress for the feast, I discovered that in my absence someone had slashed all my dresses and my caftans; not one piece of my clothing had been spared. Someone wanted to prevent me from even attending the celebration. For a moment I felt totally crushed—and yes, I cried, though mostly out of rage. However, the celebrations were about to begin, and I had to show myself there no matter what the cost. Remembering the Bedouin robes I had noticed during my stroll in the bazaar with Selim, I ordered Ali Effendi to run into town, have the shops opened in the name of the Sultan if necessary, and bring me back anything he could find.

He returned three-quarters of an hour later, stumbling under a mountain of striped silk. The peasant women who make those robes have an extraordinary poetic imagination in their choices and juxtapositions of color. Perhaps it is in that art that they seek relief from the austerity of the desert.

I chose a robe of purple, yellow, and black stripes; then I fastened three chains of large uncut emeralds casually around my waist and my arms, and mingled others in my braids.

My arrival caused highly flattering murmurs of surprise and admiration. All the women immediately recognized a Bedouin's robe, and assumed that my choice of dress had been guided by long reflection and an intention to be noticed. I was congratulated for my originality, the women gasped and cooed, and I triumphed where I—and others—had expected defeat. In fact, my improvisation was to become fashion. In the months following that evening, many women of the harem abandoned their sumptuous brocades and baggy trousers for the traditional costume of the Bedouin peasant women!

The feast itself was of a rare splendor. Nature herself took part in the enchantment, contributing the fire of autumn, so rich in reds and golds and browns. In the midst of this glowing vegetation the Palace of Joy, built of immaculate marble in the European style, stood out like a white jewel. Inside, trompe l'oeil colonnades on the walls created a perspective leading to the infinite view of the windows on the Sea of Marmara, the Islands of the Princes, Asia. Most astonishing were the hundreds of caged canaries trained to open with their claws miniature taps linked to innumerable minute fountains. Tents had been set around the palace, for the weather was still very mild. Matching the splendor of the gardens, the draperies and standards had been chosen of crimson and gold; instead of the usual candles and lanterns, the scene was ablaze with torches, which lit us as if by daylight.

While various orchestras worked through their most rousing Oriental repertories near the palace, one could see from the ramparts a spectacle which Selim had organized outside the walls, on the esplanade, where acrobats, wrestlers, and animal trainers staged their best acts for the guests perched above them.

The star attraction, however, welcomed with cheering enthusiasm, were the dances presented by the French balletmaster and the harem girls. They paced through their unfamiliar minuet with such grace that one completely forgot their obvious unfamiliarity with its figures. They were cheered so loudly they had to repeat their performance all over again from the beginning.

Mirizshah, splendid as usual, was enthroned in the place of honor. At her side sat Ali of Tepeleni's mother, Chamco, whose legend had preceded her. She was an Albanian of imposing stature, whose life of banditry and warring had marked her with an aura of ferocity, without for all that diminishing her beauty. Side by side, Mirizshah and Chamco made simultaneous impressions of resemblance and contrast. Both of them were very beautiful in spite of their years; but one of them, delicate and restrained, exuded a calm and sedate sense of power, while the other represented wild, savage strength. Although the Albanian could not but be impressed by the luxury at court, she refused to show it and remained impassive.

I sat next to Vassiliki, the Sultan's doll for the night. Under the eyes of the entire court, which I felt weighing on me like a single attentive and mocking gaze, I went to great lengths to charm her. Already seeing herself a kadin, she barely deigned to address me, and answered me only in monosyllables. Once in a while Mirizshah glanced in my direction and several times I thought I detected a questioning look in her eyes. Of all the people there to deride me and rejoice at my imminent fall from grace, she was the only one who knew me well enough to have any doubts as to the success of her plan.

Selim, sphinx-like, polite and charming to all, did not give anyone his particular attention. He was the first to leave. Soon afterward Billal Aga—looking morose, for he rather liked me—came to bow before Vassiliki; the hour had come. She rose and strode away under the stares of the entire harem, very haughty, as if she were walking toward glory.

I shall never forget the effort I had made to remain wooden. But—I think I have already said this—the resources of the human character are virtually limitless. I knew the stakes, the facts, and the consequences of that night; I remained seated, forcing myself to smile as if I were enjoying myself.

At last, when Mirizshah gave the signal, I left the party with the other high-ranking kadins. I went back to my apartment, to spend the night alone while Selim lay in another's arms. I had carefully prepared myself for that ordeal—and I found I wasn't ready. In the solitude of my room, freed from the scrutiny of strangers, I was visited by unbearable images that returned again and again throughout that long sleepless night.

It was not that I doubted Selim's love. I was not jealous, as I had been of Refet. But the man I loved, the man I wanted, was giving another the caresses that were my privilege. He was taking his pleasure with another, and the thought of it burned me like a red-hot iron. I choked with hatred for the intriguers who had forced Selim to sleep with Ali of Tepeleni's "gift"; for Mirizshah, who wanted to supplant me with a rival; for the idiot women of the harem, who rejoiced at my humiliation.

Next morning Selim came to me embarrassed and sad, and I had to be more gracious and more cheerful than ever in order to clear the air. We made no mention of the preceding night. The harem buzzed with rumors and suppositions, as all concerned tried to evaluate the Sultan's satisfaction by the richness of his gifts to Vassiliki; and all assumed I was lost.

In reality, Selim had simply wanted to honor Chamco, and, through her, Ali of Tepeleni. Now Chamco could return to Albania and tell her son that the Sultan was overjoyed with his gift.

No sooner had Chamco left Constantinople than Vassiliki was taken with a strange illness, an eruption of the skin which spread over her face and her body within a few hours and altered her completely.

The imperial apothecary diagnosed a highly contagious disease, which could be transmitted by contact. Vassiliki was put in quarantine. No one could approach her, especially the Sultan, and she was packed off to the Old Seraglio on the spot.

Today I can admit that it cost me quite a few gold coins to buy the imperial apothecary and have him first concoct, on my instructions, a potion which would produce the desired symptoms, and then make a false diagnosis. In fact, Vassiliki's spectacular illness was entirely benign, and I knew very well that she would soon recover her health—and her beauty.

There was no mention of Vassiliki's illness between Selim and me. But I did make him promise that as soon as she recovered he would marry her off to someone—some dashing young pasha, for instance. Although I had to eliminate her, I did not for all that want to condemn her to eternal imprisonment in the Old Seraglio.

The Palace of Joy, whose inauguration left me such a bitter memory, was to cause considerable problems to others, in the person of its architect. He was a foreigner, a German, Anton Ignatius Melling, who had been introduced to the Seraglio through the favor of Selim's sister, Princess Hadidgeh. It was the imperial princesses' prerogative to walk freely around Constantinople; and strolling through the gardens of the Danish ambassador one evening, Hadidgeh had marveled at their beauty and inquired as to who had designed them. She had fallen for Melling at their very first meeting. He had all the necessary traits to seduce her: he was tall, lanky, fair-haired, a dreamy artist. The romantic Hadidgeh, already once divorced (another prerogative of the princesses) and once widowed, thought, for the twentieth time, that she had found the kindred soul. She looked at Melling as if he were a celestial apparition; he himself seemed terrified both by her and by the passion he inspired. Mirizshah and Selim were upset by her display, and once again Hadidgeh became the laughingstock of the harem.

Around that time one of the harem girls, a gedikli, was caught in the act with one of the halberdiers in charge of the supply of firewood. Selim reacted unthinkingly, following centuries of tradition, and ordered immediate punishment: drowning for the girl, beheading for the man. Perhaps, even though he paid no attention to other women, he could not bear the idea that a piece of his property, no matter how forgotten, should have the impudence to give itself to another.

I did not know the girl, but her fate moved me. I explained to him that the girl's only fault was to have wanted to live. I reminded him that had I not been noticed by Abdul Hamid, my life would have been the same as that of the girl and so many others delivered to nothingness. I brought Selim around to my point of view, and together we tried to find a way to spare the couple. The most important thing was to keep the affair a total secret; but Billal Aga came to tell us that the entire Seraglio already knew its details and awaited the lovers' punishment with great anticipation. I suspected something deliberate in the speed with which the news had spread: no doubt our enemies wanted to force Selim to apply the fiercest of the laws of Islam in order to place him in opposition to his own ideals. Sparing the guilty, Selim would bring down all the tenets of Muslim tradition on his head. On the other hand, ruthlessness ran against his deepest convictions.

We discussed the details of the case with the highest religious authority, our friend Veli Zadeh, the Sheikh-Ul-Islam. He thought it too late to bury the business. We could not circumvent the law while everyone was in an uproar.

But that kind man also added that with the help of time, spirits might grow calmer; perhaps other events would push this one back into oblivion. The best thing to do was wait.

The necessary diversion came from Princess Hadidgeh. She had decided she must crown her delirious passion for the architect Melling by marrying him. An imperial princess, married to a giaour, a Christian. Almighty Allah! Already she had had him moved into her palace at Ortaköy, which he had designed for her, at the gates of the city. Mirizshah and Selim went there several times to try to dissuade her from such madness, but she swore she would throw herself in the Bosporus rather than renounce Melling.

I was the only one to smile at her folly. Mirizshah and Selim were desperate. The court, which at first had rather enjoyed the scandal, was beginning to worry about the proportions it had taken: Hadidgeh, spurred on by that mixture of rebellion and recklessness which she called love, was already announcing her engagement to whoever wanted to listen.

Poor Hadidgeh—she had to bear both the mockery of the harem and her mother's fury. Mirizshah was always after her and heaped abuse on her at every opportunity, as if she found in such behavior a relief for the resentment she could not spend on me; for she did not go without imagining the part I had played in Vassiliki's illness.

The business of the gedikli and the halberdier, which I had thought forgotten, suddenly returned to haunt us. The rumor that the Sultan afforded protection to those who broke the laws of Islam spread like wildfire, and in the end Selim had no choice but to let justice run its course. There was a brief trial, and on testimony of the eunuch who had caught them red-handed the lovers were condemned to death.

On the one hand, Hadidgeh could force the entire state to tiptoe about trying to end her absurd affair, which would have been criminal for anyone but an imperial princess. On the other, a humble girl, without past or future, was to be executed for the crime of having wanted to live—be it just for a single day.

My plan was to have the gedikli escape. A few well-paid eunuchs would take care of it, and a bag of stones thrown into the Bosporus would be enough to mislead the harem. Selim shook his head sadly at this suggestion. "A religious tribunal, acting in full legality, has condemned the girl according to the law. There is nothing I can do about it."

"What use, then, is all the power of the Sultan?"

"If the Sultan fails to obey the law, what right does he have to impose it?"

"And what use are all your reforms, my lord, if they cannot put an end to such barbarity?"

"My reforms can change civil law. They have no bearing on religious law."

"Even if those laws send an innocent girl to a cruel death? Is that the Muslim religion? Is that your faith?"

"My faith has nothing to do with it. What I believe is my own affair. But I am also the Caliph, the religious leader. I must maintain the cohesion of Islam. I can make no exceptions."

"But the Caliph can allow me to act. You don't have to know how I save the gedikli."

"That would not spare my conscience. I beg you, Aamé, don't disassociate yourself from me. If you love me, suffer with me from this act of cruelty I am compelled to allow."

How could I ignore his plea? . . . The gedikli was sewn into a sack and thrown into the Bosporus from the ramparts of the Seraglio. The halberdier was beheaded in his barracks, in the presence of his companions.

Mahmud left me, in accordance with the custom by which imperial princes are considered men from the age of eleven onward, and live alone in their own quarters in the selamlik.

First he was circumcised. Of course that ceremony, which is very important to Turkish families, took on extraordinary proportions in the Seraglio. Selim had sent to Mahmud a caftan we had chosen together, of white satin with stripes of carnations and tulips embroidered in gold. I could feel Mahmud's apprehension at the thought of the operation, although he hid it well. It was not in his nature to swagger; but there was a proud little curl to his mouth, and he had adopted a haughty look through which flashed, from time to time, a streak of fear. I wrapped his turban on his head and watched him walk off in the footsteps of the Kizlar Aga to the selamlik, where the entire court awaited him.

The gardens, turning gray with the winter, were strewn with multicolored tents. A thousand boys of his age were circumcised with him. Mahmud's foreskin, which was to be covered in gold, was solemnly displayed to the Sheikh-Ul-Islam, the Grand Vizier, and other authorities of the empire. After receiving the congratulations of the court, Mahmud watched a show of actors and acrobats. He was then introduced to his household, whose steward bore the title of Lala Pasha. He was a eunuch, Amber Aga, who had been chosen for the post by his friend Billal Aga.

From now on Mahmud would have his own court—his servants, his playmates and schoolmates and his own ulemas for his lessons.

At last he was taken to the Pavilion of Erivan, his new residence. We awaited the little boy in his apartment for a private celebration. Selim gave him a diamond aigrette for his new turban. As for myself, I teased him by first giving him a French grammar, which he accepted politely, though he was unable to hide his disappointment. Then I produced the little dagger I had ordered for him from the palace goldsmith; the hilt and the scabbard were made of gold enameled in the Persian manner, with portraits of Abdul Hamid and Selim.

I was satisfied that Mahmud was in the hands of devoted and competent men. He would live only a hundred yards from my apartment, and I was to see him every day. Everything was for the best—and I was devastated by the feeling that he had been torn from me. I could not reason with myself, although I claimed that my life here had hardened me. If it hadn't been for Selim's love . . .

Though it was only symbolic, my separation from Mahmud linked me even more closely, if such a thing was possible, to Selim. The child was gone; the man remained.

My evenings and my nights were set aside for him. We met, day after day, with undiminished impatience and joy. Affairs of state justified, in the eyes of the court, that feasts and celebrations had decreased in size and frequency; but the truth of the matter was that Selim much preferred our daily tête-à-têtes.

We had been together for more than seven years now, and every day I marveled at the constancy and strength of our love. Our secret, I think, lay in the diversity and complexity of our relationship. We were lovers at once fulfilled and forever unsated; we were friends who amused each other endlessly; and we were partners deep at work on an enormous task.

For my entertainment I still had the gossipy letters of our ambassador to Paris. My cousin Josephine was once again the talk of the town. Leaving her husband, General Bonaparte, to wage his wars in Italy, she had taken a lover, a man by the name of Hippolyte Charles, who was much younger than she, and with whom she lived love's young dream. My nature and my love for Selim could not understand such behavior, but I made an exception for Josephine. Who could have held a grudge against that lovely, incorrigible, generous little bird? She inspired only tenderness and indulgence in those around her. Let her play with her Hippolyte if it made her happy. Never mind her cuckold husband, General Bonaparte!

Actually he was not doing badly; he scored victory upon victory in Italy and occupied the Ionian islands off the coast of Albania; thanks to him, France now had a common border with our empire.

From his lair in Iannina, Ali of Tepeleni sent us alarming reports on the movements of French troops in the Adriatic and on the Albanian coast. But the bandit had the tendency to claim that the entire empire was threatened whenever he feared for his dominions. Selim, attributing Ali of Tepeleni's worrying to the fact that suspicion was second nature to him, did not comply with the latter's demands for reinforcements.

Thereupon the Russian ambassador to Constantinople, beaming with delight, came to tell the Rais Effendi, our minister of foreign affairs, that he knew from unimpeachable sources (in other words, his spies crawling all over our empire) that the French were secretly negotiating behind our backs and conspiring against us with that very same Ali of Tepeleni. It was not difficult to believe that despite his assurances and his pleas for help against the Frenchmen in question, Ali of Tepeleni might be ready to betray us. He was a warlord, and remained true to himself. But why on earth should the French wish to fight us? After all, we had been France's traditional ally since the Renaissance; and her behavior was all the more incomprehensible in light of the fact that we had maintained close and highly privileged relations with France ever since Selim had recognized her revolutionary government.

I was convinced that it was a poisonous maneuver by the Russians, an attempt to drive a wedge into our friendship with France in order to better gain a grasp on Turkey—their unchangeable ambition. Selim was quite shaken. He requested an explanation from the French government. The answer, from the foreign minister, seemed quite acceptable and appeasing. France could not forget that the Turkish Sultan had been the first monarch to recognize the revolution, and the friendship between the two states could not be altered.

The letter was signed with the name Talleyrand. Before the revolution, that same man, then the Abbot of Périgord, had saved me and Marie-Anne from the attentions of my cousin Alexandre de Beauharnais and Ishak Bey at the Palais-Royal.

No sooner had we been reassured than we heard that Bonaparte was at Toulon in the south of France, arming a formidable fleet destined to carry an army of invasion. Europe was alarmed; so were we. England sent Lord Nelson and his war fleet to set up a protective cordon in the Mediterranean. No one knew where Bonaparte meant to strike, and guesses shot back and forth between chancelleries. Would it be Sicily, Portugal, North Africa . . . or some point on a coast of the Turkish Empire?

Again Selim demanded clarification from the French. Again Talleyrand took up his pen, this time to assure us that France's preparations for war were directed solely at England. I managed to convince myself of the truth of these words; looking back, I realize that the thought of French treachery was simply unbearable to me. I accepted the appeasing phrases and the denials, and ignored the evidence.

As Selim pointed out, however, the evidence was considerable: why, if Bonaparte really planned to invade England, had he not concentrated his fleet on the Atlantic? The choice of a Mediterranean port suggested a different plan, and Selim insisted that Bonaparte meant to land on one of the coasts of his empire—probably Albania.

In May 1798 we learned that Bonaparte had left Toulon with his fleet—and having slipped through the British net, had vanished into the Mediterranean. Couriers crisscrossed the roads and seas; chancelleries, ours foremost among them, did their best to gather information, but soon we had to accept the conclusion that Bonaparte and his fleet had literally disappeared on the high seas.

We waited several weeks with bated breath, powerless to act, until one day in June the news fell; Bonaparte had seized Malta, despite the fierce resistance of the knights who had held it until then.

Selim sent a message to the French government, declaring that any landing of French troops on Turkish territory would be tantamount to a declaration of war. I could only approve this amply justified warning.

The French government then answered, through its foreign minister, that Bonaparte's actions in the Mediterranean had no other goal than to clear it of pirates. The capture of Malta, they said, was only a first step in that pious crusade. It seemed the French were mocking us, and my exasperation, like Selim's worry, grew apace. Talleyrand went so far as to ask for our assistance for Bonaparte's project.

This time we had had enough. But what were the French aiming at? Selim decided to send home all French citizens employed by the Turkish government or working in Turkey—engineers, technicians, military instructors. He did not wish to harbor spies in his ranks, and besides, it was wise to expel the Frenchmen for their own safety in case war should break out. For we now fully accepted the possibility of being attacked, without rhyme or reason, by our oldest ally—who continued to smother us in assurances of her peaceful intentions, in ever more obvious lies. While preparing other ammunition, France bombarded us with kind words.

In the meantime Bonaparte had left Malta with his fleet and vanished once again. Where was he headed, where would he resurface? We could only wonder, while Lord Nelson's fleet pursued him, in vain, on every latitude.

PART 4

POLITICS AND REVOLUTIONS

CHAPTER 13

—————————⊶⊷—————————

A STIFLING HEAT had settled on the city, and Selim decided to move
to the Summer Harem. Freshened by the breeze from the Bosporus,
the wooden palace stood near the water, within the Seraglio wall,
behind the Top Kapi, the Gate of the Cannon. It consisted of a
selamlik, the Sultan's wing, quarters for the eunuchs, apartments
for the kadins and other odalisques, kitchens, baths. Although it
was only a question of a few hundred yards, the transplantation of
the harem was preceded by weeks of preparations amid the usual
agitation and hysteria.

Vartui was no longer on earth to boss everyone about and Billal
Aga, who as Kizlar Aga had to organize the transport of three hundred women with their slaves, eunuchs, and baggage, soon found
himself completely out of his depth. There were considerable de-
lays while everything was readied. I can still see us, the odalisques
and I, rushing down through the gardens one torrid afternoon. The
cry of "Helvet," shouted by the eunuchs, had scattered all men
from our path, enabling us to unveil. We all wore the salvar, gold-
embroidered breeches under an unbuttoned caftan which left the

245

neck and part of the throat uncovered. Diamonds sparkled in the kadins' hair. Stuck against the wooden facade of the Summer Harem, marble columns imitated European architecture. I remember thinking the marble was the color of dawn.

I was given an apartment in the kadins' wing, with a view on the sea. The walls and the ceiling were inlaid, in the Persian fashion, with shards of mirror. At sunset it looked as if a thousand fires had burst around me.

The only problem was that my new lodgings were situated directly above the kitchens and I had to endure the fumes of roasting mutton at all times. The scents and the incense I burned were powerless to neutralize the smell, which had saturated the whole apartment, down to the brocaded cushions.

The promiscuity and lack of privacy in that modest-sized palace were far more constraining than in the Seraglio. Luckily we had the run of the kiosk-studded ramparts over the sea. The ladies' primary activity consisted in standing there in endless contemplation of the ships sailing up the Bosporus.

I saw Selim every day. His room was hung with painted waxed cloth, imitating his war tent. A thousand-leaved Gobelin tapestry had been spread on the floor, and I had to explain to him at length the difference between a carpet and a tapestry before it was removed and hung on the wall.

It was in that room, one day in July of 1798, that we received brutal news, brought by a merchantman recently escaped from Alexandria: Bonaparte had just landed in Egypt. So that was his target.

Egypt was the nerve center of the Mediterranean, the pearl of the Turkish Empire, and before that of the Greek, the Roman, the Byzantine empires. Yet it had always been a badly set pearl, forever ready to roll away. Three centuries ago the Turks had conquered it from the Mamelukes. Between that military caste and the administration there had settled a sort of status quo in which neither faction made too many attempts to determine who really held power. Bonaparte had made a good choice, for the equilibrium in Egypt was unstable, and the strength and agitation of the Mamelukes were a constant worry to us.

Dramatic news came streaming in. The terrified population of Alexandria had taken refuge in their mosques, and the French, mistaking this for an insurrection, had massacred men, women, and children. Then Bonaparte defeated the Mamelukes, the only force which had managed to oppose him, at Gizeh in the shadow of the pyramids. A few days later he entered Cairo. The entirety of northern Egypt rested in his hands.

Selim then summoned, to his ceremonial room in the Summer Harem, the first of those councils of war of which I retain a bitter memory. I attended the meeting, hidden in a small and terribly hot contiguous oratory. From a gap in the brocade curtains I watched the Sultan's advisers enter: Hussein Pasha; Veli Zadeh, the Sheikh-Ul-Islam; Ishak Bey, my old "enemy"; and kind Billal Aga, the Kizlar Aga.

Selim had also asked for the attendance of Mirizshah's adviser Yusuf Aga, not only out of deference to his mother but also because Yusuf Aga had influence among the janissaries and the ulemas—an important advantage under the circumstances.

Some of them demanded an immediate declaration of war against the French, stressing that the Ottoman Empire would not tolerate the invasion and occupation of one of its provinces by a foreign power. Others called Selim's attention to the soothing tone of Bonaparte's latest declaration, in which he had assured us he was working not against the Ottoman Empire but solely against England, whose route to her Indian colonies he wanted to cut. But how could we continue to believe his ever more misleading words of appeasement?

I still could not understand why France had broken her friendship with our empire; but my resentment seemed to focus instinctively on the worker of that criminal absurdity: my cousin by marriage, General Bonaparte.

Furthermore, it was painful for me to listen to Selim's advisers insulting the French in the next room. I could not bear the thought of a war, to my eyes a fratricidal war, between French and Turks.

In the middle of the arguments Selim rose and came to ask my opinion in the little oratory. I had had time enough to prepare my answer. "You must choose, my lord, between intervening in Egypt and continuing your reforms. One possibility excludes the other. Embarking on a campaign would automatically suspend your program, and besides, we do not yet have enough troops to face Bonaparte; the new army, the Nizam-i-Jedid, is not quite filled out. We cannot let that troublemaker force us to renounce our reforms. Like me, you have recognized their necessity and their urgency. The future of the empire and your success depend on them. We cannot afford to interrupt their course on any pretext. What we need to do is defer our intervention in Egypt." Selim remained silent and inscrutable while I explained my point of view, and I was convinced that he agreed with me.

I marshaled all the resources of my intellect and my meager experience to convince him to wait; I felt, besides, that he too leaned in that direction. Finally we were agreed on the solution—to abide—he because he was an Oriental, and I because I was a woman and stubborn.

Selim tersely told the council that no measures would be taken for the time being. I heard Yusuf Aga's reedy little voice spring up:

"My lord, all of us here respect your decision; but please allow an old and faithful servant to dare make a remark at this difficult and dangerous juncture; take counsel only from yourself and beware of foreigners. Take counsel only from your conscience, and accept help only from God."

Selim did not reply to that insolent attack, obviously directed at me.

CHAPTER 14

————⊶⊷————

THE RESPITE was short-lived. In Cairo the population had risen, massacring the officers and soldiers billeted on the inhabitants with cries of "May God make Islam prevail!" Peasants surged in from the countryside and joined forces with the insurgents to chase out the French. Bonaparte shelled the city from the citadel. Mosques, palaces, and caravansaries crumbled, while fires broke out in every quarter. In the midst of the deafening noise one could hear the wails of the women and the terrified cries of the children. A storm of terrible violence—unheard of at that time of year—brought the population's panic to a climax. Torrential rain transformed the streets into rivers of mud, the crash of thunder echoing that of the guns and the toppling buildings. Then Bonaparte surrounded the city; his soldiers worked their way methodically through every street, destroying and killing everything in their path. Those who attempted to flee the city were cut to pieces by the French cavalry posted at the walls. As one functionary wrote to Selim: "The French did things to make one's hair turn white." The reprisals went on for fifteen hours and left Cairo wrecked, bloodied, and sobbing in ruins.

Selim immediately gave orders to stifle any news of the disaster. But nowhere does news travel as quickly as in the Orient. It slips under bolted doors, hurdles the highest walls, leaps from terrace to terrace, runs in streams through the streets, swelling with rumor and confabulation; and everyone comments on it while the powers that be imagine it still a secret. The Turkish population knew all about what had happened in Egypt, and judged the Sultan severely. I was furnished proof of this by Ali Effendi's behavior: That incurably jolly eunuch suddenly became morose, and finally admitted how disappointed he was by the Divan's—he did not dare say the Sultan's—weakness before the French invaders. All his admiration went out to the inhabitants of Cairo, who had resisted to their deaths. "They've won Allah's paradise, those courageous fighters," he said.

"It won't be easy to defend the empire from up there," I retorted.

Yet I was more affected by Ali Effendi's opinion than I wished to admit. He was a man gifted with great common sense, and furthermore he was a man of the people; through his voice I could hear that of millions of Selim's subjects who reproached him for his inertia.

Even Mahmud disapproved of my attitude. I had taken the habit of keeping him abreast of current events. At thirteen he was just beginning to grow into manhood. The time for French grammar and arithmetic had passed. I left to his tutors the task of teaching him history, poetry, mathematics, and other sciences. With Selim's approval I had decided to make of him a modern prince opposed to the traditions of the Seraglio and, unlike his predecessors, aware of the politics of the modern world. I saw his mood darken when I told him of our decision to remain aloof from the conflict.

"We should have made concessions, even if it meant declaring war on the French in order to buy a little time," he said.

"Do you want the Sultan to renounce his reforms?"

"Never! But he ought to postpone them under the pressure of those events." He backed up that opinion with reasoning that showed so much wisdom and maturity for a thirteen-year-old that I remained speechless. Could it really be that this child, my child, had become a man that skillful at manipulating concepts, capable of speaking to me of adversity, of time, of destiny?

It was then we received news of the battle of Abukir. After months of search on every latitude, Admiral Nelson had found the French fleet and blown it up in the Bay of Abukir. Thus Bonaparte had been deprived of his transport and cut off from the rear. Selim sent the victor a jeweled sword, and I made the mistake of thinking this merely a gesture of protocol, failing to see its deeper significance.

Mirizshah made a gift to Nelson of a very large diamond and ensured that word of her gratitude was spread. She had wanted a war with the French since the very beginning: perhaps she hated them for being my compatriots, or perhaps because she knew that I wanted to keep peace.

Shortly after the Cairo massacre she had herself announced at Selim's door, and I barely had time to leap into the adjoining closet and hide before she burst in to throw a violent scene.

"Are you not ashamed, my son! Your empire is attacked, your authority mocked, your subjects massacred—and you do nothing! Instead of doing what everyone expects of you—instead of sending our valiant troops to wash away the French insult, instead of behaving like a man—you prefer to listen to the advice of a woman, a Frenchwoman, an enemy!" Yes, she used the word "enemy." Then, turning to the curtain behind which I hid, she shouted: "And you come out of there. I hate these little mysteries. I don't have anything to say to the Sultan that you shouldn't hear."

There was nothing to do but emerge from my hiding place like a guilty child, weak with shame. Mirizshah didn't even look at me before resuming her tirade. "Is it possible, my son, that you have fallen under the influence of this woman to the point of growing blind? Is it possible that you mean to rush down the path of dishonor for the charms of a giaour, an infidel? I refuse to stand by any longer while the Selim I once knew is destroyed before my eyes. Rather than see you sink ever deeper into lust I shall leave the court and retire to the Old Seraglio. You must choose, my son, between the Frenchwoman and me."

Thereupon Mirizshah stomped out of the room, leaving behind her the scent of her musky perfume. Selim had weathered the storm without losing his customary impassivity. He remained standing, very straight, lost in thought, his eyes to the window. I started toward the door and was about to leave when Selim, without turning, said, "My mother is a little quick-tempered, but don't worry, Aamé. There won't be a choice between you and her."

Mirizshah was not the only one who believed that I was betraying Selim and the empire to France. The entire harem was convinced of it, including, I knew, several of Selim's advisers. Yet I had lost all sympathy for the French since the horrors my former compatriots had perpetrated in Egypt. On the other hand, nothing could make me renounce the reforms. They were Selim's task, my task, and their success would make Selim one of the best, one of the greatest sultans of all Turkish history.

The dilemma grew even more spiny when Russia declared war on France. The Russians' Black Sea fleet sailed toward our coast, planning to cross the Bosporus on its way to fight the French. Since it was out of the question that they cross the straits without our authorization, we found ourselves compelled to make a stand. Letting them through was tantamount to declaring war on France, and would have forced us to accept the burdensome protection of our traditional enemy. On the other hand, a refusal would have alienated our allies.

A second time Selim assembled his council, and I regained the oratory off his room. Even in such dramatic times we could not spare ourselves the proprieties imposed by Turkish tradition. No woman, not even a valideh, had ever been allowed to attend a meeting of the government. Even if it was known to everyone that I was taking notes in the oratory, at least I was hidden and the rule remained unbroken.

Those who wanted war, Mirizshah's adviser Yusuf Aga foremost among them, attacked vehemently any suggestion of another course of action. Not only did they insist on allowing the Russian fleet passage, but they wanted to sign an aggressive alliance with Russia and England. Veli Zadeh, the Sheikh-Ul-Islam, and Grand Vizier Izmet, a friend of Hussein Pasha's, replied with equal vehemence that they would never tolerate the presence of the Russians in the Bosporus. For them the question of war was secondary; keeping the Russians from setting foot in the empire, the object of their hereditary ambition, was more important. As for the advocates of peace, they were visibly shaken by the recent events. Even Hussein Pasha wavered.

Abandoning his reserve, Selim announced his intention of declaring war on the French while carrying on with his reforms. This left me stunned; never had my beloved's lack of realism seemed so flagrant. Nevertheless I detected, in his search for an impossible solution, a desperate attempt to save those reforms, and this only strengthened my certainty. Hussein Pasha spoke up for us both, affirming that war and reforms were mutually exclusive. A choice had to be made.

At this point Selim joined me in the oratory. "The empire has seen quite a number of wars and invasions," I began. "But it has never seen reforms such as those you have begun, my lord! Never in her entire history has she enjoyed such opportunity. And at this point they are still too fragile, too recent. To give them up now would be to destroy everything you have already built, and you would have to start all over again. And for what? For a dangerous war, a war we are not prepared for, a war we might lose. Let the British and the Russians fight the French, and carry on with the main purpose of your reign." I had wanted to shout, but in fact I had to whisper my harangue in order not to be overheard by the others. Selim listened to me in silence, his face inscrutable. He neither approved nor contradicted. When I had finished, he left in a rustle of silk. His silence suddenly brought doubts. Had I disappointed him? I started when I heard him tell his council that he was off to consult the Valideh.

For the first time since I stood at his side the scales tipped toward his mother, and I was assailed by tempestuous thoughts. Next door

Selim's advisers, freed by the absence of their master, opened up. Advocates of war and advocates of peace argued with terrible violence, hurling insults, accusations, and threats at one another. Hearing them, one would have thought that all those notables were corrupt, traitors, sold to the British, to the Russians, to the French—which, in certain cases, was not entirely false.

Selim's advisers tore at one another, and I myself was torn by my own thoughts. Evening had fallen, and yet the heat remained unbearable. I suffocated in that small oratory. I looked at my watch—a present from Selim—and examined absentmindedly his enameled portrait inside the watch case. Suddenly it struck me that despite the late hour it was still light. Outside, the sky glowed red. I ran to the window and saw the low quarters of Constantinople ravaged by enormous flames which rose straight up into the still night like cypress trees made of fire. A plume of thick black smoke covered the city's outskirts, from the Mosque of Sulemanye to the ramparts of Theodosia. Then I heard drumrolls spreading through the city, taken up from street to street like an echo—Constantinople's fire alarm. Then came the hammering of the night watchmen's iron-tipped sticks on the cobblestones, and their endless lugubrious cries of "Yangum war!"—"Fire!"

According to an age-old custom it was the Sultan's duty to drop everything and go in person to the site of the disaster. From my window I saw him cross the gardens of the Summer Harem, surrounded by a handful of guards, and disappear through the Gate of the Cannon. The summer night, filled with fire, was breathtakingly beautiful. Before me the flames grew taller, stretching into a clear sky riddled with stars. We were too far away to hear the people's cries of terror, and only the incessant roll of the drums accompanied the fearsome and superb spectacle. The walls of Selim's room, hung with waxed cloth, seemed to dance in the flickering light; the mirrors and the crystal chandeliers glowed and sparkled in the magic of the fire.

The blaze had put a stop to the dispute among Selim's advisers. In the ceremonial room, now metamorphosed by the fire, they remained silent, and I could hear only the clicking of the amber or emerald chespis, the beads they fingered. We waited an hour, and then another, before Selim reappeared.

His face was black with soot, his caftan of white brocade was stained and streaked, and the feathers of his aigrette were singed; but no one even thought of smiling. He began to tell what he had just seen in the city. His low monotone only made the description more dramatic. He told of houses turned into torches, of flames leaping from terrace to terrace, of charred corpses pulled from the ruins, of devastated families searching for the missing. He told of all the misery, the ruin, the blood and tears and horror of that night. It was as if he could speak of nothing else, as if he were hypnotized. And we all listened, fascinated despite ourselves.

He spoke to us of an old woman who had hailed him as he walked through the smoldering ruins. Sitting next to the remains of her shack, like a statue of desolation and reproach, she had called to him: "Mecca is taken, my lord. What are you waiting for?"

Mecca was not taken—that was just an exaggeration of popular rumor—but Egypt had been taken.

Suddenly, he told us, everything had become clear to him. He had seen what must be done. No one in his entourage, he said calmly, had shown him as clearly as that ragged stranger.

Without raising his voice, he declared that he would authorize the passage of the Russian ships through the Bosporus and declare war on France.

This decision, uttered with a determination to which there was no appeal, unleashed a storm. Veli Zadeh declared that he would never sanction such a decision. The Grand Vizier added that he would refuse to sign the order allowing the Russians through the Bosporus.

Selim, gazing into the distance, did not react to his companions' insubordination. He limited himself to declaring the session adjourned until the following day.

The advisers rose and retired in silence. I didn't move; I waited, as usual, for Selim to join me in the oratory. I waited long, in vain, writing in the heat of the moment.

From the window I see him pacing alone in the courtyard—up and down, with an even step, always turning around at the same intersection of two marble paths and starting all over again, like an automaton. He's been doing this for hours, though he must be exhausted. Above him the sky is still aglow from the fire.

Though there is nothing I would do more readily, I cannot join him; I could be of no help. Without wanting to, I've carved a gulf between us. I've been obsessed by Selim's obsession with reforms; I've been blinded by my enthusiasm at the idea of participating in his work. I failed to understand how much he suffers at the knowledge that Egypt—his Egypt—has been invaded. It is not only the integrity of the empire which is at stake; it's also his own integrity.

When he asked for my advice, he hoped I would give him the courage to renounce his reforms in order to defend Egypt. He hoped for the strength to sacrifice his convictions for his duty. I gave him neither. With all the power of my lack of experience, I defended the reforms and only worsened his dilemma. I failed him. It must have been a heartrending decision to make—against his most loyal advisers, or against me. Of course he cannot doubt my loyalty and my sincerity. But a crack has appeared in his trust in me. . . . Still he walks, and still I wait. I find myself returning to the prayers of my childhood—praying that God put an end to the solitude and the suffering of the man I love, and praying that he be returned to me. Still Selim doesn't come. . . .

I was wakened by a hand on my shoulder. I had fallen asleep crouched by the window, my writing chest slipping off my knees. Ali Effendi had come to ask me gently to return to my apartment. Selim had stayed up all night without returning to his room. The courtyard was empty. The gray-and-pink glow of dawn was mingled with that of the blaze, which refused to die. Bright-eyed, waving his arms and babbling, too excited to take notice of my state, Ali Effendi gave me the news which all the harem was already repeating: Selim had just dismissed the Sheikh-Ul-Islam and the Grand

Vizier, a reformer and a friend of Hussein Pasha's, and was sending them both into exile.

Selim, then, had not hesitated to take action against two of his most loyal collaborators, who had dared oppose his decision. But had he punished them on his own initiative? Ali Effendi struck the last blow by telling me that while I slept, Selim had gone to see Mirizshah and had spoken to her for more than two hours.

At noon on that exceptional day—I had still not seen Selim—I heard of the outcome of the night. Selim had appointed a new Grand Vizier, Ziya Pasha. It was as if Mirizshah herself had signed the Hatif Sherif, the decree nominating him. Ziya Pasha was known to be hidebound, and hand in glove with the janissaries, the ulemas . . . and with Yusuf Aga, the Valideh's adviser. I had been defeated. Yet it was not Mirizshah, despite her triumph, who was the victor, but that old woman who, in a disaster-filled night, had hailed Selim: "My lord, what are you waiting for?"

Selim addressed a decree to the new Grand Vizier and had it posted at every corner in the city: "It must be known that all true believers are to wage war on the French and I consider it my sacred duty to make every effort to free my empire of their impious hordes. You shall notify every Muslim that I have declared war on the French, and you shall labor day and night to exact a brilliant vengeance."

The program for reforms was suspended, and war declared on France. Amid the general joy Mahmud, Ali Effendi, and even Zinah were delirious with excitement.

The ground was giving way under my feet. I didn't even know what justified my presence anymore, since Selim ignored me.

I count those days of the summer of 1798 among the most unpleasant of my existence. Selim did not come to see me, but only sent an occasional message. I stayed alone, cloistered in my over-heated room, breathing in the smells from the kitchens below me. The very memory of those smells of roast mutton is enough to nauseate me, even today. The heat was stifling, so much so that I had given up all resistance, and let streams of sweat roll down my face and body. I did not even make the effort to change my damp clothes. Mostly I spent my days reading memoirs of the past century. The incredibly prolix authors of that period immersed me in worlds mercifully distant from my own. But one that they described—the court of the Sun King—invariably brought me back to the Seraglio, for I found there the same petty existence of intrigues and jealousy. I even managed to recognize, among the great writing lords of the seventeenth century, the perfidious and gossiping eunuchs who surrounded me.

These last submitted me to the bombardment of false news which the Seraglio swallowed so avidly, and which filtered down to me through the wall of my servants. The Russians, it was said, were preparing to shell Constantinople, a revolution would break out at any moment now, Selim was about to be deposed, there was a plot afoot to assassinate him.

The greater its enormity, the flimsier its foundation in truth, the more glorious the career a rumor shall have in the Orient. The public savors rumors with a delicious little shiver, for its credulity is matched only by its love of catastrophe. I had long since become hardened to that sort of foolishness, but my distress weakened my resistance to hearsay. I trembled and panicked every time I heard one of those absurdities.

Those around me were no help. They were swept away by the general excitement which, as if to make up for its traditional passivity, periodically inflames the Orient. Ali Effendi imagined that he was doing his duty to entertain me when he brought his parcel of news—at the time the rule seemed to be that good news was false and bad news true—and then would grow horribly offended when I shouted, "Be quiet! Leave me alone! I don't want to hear!" I would have wished to keep Mahmud ignorant of the distance that now separated me from Selim, but he could tell; there was no way of hiding such things from a sensitive child. He did not understand, however, and he did not understand me, even though his trust in me remained unaffected. He seemed to avoid me instinctively, and perhaps that was the best thing he could do. Zinah too could see that I was in pain, but my torment was too deeply internalized to allow me to express myself and confide in her. Thus I spent those stifling days roasting in a sort of torpor, a volume of memoirs on my lap.

I could have thought I was very far away from here, had it not been for the chants of the muezzins who echoed one another from minaret to minaret four times a day. "O illah kibiz ... Allah salah"—God is great ... come to prayer. Even those words seemed out of context. What did seem in context at the time was Monsieur Quinteux, the Seraglio's French gardener.

French citizens still living in the empire had been put under arrest. Even poor Ruffin had been incarcerated in the Castle of Seven Towers, a prison set aside for diplomats.

How pleased the eunuchs must have been to whisper to my servants that Selim himself had stood on the path of the procession of French prisoners in order to enjoy the sight of their humiliation. I had trouble imagining such pettiness in Selim, but I no longer knew whom or what to believe.

More than a hundred and twenty prisoners—among them Ruffin's wife and his pregnant daughter—were crowded into the Maison de France in Constantinople, without food or bedding. Elsewhere French engineers, merchants, and technicians were hunted out and mistreated and saw their belongings confiscated.

One afternoon a group of eunuchs began to pick on Monsieur Quinteux. An epic chase through the grounds of the Seraglio ensued, with considerable damage to the flowerpots. Monsieur Quinteux was convinced the eunuchs were after his life; in fact, they would never have dared massacre the Padishah's gardener, and simply wanted to rough him up and frighten him. Finally Monsieur Quinteux was saved by Idriss, Zinah's husband, whose path he fortunately crossed in his flight. I ordered that he be brought to me, and hid him in a small room off my own, which was then empty of the eunuchs who normally occupied it. Monsieur Quinteux had been there ever since, making his presence known during the day only by fits of his dry cough. In the evening he would appear at my door, meek and timid, his customary arrogance vanished. He looked so miserable that I would take pity on him and ask him in, and he would launch into a litany of complaints and recriminations.

"Why did I come here? Why did I leave France, where I was happy?" he would wail, forgetting that revolution had driven him from his country. "Here they're all a bunch of savages. You understand that, Madame Nakshidil, you're French like me . . ." and indeed he was right. I had come once again to look upon the French as my countrymen, and on the Turks as barbarians, all because of that stupid war begun by Bonaparte. I was consumed by hatred for that man.

One evening Mahmud interrupted Monsieur Quinteux's lament by suddenly appearing in my room, stumbling, and yelling, "Vive la France!" Then he collapsed on the carpet, blind drunk. I ordered Ali Effendi to throw a bucket of cold water at him; but he refused, fearing that such disrespect would send him to the executioner. Furious, I did it myself. Somewhat sobered, the young drunkard managed to give me the explanation I demanded, though it was interrupted by much hiccuping and belching. That afternoon, abetted by his half-brother Mustafa, Sineperver's son, he had found the closet where we kept the champagne, picked its lock, and, with the aid of his accomplice, emptied half a dozen bottles.

I scolded him harshly, only to hear him answer: "You can't say anything, Mama Nakshidil—you look worse than I do."

Unfortunately he was right. With my matted hair, my face streaming with sweat, and my soiled clothes, I looked like a drunk.

That very evening it was my turn to be scolded, by Zinah. "Aren't you ashamed, Aimée! To let yourself go like that and set such an example for your son!"

"Oh, why should I make the effort!"

But Zinah remained invariably optimistic. "All men are alike. Don't worry, Aimée, the Sultan will come back to you."

In the meantime I felt like the outskirts of Constantinople—ruined by fire, reduced to ashes.

CHAPTER 15

ONE AFTERNOON he came back. He walked into my room, silently as always. Suddenly he was there. I barely moved, as if I were indifferent. I had dreamed of this moment with too much intensity, I had awaited it with too much suffering. I was too exhausted, too drained to react. To dissipate our embarrassment, he led me to the window to see the arrival of the Russian fleet. Standing side by side, we watched the ships anchor below the very walls of the Seraglio, and saw the yellow imperial standards, stamped with the two-headed eagle, flying in the sky of Constantinople. We heard the sailors' shouts, and the orders of the officers directing the maneuver. Selim was silent before the extraordinary, sacrilegious sight of the hereditary enemy quietly camping under our noses, and I was unable to pierce his thoughts. Suddenly I felt ashamed of my neglected appearance and the disorder of my room, and I stepped back.

Selim misunderstood my gesture. "Don't turn away from me, Aamé," he said. He put his hand on the nape of my neck, and as I turned to face him, I saw in his eyes something I had almost forgotten—desire.

We made love with an intensity we had never reached before—
at first with the fever of two strangers exploring one another, and
later with the rage of lovers reunited after a long separation. Our
bodies sated, we were lying side by side when I was assailed by
dark thoughts. Selim had returned, but he had not brought the
happy past with him. The thing that had drawn us apart still stood
between us. I had lost the privilege of his confidence and the privilege of advising him. He felt me growing taut.

"I can't live without you, Aamé. I just can't do without you."

"You can't do without my body, my lord. I can't say that it isn't
flattering, since you command so many beautiful kadins."

"Do you think I came back for your body alone? Do you think I
love you only for your body?"

And yet when he tried to rise, I folded my arms about him and
held him back. I didn't want him to leave me again, ever. He
stayed, and spread out for me the treasures of his tenderness. Could
he ever be anything but tender, that Sultan Selim III?

"Shall we dine together, Aamé?" he asked, in a perfectly natural
tone of voice, as if we had done so every night in the past few
weeks.

"If the Padishah will allow his slave to dress . . . " I answered.
Once he left, I examined myself in the mirror. I looked a fright. I
called Zinah, Cevri, and my slaves, and they quickly set about making me presentable once again. Hammam, massage, makeup, scent,
dress—breeches and a bolero of white silk embroidered with silver,
a blouse of white muslin with diamond buttons, rivers of pearls . . .

Selim himself had also made preparations. He had chosen to eat
not in his ceremonial room but in one of the kiosks which stand on
the big stone towers guarding the Gate of the Cannon. It looked out
over the Bosporus, open to the breezes from the sea. The dark waters of the night, lit up here and there by the lanterns of a barge,
lolled under the lights of Pera, of Galata, of Scutari on the Asiatic
shore. We did nothing but laugh and tease each other. The relief of
having at last emerged from the nightmare of the past weeks, and
the joy of being together, made us lightheaded.

Later I managed to overcome my scruples and unburden myself

of a question which had weighed on me for several days; I asked him about his presence at the procession of French prisoners. He burst into laughter—youthful, happy laughter—before explaining that he had been there not to gloat but only to make sure that the prisoners were not ill-used. It is true, there was nothing petty in Selim's character—but was I certain I had always believed that? Emboldened, I went so far as to intercede in favor of the prisoners at the Maison de France. Selim promised to watch over their welfare and make sure they were treated as humanely as possible.

"Don't you have another favor to ask of me, Aamé?" he said. I shook my head.

"And what about my gardener? Do you plan to keep him locked up in that cubbyhole much longer?"

And yet Monsieur Quinteux had made no noise, had not coughed a single time since Selim had arrived in my room. But Selim always knew everything about me. I blushed. He smiled.

"Perhaps Monsieur Quinteux"—a name he was quite incapable of pronouncing—"would feel more comfortable at the Maison de France."

There was joy in his voice. By interceding on behalf of those prisoners, I acted as if nothing had ever come between us. Selim's haste to comply showed clearly that he only wanted to forget the recent past.

Came the hour which seems the deepest of the night. Almost all the lights in the distance had gone out. Even the dogs had stopped barking, and no sound troubled the thick silence. Sweet darkness enfolded us as the lamps on our terrace died out.

"I've been so alone," said Selim in a low voice.

"And I, my lord—I was all the more alone for knowing it."

"I had to make the decision to abandon the reforms on my own. I was torn by the knowledge that you opposed it. I was afraid that your arguments would rob me of my firmness. And then over the weeks it became difficult for me to see you. I had to face a war that was costing me too much, a war I hadn't wanted. Besides, I knew that you were suffering because of me, and remorse kept me away."

"You speak of remorse, my lord. It is I who should have felt it. I was unable to help you make your decision and hold to it. It was my own fault I was of no use to you. Your absence made that clear to me. By right the remorse was mine, not yours."

"I love you, Aamé."

"I love you, my lord."

Monsieur Quinteux was smuggled out of the Summer Harem and sent to join his compatriots. Food, clothes, and money were brought to the French prisoners, and soon their existence at the Maison de France was organized as comfortably as it could be. Thanks to Selim, not only had they avoided the worst—the traditional massacre, almost inevitable under the circumstances—but their detention was made more bearable by a little material comfort. They did not show their gratitude until many years later, when a few of them published memoirs in which they described in detail the Sultan's terrible cruelty toward them. My compatriots always need to complain. Only Ruffin was truthful and paid homage to Selim's magnanimity.

When autumn came we left the Summer Harem, and I regained the Kiosk of Osman III with relief. Selim and I resumed our daily tête-à-têtes, recovered the sweetness of our embraces, and showed to those around us the same unchangeable harmony as before. Nevertheless Selim still did not solicit my advice or opinions, although he wrapped my exile from public affairs in the most disarming kindness. I discovered, by the boredom I experienced at no longer participating in his deliberations, that I had a taste—both natural and acquired—for politics. My love for Selim allowed me to accept this new situation with relative good grace. But that very same love told me that I must recover my role of adviser. It was not that I thought myself more qualified than his experts. But I knew that he needed to trust me. There was no one else in whom he could have as much confidence, for no one around him was as disinterested. I sought not power but love, and knew that Selim's love could not survive without his trust. I did not have to wait very long for an opportunity to regain it.

The Russians, on the strength of our alliance and their success, announced their intention to install one of their armies permanently in the Balkans, under the pretext of protecting the interests of the empire in that region. We now found ourselves in precisely the situation Veli Zadeh and the former Grand Vizier had sought to avoid, and which had brought them disgrace and exile. The conservatives, those skillful intriguers, and even Mirizshah, whose subtlety and ability to neutralize her rivals were fiendish, were unable to solve the dilemma, which consisted in finding a way to protect ourselves from the Russians without offending them. Turkish diplomacy, wily and experienced as it was, reacted in a timid and hesitant manner.

Several times Selim tried to extract advice from me, though he wouldn't ask me directly. He beat about the bush, retreated, charged again, without ever really broaching the subject. I let him stew, and I admit with shame that I even derived a certain pleasure from watching his efforts. Meanwhile pressure from the Russians increased. His back to the wall, Selim finally asked me what he should do. Only then did I consent to lay out the plan I had elaborated on the basis of information supplied by Hussein Pasha, who had continued to keep me abreast of the situation.

"The Russians and the British are not only allies; they are also rivals and highly suspicious of one another. You ought to intimidate the Russians by threatening to strengthen your ties with the British, and threaten the British by hinting at improved relations with France." Selim protested: "I shall never negotiate with the French as long as they don't evacuate Egypt." "Who is talking of negotiating with France, my lord? It is simply a question of making the British believe." "And what card shall we play against the French, then?" "War, my lord. Not the little halfhearted war we are waging on them now, but total war, without quarter."

The British against the Russians, the French against the British, and war against the French—our game of skittles, which Selim played admirably, soon resulted in two treaties of alliance, with the Russians and the British, signed on Selim's conditions. He and I had won all along the line: I had recaptured my lord's ear, and he had neutralized the Russians.

The British concocted a delightful, witty gift for us. In Egypt,

Lord Nelson's sailors had intercepted the French army's mails, and found among them Bonaparte's letters to Josephine, which they then published and distributed openly. In clumsy prose, a furious and passionate Bonaparte reproached my cousin with being unfaithful to him while he was away. He knew all about handsome Hippolyte Charles, Josephine's lover. He pleaded, he threatened, and managed to make himself utterly ridiculous. Cuckolds always have a difficult time, and I was deeply gratified to know that a man responsible for so much unhappiness was not particularly happy himself. His conjugal discomfiture, unfortunately, had not lessened the conqueror's combativeness.

Early in 1799 Bonaparte marched into Syria. First Gaza fell, and then Jaffa. Bonaparte then turned toward Acre, our last important stronghold in the Middle East. It was defended by a notorious scoundrel, Djezzar Pasha, a Bosnian who had fully justified his nickname—the Butcher.

Several times before, sultans had sent messengers to this professional rebel with an order to execute him. And regularly their heads were sent back to Constantinople, sewn into sacks. The siege Bonaparte laid to his hideout placed Djezzar Pasha, this time, on the Sultan's side. But the indisputable bravery of this old man and his meager forces offered thin resistance against an army which had proved itself invincible until then.

The Divan held feverish meetings, and passively awaited disaster. The elders invoked kismet, that fate which always cropped up so opportunely. Others were sincerely prepared to die for their country and their Sultan, but that was the limit of their initiative. Burdened by their education, mired in tradition, the more zealous among the reformers could not bring themselves to make a decision, to take a risk. Once again I saw that in spite of his friends, Selim stood alone, in the same solitude Abdul Hamid had endured. But Selim had youth, ardor, and my love. Perhaps because I was a foreigner, a European, or perhaps because I was a woman, I was always the only one who encouraged him to take the necessary risk. We had nothing to lose; I persuaded Selim to send Hussein

Pasha with a squadron of the Nizam-i-Jedid to reinforce Acre.

No sooner said than done—almost. A few weeks later we learned that the new army had managed to breach the French lines and enter Acre. Still, that did not improve matters very much. Selim and I, though we dared not admit it, thought the fall of Acre inevitable. And then? If Acre fell, there would be nothing standing in the way of Bonaparte's triumphal march to Smyrna, to Anatolia, and to Constantinople—his declared aim. But at least we would have tried. . . . Once again we settled down to an interminable, anguished, unbearable wait.

This time it was I who suggested a little excursion, to take Selim's mind off his troubles. My idea was to lure him to Scutari, on the Asiatic shore of the Bosporus, where a fair was being held. He was too preoccupied to accept with any enthusiasm, but he accepted nonetheless. Again we disguised ourselves carefully, slipped discreetly out of the palace, and walked to the docks, dominated by the Mosque of the Valideh, through winding, ill-paved streets.

The crowd milling about among starving stray dogs seemed quite different from the one we had seen in the bazaar; it appeared sullen and colorless. The browns, beiges, and dark blues, the colors worn by the Turks, only reinforced that impression. The Turkish populace seemed to want to escape notice, to fade into the scenery.

We waited for a moment among a disciplined and patient throng; then we all embarked—calmly, without haste—on a bazaar caïque, one of those big boats which ferry passengers across the Bosporus. With us were women coming home from the bazaar and comparing their purchases, Anatolian peasants on their way back to the mountains of central Turkey, burghers and their families going, as we were, to the fair at Scutari. The discomfort of the passage—we were all crammed together in insufficient space—did not cause the slightest quarrel, or a single brusque movement. The Turks are nomads in soul and have an instinctive aptitude for travel.

As soon as our bazaar caïque left the pier, Selim assumed the expression of an enchanted child. He was no longer the Grand Signor condemned to majesty, sailing in the enormous red-and-gold imperial barge. Pressed among his subjects, he discovered his city. Constantinople, Galata, Scutari—like three sisters separated by a whim of the oceans—appeared as strange bare forests of minarets and cypress trees reaching for the sky, interspersed with terraced gardens and red-and-white houses.

The shores of Scutari are bordered by yalis, the summer houses of red-painted wood that belong to the richer citizens of Constantinople. We strolled through the fair, mostly to open our appetite and make us impatient to sit down in one of the humble taverns which grow like weeds between the sumptuous yalis. We settled at an uneven table in the shade of a canopy of dried palm leaves. Our feet almost touched the water lapping quietly at the shore. We paid homage to the dolmades—vine leaves stuffed with balls of rice—to feta—the famous goat cheese marinated in salt water—and to the kebabs, skewers of grilled lamb. But what delighted me most was a dish completely unknown in the Seraglio—that famous flatfish found only in the Bosporus, which looks swollen and rather distasteful to the eye but whose flesh is delicious.

We delighted in the warmth of spring, in the soft sunlight, in the smells of the sea, in the raki, in the faraway sight of Constantinople, and in each other's presence. Toward the end of the meal the innkeeper came to our table to strike up the traditional conversation with his customers. Following the custom, Selim began by asking him how business was.

The innkeeper was a sort of giant, his skull shaven except for the single tuft of hair by which Allah would one day yank him into paradise.

"How do you want business to be," he asked, "with a sultan like the one we have? He might be a good man, but after all he's incompetent. Imagine! It's not only in public affairs that he's impotent. He doesn't even visit the women of his harem!"

I saw Selim redden, and for a moment I feared the worst. But Selim merely pointed out that perhaps the Sultan loved only one woman.

"Rubbish," answered the innkeeper with a fat laugh. "A true

Muslim is never satisfied with one woman! No, no—he's incompetent! Thanks to him we shall soon see the French, those damned giaours, in Constantinople. Soon Acre will be in the giaours' hands, and there will be nothing left for us but to submit."

"The Sultan," Selim murmured, "has sent a squadron of his new army to defend Acre."

The innkeeper sniggered. "You don't really believe that a handful of young tenderfeet will show themselves capable of withstanding a siege from that French devil! No one believes that but the Sultan. . . . The truth is that the janissaries should have been sent to Acre; they at least know how to fight. But the Sultan is afraid of the janissaries."

Suddenly Selim leaped to his feet, knocked over the table, and, his voice hoarse with rage, yelled that the janissaries were cowards capable only of terrorizing the population, rebelling against the Sultan, and losing battles.

The innkeeper choked with indignation. His face scarlet with rage, he began to abuse Selim, accusing him of treason, and rousing the other customers' ire against that spy in the pay of the giaours. I was petrified. The families at the nearby tables remained silent, afraid to involve themselves in the quarrel. Half a dozen drunks emerged from the depth of the tavern, heading straight for us, knocking over hookahs, tables, and backgammon boards in their path. Selim drew his dagger out from under his frieze robe. His movement, and the sight of the jeweled dagger, stopped our attackers in their tracks, and Selim took advantage of their hesitation to grab me by the wrist and drag me in a mad race down the streets of Scutari. It was more fear of scandal than of the hoodlums on our heels that propelled us. Our assailants had rushed after us as soon as they had recovered from their surprise, but they were weighed down with raki; eventually they gave up the chase, and we were able to reach the piers—out of breath, our hearts pounding—without further incident.

Jumping into the first bazaar caïque to push off, we elbowed our way to the only remaining free spot on the crowded boat and settled gratefully into the passengers' resigned silence. Just as the order to leave had been given by the chief oarsman, a janissary appeared on the pier and, without a second to spare, leaped into the already overloaded boat. He had the arrogance of those who know that nothing is forbidden them, and sure enough, the boatman did not dare protest. The rowers arched their backs in unison, and the boat drew away from the pier. The janissary, steady on his feet, both hands on his sword, glanced over the passengers. He was standing not far from us, and just as I feared, his gaze came to rest on Selim, whom he spoke to sharply:

"You, dervish, tell your hanun to get up and leave me her seat."

Wishing to avoid another scene, I started to stand up, but Selim's grip on my shoulder stopped me. He answered the janissary calmly:

"My hanun was sitting here before you arrived. If you wanted a seat you should have waited for the next boat."

The janissary became threatening: "I find you very insolent for a dervish. Do you know I could slice you in two with this sword?"

The passengers were silent and afraid, and looked down at their feet. Selim was squeezing my shoulder so hard that it hurt. He had lifted his head and stared the janissary in the eye.

"And where did you fight, you janissary, to earn such pride? Did you fight the enemy, or the innocent? You and yours have furnished sufficient proof of your cowardice in battle. On the other hand, you don't mind oppressing the people, or taking on an unarmed dervish and his wife."

Selim's speech—an unheard-of audacity—had begun to change the atmosphere aboard the bazaar caïque. Though they didn't dare show it openly, the passengers approved of Selim's attitude.

Apparently the janissary realized that the majority of the passengers were hostile, for he said, "I'll let you go, dervish. You're a foreigner; you don't even speak proper Turkish."

And on that parting shot, he gave up the game and made his way to the bow, jostling everyone in his way. His last insult referred to the fact that Selim used only the court language, which is different from popular Turkish. Selim was extremely upset, whereas I was only relieved. We had avoided an incident which would have had impossible ramifications in scandal.

In the following days both Selim and I were overwhelmed by a flood of disturbing thoughts.

"When I think of the disenchantment and despair of our people," Selim told me, "I begin to doubt the value of what I'm doing. Perhaps I have sinned through pride or excessive idealism. I wonder whether there is in fact a connection between my reforms and the needs of my people."

"Whereas for me, my lord, our escapade was most edifying, since it gave me a rare chance to mingle with the crowds. Your people are suffering; they need to be looked after and defended. I am more convinced than ever of the necessity for urgent reforms."

"I envy your certainty. I've started to think my hopes are false. I'm losing my self-confidence."

"You mustn't let yourself be pressured by events or by the lack of news from Acre. Look at the positive results of those reforms which have already been enacted. You must keep to the just and generous path you have chosen. Be confident."

"My confidence is you, Aamé."

One morning in May, just as dawn cracked, I felt someone shaking me brutally out of sleep. My eyes half open, I saw Selim bending over my bed and heard his hurried words without immediately understanding them.

"Wake up, Aamé—I beg you, wake up. A messenger has just arrived from Acre. Bonaparte has lifted the siege!"

I stared at Selim stupidly, my mind still swollen with sleep. He called Cevri. "Bring strong coffee for the kadin."

Then he sat down at my side, took my hand in his, stroked it, and without waiting for me to regain my spirits, he continued: "Listen, little Aamé, hear the news. Acre is saved! Bonaparte has evacuated Syria!"

When my lucidity returned I was able to read Djezzar Pasha's letter, in which he praised the soldiers of the Nizam-i-Jedid for their combative ardor, their courage, and their discipline, and declared that they had greatly contributed to the defeat of the invaders. Djezzar Pasha was not prone to flattery—it was the only vice the old bandit lacked—and Selim beamed.

In order to celebrate the victory of the Nizam-i-Jedid, his victory, I asked Selim the favor of allowing me to hold a celebration. At least the idiots and intriguers of the harem would learn once and for all that the French kadin's heart was no longer French, but Turkish.

The evening began in the usual venue of the Sultan's Hall, with an excellent concert of Oriental music which only Selim and I appreciated. All the ladies of the harem, from the Valideh down to the last gözde, impatiently awaited the surprise they had been promised, and in fact couldn't have cared less for the melodious preambles. When the orchestra stopped playing, I let the audience exchange disappointed glances for a few moments before the Kizlar Aga came to bow before Selim and ask him to follow him with the court. Eunuchs stood at the door, helping the guests on with their pelisses. The chattering throng followed Billal Aga down the Golden Road to the selamlik, that vast terrace which hangs over the city between the Hall of Circumcision and the Pavilion of Baghdad. Selim took his seat under the Iftariye, a sort of canopy of golden bronze topped with the Turkish crescent, from which the Sultan traditionally witnesses the ceremonies of Ramadan. The ladies sat down along the marble balustrade. Under a star-studded velvet sky, the luminous Oriental night revealed tall bare trees below, and beyond them entire neighborhoods shut down in sleep and the masts of the ships anchored in the black water of the Golden Horn.

I let a crescendo of whispers, of giggles and questions, rise around me; when it died down I raised my hand. At that signal the quiet night was shredded by explosions as rockets shot up from the four corners of the dark city. They burst very high in the sky in sparkling multicolored bouquets, each one more surprising than the last. After a moment of speechless admiration my guests began to gasp; they were echoed by shouts of enthusiasm from the town below us. The population of Constantinople, awakened by the explosions, had rushed to its terraces to cheer the spectacle.

Although the crowd could not be seen from the terrace, I pictured it with delight—eyes lifted to the sky, shuddering, marveling.

The people were participating in the festivities, as I had wished. The explosions continued to rock the city, and the sky turned into a canopy of lights and colored smoke. Later I learned that Constantinople had never seen such fireworks. The French pyrotechnists, whom I had found locked up in the Maison de France, had served me well. Released on my authority, they had labored day and night to produce that single evening's wonderland.

Then came the highlight of the evening: The rockets stopped, and suddenly fiery letters appeared in the sky over the entire city, spelling out the tugra, Selim's stylized signature which is stamped on all coins; the Sultan was signing his victory. The apparition was followed by a thunder of cheers and hurrahs, in which one heard an entire people shouting its traditional formula: "A thousand years to our Padishah!"

The unanimous—and, for once, sincere—congratulations of all the ladies provided me with a moment of glory, as fleeting as the fireworks themselves; but the only reward I wanted was the matchless smile Selim gave me as he walked by. The sparkle of that celebration restored the harem's consideration for me, which Selim's temporary coldness had destroyed.

Events began to accelerate after the liberation of Acre. Abandoning his army, Bonaparte disappeared from Egypt, reappeared in France, overthrew the Directoire government and took power as First Consul—a title he had invented himself. Our troops embarked for Egypt, where they joined the British forces and pushed the French into retreat, retook Cairo, then Alexandria, and finally forced the French back onto their ships. Egypt was freed. And yet . . .

Our secret services intercepted a letter from the commanding officer of British troops in Egypt, General Hutkinson, to his ambassador in Constantinople; Selim and I read it together:

"The Turks, without help, will never be able to keep Egypt in their possession. That jumble of automatons the Grand Vizier calls his army is rapidly dispersing. The more I think about it, the more I am convinced of the absolute necessity of supporting the Mamelukes."

The Mamelukes were that fierce and bellicose military caste who had occupied Egypt before the Turks and still hoped to recover it from us. Of course the situation in Egypt was confused, as a result of the French occupation and subsequent evacuation; our pashas and our functionaries were experiencing difficulty in reorganizing the administration. But what were the Mamelukes doing in all this? And why, thought Selim, could the British not mind their own business?

"They simply want to stay in Egypt," I told him. He did not believe me. For him, the enemy had always been the Russians. For me, the hereditary enemy was England. I had, in a sense, experienced the furious colonial rivalry that had pitted her against France in the Caribbean. My ancestor Pierre Dubuc had played a role in it, and my family had told me of it. I could remember the Anglo-French war of hegemony which, in my childhood, had cut us off from France.

"And when the British step ashore, they stay," I added for Selim. I begged him to send troops, arms, and a strong man to Egypt immediately. Once again Hussein Pasha volunteered and left with our fleet. In any case Egypt sorely needed to be put in order, and Hussein Pasha was ideal for the mission. Selim, however, remained skeptical.

"The British freed us of the French. Surely they're not going to occupy Egypt against us."

"They are more subtle than that, my lord! They are going to take advantage of the confusion in Egypt, prove that we are unable to restore order, and strike a bargain with our adversaries the Mamelukes—or so I understand from the letter of their commanding officer, General Hutkinson."

The near future was—to my chagrin—to confirm the predictions of Casssandra Nakshidil. The British and the Mamelukes were soon as thick as thieves, and signed an agreement behind our backs, at our expense: The Mamelukes recovered all their belongings and former rights, in exchange for which the British were allowed to settle in Alexandria, Rosetta, and Damietta—in other words, to occupy Egypt.

His eyes opened, Selim conceived a great admiration for my gift of prophecy and an equally great rage at the treachery of his British "allies." Lord Elgin, the British ambassador to Constantinople, was summoned for explanations; he calmly declared that the commanding officer in Egypt had overstepped his powers, and then gave Selim a superb crystal chandelier, a present from his master the King. My first impulse was to shatter the object, but in the end I suggested to Selim that he give it to his mother for the Palace of Joy. The chandelier hangs there to this very day.

Sensing, however, that the present would not be enough to soothe Selim, Lord Elgin pushed the incoherence or the perfidy of British foreign politics as far as to publicly disavow the agreement his compatriots had signed with the Mamelukes. Thereupon he left Constantinople in a hurry, claiming he wanted to make a tour of Greece.

There was nothing to do but sort it out ourselves—or rather have Hussein Pasha sort it out. But he lacked sufficient troops to reduce the Mamelukes, and therefore he opted for ruse, which he used as effectively as he used force. He invited the Mamelukes' two hundred and fifty leaders to a banquet on his flagship in Alexandria harbor. The Mamelukes donned their glittering ceremonial clothes and, embroidered to the teeth, headed for the port, between hedges of Hussein Pasha's soldiers, who served as their honor guard. Embarking in launches of the Turkish imperial navy, they were rowed out to the middle of the harbor, at which point a few of them sensed a trap. Ordered to turn back, the rowers refused. The Mamelukes drew their daggers and threatened them. Hussein Pasha, watching the scene through his spyglass from the deck of his ship, had foreseen this eventuality and gave orders to shoot. The soldiers, hidden behind gunwales, opened fire. The Mamelukes offered little resistance, and Hussein Pasha was able to capture most of them without too much loss of life. Instead of a banquet, the Mameluke leaders had been invited to irons belowdecks.

No sooner had we begun to congratulate ourselves on that haul than we learned that Hussein Pasha had been forced to release the Mamelukes. Hutkinson, the British commander, outraged to find his maneuvers foiled, had reacted brutally and threatened to throw his army against Hussein Pasha if the good Mamelukes were not freed on the spot. Hussein Pasha had no choice but to comply; and we beheld, with astonishment, the British dealing with us as enemies, when they had come to Egypt as our friends.

Nevertheless Hussein Pasha and our imperial fleet were there to stay. General Hutkinson understood that he could not continue with his plans to grab Egypt as long as our sentinel watched over him. The British government saw that its stratagem had failed, and ordered its troops to evacuate Egypt.

"That was close," I told Selim. "If Hussein Pasha hadn't been there . . ."

"And if a little girl from France hadn't remembered the history lessons of her childhood . . ." added Selim.

Thank God it was all over; but I still held a deep grudge against Bonaparte, the cause of all our trouble. Mother Marie-Agnès tried to soften my rancor.

> You cannot imagine, my child, what General Bonaparte represents for us, the French. Yes, it is true he is a usurper occupying the place of our legitimate kings. But remember he has extinguished the bloodletting fires of revolution; he has reestablished the clergy and returned the country to religion; he has conquered anarchy and brought back order and security. You do not know what it is to have to live in constant terror. He has put an end to the civil war that was tearing the provinces apart. He has imposed his terms and put an end to the war with England. He controls the affairs of Italy, of Switzerland, of Spain. Austria, Prussia, Russia, who wished to take advantage of the revolution to invade France and apportion her, have put down their arms. Thanks to Bonaparte there is peace everywhere. From the height of her new position, his wife, your cousin Josephine, spreads the benefits of her generosity; her door and her purse are open to all who are in need. At last we have received news from Martinique. Revolution did shake the island of your birth, but somewhat less violently than the home country. Your family are safe and well and flourishing in the long-awaited return of calm and prosperity.

CHAPTER 16

MY MOST important task was to assist Selim in his work, and I re-solved to accomplish it with greater energy in order to compensate for deficiencies and lapses. From now on I would take the initiative instead of waiting to be asked for my opinions. I wanted to serve as Selim's guard, so as to allow him to give his all to the reforms. Now that peace was restored, he had returned to them with determina-tion, tackling simultaneously the army, the administration, and the provinces, making innovations here and improvements there. My sex forbade me to act directly; I could work for Selim's welfare only through intermediaries. Hussein Pasha was no longer there to help me. Having driven himself to exhaustion, he had collapsed and died, though barely forty. Selim lost his best friend—perhaps his only friend; I lost an accomplice who from the very start had shown me affection and trust. I now set my sights on Ibrahim Nes-sim, an unconditional partisan of the reforms.

I got into the habit of receiving him to discuss affairs of state. With a Roman emperor's head on a squat and powerful body, slightly running to fat, Ibrahim Nessim was all boldness and ardor, quick in his decisions and his movements, and gifted with a character of steel.

The second assistant I chose was almost Ibrahim Nessim's opposite. Ahmed Effendi, Selim's private secretary, Selim's shadow, was a creature of calm reflection, of solid ethics and convictions, of discretion. He was endowed with a prodigious capacity for work, and could spend entire nights without rising from his desk. With a big round head, bushy blond hair, and an eagle's beak for a nose, Ahmed Effendi was a nobleman; while Ibrahim Nessim was a warrior fighting with a sword in politics as in battle.

The former was to be the relay between myself and Selim, while the latter served as my ear and my voice in the Divan.

I had asked Selim to have Mahmud participate as much as possible in the deliberations of the Divan, and Selim had been only too happy to oblige and break yet another outdated tradition. Both he and his predecessor Abdul Hamid had been the victims of the rule that took care to keep imperial princes out of affairs of state. Now the friendship between the two cousins, born on the playing fields, flourished in the council chambers. Mahmud became imbued with political sense as he watched the workings of the state's innermost mechanisms. He was eighteen years old and I wanted to prepare him to become the Sultan's collaborator—another plan inconceivable under preceding reigns. Perhaps he too would reign one day, after Selim's successor, Sineperver's son Mustafa. I wanted to bring the half-brothers closer together, but I was held back by the shadow of Sineperver. Selim did his part through sports, inviting both his cousins to join him in his exercise. The results were not what we expected; Mustafa came to like Selim in his way, but the brothers, reflecting their mothers' attitudes, remained wary of each other.

I deplored the conflict between Mirizshah and me, between the mother and the "wife," for Selim was the first to suffer from it. She wanted Selim's welfare as much as I, and I thought it ridiculous that we should be enemies when in fact our aims were the same. Therefore I undertook to make it up with her. First I sent her a braid of pink India silk for her drawing room, claiming that it was I who had embroidered it with carnations of gold thread. She knew very well that I was incapable of threading a needle, but that did not prevent her from praising my talent and raving about the beauty of the braid.

Furthermore, she could not fail to invite me once it had been installed. I was received, then, apparently as a friend, and after the customary greetings and compliments I turned to Selim and reproached him with the cramped proportions of his mother's apartment. It consisted only of a sitting room and a bedroom, which was separated from a minute oratory by a grille. Yes, the place seemed unworthy of the Valideh, the second personage of the empire, and I suggested that it be enlarged. The bait was a little obvious, but the Valideh in question bit. Just hitting my stride, I offered to oversee the new apartment's decoration myself. The Valideh deigned to accept with gratitude.

I drew up some specifications, and a wooden overhang was built above Mirizshah's old apartment to house two large sitting rooms, one an antechamber to the other. I knew Mirizshah's taste for luxury and her weakness for the French style, which still survived her hatred of France. Through an intermediary I turned to Pierre Ruffin, who had recently been released after three years' imprisonment in the Castle of Seven Towers, and he provided me with a team of French workers who built, in record time, a sumptuous decor in the purest rococo style, which had been all the rage in France fifty years before. Everything was smothered in green and gold, and I had French-style views of parks and large mirrors set in the woodwork. The chandeliers and candelabra were imported from France, as well as the ceramic tiles which covered the fireplace and ran along the walls, bearing a dedicatory inscription: "Sea of constancy, crown of continence, mine of kindliness, star of the seventh heaven, mother-of-pearl of the empire . . ." and so it read on; I did not skimp on the Valideh's attributions.

The new apartment, the acme of the persistent vogue of the Louis XV style, dazzled the harem and disarmed Mirizshah. The touch which moved her most was the opening—on my instructions—of a corridor linking her sitting room and Selim's apartment.

Mirizshah was quite subtle enough to understand that with that symbolic corridor I was letting her know I wanted neither exclusive power over Selim nor competition with her, intentions she had always suspected in me.

The composition of the new government sealed our reconciliation. The extraordinary stupidity of Ziya Pasha, his disastrous brainstorms, his criminal negligence, amply justified an ignominious dismissal. Nevertheless I advised Selim to keep him in order to flatter Mirizshah, who had secured the grand viziership for him. Mirizshah was grateful, and furthermore Ziya Pasha's very incompetence was a guarantee of his docility. From one day to the next that dyed-in-the-wool conservative became a zealous reformer, utterly astonished at having escaped disgrace.

This reorganization enabled us to recall Veli Zadeh, who had been sent into exile at the start of the Egyptian war. Mirizshah was as happy as we to see her oldest friend reinstated in his post as Sheikh-Ul-Islam.

Mirizshah gave a party to inaugurate her new apartment. In the first sitting room, an orchestra composed of the prettiest girls of the harem played for the guests, who sat in the next room, around trays laden with pastries. This was not the usual large assembly but a small reunion limited to Selim's kadins and the powers of the harem. In fact, Mirizshah had wanted a pretext to see me and show me her satisfaction without having to stoop to coming to me nor having to summon me from the height of her authority. While the music played and the women gorged, she leaned over:

"I've always wanted harmony, but it's you who have brought it back."

"Venerable Sultana, I've sought only to serve two people I love and respect, the Sultan and his mother."

"In short, you've returned me my son. Thanks to you, I've regained his submission . . . and his attention." She spoke in a bantering tone, but I knew what this admission cost her pride.

"The Sultan has only devotion and veneration for you. It's just that sometimes he's afraid of incurring your disapproval."

"Let us hope then that your impulsiveness and my wisdom, after clashing, will now work together for the good of my son and the empire."

I took her hand and kissed it.

After contributing to concessions to Mirizshah and her allies, I was able to move my own pawns forward. Ibrahim Nessim was appointed Kehaya Bey, minister of the interior. Since all those who have or want power in this country make use of a network of spies, I could not do without one myself. I therefore instructed Ali Effendi to build me a small and discreet but efficient service, and supplied him with quite a number of gold-filled purses for that purpose. That virtuoso of intrigue immediately picked out and bribed the most venal slaves and eunuchs in every wing of the Seraglio and every palace of the capital, and thus I acquired my own shadowy hirelings in the ministries, at the Divan, at Mirizshah's, in Sineperver's circle, and in foreign embassies.

It was thanks to those spies that I learned, before Selim, of the agitation reigning in the embassies early in 1804. Despite the peace treaties he had signed, Bonaparte was growing ever more belligerent, and all Europe was in a state of alert as the powers prepared for battle. It was becoming evident that the Turkish Empire would not be able to stand aside, and thus we followed with anxiety the development of the crisis from day to day. Therefore I was most annoyed when our dealings with the Americans forced us to turn our attention away from Bonaparte.

The Americans had been working energetically to develop trade with the Turkish Empire, but they refused to pay any tribute to the Barbary corsairs, who were, in theory, our vassals. The corsairs were outraged at the Americans' ruinous infringement of the rules, and had seized a number of United States ships; to which the Americans responded by sending a fleet under the command of William Baynbridge to blockade Tripoli in Libya. The pirates captured the sailors encircling them and kept them under lock and key; until, that is, a small American commando succeeded in freeing them. The operation was led by George Wainscott, the privateer who had formerly fought with the Russians and had so heavily contributed to Hassan Pasha's defeat. It was a remarkable though intolerable exploit. We could not simultaneously fight the Americans and trade with them, and it was my opinion that we should send the Nizam-i-Jedid to clear the Mediterranean of those unwelcome guests.

Selim refused, wishing to avoid belligerence at a time when the situation was becoming very tense.

Then Bonaparte proclaimed himself Emperor of the French, and demanded that we recognize him as such. The Russian and British ambassadors rushed to the offices of the Rais Effendi, our minister of foreign affairs, to protest. For weeks we sat in the midst of a sort of diplomatic ballet while they took turns to come, insist, demand, and cajole. Voices were raised, threats in diplomatic notes grew less subtle, and Selim, clinging to neutrality, let the Divan indulge in endless palavers.

What the European powers wanted to know was not whether we would recognize the title Bonaparte had usurped, but what side we would choose in the now inevitable war. Selim shied at the thought of an alliance with Russia, the hereditary enemy, or with England, whose "friendship" he had tasted in Egypt. I advised him against strengthening our relations with France, having already seen Bonaparte disregard a solid alliance with Turkey in order to satisfy his ambition. The interests of the empire would best be served by neutrality. Selim decided not to take sides, to the European powers' dismay.

Our ambassador in Paris sent us a caustic description of Bonaparte's coronation in the Cathedral of Notre Dame. Yesterday's ardent revolutionaries, plumed and laden with newly acquired titles and decorations, proudly paraded with yesterday's aristocrats, whom they had so recently wanted to send to the guillotine, and with the prelates, whom they had wanted to disembowel.

The Corsican tribe, brothers and sisters of the "emperor," fought one another almost all the way to the altar, and Madame their mother, displeased with her son, had not attended the ceremony.

The only person who transcended the grotesque carnival was my cousin Josephine. All were agreed in praising the grace and dignity of her appearance. "You shall be more than a queen," had said

Euphemia David. Now Josephine was Empress, with all the rights bestowed by nobility of bearing and of spirit.

One strange consequence of Bonaparte's coronation was that Constantinople's social life was seized by frenzy. The kickoff was the banquet given by General Brune, the French ambassador, to celebrate the accession of his emperor. Representatives of powers locked in bitter conflict with his master rushed to attend. Next came the ball, to which the entire Seraglio was invited, given by Princess Hadidgeh, Selim's sister, on the pretext of inaugurating the palace of Ortaköy, which she had built from the plans of her architect, Melling.

Princess Esmee did not want to be outdone. At the death of her husband, Hussein Pasha, she had displayed dramatic—and perhaps sincere—despair. She had been making up for it ever since.

Her ball was the choicest and the best of all. The court, the city, the government, and the ambassadors stampeded into the palace she had inherited from Hussein Pasha, behind the Blue Mosque of Sultan Ahmed. I attended, and it seemed a fitting opportunity to use the coach of crystal and mother-of-pearl that Selim had given me. Reflections from the guards' torches sparkled on its facets, so that it seemed as if it were made of fire, and it drew cheers from the citizens of Constantinople who were massed along the path to the palace. The other kadins and I were confined to a trellised balcony from which we could see the ballroom without being seen. Our dignitaries, wearing their most heavily embroidered caftans, mingled with foreigners dressed in every color of the rainbow. Ambassadors of rival powers, who spent their days wreaking diplomatic havoc on one another, conversed amiably that night, and beamed cordially at our viziers, whose harassment with impossible demands they planned to resume the very next day. Billal Aga, our Kizlar Aga, who had insisted on personally shepherding his flock to the ball, pointed out Arbuthnot, who had replaced Lord Elgin as British ambassador, General Brune, Bonaparte's representative, and the Russian ambassador. I was more interested in examining the Europeans' manners and their clothes, which I had not beheld for so many years.

The foreign youths danced, or rather hopped about in the fashion inaugurated under the Directoire, which had replaced our graceful minuets. I thought those dances simply obscene, and then smiled at the realization that I was reacting like a dowager. All the women were dressed in the latest fashions, dictated, as always, from Paris. I found the high waists, pinned under the breast, and the straight dresses lacking in elegance and femininity; but then those qualities were lacking in the period itself, dominated as it was by a soldier. A very handsome man in the British ambassador's retinue drew stares by the somewhat affected simplicity of his dress. I inquired about his identity; it was the American privateer George Wainscott, who had the audacity to come to taunt those very same Turks he had so happily shelled not long ago. However, he soon found a high-placed protector in Princess Esmee, whose lover he became—I would learn it from Esmee herself. Hussein Pasha's no longer tearful widow at last caught the corsair she had dreamed of for years.

Suddenly I noticed a guest whose dress was that of the *ancien régime* of the prerevolutionary years—knee breeches, silk stockings, and powdered wig. Something in his silhouette, something in his features, jolted my memory. Where had I seen that gentleman? For I was certain I had seen him somewhere before. Now I remembered: I had seen him at the Nouveau Théâtre in Nantes, one evening when my cousin Marie-Anne had taken me to see *Phèdre*. The years had not altered his fatuous Don Juan's features. It was the Count d'Antraigues—the Count of Intrigues, I should say. What on earth had brought that meddlesome spy to Constantinople? Certainly not, I knew, the pleasure of whirling about the dance floor of Princess Esmee's palace.

As I watched those Westerners, those foreigners of my own race, dance, laugh, and speak French, I was seized by a sudden wave of regret, by a fit of nostalgia, aggravated by my inability to mix with them and by the chatter of the kadins. I wished to stand among them for a moment, for an hour, to speak to them, to attempt a mazurka or a polonaise, even to wear one of those awful Empire dresses. The thin gilded trellis separating me from the society of my birth seemed the bars of a most cruel prison. I left the ball. The guards' torches had nothing left to illuminate but the dirty, trampled snow of the empty streets.

Selim was waiting for me. He sensed my sadness immediately, though I used every artifice to paint an attractive picture of the celebration. He found the right words, the right gestures to comfort me, as always when I felt the pangs of nostalgia. Not listening to my tales, he took me in his arms, caressed me gently, tenderly, made love to me. I gave myself to him with a sort of rage, as if my torn and suffering soul was to be restored in him, denying any other allegiance.

The ball made a far more pleasant impression on Mahmud. Throughout the show of Oriental dances organized by Princess Esmee he had seemed fascinated, riveted by the star of the ballet, a nervous beauty named Husmumelek. On the following day his kind sister Esmee gave her to him as a present. Selim was furious, and wanted to refuse the gift on Mahmud's behalf. Even though Selim had already given the order to assemble a meager harem for Mahmud, he still refused to accept the fact that the latter had reached manhood, and persisted in his overprotective ways. I faced the matter with more humor and resignation. In the end Selim consented to keep Husmumelek; Mahmud was in the throes of his first passion, the frenzied one, and when separated from her spent his days writing her letters delirious with love and naiveté.

The lanterns of the last ball were still warm when General Brune, who had been such an enthusiastic guest at the imperial princesses' palaces, presented us with an unmistakable ultimatum. Besides our immediate recognition of Bonaparte as Emperor of the French, he demanded that we forbid the passage of any military convoy through the straits.

Bonaparte's brutality made me choke with indignation, but I had learned to moderate my reactions. Though my first impulse was to tell Selim to answer the "Emperor of the French" with a stream of insults, I approved of his caution; clinging to neutrality, he did not want to give in to France or break off relations with her. The Rais

Effendi was therefore instructed to keep the French hanging, and to use all the age-old science of Turkish diplomacy to that effect.

As we persisted in procrastination, General Brune suddenly slammed the door of the Maison de France—loudly announcing that he was leaving this hostile empire forever—and moved into a yali on the outskirts of Constantinople to await our proposals, which he expected very soon. He was not mistaken. Selim invited him to a secret meeting, which he asked me to attend, hidden, and thus General Brune was led one night to the Pavilion of Baghdad, where the Sultan awaited him.

Followed by Cevri, I walked through the gardens, stripped bare by winter and heavy with snow, to a terrace from which a half-hidden stairway climbed to a narrow closet within the pavilion. Once inside that listener's cubbyhole, however, I found that I was not alone. A thin and modest shadow had preceded me, that of a silent, immobile woman. I shone my lantern on her and recognized Firuz, one of my slavewomen. A strange reflex—which I was later to look upon as a miracle—made me check my anger and surprise, and I beckoned the girl into the complicity of silence by putting my finger to my lips. Then, with a wave of my arm, I motioned her to follow me. She was too stunned and frightened not to obey.

Back at the Kiosk of Osman III, I found Ali Effendi and Idriss and regained my imperious manner. I demanded an explanation from the girl.

Insolence and slyness fought for a moment on her features; then, looking me straight in the eye, she said, "You can question me, you can threaten me, but I won't answer. I have powerful friends here, and I'm not afraid of you."

She had spoken in faultless French.

"Oh, yes," she said, "I speak your language! Today I am only a slave, but my parents were nobles of the Caucasus and they gave me a good education before I was captured. I know exactly who you are and what you do—I know everything about you!"

I turned to Cevri. "This is a most arrogant child. Try to make her understand that she had better be a little more talkative, not to mention respectful."

Cevri grabbed the girl and started to beat her, conscientiously, the way she did everything else. Her huge fists pounded rhythmically at the girl, who shrieked, struggled, tried in vain to free herself from Cevri's formidable grip. After a few minutes of that treatment I told Cevri to stop. The girl lay gasping on the carpet, all resistance beaten out of her.

"Now you know how I treat those who resist me," I said. "But I also know how to reward those who serve me. I imagine you have been paid for your spying. Just tell me what you were given and I will double that sum if you agree to speak. Work for me from now on, and one day I shall send you back to your people in the Caucasus."

The alternation of Cevri's blows and my promises convinced the girl to tell me what she knew.

"Whom are you spying for?" I asked.

"For Ristoglou."

So my old language teacher, my old enemy, had resurfaced. He had hired Firuz at a high price and entrusted her with informing him of my every word and move, as well as Selim's. She also revealed to me that the information she harvested was sent on not only to Sineperver but also to certain foreign powers. Ristoglou, now inhabiting the Old Seraglio, could come and go as he liked at the Hall of Circumcision, where Prince Mustafa lived; as the residence of an imperial prince it was inviolable, and Ristoglou had made of it the center of his activities.

His organization consisted of underground cohorts of women of every rank, of slaves, of eunuchs. I ordered Firuz to bring me a complete list of them, in exchange for which I would quadruple the sum of money I had already offered her; and I renewed my promise to return her, once her mission was accomplished, to the Caucasus.

Then she left, melting in thanks and assurances of devotion, clutching a gold-filled purse.

The following morning I was drawn out onto my balcony by a concert of exclamations below. A small gathering of people gesticulated around the Gözdes' Pool, in the middle of which floated something which at first I mistook for a bundle of linen. Someone came to tell me that one of my slaves had drowned by accident. I did not need to ask for the victim's name. Firuz had been assassinated.

Ristoglou and Sineperver must have learned through their spies that she had been discovered and interrogated by me. Trusting my powers of persuasion, fearing her betrayal of them, they had got rid of her. If once before they had dared to make an attempt on my own life, it was clear that they would not take pause at the murder of a mere slave.

I told Ibrahim Nessim, the minister of the interior and my faithful secret collaborator, of the incident. It stood to reason that Ristoglou should spy, that Sineperver should intrigue—but how and why was the information collected in the Hall of Circumcision transmitted to foreign powers?

"They pay well," answered Ibrahim Nessim.

"But why are they so interested in what we do?"

Ibrahim Nessim explained. We were the only power that had not yet decided for or against recognizing Bonaparte's imperial dignity, that had still to take a stand for or against France. As such we had become the focal point of European diplomacy, a sort of object to be bid for . . . and a magnet for spies.

Constantinople was riddled with them—spies of every persuasion and every nation. Each embassy had its own intelligence agency, every ministry, every pavilion was infiltrated by foreigners, and it was quite impossible to find out who the spies were or do anything about it.

That explained the presence of Count d'Antraigues, whom I had noticed at Princess Esmee's ball. Ibrahim knew that he was in Constantinople, and told me that, through love of gold and hatred of Bonaparte, he had become one of the most important figures in the British secret service. There was not a single intrigue against France in which d'Antraigues had not dipped. There was not a single conspiracy against Bonaparte that did not include him. The stakes must have been enormous if they had brought him to Constantinople.

"Tell me, Ibrahim Pasha, what are the roles of Ristoglou and Sineperver in this chess game?"

"The foreign powers are making use of Kadin Sineperver and the conservatives in an attempt to lure Turkey into their camp. As for Sineperver and the others, they use the foreigners in their quest for power. Every crisis, every pretext is fuel for their ambition. Did you notice, Nakshidil Kadin, who was invited to Princess Esmee's ball? All the ambassadors, all the important foreigners were there. The Princess is like a window that opens on Sineperver. Mother and daughter work together. In this skein of intrigue, the Padishah will have much trouble containing his enemies within the empire and maintaining his wise neutrality among the foreign powers."

"Are you sure, Ibrahim Pasha, that the Padishah, in his heart of hearts, is still neutral? Are you sure he has not chosen?"

Ibrahim Nessim looked at me with a surprised, questioning eye. I could not yet tell him what I detected in Selim—a secret admiration for Bonaparte. The invader of Egypt, the tyrant of Europe, was also the hero of our time, the conqueror with a hundred victories to his name, the welder of a continent, the standard-bearer of daring and success—the image of what Selim wished to be.

I was a woman, and Bonaparte had wronged me, but still I could understand that he might represent an ideal for an entire generation of men, from the humblest of his foot soldiers to the Sultan of Turkey.

Strangely enough, someone else, who barely knew Selim, also thought that he was secretly leaning toward Bonaparte, toward France; it was the British ambassador, Arbuthnot. He was well informed, but so were we. We knew that within the intimacy of his cabinet he indulged in threats. He would use every means at his disposal to prevent an alliance between Turkey and France. Was it d'Antraigues who had awakened Arbuthnot's suspicions? Had Arbuthnot been warned by Ristoglou? And in that case, what had Sineperver's henchman told him? Had he managed to pierce the wall of silence around the Seraglio? Had he told Arbuthnot of my presence? Of my role at Selim's side? In what terms? What lies had he told?

Ibrahim Nessim told me that Arbuthnot, in private, made very specific threats, to this effect: "I know from unimpeachable sources that within the Seraglio itself the Sultan is subject to French influences. That is something England cannot tolerate. Upon my word, we shall eliminate those influences, no matter how powerful or secret they may be!"

CHAPTER 17

IN ORDER to escape the cold of the winter months, Selim was in the habit of holding the meetings of his council in the Cage, the prison of his youth, where he kept his books and his documents.

One evening while the council sat in the drawing room, I waited by a joyful blaze in an adjoining chamber. It was a moonlit night, wan and cold, and I remember looking out for a moment over the snow-dulled Gözdes' Courtyard. The big pool, covered in ice, reflected the metallic rays of the moon. Even the djinns, whose alleged meeting place was nearby, would not have set foot outside in that cold. It was already very late when a commotion in the next room informed me that the session was coming to a close. I then heard Yusuf Aga, Mirizshah's adviser, request from Selim the favor of speaking to him without witnesses. I decided not to wait and returned to my apartments, where Selim would join me after his private audience.

I found Zinah and Cevri waiting for me outside, freezing in the drafty corridor. Smitten with remorse at having left my Zinah, my tropical flower, outside to shiver in the cold, I wrapped her up in my chinchilla-lined red satin pelisse and my veils. I had stored enough warmth to resist the murderous drafts with no more protection than my Bedouin robe. My two servants walked ahead, each carrying a lantern, Zinah dressed as a sultana and I following in peasant's clothes. We crossed the gözdes' quarters and then continued through a series of small apartments and deserted hallways, for I did not want anyone to learn of my presence in the Cage during meetings of the council. We walked on in single file, Cevri's massive silhouette preceding that of Zinah, which wavered like a flame. I trotted behind, hurrying in order to fight the cold that was already beginning to grip me. And suddenly they materialized—three in front, three behind—six black-veiled men. The first three tackled Cevri, while those who had sprung up behind me brutally pushed me aside and grabbed Zinah. I saw her pinned to the ground, I saw those shadows milling about her, and I heard her shout, "Run, Zinah—run, Zinah!"

Then, propelled as much by instinct as by her order, I began to run, and ran until I lost my breath, crashing into walls and stumbling over invisible obstacles. I ran on and on, until I came to a dead end. I could neither go forward nor retrace my steps. Trembling and exhausted, I leaned against a wall and waited, struggling to melt into the shadows, to make myself invisible. After a few moments I heard a heavy tread approaching, I heard someone's muffled breathing drawing closer; my heart, like the big pool, iced over. A dusty moonbeam picked out a silhouette in the doorway; it was Cevri. She came toward me and I was so petrified that she had to take me by the shoulders to move me from the wall. Her features were distorted by rage and hatred.

"Zinah?" I asked; she dropped her chin without answering. Then she took me by the hand and, half-dragging, half-carrying, brought me back to the scene of the attack.

With a single glance I took in all the surroundings, which retain in my memory the fixity of a painting: There was a silhouette sprawled on the ground, covered in the flame-colored pelisse; beside it lay a bowstring of red silk, a scarlet serpent. It was Zinah, and she had been strangled to death. She had saved my life by tricking the assassins. "Run, Zinah!" she had cried; and it was she who had died instead of me.

She was buried on the following day, and I was not even able to walk with her to her grave. I had to be content to watch her funeral procession from my window. Her husband, Idriss, and Ali Effendi carried her body, wrapped in a white shroud, on a stretcher. They crossed the harem hospital's courtyard on a drab snowy morning. One detail which made me smile despite myself would have elicited laughter in Zinah herself: The very small Ali Effendi was unable to keep the stretcher horizontal behind the very tall Idriss, so that Zinah's body threatened to slide back into Ali Effendi at any minute.

My eyes followed them until they crossed the Corpse Gate, which opens only for those who die within the Seraglio. They buried her, I was told, somewhere in the park, near the Kiosk of the Pearl, under a bed of carnations. Come springtime, her favorite flowers would bloom over her remains.

I asked Selim to let me conduct my own investigation, which I placed in the hands of Ali Effendi. His affection for Zinah was sufficient guarantee of his zeal for the mission. I gave him carte blanche and unlimited funds to bring back the names of the men who had attacked us and killed Zinah.

He vanished for three days. When he returned he wordlessly handed me a piece of paper on which he had scrawled six names. Without reading them, I passed the list on to Selim. He gave his order and the culprits, six eunuchs, were arrested. The pay for the crime was found in their quarters—gold coins stamped with the likeness of the King of England, George III.

I was not surprised that the British, misled by the rumors and their rage, should have wanted to eliminate the person they mistook for their main obstacle and the artisan of the alliance with the French. They were skilled at assassinations by proxy, and with the help of an expert such as d'Antraigues they could develop plots of extreme boldness.

Mahmud wanted to torture the eunuchs until they divulged the names of their patrons. Selim backed him up: "Justice must be done."

"But would justice be done?" I asked bitterly. "Who guided the hand of the British? Who found them their agents within the Seraglio? Who broke the harem's law of silence and brought my presence to their attention? An anonymous, invisible person. Even if the eunuchs identify him under torture, he will have disappeared in the meantime. As always, there will be a rustle of rumors, of suspicions . . . and nothing more. It is easier to reform your empire, my lord, than your court. You can turn everything upside down in the former, but you can't change a single thing in the latter. The three of us don't have to tell each other that Sineperver is, as always, behind all this, and that she is, as always, out of reach. What is it you want? To cause a massacre in the Old Seraglio? That's not really what you want—"

Mahmud interrrupted: "And why not? Why not purge the Old Seraglio? Why not even a purge here in the harem? It might instill a salutary fear in our enemies. If we cannot confound them, at least we can intimidate them."

"That would be of no more use than their assassination attempt," I answered. "Our enemies must be very crafty if they thought of using the British in order to get rid of me. But their hatred led them down the wrong trail. It's not only that they made the mistake of killing Zinah in my place; killing me would have been a mistake in itself. Am I really the obstacle the British think I am? Am I the cause of our ties with the French? Am I responsible for the Sultan's politics? You and I know better. And it's all for the best if the British think that way. It is better that they attack me and not the Sultan."

Selim said, "I won't allow another attempt on your life, Aamé. I want an exemplary punishment."

Had our enemies succeeded at last in transforming Selim the Just, Selim the Magnanimous? I had never seen him like this. He was not even to be outdone by Mahmud, who cried, "And I want Zinah to be avenged! I loved her!"

"I beg you both to reconsider. Vain is the vengeance that doesn't return Zinah to life and to me." Sorrow had made me apathetic.

Selim simply ordered the execution of the six black eunuchs, and had their heads exhibited in the niches on either side of the Imperial Gate.

The British refused to understand their mistake. Enraged at their failure, they took their revenge in characteristic fashion: Two years later, their newspapers spread the rumor that in the Grand Signor's harem there was a Frenchwoman, an all-powerful Creole, who ruled the empire. Ironically, I was in prison, utterly powerless, by the time I came to read those "revelations."

For weeks after Zinah's death I was unable to sleep, and had to resort to opium in order to get a few moments' rest from time to time. The hours of darkness were filled with nightmares, and daylight brought visions that wavered between memories of my earliest childhood and the violence of the recent tragedy. During the day I wrote somber notes in my diary.

> I think of Zinah with the despair that filled my thoughts of my parents when I was a prisoner of the pirates; Zinah was a refuge, a source of warmth, that is now lost to me forever. I mourn her more than I would mourn my mother. An entire side of my personality, which opened only for Zinah, is now locked shut for all time. It is a large part of myself she carried to the grave. I am overwhelmed by solitude, despite Selim's presence—or perhaps because of it. For my love for him is heavy to bear, like any all-encompassing emotion, and I could share it not with the man who inspires it but only with my sister, my friend, Zinah. Now she has gone and I am overcome by lassitude, as if I had already lived too long.

In Idriss I found a semblance of solace; he soon replaced his wife, not in my heart—no one could replace Zinah—but in my habits. The young widower asked for the privilege of taking over Zinah's work in caring for my wardrobe and my jewels. He fulfilled it with a delicate feminine grace astonishing in a man so large and vigorous. Perhaps he found some comfort, some illusion of proximity to Zinah, in handling the dresses that had run through her fingers so often.

In the harem, where Selim's love had reunited us, where she had lived and given her life for me, a flowered inscription in white marble stands in honor of my "da."

> Erected by Nakshidil Kadin in memory of her faithful servant Zinah who died in order to save her. This plaque was set in the year 1220 of the Hegira and the sixteenth of the reign of the glorious Padishah Selim son of Mustafa.

Zinah's death left me indifferent to the situation, to everything, for weeks. Mirizshah's illness brought me back to reality and activity, for Selim needed me more than ever.

The summer of 1805 was drawing to an end when the Valideh fell into a long loss of consciousness, from which she emerged with great difficulty. The disease that had gnawed at her for months, perhaps years, had gained the upper hand. During the weeks of her illness Selim and I took turns at her bedside, so that she was almost never without one of us.

Mirizshah was dying. No one thought otherwise, and inevitably her approaching death gave rise to speculation and intrigue.

She called for me several times. I would find her lying on her pillows, elegantly dressed and, as always, covered in jewels. Dressing up was exhausting for her, but it was something she would never give up. She painted her face carefully to hide the ravages of disease and wore more perfume than ever. "I hate the smell of sickness. . . . My doctor is in despair; following the custom, he will lose his post when I die. But I myself am not afraid of death." I did not protest, for I knew that with Mirizshah it was useless to voice false hopes. "And yet," she continued, "I am sad to be leaving. I would have wished that Allah grant me a little more time." She said those words with such bitterness that for a moment I mistook their sense and imagined that she was desperate at the thought of leaving me to triumph in Selim's heart.

"No one could ever replace you, venerable Sultana! I would be stupid indeed if I thought I might succeed."

She understood my mistake and smiled weakly. "I've never been jealous of you, Nakshidil. Only sometimes I disapproved of your influence on my son."

"No one has influence on Sultan Selim—I remember telling you that once already. Perhaps you did while he was growing up. But now he makes his choices and his decisions alone."

"I am aware of that. He works for the welfare and the future of the empire with the courage and determination his ancestors showed in waging wars and subjugating nations. Selim thinks far ahead. It is with the present that he has difficulties. It will be your task to advise him about daily matters, to steer him away from the shoals, to keep him from the enemies who stir up the shadows. And you yourself have many enemies—the same enemies as he— and you are alone."

"They've tried to kill me several times, and yet I am still alive."

Again she smiled. "You have harabra, Nakshidil, you have good luck. The entire Seraglio says so."

"Then I shall bring good luck to the Sultan." I wanted to inspire confidence in Mirizshah in order that she might die in peace. But she was not easily convinced.

"You are young, Nakshidil. So is my son. Neither you nor he is distrustful, and even experience has not convinced you of the perfidy of your enemies. I am proud of my son, proud of the path he has chosen; I would not have wanted him to choose any other. He has turned the page and begun a new chapter in the history of the empire. He's a precursor, and I'm afraid of his meeting a precursor's fate."

"You are proud of your son, Sultana, and I shall be proud to follow him always, anywhere, no matter what the consequences."

"May Allah bless you, my child. And now leave me. I am tired, and fatigue is ugly."

The negotiations between Selim and General Brune had come to a sudden end. Informed of their progress by his spies, Ristoglou had alerted the Russians and the British, who howled in protest, and Selim was forced to break his no longer secret contacts with the French.

Meanwhile war had broken out between France and the most

formidable coalition ever assembled against her. Despite his genius, it seemed highly unlikely that Bonaparte could resist the combined assaults of England, Austria, and Russia. Our old allies put pressure on us to join them. General Brune was no longer there to defend France's position.

Pleas for an alliance with Russia and England were heard in the Divan, and events soon justified the viziers' predictions. Lord Nelson annihilated the French fleet in a superb victory at Trafalgar in Spain—a victory in which he lost his life. Again the allies demanded that Selim join them, and they were backed by the Divan. Time was running out, events were unfolding too rapidly, and I did not know how to counsel Selim on the matter. I have always needed time to think before making up my mind.

Besides, I was mired down in the rites of the harem, held back by its perennial slowness. Facing Ahmed Effendi, Selim's secretary, I was unable to restrain myself: "I envy you, Pasha. You're a man and you can do anything. I'm a woman, and powerless. Any news I receive is already old, and my advice has to wait until the Sultan has discussed the matter with his collaborators. Only then does he inform me of their opinions, and only then can I add mine. These comings and goings blur my vision of events and muddle decisions when every day, every hour is crucial. What I would give to be always with the Sultan, in the fires of discussion, in the midst of the fray! But no—I have to stay hidden in my rooms, where I feel powerless to help my lord."

Shaken by the news of Trafalgar, exhausted by his mother's slow agony, Selim finally gave in. A new treaty of alliance was signed with England and Russia.

Mirizshah passed away at dawn on October 24, 1805. Selim and I had stayed at her bedside throughout the night. I admired her beauty, which neither age nor imminent death could alter, and I admired Selim's courage and his self-control in disguising his grief. He spent his mother's last hours reciting verses of the Koran beside her.

Already Mirizshah was unable to speak. Yet at one point I detected a gleam in her eye; she was calling me. I moved closer, leaned over her, and pressed my ear against her lips. She managed to whisper, "Be his star. He has such need for a lucky star."

At the gates of death, the mother had entrusted her son to me. That highest testimony of her trust moved me more than I can say, and suddenly I recovered all the attachment I had once felt for the grande dame who had adopted me upon my arrival in the harem.

Her disappearance had consequences. Out of regard for the late Valideh, it was with kid gloves that her adviser, Yusuf Aga, was shunted aside; it was suggested to him that he go on a pilgrimage to Mecca—and that he stay there as long as possible.

Mirizshah's death weighed on me. "I miss her," I told Ibrahim Nessim.

He seemed deeply surprised. "She opposed you, and she opposed you harshly."

"Perhaps she did. Yet her vast experience was a support, her will to serve Selim an inspiration. Now I feel more alone at his side than ever before—alone to sustain and advise him."

"Don't let the responsibility intimidate you. We're all behind you, I and the others around the Sultan. By Allah, we shall sustain him."

Ibrahim Nessim's enthusiasm was comforting, but I knew that no one could ever replace Mirizshah's sharpness and penetration—not into the affairs of the empire, but into the mind of her son.

Staggering news arrived from Europe. Against all odds, Bonaparte had crushed the Austrians and the Russians at Austerlitz, forcing the former to sign a hasty peace and the latter to flee in shame. Our assessment of the situation had been mistaken, and we found ourselves stuck in the camp of the vanquished. The allied ambassadors tried to make themselves as small as possible, and the viziers' cockiness melted like spring snow.

A letter from Mother Marie-Agnès did nothing to diminish my helplessness.

Napoleon, not content with taking the place of our kings, has taken their crown as well. It would be in bad taste for us to take umbrage, since our Holy Father the Pope came to Paris expressly to bless him. Just think, my child: young Czar

Alexander and the Emperor Francis joined their formidable forces against him—and were crushed. Russia and Austria are at his mercy. Warlike Prussia quakes at the thought of meeting the same fate. The smaller nations crawl before him on their knees. England has destroyed our fleet—but with a mad king, an unpopular regent, and incompetent ministers since the recent death of William Pitt, she cannot risk her armies on the continent. Europe bows before Napoleon, and the French are ecstatic.

Mother Marie-Agnès's enthusiasm annoyed me, but it was nevertheless indicative of the mood in France. The picture she painted of the situation from inside the walls of a provincial convent was far more accurate than the one we could see from behind the walls of the Seraglio. Mother Marie-Agnès continued on a more personal note:

Grace and kindness shine forth from the throne of your cousin Josephine. Remember, too, that she was the same when she was only Madame de Beauharnais and barely managed to keep her children fed. Eugène is now Viceroy of Italy; his sister Hortense has married Napoleon's brother and thus become an imperial princess. I hear she will soon be Queen of Holland. I prayed for Sultana Mirizshah; her death increases your responsibilities toward the Sultan—I know him well through your letters, make no mistake. Now you must be not only a companion but also a mother to that powerful ruler. The first piece of advice you may give him is to link his fate as quickly as possible to Napoleon's triumphant star.

That was a fine idea, now that we had just become the ally of his adversaries! Yet Mother Marie-Agnès was right. The path she pointed to was the one to follow. But how could we step onto it?

Suddenly we heard melodious sirens' songs emanating from the Maison de France. In hiding there since General Brune's departure, Pierre Ruffin made us understand through the most tortuous channels that the Emperor Napoleon might be induced to forget the past and come to an agreement with the Grand Signor. This time I did not let the opportunity slip by and made up my mind in a hurry. I encouraged Selim to take Ruffin's proffered hand. Our "allies" had not allowed us to keep the neutrality we wanted. They had subjected us to numberless pressures, and it was now within our rights to discard an alliance that had been forced on us. After all, was it not wiser to stand at France's side in the winning camp? Those words were what Selim had hoped to hear. His secret admiration for Bonaparte did the rest.

Early in 1806 the Turkish Empire recognized Bonaparte as Emperor of the French. I am compelled to admit I was pleased. I continued to detest that Bonaparte, that pitiless tyrant, that oppressor; still, though I hated the French, though I had suffered because of them, they had once been my compatriots. I felt more comfortable as a friend of the French than as their enemy.

Once our minds were made up we decided to do things in style. Selim chose the gifts for his new ally the Emperor Napoleon with munificence, and I, relying on memory, picked out those for his wife, my cousin Josephine. They were sent to Paris in the care of an ambassador extraordinary. I quote the French newspapers of the period:

"For the Emperor an aigrette with a central diamond worth fifty thousand crowns, a snuffbox inlaid with precious stones, Arab horses with gold-trimmed harnesses; for the Empress a pearl necklace worth eighty thousand crowns, cashmere shawls, pelisses of sable and chinchilla, and samples of all the scents manufactured in the Grand Signor's Seraglio."

The court and the newspapers went into raptures over the splendor of the gifts, and I heard that everyone was surprised at the accuracy of the Sultan's guesses as to the tastes of the Empress of the French. In return Bonaparte sent Selim two enormous vases of Sevres porcelain painted with scenes of his recent victories. Selim wanted to place these cumbersome and pretentious gifts in his drawing room. But there are limits to euphoria, and I had them exiled to the Sultan's Hall.

Our reconciliation with France was not to please everyone, our former allies in particular. A systematic campaign of slander was unleashed against Selim. Armed with calumny as corrosive as acid, our enemies made use of any material they could find. First the word was spread that Selim was an alcoholic, whereas he was sobriety itself. In response, Selim put a tax on alcohol. Then it began to be said everywhere that Selim was sterile—in other words, damned. That old rumor, trotted out for a new round, became so popular that Selim was not able to turn a deaf ear.

The campaign was also indirectly aimed at me, for Selim's "sterility" had no cause other than his devotion to me. The affair was too delicate, and too close to home, to allow me to interfere. I could not demand that Selim remain faithful to me when that very faithfulness threatened his throne; on the other hand, I couldn't very well encourage him to be unfaithful. Thus I had to listen, without flinching, while his councillors advised him to make use of his harem, sire a child, and put an end to the rumors. Selim, wounded in his pride and annoyed by the fact that some thought it their duty to meddle in his private affairs, refused to comply. Although his reaction did not surprise me, I felt singularly relieved. Meanwhile the danger grew, and finally the Grand Vizier suggested that we falsely announce the birth of a son to Selim. The wall of silence separating the Seraglio from the rest of the world was such that this solution, though unlikely, was not impossible. Its advantage lay in the fact that it would stifle the rumors without forcing Selim to change his habits. And yet the crafty stratagem made me uneasy. Selim, however, was compelled to accept it. In the end the unbelievable, pitiable farce was played to the hilt. All over Constantinople town criers shouted news of the birth of Ahmed, son of Selim, and the arrival of the phantom prince was greeted with cannon salvos and other ritual celebrations. We waited for the news to take effect, and three weeks later we announced, in passing, the prince's death. It caused no great surprise, for infant mortality in the harem was very high.

My uneasiness, however, remained. The imposture so cunningly organized by the Grand Vizier cruelly reminded me of the fact that

Selim and I were childless, and that my equivocal position could always endanger him.

The campaign against Selim also left me anxious and agitated. I could no longer suspect Sineperver alone. Her perfidy was limited to the old methods of bygone days—underground intrigue and discreet assassinations. The recent campaign of slander bore the mark of political experience, of a knowledge of the people, of a modern turn of mind, served by powerful means and an extended network. Of course Sineperver lay behind it all; but it was clear that she now disposed of partners who were incomparably more able and dangerous than those she had enjoyed before. Who were they? How far would they go?

Thereupon a rebellion broke out in the province of Rumelia, not far from Constantinople. The warlord Ismaël Aga burst on the scene with eighty thousand of his fellow bandits and designs on nothing less than Adrianople, the second city of the empire, a hundred leagues from Constantinople. How had he assembled such manpower? Whose secret support did he have? No one could enlighten us.

Selim reacted with firmness. He sent the Nizam-i-Jedid, with its commander, Cadi Pasha, to put down the rebellion. Cadi Pasha led his troops on a forced march, planning to take the rebels by surprise. In fact it was they who surprised him. They swept down on Cadi Pasha in the most unexpected place and, inflicting heavy losses, threw him into retreat. It was obvious they had been warned of Cadi Pasha's plans. By whom?

We turned to our various intelligence services, but we did not know where to look, or what to look for.

Ismaël Aga took Adrianople. News of the city's fall echoed throughout the empire, and Selim's name was openly derided.

Ismaël Aga threatened Constantinople, and the Divan sat in session without interruption. One morning Selim and I witnessed the debates from the Sultan's trellised box above the Grand Vizier's seat. Watching those incompetents indulging in useless conjecture and ridiculous suggestions infuriated me. Then a dusty messenger burst into the room and placed a shapeless sack at the feet of the

Grand Vizier. It contained filthy rags which, unwrapped, revealed a revolting ball of dark hair and brownish matter. Then I understood and managed to distinguish in the terrible object a hole that had once been a mouth, glassy globes that had once been eyes, a nose: I was looking at Ismaël Aga's head.

It was a dramatic turn of events. At the very moment when he began to believe in his victory, Ismaël Aga had been assassinated by his second in command, Mustafa Alemdar, known as Baraïktar.

With the head of his chief, Baraïktar sent us a proposal. He was willing to pull back from Adrianople and submit to the Sultan's authority, provided he was recognized as the only heir to Ismaël Aga's possessions in Rumelia.

Selim took advantage of the offer, granted the repentant rebel his request, and even appointed him pasha of Ruschuk.

At last our spies began to obtain results, and informed us that the origin of a good number of our troubles could be found in the Russian embassy in Constantinople. Unwilling to forgive us our alliance with France, Russia had poured oceans of gold into operations designed to sour public opinion against Selim, into Ismaël Aga's rebellion, and into the pockets of our highest functionaries in order to buy knowledge of our plans.

Intrigued, Selim called the new champion of his throne to Constantinople and received him. He asked him where his nickname came from. Baraïktar answered that it was Selim himself who had indirectly bestowed it upon him. Seventeen years before, while speaking to his troops leaving to fight the Russians, Selim, conforming to the custom, had entrusted them with the sacred Standard of the Prophet, the Sanjak-i-Sherif. He had placed it in the hands of a young officer of Albanian origin, who ever since that day had been called nothing but Baraïktar, the Standard-Bearer. Selim was delighted by the interview. He sang the praises of his visitor tirelessly: he was sincere, whole, passionate, faithful, dauntless, a man of integrity, with a superb bearing and eyes of steel.

The talk of the Divan had informed me of the fact that Baraïktar, the fierce warrior, bore unlimited love for an Albanian girl named Vassilo. A sudden inspiration made me open the doors of the Harem to her for a visit. She was a slight young woman, a child really, whose youthfulness hid the bones of an extraordinarily strong character. I understood very well how her rare combination of beauty and spirit had chained the heart of the dauntless adventurer. She loved him as much as he loved her, but she knew him well, and with a lucidity almost disconcerting in a girl her age she told me of his faults.

Her visit brought me the bracing air of the mountains where she was born, and allowed me to forget, for a moment, the women around me, their gossip and their sweets.

As she left I slipped into her hand a pair of emerald earrings, which she accepted with a grave, dignified gratitude. I hoped that this new ally would inspire fidelity to the Sultan in her strange lover.

Ismaël Aga had been eliminated, Adrianople freed, the Holy Cities recaptured; yet public opinion, poisoned with Russian gold, refused to quiet down. Ali Effendi whispered to me the name the bazaar had bestowed on the Sultan: Selim the Weak. Selim weak! I ask you, could I have loved a weak man? Selim the Unlucky was another name one heard in the bazaar; and the superstitious Orient does not forgive the unlucky. Opinion must have been manipulated with science in order to spread such lies.

In their barracks, the janissaries grumbled. In the mosques, the ulemas harangued the population and incited it to revolt against the heretic Sultan, against his impious reforms and his new army.

The Sheikh-Ul-Islam, our friend Veli Zadeh, took it on himself to suggest to Selim the solution he dreaded most: to dismiss his conservative ministers and install in their place the janissaries and the ulemas who hated him, to quiet them down. There was no other way to save the throne. But it was our turn to make a move, and it was best to limit the damage.

Veli Zadeh insisted on his own dismissal and suggested that Selim replace him as Sheikh-Ul-Islam with Atallah; though an ulema and a conservative, the latter was intelligent and enlightened, and a man of integrity. Furthermore, if the new Grand Vizier had to be the aga of the janissaries, then at least his deputy Musa Pasha, an officer open to new ideas, would occupy an important post. If there had to be a conservative government, at least it would be dominated by two men, Atallah and Musa Pasha, whom he thought favorable to our ideas.

"And now," Selim asked bitterly, just after appointing the new government, "what shall we do? The Russians are back to their intrigues, and the conservatives are winning on every front. What is there left?"

"France, my lord! You need support. Accept what Bonaparte offers you. Until now we have been wary of strengthening our ties with France. Until now I have warned you against Bonaparte. But now the Russians, by their subversive actions, are throwing us into his arms. Perhaps he really wants a concrete and dynamic alliance with us that will allow you to pursue your political course. The stakes are worth it. In any case, there is no alternative."

Once again, in praising France and her leader, I was telling Selim what he wanted to hear. He found the idea of friendship with Bonaparte very appealing. An opportunity to lay its foundations presented itself when a new ambassador—there had been none since General Brune's departure—arrived from Paris. Bonaparte's choice showed his desire to flatter and win the heart of the Sultan. He sent us his friend General Sebastiani. A handsome Corsican, a noble-mannered soldier, Sebastiani had married Fany de Coigny. That name brought back to me the still-vivid image of that little girl who had moved me so deeply, one day long ago in the dressmaking workshops of Mademoiselle Bertin.

CHAPTER 18

———⊶✦✦⊷———

THE FRENCH AMBASSADOR'S ceremonial audience with the Sultan took place amid the customary pomp, to which several unprecedented details had been added, testifying to Selim's desire to make an exceptional event of greeting Sebastiani.

On the appointed day the ambassador left the Maison de France, embarked at the Galata arsenal, crossed the Golden Horn on the barge sent by the court, and landed at the pier of the Grand Vizier, where he was served coffee and sweetmeats in the Imperial Kiosk while waiting for the procession to form. He entered the Seraglio through the Imperial Gate and dismounted at the Middle Gate. There he was shown the Grand Signor's horses; they were thirty-two in number, all splendidly harnessed and saddled. At their side stood the Grand Equerry, in a caftan trimmed with black fur. Seven thousand functionaries and court servants in ceremonial dress were lined up along the ambassador's route. He was led to the Divan's chamber, where he was introduced to Ziya Pasha, the Grand Vizier.

After the customary greetings, the Grand Vizier bade the ambassador sit down at his side. All the viziers, judges, ulemas, generals, and functionaries took their places according to rank. The Grand Vizier and the ambassador first exchanged a few inquiries about each other's health; then General Sebastiani solemnly requested the honor of being brought to meet the Grand Signor.

He was served a meal which included twenty meat dishes; to cut them the guests were provided with gold knives and forks with jeweled handles, something which had never been done before. The organization of the meal was supervised by the Grand Chamberlain, the Grand Bread-Store Keeper, and the Steward of the Imperial Kitchens. After the sweetmeats and the sherbets, finger bowls were brought for the guests to rinse their hands, and the Grand Master of Ceremonies sprinkled the company with rose water.

Meanwhile I dressed. I had heard that Sebastiani's wife, Fany de Coigny, had obtained Selim's unofficial consent to attend, disguised as an aide-de-camp. Thereupon I too was seized by the desire to be there, hidden in the clothes of a page of the first chamber, and forced Selim to allow it.

The pages in question were all very young, and I worried that my years might betray me . . . but Selim assured me there was nothing to worry about, and said I would certainly be the prettiest of his pages.

I put on the long gold-threaded skirt over baggy trousers, and piled my long hair up under the conical beribboned turban. Despite the protestations of Ahmed Effendi, Selim's secretary, who was extremely upset by the mystification, it was behind him, carrying his morocco portfolio and his ivory flyswatter, that I left for the ceremony. We crossed the Third Court, where I had never been before, for it is reserved for the Sultan's official duties. It was already crowded with functionaries, dignitaries, and servants. Quite a few people were there, not because of their position or because they had something to do with the ceremony, but simply to watch. The Orient is filled with onlookers, to the point where the love of pomp can overcome protocol, even here in the Seraglio, where protocol is so severe.

I installed myself with Ahmed Effendi under the colonnade reserved for the high dignitaries, which surrounds the throne room. I could see the chamber through its trellised windows, and at first I was surprised by its smallness. It was a sort of treasure cave, filled with gold: gold thread in the carpets and the tapestries, gold-painted ceiling, gold chandeliers. In a corner, the gilded throne inlaid with precious stones, covered with pearl-embroidered brocade, sat under a canopy from which hung chains studded with diamonds, glittering in the light of the candles. Selim wore a red satin caftan with a wide gold braid, open on a long robe of white satin, and his turban was topped with the three aigrettes only the Sultan is allowed to wear. Oblique sun rays penetrated the room through a high transom, to fall exactly on the throne. Ahmed Effendi whispered to me that the peculiar lighting was designed in order that foreigners admitted to the Sultan's presence should see only his profile in silhouette, and be unable to detect his eventual decrepitude.

Before the throne, on an emerald-blazoned cushion at Selim's feet, lay the sword he had been given on the day of his enthronement.

Two rows of white eunuchs and pages dressed in gold and silver left the throne room, crossed the nearby Gate of Felicity, joined the rows of janissaries, and marched to the Divan, where Sebastiani was just finishing the traditional meal.

The janissaries' aga appeared before him and announced that the time for the audience had arrived. It is a tradition that no foreigner may appear before the Sultan if he is not wearing a ceremonial caftan. The ambassador was therefore given twenty-four brocade caftans for himself and his retinue. Nevertheless Sebastiani was excused from wearing his as a mark of exceptional favor, and thus it was in his gold-braided dragoon's uniform that he went to the audience.

Into the throne room came, by order of protocol, the Aga of the Janissaries, the Judges of the Army, the Grand Vizier, the Grand Admiral, and at last Sebastiani himself. He was held up on either side by a dignitary of the empire, in order that his feet need not touch the ground. By another unprecedented favor he had been allowed to wear his sword. No foreign ambassador had appeared armed before the Sultan since the days of the Conqueror. I recognized Fany without difficulty in Sebastiani's train of officers. She was betrayed by her overly pretty silhouette squeezed into a dragoon's uniform; the tight red knee breeches suited her to perfection. The shako placed too jauntily on her head confirmed my suspicions. No longer the skinny, sad child I had once seen at Mademoiselle Bertin's, Fany Sebastiani had blossomed into a woman of soft, luminous beauty.

Meanwhile Sebastiani, after bowing three times before Selim's throne, had begun a short speech, in which he voiced his wishes for Franco-Turkish friendship. Then he presented Selim with a small bag made of golden cloth, which contained a letter from Bonaparte. Next came an exchange of vows, and Selim's reply to General Sebastiani was accompanied by a gift: a gold box inlaid with a pattern of diamonds in the shape of a dove, the symbol of peace.

Was it the Frenchmen's martial appearance? Was it their uniforms, which had seen all the victories that were the talk of Europe? I felt that a rousing chorus of glory and futurity had suddenly burst into the venerable throne room of the Turkish sultans. Our own court seemed by comparison a miniature forever fixed in old-fashioned pomp. Selim's task was truly a heavy one, and I was not certain that his strength and mine would suffice to fulfill his desires for renewal.

The Grand Vizier gave the signal indicating the end of the audience. The ambassador again bowed three times, and backed away toward the throne room's door.

Sebastiani's arrival brought us what we expected of it: a support. A genuine friendship sprang up between Selim and him, and the relationship between the soldier of fortune and the Reforming Sultan soon overran the boundaries of the official ties of France and the Turkish Empire. Sebastiani was a fountain of advice and initiative. He encouraged Selim to be firm, assuring him of his power and of France's unconditional support. When Selim told him of the Russians' subversive actions, Sebastiani insisted that he be ruthless in cleaning out their nest of intrigue. It was especially necessary to put an end to the carryings-on of the hospodars of Moldavia and

Walachia, Princes Ypsilante and Muruzi, who administered Rumania for the empire but worked for Russia almost openly. With Sebastiani's encouragement, Selim felt strong enough to dispossess them. They managed to escape and take refuge with the Russians; Prince Ypsilante's father was arrested, convicted of complicity, and beheaded. Russia had to be shown that the Turkish Empire would not tolerate her scheming.

The sight of Fany Sebastiani during the presentation of credentials and the memory of her that I had kept through the years led me to receive her in private. It was not only a pleasure, but also a political gesture: Bonaparte's ambassador could only be pleased to know that his wife had been allowed inside the imperial harem.

I dressed according to the other kadins' sartorial taste rather than my own in order that she would not suspect my true identity, and I brought Mahmud with me as interpreter. Fany's entrance was like the arrival of spring. She wore a flower in her hair, and a simple white dress which enhanced her gracefulness and freshness. Through Mahmud we exchanged the usual compliments, and I had the cardamom-flavored coffee served with the harem's finest pastries. Very soon I realized that I would be disappointed with this interview, which I had looked forward to so much.

Convinced she was speaking with a Turk such as had been described to her, Fany consulted me like a guidebook on the customs and traditions of the harem. When, in turn, I questioned her about France, she behaved as a perfect ambassadress, painting idyllic images of her country and the imperial court, drowning me under the propaganda inevitably reserved for foreigners. When she praised the touching union of the Emperor and Empress of the French, I was unable to contain myself any longer.

"Madame Ambassadress," I interrupted, "I am not unaware that the Empress of the French had renounced her lovers, but I also happen to know that the Emperor is unfaithful to her, and that he neglects her more and more." This sally stunned Fany, and Mahmud had to come to my rescue.

"Don't be surprised, Madame Ambassadress. I've taught my mother a little French."

"A little French"—when I had spoken without the trace of an

accent. "My mother"—when I looked barely older than Mahmud. But Fany did not seem to notice anything strange. No doubt she had heard so much nonsense about the Seraglio that she had armed herself against surprise.

The conversation was steered back toward reassuring platitudes, but it was difficult for me to sustain my interest and hide my frustration. After years of confinement in a world infinitely removed from that of my childhood, I found myself by chance in the presence of a young woman my age, from my country, from my own background. Here was an opportunity to speak my language, to make a friend. Although the possibility of breaking my hard-kept rule was enticing, my position more than ever forbade giving in to temptation. Had I told Fany who I was, the entire world would have known of my existence. I would have ruined the work of seventeen years of secrecy. Yet for a moment, I had stupidly hoped that Aimée Dubuc might talk with Fany de Coigny, and I had lost the habit of finding obstacles to my desires. I almost came to hold a grudge against Fany. But after all, the poor girl was not to blame. I was the cause of the misunderstanding, and I would have to endure it to the bitter end.

The only amusing aspect of our conversation was the effect Fany had on Mahmud. The man—my child—blushed, stuttered, tripped over his sentences, beamed with admiration before the flowered apparition, and I could see him literally falling in love before my eyes. Thank God Husmumelek, the siren so affably provided by his sister Princess Esmee, continued to rule over his senses, if not his heart. Otherwise we would have been headed for a sticky diplomatic incident.

Suddenly the cloud burst. Outraged by Selim's rough treatment of her clients the hospodars of Moldavia and Walachia, Russia opened hostilities without a prior declaration of war.

In the last weeks of November 1806, Russian troops poured into the Balkan provinces and took a whole chain of strongholds. Violent riots burst out in Constantinople, where an enraged population clamored for the arrest and execution of all Russians living on

Turkish territory. But Selim wanted to break with the past and show himself to be a modern sovereign. Despite the pressure of opinion, he refused to arrest, the Russian ambassador and limited himself to expelling him with the members of his embassy; he even offered them the opportunity to leave Turkey on board a British merchant ship.

Meanwhile, on his own initiative, Baraïktar had thrown himself on the Russians and had managed to hinder their advance.

A formidable army set off from Constantinople under the command of the Grand Vizier, just after the traditional presentation of the holy Standard of the Prophet, the Sanjak-i-Sherif, which was also going off to war. The army's spectacular departure was cheered by an enthusiastic, almost hysterical crowd—the very same crowd which, a few weeks before, had been shouting slogans hostile to Selim and talking of overthrowing him. Once again a threat to the empire and the humiliation of invasion had gathered the population around the Sultan.

Ibrahim Nessim, though no longer a minister, retained his position as a trusted adviser; he exhorted Selim to follow the example of his distant ancestors and assume personal command of his armies. With the halo of victory on his head—a victory Ibrahim Nessim did not doubt—Selim would become immune to all opposition, to any attack. All my life I shall regret not encouraging Selim to go. But I knew him too well. He was aware of his incompetence in military matters, and could not see himself as commander in chief. His refusal stemmed from humility and not from fear, which was unknown to him. Furthermore, his long years in the Cage had made of Selim a reclusive man accustomed to the confinement of the Seraglio. He dreaded the outdoors, open spaces, crowds; all those things made him gauche and unnatural and filled him with apprehension. Selim let the opportunity slip, and I did not intervene.

One night in December, Selim and I were talking in the Pavilion of Baghdad when I saw through the window, far away, a ship trying to cross the Bosporus despite the darkness and the stormy winter weather. Time and again, dangerous winds drew it toward the rocks, and we feared it would run aground, under our very eyes, on the Seraglio's headland. All torches blazing, abandoned to the raging elements, the ship seemed like myriad will-o'-the-wisps twirling on the waves.

Suddenly I was overwhelmed by the vision of another shipwreck—my own, that of *La Belle Mouette*, years ago. The horror of the memory was still sharp, and goaded me into action. I had to do something. An impulse pulled me outside. Whipped by the wind, suffocating from the cold, Selim and I ran through the gardens to the Kiosk of the Pearl in order to watch the ship's struggle from close up and sound the alarm if necessary. We were only a few cables' lengths away, and we could see and hear the cries of the sailors running on the wave-beaten deck. It seemed to me that I heard some English words, but I couldn't be entirely certain. We prepared to rush for help, but the ship managed to straighten out, drew away from the murderous shore, and sailed off toward the Dardanelles. As she turned about, we caught a glimpse of the word *Endymion* on her hull. We could not guess whose dangerous daring had caused her to sail, flagless, on such a night. But we were provided with an explanation on the very next day.

In the past weeks the British ambassador, Arbuthnot, the man responsible for Zinah's death, had been harassing Selim with exorbitant demands: the renewal of our alliance with England, the cessation of hostilities with Russia, the expulsion of Sebastiani, the handing over of the Dardanelles forts to the British, and other requests which Selim refused even to consider. Then Arbuthnot became aware of the general exasperation with the enemies of the empire, and witnessed the turnabout of public opinion toward Selim; and he grew afraid for his freedom, if not for his life.

He had himself invited to dinner aboard the *Endymion*, a British frigate anchored, by chance, at Constantinople. In the middle of the elegant and solemn reception reuniting the members of the embassy with the ship's officers, Arbuthnot announced to the astonished assembly his intention to leave Constantinople that very minute, aboard the *Endymion*. One can imagine the captain's stupefaction, having not been warned of this project yet having no choice but to obey. Without delay they hoisted the sails and weighed anchor in the middle of the storm, in the dead of night, and the ambassador slunk out of Constantinople with his collaborators, leaving his wife and children behind at the embassy. I almost regretted that the ship had not foundered at the foot of the Seraglio. I could imagine the eunuchs rescuing the drenched and frozen ambassador with utmost deference, and leading him to Selim. . . .

Two months passed. One afternoon Ali Effendi woke me from my sacrosanct nap to invite me, on Selim's behalf, to the top of the Tower of Justice. The peculiar time and place for this summons quickly roused me from my stupor. At the top of the tower, on the terrace which dominates the capital, its outskirts, and the Bosporus, I found Selim waiting for me, a spy glass in his hand. He gave it to me and showed me where to look. A war fleet, flying the Union Jack, was sailing straight for Constantinople. When they came within a few leagues of the Seraglio, the fourteen ships began maneuvers to anchor in the bay of one of the Islands of the Princes.

Arbuthnot, whose flight we had found so comical, had returned with reinforcements. He immediately sent a note to the Divan, repeating his demands, only louder. It was in fact a genuine ultimatum. If we did not comply within twenty-four hours, the British fleet would bombard Constantinople.

Our armies were fighting in the Balkans, and Constantinople had virtually no defenses . . . and the Seraglio happened to be within easy shot of the British guns. The Divan plodded on in fruitless discussions, and of course failed to come up with any coherent strategy.

The highly secret threat of a bombardment spread like wildfire through the Seraglio, and the most alarming rumors shot back and forth among the hysterical population of eunuchs, women, and slaves. Ali Effendi jumped up and down, took flight, and returned a moment later to squeal the latest and most farfetched fabrications with horror and delight.

No decision had been made, and the hour set by the British crept up on us inexorably. In the early evening I joined Selim in the

Pavilion of Baghdad, where he had summoned his closest collaborators, Ibrahim Nessim, Ahmed Effendi, and Billal Aga. Selim had already sent Ishak Bey to warn Sebastiani that he must be ready to leave in case the British should force Selim to arrest him.

Selim cringed at the idea of submitting; and he was filled with horror at the thought of letting his capital be destroyed. Despite his reluctance, I thought him more inclined to give in, so as to avoid the shelling and the massacre of his people; all the more so because his advisers were not helping him extract himself from the dilemma.

I exhorted him to resist. Once again he objected that there was nothing and no one to defend us. My reply sprang to mind and issued from my mouth instinctively: "Yes—there are the people of Constantinople!" Then, to my own surprise, I developed the idea on the spot, as I spoke. On many occasions already, the population of Constantinople had proved its will and its ability to resist, for good or for evil. Until now no one had thought of calling on its support. Yet we needed only to try—to entrust to it the defense of its own city, and help it organize its efforts. I was convinced it would answer our call. Ibrahim Nessim concurred immediately, with great warmth. Ahmed Effendi, normally so reserved, welcomed the suggestion with enthusiasm. He respectfully pointed out to Selim that if he had been unable to leave Constantinople to lead his armies, the opportunity had now arrived for him to become the leader of his people in the defense of the capital. Selim wavered, but still insisted that we lacked time to elaborate a plan and put it into effect; the British ultimatum was to expire the following morning.

Heated by the argument, Ibrahim Nessim had risen to take a few steps on the terrace. Through the window I could see him pacing the marble floor, his head bent, his brow furrowed. Suddenly he stopped, turned around, and came inside to join us. "We have an ally," he said.

"Who?" Selim asked, amazed.

"The wind," answered Ibrahim Nessim.

A corridor between two continents, the Bosporus is subject to the alternation of two strong winds. The southwest wind, which had drawn the British fleet until then, had just shifted to the northeast, blowing toward the Islands of the Princes. It would paralyze the British fleet for several days, and thus we had time to organize the defense of the city while the enemy lay helpless. That thin ray of hope was enough to make us all euphoric.

Billal Aga, the first to return to earth, suggested that we keep the British in suspense for a time by sending them a negotiator to lead them astray.

Selim and his advisers settled down to compose the proclamation that would call the population to enlist for their own defense and that of the city. As for myself, I was suddenly invaded by grave doubts. Who was to coordinate and direct this desperate enterprise? Who among us could issue the necessary orders and instructions? It was not enough that the people consent; they needed leaders.

In the middle of the night Selim received a message from the dragoman, the secretary at the French embassy, a double agent by the name of Franchini. He warned us that his master, fearing arrest from the Sultan, was preparing his departure in secret on a merchant ship. Already he had burned the embassy's archives. Pierre Ruffin had tried, but failed, to convince him of the Sultan's honorable intentions.

Selim was shattered by Sebastiani's mistrust—by what struck him as treason from a friend. My rage became so violent that I lunged to my writing desk to dash off, in my best French, a note addressed to General Sebastiani, His Majesty the French Emperor's ambassador:

Monsieur l'ambassadeur,
A Frenchman does not run away. Do you really wish to imitate the British ambassador by slinking off like a criminal? Why don't you come to see His Highness instead, and give him the benefit of your advice, which would be welcome and gratefully taken.

Ali Effendi immediately went to bring the note to the Maison de France, with orders to let it be known that it came from the Grand

Signor's very entourage. I left it to Sebastiani to guess who had written it.

Less than two hours later a message came from Sebastiani, urgently requesting an audience.

I hid in the closet where I had once surprised my slave Firuz spying on Selim. Sebastiani was led into the chamber in total secrecy. In order to relax the atmosphere, he began with a jest:

"The Grand Signor has not only England and Russia for enemies, but also the fatalism and the wait-and-see attitude of the Turkish people."

Selim could not help but smile; Sebastiani could now lower his guard. He did exactly that, offering to put his experience, his ability, and whatever power he disposed of to work for the defense of Constantinople. Far from making vague suggestions, he had come with a definite plan, which he now described to Selim: First of all, cannon had to be moved into the Seraglio, which meant that all the women would have to be evacuated to the Old Seraglio. Ahmed Effendi and Billal Aga lifted their arms to the skies and began to shriek. Even a miracle from Allah could not have shifted the harem in a few hours. I myself shuddered at the thought of the pandemonium to come. But Selim ordered the evacuation. Thereupon I went back to my apartment to rest, triumphant at the idea that it was my own bold initiative which had brought us the organizer we needed.

It was barely first light on the following day when I was wakened by a terrible racket. The migration had begun. The ladies were leaving the harem and the reasons for this unprecedented move as much as its suddenness had caused the general hysteria to reach an excessive pitch.

Nothing in the world could have convinced me to follow them to the Old Seraglio. I rushed over to beg Selim to take me into his own apartment. He did not resist for long, and soon I was installed there, in the large yellow-and-silver room on the second floor, the only remaining woman in the Seraglio, which was presently invaded by soldiery.

The din which had presided over the women's departure now

gave way to an unusual silence. I took a stroll through the deserted harem, which seemed disfigured by the strange calmness. I wandered through apartments abandoned in a great hurry, where closets and chests had been left open on piles of brocade, velvet, and silk. Empty jewel boxes and small objects were strewn everywhere, and from time to time the cavernous silence of exodus was broken by the song of a caged bird, forgotten in the panic by its mistress.

I regained my refuge at Selim's. Soon afterward I heard a rumble so powerful that it shook the walls like an earthquake: Cannon were being dragged from the neighboring forts to be placed at strategic points around the Seraglio. French voices—those of Sebastiani's officers—mingled with the janissaries' Turkish in a profusion of orders, calls, oaths.

Later in the morning Ali Effendi told me that the Sultan's proclamation had been read at all the crossroads in the city to an approving and enthusiastic crowd. Already a large throng of men, women, old people, children, peasants, burghers, storekeepers, had massed at the wide-open gates of the Seraglio.

Two immense tents had been pitched in the gardens of the selamlik, from inside which Selim and Sebastiani directed operations.

The placing of the guns on the Seraglio's flank, the point most exposed to the British shells, was entrusted to Mahmud. He was extremely happy to have, at last, an outlet for his energies. He was beaming when he came to see me in the evening. He told me of the ardor with which the populace had set to work, carrying cannonballs and munitions, dragging heavy sandbags to build embankments. The wonder had been worked: The people of Constantinople had answered Selim's call as one, and were already actively engaged in preparing the defense of the city.

Next morning, unable to resist any longer, I went to see the sights with my own eyes. I threw on a long black abaya which would allow me to melt into the mass of peasant women, and dragging a more than reticent Ali Effendi in my wake, I set off through the gardens.

The beds of rare plants had been trampled, the lawns torn to shreds; the fat China vases were broken, and the pavements of pale marble muddied. Eunuchs in silk, bejeweled kadins, dignitaries in brocade—all had disappeared. In their place halberdiers and janissaries labored together with men and women of all ages, races, and ranks, joined in a single collective effort.

I stopped by the Kiosk of the Pearl, which swarmed like an anthill. A wall was being built to protect a battery of guns. The impromptu construction workers had formed a chain and were passing the sandbags from hand to hand with extraordinary speed. Suddenly a merchant from the bazaar, who was sweating blood in the middle of the chain, shouted at me, "Hey! You, the hanun! Are you here to work, or to watch us!"

The whole chain burst into laughter. Despite Ali Effendi's protests, I chose a spot among the others and began to pass the sandbags along. Harassed by jokes, Ali Effendi himself had to follow suit. He tripped, sweated, and swore, and I thought I heard my name muttered among his imprecations. I was not really that much braver than he. I would never have thought sandbags could be so heavy; you should try. I bent my shoulders into the effort, hoping to avoid the shame of dropping one, but my hands shook and my arms and my back burned with the pain.

We worked on, and a rumor traveled down the chain: The Padishah was coming. Soon I saw Selim's tall silhouette approaching. He walked slowly, stopping to talk with the workers, encouraging here and thanking there, and I saw the crowd, which at first had been almost paralyzed by the presence of the Grand Signor, the Shadow of Allah on Earth, relax little by little and smile, incredulous, delighted, seduced.

Selim recognized us almost immediately, as I saw by the amusement that flashed in his eyes. He walked up to Ali Effendi, who was about to faint from exhaustion, and having ordered that a gold coin be given to him, he said, "May Allah reward you for your trouble. I hope you shall recover from it."

Then, turning to me, he gave me a coin too. Smiling, he said, "The Sultan thanks you, Hanun, for having left your husband and your home to come and help him defend the empire."

At lunchtime a meal of mutton and rice was brought from the imperial kitchen. It was quite different from the refined dishes concocted daily for the women of the harem, and yet I have never had a better meal or eaten with more joy and appetite. The comments and the thoughts of those around me were the best spices imaginable: Everything I heard told me that Selim had never been more popular. By the end of the day Ali Effendi was so exhausted that he did not even have the energy to bring me back to Selim's room. I was at the end of my strength myself, and barely made it back on my own, my knees like jelly and my heart filled with joy.

On February 23, 1807, we were ready: six hundred guns now defended the approaches to the Seraglio, to the Golden Horn and the Port of Constantinople. During the day, Ishak Bey went aboard the British flagship to confer with Arbuthnot, but instead of the prevarications and the moanings he had served up in the past few days, he transmitted a regal message: The Padishah would not negotiate under the threat of the guns, and refused to hold any talks until the British recrossed the Dardanelles.

Ali Effendi awoke me at dawn the next day. Selim was waiting for me on the Tower of Justice, scanning the horizon through his spy glass. The northeast wind had given way, and the British ships flew toward Constantinople. The hour of the decisive trial had struck.

The courtyards and the gardens of the Seraglio were black with people. There was total silence and stillness as everyone, at his post, awaited the assault.

Billal Aga rushed over to beg his master not to stay in such an exposed spot and to take shelter. Selim refused; I stayed at his side, impassive and yet weak with terror. The British fleet drew closer. Already we could see the open hatchways, the guns aimed at us, the sailors with their fuses at the ready.

And then something inexplicable happened: Suddenly the British fleet turned about and headed for the high seas. At first we thought it was a maneuver, and it wasn't until the fleet had disappeared on the horizon that we realized the battle would not take place. An enormous cry rose from the crowd below us, as if from a single breast—the voice of all Constantinople. The townspeople had understood they were saved.

The British themselves had understood that once again they were to fail. Seeing through his telescope the Seraglio bristling with guns and the crowd massed on the improvised ramparts, Arbuthnot had not dared force the issue. The jubilation that ensued among the crowd caused even more damage to the harem gardens than had the preparations for battle. But no one minded. That victorious joy was the most spontaneous, the most extraordinary sight the Seraglio had ever seen.

Little by little, the harem was restored to its former self. The women returned to their apartments with their eunuchs and their slaves. An army of gardeners repaired the damage wrought by the brave and industrious crowds of Constantinople.

To reward Sebastiani, Selim gave him a yali at Therapia on the Bosporus. The Sultan was simply giving his friends what he had taken from his enemies, for that splendid palace, with its famous park and its inestimable treasures, had been confiscated from Prince Ypsilante, the hospodar who had been dispossessed for having served the Russians too well.

"It is to you, Aamé, that I should give that yali. It is you who thought of calling on the people. It is you who brought Sebastiani to our rescue. It is you who saved Constantinople, and you who deserve the yali."

"I need no other palace than the chamber of my lord."

"Little girl"—in spite of my thirty-three years of age, Selim still thought of me as I had been on the day we had met—"little girl, how is it that you always come up with the solution my most renowned councillors never find? What do you have that they lack?"

"My love for you, my lord. It puts wings on my imagination. And that's not all. If you find any merit in me, it is in yourself that you must seek its cause. Your courage, your calmness, your integrity, your faith in your mission, inspire me."

I saw Selim begin to flinch. That humble, inspired man hated to hear people speak of him—especially in praise. Quickly I changed my tone.

"And then, my lord, I like to take risks, I like to wager success on a throw of the dice. Surprises and emotions never lack when one lives at the Sultan's side. One has to get used to it, or else give in to panic. One has to learn to react to emergencies."

"If only those emergencies would stop! I ask only for a little peace in order to work seriously for the good of the empire. Perhaps I shall at last be able to do something while my enemies are at bay."

Indeed, the British were beaten and the Russians on the run in the Balkans, pursued by our armies under Baraïktar and the Grand Vizier.

In the spring of 1807 two deaths struck us. Veli Zadeh died of old age. We lost not only an old friend but also a powerful support, and irreplaceable wisdom and experience.

Then, in faraway Mecca, we lost Rusah, Abdul Hamid's favorite kadin, who had made him suffer so before leaving on a pilgrimage from which she had never returned. I hoped that in Allah's paradise she would at last join her lover, who had pined for her until the end of his days.

Allah takes with one hand and gives with the other. In May Fany Sebastiani gave birth to a daughter in her yali at Therapia. The birth rewarded a united couple, and seemed to crown Sebastiani's success in Constantinople.

At the same time, while a little French girl opened her eyes to the world on Turkish soil, the Grand Vizier and Baraïktar retook Bucharest from the Russians and chased them from Rumania. Our enemies were in trouble, all the more so because Bonaparte, after crushing their Prussian allies, hounded them from battle to battle and made their proud armies melt away in the snows of Eylau.

It occurred to Selim to coordinate the movements of French and Turkish troops: Simultaneous assaults would deal a final blow to Russian ambitions. He suggested to Bonaparte that they change their defensive alliance into an offensive one, and asked him for twenty-five thousand troops to help the Grand Vizier throw the Russians out of the empire. We expected a prompt and enthusiastic response, for the plan was to Bonaparte's advantage as much as to ours. In lieu of the reinforcements we expected, he sent Selim a marble bust—of himself!

Once again I could not understand. Was our empire not Bonaparte's strongest and most faithful ally, the ally whose friendship he had sought for years? Now he had gained our friendship; and yet, in response to our proposal to unite our forces toward a common goal, he sent us a knickknack. Did he have second thoughts? Was he nursing some secret design, again at our expense? My mistrust of him was renewed. Selim was more than puzzled, which did not prevent him from placing the great man's bust in his sitting room, ignoring my loud protests.

Tragedy struck Sebastiani: Fany died of the aftereffects of childbirth, felled by a fever. Crazed with grief, the French ambassador locked himself in his yali at Therapia and refused to receive anyone. The palace that had welcomed his happiness had become the scene of his despair. That active martial man sank into melancholy, and it seemed that nothing could draw him out of it.

Selim's condolences to his friend were expressed in deeply moving terms, but words had no power to lighten his distress. We did not know that Fany's brutal, unfair death was to sound the alarm for us.

CHAPTER 19

———⊶⊹⊷———

MAY 25, 1807, fell on a Thursday, the day I devoted, each week, to accounting. My kadin's pension and Selim's generosity had enabled me to accumulate quite a little fortune. Instead of buying lands, estates, and residential property, like the other speculators of the harem, I had kept my crowns—my Norman blood made me like them—and placed them in a bank, from which I received a comfortable income. That Thursday, then, I went over the statements with Ali Effendi, and as always, the chubby imp muddled his accounting and forced me to do the sums myself. When Selim interrupted us, it was to tell me that the Yamaks at the fort of Rumeli Kovak had rebelled.

The Yamaks were fierce Albanians, traditionally used as artillerymen, who were garrisoned in the forts of the Bosporus. Selim, as part of his reforms, had decided to integrate them little by little into the Nizam-i-Jedid.

That morning the Commander of the Bosporus had gone to Rumeli Kovak, and after enticing the Yamaks with various promises, including that of doubling their pay, had invited them to don the uniform of the Nizamites. The Yamaks balked. The Commander of the Bosporus thundered. The Yamaks grumbled. The Commander of the Bosporus threatened. The Yamaks threw themselves upon him and massacred him, with several of his officers.

Selim informed me that he had just sent the chief of the domestic soldiers of the Seraglio, the Bostandgy baj, faithful Chakir Bey, to make his inquiries at the scene. This sort of incident being, alas, too common for alarm, I returned quietly to my accounts. But evening brought more troublesome news. Having heard of the mutiny at Rumeli Kovak, all the Yamaks in the various forts of the Bosporus had risen, massacring their officers and chasing off the soldiers of the Nizam-i-Jedid, who had taken refuge in their barracks around Constantinople. At the village of Buyukdere, which was now the mutineers' headquarters, Chakir Bey, sent by the Sultan, was greeted with cannon fire and had to turn back without even setting foot ashore.

From the Pavilion of Baghdad, Selim summoned Ibrahim Nessim, his secretary Ahmed Effendi, Billal Aga, and Musa Pasha. We had recently brought Musa Pasha, a conservative janissary with a reputation for an open mind, into the government as Caimacam, aide to the Grand Vizier—who was now fighting on the Russian front. Musa Pasha's presence forced me to hide in the closet off the room where the council was being held. For Ibrahim Nessim there was only one solution, and as always it was radical: The Nizamites had to be sent against the Yamaks to restore order with cannon. Musa Pasha objected, claiming that the Yamaks wanted only to safeguard their autonomy; Selim's assurance that they were not to be incorporated into the Nizam-i-Jedid would be enough to appease them.

I was impressed by the authority emanating from that round little man. Insignificant as he seemed, he dominated the meeting by his rigor and his firmness. The revolt of the Yamaks, he explained in his reedy voice, was in fact a rather simple event, caused by excessive haste and clumsiness. Calm and a little tact would allow this isolated incident to die a natural death without any consequences.

As if to confirm his words, a eunuch arrived with a message from the mutineers' headquarters in Buyukdere: The Yamaks had elected as their chief a certain Kabadji Mustafa, who professed his loyalty to the Sultan and begged only that the Nizamites be ordered to return to their original quarters. Musa Pasha suggested that we temporarily confine the Nizamites to their barracks in order to avoid stirring up the Yamaks to no purpose.

When Selim came to consult me, I advised him to follow Musa Pasha's suggestion. Those Albanian devils the Yamaks were touchy in the extreme, and it was pointless to make life difficult for that handful of savages. Containing the incident seemed by far the best policy, especially if Musa Pasha promised to settle the Yamaks by force in the unlikely event of their not calming down on their own.

Selim opted for the voice of wisdom and had an appeasing proclamation drawn up for the Yamaks.

It was past ten o'clock when I returned to my apartment, and I was surprised to note Ali Effendi's unusual absence. He reappeared only when I was readying for bed. He had been loafing about the city, trying to gather news. The rumors he had brought were not reassuring, but then I never knew when Ali Effendi's taste for the dramatic got the better of his truthfulness.

According to him, the business was more serious than we had thought. Far from being spontaneous, the revolt had been carefully organized, and probably the Yamak mutineers had been paid to make trouble. Anonymous tracts encouraging the janissaries to follow the Yamaks' lead were making the rounds of the barracks. A few of the janissaries' officers had traveled to Buyukdere to contact the mutineers.

Ali Effendi's news left me sleepless, and I slipped back into my clothes and went to report the rumors to Selim. He reassured me. If we were to believe every piece of gossip there would be at least one war or revolution every day. I knew that as well as he, but still I was edgy and took a long time to fall asleep.

Selim's confidence seemed justified, for the next day was quiet. I scolded Ali Effendi for his alarmist chatter. He shook his head silently. Since there was no news from Buyukdere, I concluded that

Selim's proclamation had appeased the mutineers, and that following Musa Pasha's prediction the incident was resolving itself on its own.

I spent the afternoon pacing up and down, incapable of concentrating on any task. Although there was no longer anything to worry about, I was gripped by a strange and unjustifiable apprehension, by forebodings which I did my best to ward off. Perhaps they were no more than the seeds planted by Ali Effendi's gossip.

That evening Pierre Ruffin had a message carried to Ahmed Effendi. After paying a visit to Sebastiani, who was still prostrate with grief in his yali at Therapia, Ruffin had made a detour through the neighboring village of Buyukdere to see what was happening there. Far from quietly breaking up, the Yamaks' revolt seemed to be solidifying and growing by the hour. Ruffin's news drove me wild with anxiety.

"Time is short," I told Selim. "Call your advisers. We must take swift and energetic measures. This very evening. Right now."

"Calm down, Aamé. I know Ruffin; he's a pessimist by nature, and probably he's been misled. As a foreigner, he's not familiar with the ebullient nature of the Yamaks."

"But we've just seen what those Yamaks are capable of!"

"Don't worry, Aamé. They're still seething, but in fact they've already been quite appeased by my proclamation and my acquiescence to their demands."

I went to bed, calm, resigned, but not at peace.

May 27 was a hot, heavy day. It seemed as if a suffocating summer had settled on the city. I had slept badly, and dragged myself about without energy or purpose.

Evening brought Selim with unexpected and worrisome news. In the morning, six hundred Yamaks, led by Kabadji Mustafa, had left their headquarters at Buyukdere and marched to the suburb of Ortaköy, where they were joined by three hundred other Yamaks from different Bosporus forts. Why were they marching on Constantinople? Why had they stopped at Ortaköy?

Selim received Caimacam Musa Pasha, who came with the offi-

328　SULTANA

cers commanding the regiments of janissaries garrisoned in the capital. They proposed to go to Ortaköy in person to order the Yamaks to disperse. Musa Pasha claimed, besides, that according to reliable information, the Yamaks were already trying to negotiate a pardon. His plan was to soothe them with the (false) promise of dissolving the Nizam-i-Jedid once and for all. Would the ruse restore order? Would that order be maintained in the face of such a confession of weakness from the government? I could not understand why Musa Pasha, who had been so firm until now, advocated such a solution. I did not understand how he had secured Selim's consent. But it was already done, and I tried to keep my peace, for Musa Pasha had committed himself to dispersing the Yamaks by force if necessary.

Later, when he returned from his daily excursion through the town, Ali Effendi came to report. He had seen artillery regiments on the march toward Ortaköy. I felt somewhat reassured, if not completely serene. Musa Pasha was keeping to his word: It would be either negotiation or dispersal by force. Perhaps he was right. In any case he seemed in control of the situation.

The hot night drew us, Selim and me, out onto the terrace. What secrets crawled through the sleeping city? What did the stars shining in the sky hold in store for us? Across the Golden Horn, at Tophane, there was either a fair or a celebration. The quarter was all lit up. From time to time we could hear, or guess at, a crowd. Barges sailed across the Bosporus, ferrying the celebrants back and forth despite the lateness of the hour, and we followed the comings and goings of their lights on the dark waters.

Late to bed, I slept almost well, but bad news hit me with full force as soon as I awoke. Not only had the Yamaks not dispersed; they had been joined by the artillery regiments sent out against them. Their ranks had swollen further with Yamaks who had crossed the Bosporus from the forts on the Asiatic shore. What we had mistaken for a celebration the night before were in fact the fires at their point of assembly in Tophane. It was no longer a troop but an army which crossed the Golden Horn on hundreds of boats and climbed through the city toward the Seraglio.

At ten o'clock I learned that an entire crowd of merchants, shop-keepers, and artisans had rallied to the Yamaks and locked step with them. There was no doubt that we were facing a general revolt.

From that moment events began to accelerate. Late in the morning we were told that Kabadji Mustafa, the leader of the Yamaks, was conferring with the officers of the janissaries in the Mosque of Sulemanye.

At noon the bazaar shut down—an infallible sign of imminent trouble. Musa Pasha sent emissaries throughout the city to fetch the reformers, Selim's collaborators, who were all in grave danger from the insurrection, and bring them to the shelter of the Seraglio.

An hour later it was the janissaries' turn to join forces with the insurgents. From my windows I could hear the sinister and characteristic din they made beating on their upturned caldrons.

Selim summoned his council to the Pavilion of Baghdad. The presence of Caimacam Musa Pasha and Sheikh-Ul-Islam Atallah compelled me to hide in my closet. Ibrahim Nessim demanded the use of the Nizam-i-Jedid to put down the revolt. Musa Pasha objected; it was too late, he said. Dispersed among the forts outside the city, the new army would not arrive in time. Only a proclamation from Selim announcing the promised dissolution of the Nizam-i-Jedid would defuse the rebellion by stripping it of its purpose.

Cooped up in my dark closet, I listened to Musa Pasha's reedy, quiet voice, and suddenly the truth dawned on me, as if a door had swung open to reveal the obvious. Who had deprived Selim of his last recourse by confining the Nizamites to their barracks? Who had procrastinated, who had minimized the danger in order to mislead Selim and give the Yamaks enough time to organize themselves? Musa Pasha, the energetic Caimacam who had our fullest confidence, had betrayed us! He had stood behind the revolt of the Yamaks from the start. From the start he had pulled the strings of the conspiracy. I wanted to shout the truth, to leap out of my hiding place, but I was stunned by the enormity of my discovery, and my body would not obey me. I was afraid—afraid of my discovery, afraid of Musa Pasha. Paralyzed, unable to move or to speak, I listened while Selim acceded to Musa Pasha's arguments. The net was closing. Musa Pasha, followed by Atallah, the Sheikh-Ul-Islam, set off to announce the dissolution of the Nizam-i-Jedid. I left my hiding place. I was about to speak, but Ibrahim Nessim was quicker than I. He too had understood. Selim himself had understood. But it was already too late. All we could do to save ourselves was organize the defense of the Seraglio.

Orders were given to shut the doors and man the ramparts. Between the halberdiers, our soldier-servants the bostanjis, and the pages, we could deploy ten thousand defenders on the towers and behind the crenels. We could withstand a siege—but for how long?

I returned to the Kiosk of Osman, with an obscure, instinctive desire to go to ground in my own room. I was paralyzed by the terror of what might happen, by the threat hanging over Selim and Mahmud.

Ali Effendi stormed in at seven o'clock, returning from the At Meydan, the wide esplanade at the edge of the Seraglio, between Saint Sophia and the Blue Mosque of Sultan Ahmed. The insurgents had massed there by the thousands, listening to the harangues of their leader, Kabadji Mustafa. He was exhorting them, in the name of Muslim orthodoxy, to the murder of the reformers, of the Nizamites, of Selim's followers. A bit later he made a straightforward demand for their heads, by throwing a message, wrapped around a stone, over the Seraglio's wall. None of our friends had been omitted from his list: Ibrahim Nessim, Ali Effendi, etc. There was no need to wonder who had composed it. By inviting his victims to take refuge in the Seraglio that morning, Musa Pasha himself had lured them into a trap. Besides, he had not returned from delivering to the Yamaks the announcement of the dissolution of the Nizam-i-Jedid: He had lowered his mask and thrown his lot in with the rebels, his clients. Selim, of course, would not give in to blackmail and exchange the lives of his followers for his own.

I stood at my window, leaning out into the fresh May night, into the scented, innocent breath of spring. The sparkling of the lights in the silent city echoed that of the stars. Constantinople spread out below me, calm, motionless, a sort of sleeping beauty. It was difficult to imagine that over there, on the other flank of the Seraglio, a lust for blood and destruction coursed through the rebels on the At Meydan. Could it be only a nightmare? Would God that it had been! Suddenly my attention was drawn to furtive movements in the gloom of the gardens beneath my apartment. Vague shadows followed dimmed lanterns along the paths running to the sea.... Selim was spiriting through the best-hidden gates those of his friends who had been marked by the rebels.

He came back to my room around eight o'clock. He himself had made sure that all of them had left the Seraglio. Only one had refused to obey: old Chakir Bey, the very man who had been welcomed by cannon fire upon arriving to make inquiries at Buyukdere. He had hoped his death would be enough to calm the insurgents, and delivered himself to the executioner. His severed head had just been thrown over the wall to be brought to Kabadji Mustafa.

Selim was crying like a child, and I was too horrified to console him. We spent the whole night in the Kiosk of Osman, listening to the news which filtered into the Seraglio in arms, as securely locked as a prison.

Having received only the head of the Bostandgy baj, Musa Pasha and Kabadji Mustafa understood that Selim would not hand over his friends—whose escape soon became known to them. In their rage and frustration, they ordered a manhunt throughout the city. All night long Selim's supporters, those who had participated in the great work of his reforms, were hounded, tracked, flushed out, tortured, massacred. Ibrahim Nessim took refuge with a Jewish moneylender, who, believing he was carrying gold and jewelry, denounced him, thereby condemning him to be hacked to pieces there and then. Ahmed Effendi, chased into the house of a Greek, leaped from terrace to terrace, lost his grip, and fell to the street, where he was finished off by the crowd. Only our former minister of foreign affairs, one of the earliest of the reformers, escaped death, thanks to a gardener who smuggled him away through a sewer. All that remained of the others were beheaded, disfigured, mutilated corpses, around which the blood-crazed rebels danced exuberantly. Selim, stiff, frozen, but still undaunted, grew paler and paler as he heard the news. The horror of it was such that I was incapable of feeling anything or reacting.

Every so often Mahmud, boiling inside, suggested some plan of action. Impelled by my spirited nature, or simply spurred by fear and danger, I latched on to each of these impossible projects, born only from despair. Why didn't Selim go to the square of At Meydan to speak to the insurgents? Why didn't Selim travel to the front to take command of his armies? Why wouldn't he try to retake the city with the regiments of the Nizam-i-Jedid garrisoned in the near-by forts?

Calmly, almost with indifference, Selim pointed out the inanity of these proposals and rebuffed them. He grew lively only when I suggested pure and simple flight. To flee the trap closing in on us! A simple animal instinct demanded it. To keep my freedom, to keep my life and the life of my loved ones. . . . There would always be time for action later. To flee!

"Never!" said Selim. "I would sooner die on my throne!"

At dawn we were alone, without friends, without support, besieged by the insurgents.

The following morning Selim left me very early to go to the Pavilion of Baghdad. Before going, he implored me not to leave the harem, no matter what happened. The harem enjoyed a sacred immunity. It was always spared in the empire's revolutions, and I would be safe there even if the Seraglio was invaded.

I was left alone, overcome by successive waves of hope and despair, prey to the most fantastic thoughts and suppositions. First I thought the dissolution of the Nizam-i-Jedid would be enough to take the wind out of the sails of the rebellion; then my imagination would run wild, letting the insurgents into the palace to massacre Selim and Mahmud.

I did not leave my room, but still I could feel the strange silence which had settled over the harem, the silence of animals who await an earthquake. There was no chatter, no call, no footstep; all were hiding in silence in their rooms.

Ali Effendi came to interrupt the torment of waiting. He had managed to slip down to the square of At Meydan, and there he had heard Kabadji Mustafa harangue the overheated crowd in front of the bloodied severed heads of our friends. He no longer asked for the repeal of the reforms or even for the life of the reformers; now he demanded the deposition of Sultan Selim, who, he claimed, "in contempt of our laws and institutions, and disregarding the counsel of his wise ulemas, has sought to establish among us the barbarous institutions of the infidels." He craftily ended his indictment by placing the matter under the authority of the Sheikh-Ul-Islam, asking for his fetva, the sanction traditionally required for any important decision.

We had not yet been informed of the answer the Sheikh-Ul-Islam, Atallah, would give. He was locked in the Grand Vizier's palace, debating the question with his ulemas. "Does Sultan Selim deserve to remain on the throne?" Selim's fate rested on Atallah's answer, which had to be delivered in a single word: yes or no.

Mahmud appeared. He had heard that many among the janissaries' officers, alarmed at the turn of events, had disassociated themselves from the rebels and joined the Nizamites in their barracks, to launch a counterrevolution in Selim's favor. Could we latch on to this hope? I no longer knew whom to listen to, whom to trust.

In early afternoon, a clamor outside drew me to my window. It rose, like a pestilential vapor, from the area of the At Meydan, from the rebels' camp.

I could clearly hear the crowd chanting: "Sultan Mustafa! Sultan Mustafa!"

Constantinople wanted to make Mustafa Sultan. The revolution had found its figurehead: Mustafa, son of Sineperver. "So it's Sineperver!"—an accusation I had initially made at the time of the attempt on my life, when I had first found favor with Abdul Hamid. It had returned to my lips when Mahmud was poisoned, and yet again when I was poisoned myself. I shouted it once more when I heard the crowd demanding that Mustafa be made Sultan, thereby divulging who stood at the origin of the rebellion. Sineperver had been jealous of me, jealous of Mahmud, from the start. Now her ambition had returned to her in retirement. She wanted power for her son—or rather for herself, through the vessel of weak-spirited

Mustafa. Selim was young, and she did not want to wait until he died and Mustafa came to the throne legally. Therefore she had planned to overthrow Selim. Accomplices, attracted by the gold she distributed freely, rushed to take their stand in secret under her dark banner along with the conservatives who were determined to prevent Selim's reforms by any means. She had approved and encouraged the campaign of lies waged against Selim, Ismaël Aga's rebellion, the rebellion of the Yamaks. When had she enlisted Musa Pasha? Before, or after, he had become Caimacam? When had she enlisted Atallah, the Sheikh-Ul-Islam? For now I understood at last that he too was betraying us—and that Kabadji Mustafa's request for a fetva and Atallah's discussion with the ulemas were only a pretense.

Selim walked in. I could tell by his expression that he had already heard the verdict. To the question "Does Sultan Selim deserve to stay on the throne?" the Sheikh-Ul-Islam had answered, "No. God knows what is best." When Kabadji Mustafa read the fetva to the insurgents in the square of At Meydan, the crowd let fly an enormous shout which abolished Selim: "Sultan Mustafa! Sultan Mustafa!"

Atallah had acquitted himself of his part of the bargain with the rebels. Selim and I had thought of him as an ally, whereas like Musa Pasha he had been betraying us since the very beginning. Under Sineperver's supervision, Musa Pasha, the civil power, and Atallah, the religious power, had together staged this comedy which unfortunately deserved the name of revolution, taking advantage of their position at Selim's side, suffocating him with assurances of their loyalty, entrapping him with their lies.

Exhausted, his features drawn, Selim maintained a proud, dignified calm which flooded me with respect and tenderness. I wanted to throw myself into his arms, but his noble composure restrained me. And what use were gestures and words anyway, when our hearts understood very well what we said in silence?

Selim wanted to avoid any further bloodshed and spare the lives of his defenders. He told me he would oppose no resistance even to an illegal movement, to a treacherous Sheikh-Ul-Islam: He would let himself be deposed. I said nothing, I didn't argue. I simply bowed before him, for he had never shown as much courage as he was showing now. His decision was neither fatalism nor cowardice, but lucidity and integrity. With it he lost his throne, but kept his honor and an unsullied conscience.

A eunuch entered the room with a message from Atallah, begging Selim in the name of Allah to spare the life of Prince Mustafa. This time Selim was wounded. Did Atallah really think he would imitate his ancestors and massacre his relatives in order to keep his throne? Did he really think Selim capable of such a thing? It is true that a traitor can imagine only treachery. I saw a bitter smile, or perhaps a grimace of pain, alter my lord's features. In answer to Atallah, he wrote quite simply: "May Allah make Prince Mustafa's life a long one."

Still calm, Selim dressed. He donned the gold-trimmed white caftan he had worn on the day of his coronation and pinned the three-rubied aigrette to his turban. He entrusted me to Mahmud's care before leaving. He would await further developments sitting on his throne. During those tense seconds while we took leave of each other, without much certainty of ever seeing each other again, we exchanged neither a sign nor a word; we knew we loved each other.

He returned two or three hours later. To me it seemed that centuries had elapsed, centuries during which I had had to make superhuman efforts to hide my terror from Mahmud.

Selim looked strangely detached, as if all he was going through were no concern of his. Without emotion, he said: "The eunuchs came with their trophies—the heads of our friends. I came down from my throne and kissed those hideous remains and gave them to my chamberlain to be buried decently." Selim's voice remained flat and low. "Then I went to fetch Prince Mustafa in the Hall of Circumcision, to bring him to the throne room. Atallah was announced. He had come to inform me officially of the response to the fetva—you see, the conspirators had misjudged me. They feared my resistance, a long siege. Only the Sheikh-Ul-Islam had the authority to have the bronze doors of the Seraglio opened. So they sent him. He came and made a great show of humility and sorrow, eyes downcast, kneeling in front of the throne. He said:

"'My lord, I come on a painful mission I have been forced to accept in order to prevent the furious crowd from penetrating these sacred walls. The janissaries and all the population of Constantinople have just declared that they recognize no master other than your cousin Prince Mustafa. Any resistance would be pointless, and would serve only to spill the blood of your faithful subjects. What power have we, as poor mortals, to oppose God's will?'

"I didn't say anything. What could I answer to this anthology of hypocrisy? I turned to Mustafa and announced that I placed the empire in his hands. Mustafa protested vehemently—and he appeared sincere. I had to take him by the hand to lead him to the throne. I told him I entrusted him with the lives of my loved ones."

Then Selim stepped out of the throne room and out of the history of the empire. He finished his account of the disaster as if he were out of reach, as if he had already stepped beyond the boundaries of reality.

Billal Aga arrived, bringing, on Selim's order, a lemon sherbet. I could see him staring with horror at the precious cup, I saw his hand tremble as he gave it to Selim. I heard him mutter, "In the name of Allah, my lord, don't do it."

Selim brought the cup to his lips, and I understood, not a moment too soon. Softly, I said, "My lord, for the love of me, don't do it."

Slowly, avoiding any sudden gesture, I took the cup of poisoned sherbet from his hand. He did not react, did not leave his trance, as indifferent now to life as he had been a moment before to death.

Suddenly we heard voices and noise emanating from the Second Court. Had the rebels attacked the Seraglio? Were they coming to massacre us? My heart stopped.

Mahmud explained. The rebels had indeed invaded the Seraglio, in order to witness the enthronement of the new Sultan, Mustafa IV. At least the conspirators didn't waste time. Perhaps they were afraid of the shadow of the Sultan they had just deposed. Mahmud stayed with us. Unknown eunuchs stood guard at our doors; our familiar servants had been dismissed. We were prisoners.

We did not notice the hours passing in Selim's drawing room. Each of the three of us was absorbed in his own thoughts, and left them only to try to reassure and comfort the other two. Selim had returned to reality and did not really seem to remember having tried to poison himself. His serenity dominated us, his confidence warmed us. He did not fear the future. He believed Mustafa a nice boy who did not mean us any harm. He was willing to accept his new condition as long as we were not separated. I wanted only to be allowed to share his fate. To live with the man I love, whether he be a sultan or a prisoner, was still my only ambition. Mahmud, taciturn, thought only of risking his life in defending us.

Those two beings—my entire life—fell asleep. I envied them, for I myself could not find rest. What did tomorrow hold for us? That very word—tomorrow—frightened me.

CHAPTER 20

ON THE FOLLOWING day, May 30, 1807, cannon salvos shook the city to salute the accession of Sultan Mustafa IV, and very soon order returned to Constantinople. The janissaries righted their caldrons, and the Yamaks returned to the Bosporus forts, whose command had been given to their leader, Kabadji Mustafa. The Nizamites, fearing reprisals, abandoned their barracks and their uniforms and disappeared.

The shops of the bazaar reopened, and the population returned to its business. The revolution had fallen like a soufflé, and within a few hours the capital had recovered its usual physiognomy, as if nothing had happened, as if no insignificant usurper, propelled by the machinations of power-hungry conspirators, had replaced a popular and good sultan on the throne. Over the centuries, Constantinople had seen so many revolutions that she had earned the right to treat them lightly. Nevertheless I shall always be surprised by the capacity of the Orient to digest almost any event with extraordinary speed. The Orient is so old that she is surfeited with history. Nothing can surprise her. She has seen it all. Wars succeed invasions, empires wax and wane, dynasties overthrow one another. Through all these events the Oriental people remain unchanged; they have learned to let history pass them by. From time to time, however, the Orient begins to boil without apparent reason. Thus she shows her eternal volatility; and thus, perhaps, she rebels against her centuries of submission. Her agitation runs the risk of degenerating into wholesale slaughter. Then, when her cities are ruined and bloodied, the people again fall into apathy and lick their wounds in silence. But the agitation can also stop short and find expression in a simple palace revolution. In that case the people of the Orient, knowing that their lives and their chattels are not threatened, knowing too in their wisdom that the games of power escape them, react with indifference. Because of the infinite distance separating them, the governed ignore the changes among their masters, and forget in one night the hatred or the love they bore them.

That afternoon a great bustle alerted us to the fact that the new Valideh, the mother of Sultan Mustafa, was taking possession of her apartment. How often she must have dreamed of this moment, the supreme fulfillment of her ambition! What efforts, how much plotting, had been necessary to bring it about! Even crime had not stopped her. May she wait, I thought; may she wait, in the gold of her apartment and the glory of her position, for God's punishment! Sineperver was installed with the same pomp and ceremony which had accompanied Mirizshah's move years before. Princess Esmee shared in her mother's and her brother's triumph.

In the evening we received a visit from Ristoglou, in the guise of Kizlar Aga. His long efforts to erode Selim's power had earned him this promotion, which, if intrigue and malevolence were the measure, he amply deserved. He had come to inform us of the arrangements that had been made for us. Selim was to remain "voluntarily" in his apartment, keeping Billal Aga, his eunuchs . . . and his harem. Mahmud and I would be kept in a different apartment, but were granted a short daily visit to Selim. I was allowed to keep Cevri and Idriss, but Ali Effendi, who no doubt was thought too dangerous, would be taken from me. Mahmud, whom Selim's fall had made crown prince, was granted a certain decorum—his Lala Aga, the inoffensive Amber Aga, his old tutor; his women, his slaves. Ristoglou fidgeted; he was in a hurry to tear me from Selim. We parted, he and I, without effusions, reluctant to display the extent of our distress to our enemies. The new Kizlar Aga led Mahmud and me under the eaves of the harem to old outbuildings of the Cage which had been abandoned years before. The lugubrious rooms, airless and windowless, had no light except from a glass-covered opening in the ceiling of the central room, pompously called a drawing room.

For months, for years afterward, I was tormented by a double question: What had happened, and what could we have done to prevent it?

When I asked Mahmud, he said it was very simple. "The janissaries and the ulemas could not forgive Selim the reforms that had bitten into their privileges. As for the Russians, they wanted nothing more than to sow disorder in an empire that is their hereditary enemy—and an ally of France to boot. Clever manipulation of public opinion did the rest. The conspiracy, I think, had not one but many heads, each of them bent on the common goal of overthrowing Selim."

"You're forgetting Sineperver, who always dreamed of placing her son on the throne. She was behind it all from the start. She enlisted Atallah, Musa Pasha, and the active participation of Princess Esmee. Don't think she wasn't the head. But why did she remain hidden for so long?"

"Probably she feared your vengeance and Selim's against Mustafa and herself. She waited to appear only when the danger was over and she could safely reap the fruits of her machinations."

"Perhaps I should have encouraged Selim to resist. And yet—"

He interrupted. "It's your nature, Mama Nakshidil, to resist. And mine too. I would have resisted, I would have struck. . . ."

I thought of Selim and wondered what more I could have done for him. Mahmud, thinking not only of Selim but also of the empire, wondered what he would have done in his place. It was my duty to try to give Mahmud a better grasp of Selim's attitude.

"Selim knew what he was doing. It isn't that his character failed him; his decision not to resist was guided by his philosophy, and is therefore a decision I respect. Selim was aware that abdication was failure; but he also knew that he had paved the way to modernization and progress. Now it is up to others to follow him. It will be up to you, my son, when the time comes."

"But why did he want to poison himself?"

I tried to hide from Mahmud the pain that overcame me at the memory of that incident. "I think that in his bewilderment, the fact of seeing his work ruined and the future of the empire in jeopardy drove him to despair." I did not add that at the time Selim had forgotten even my love for him. . . .

My existence settled into a routine. I managed to adapt, eventually. After all, I had already known captivity with the Barbary pirates and at my beginnings at the harem. At that time I was carried by what I believed destiny held for me, and my patience was not in vain since it had rewarded me.

As for now, idleness weighed on me—the idleness which is thought to be the rule of the harem, but which I had never known until now. Having nothing to do disconcerted me. I tried to fight against the black thoughts that lay in wait for me during those long, slack hours by keeping to a timetable and by getting engrossed in the smallest daily tasks. I would get up early, wash myself in our minuscule hammam, get dressed, read, give orders to my slaves, and write in my diary. But often I couldn't maintain this self-imposed discipline. And then I had Mahmud on my hands. He prowled about like a caged lion, which is what he was. A recluse at twenty-two years of age, bursting with vitality and energy, he adapted even less well than I to our new existence. I tried to entertain him—but without much success, I must admit. I would begin conversations, force him to speak, ask him questions, but he would soon lapse back into silence; my very inability to draw him out again made me morose. And perhaps we were better off that way, each locked within himself rather than softened by contact with the loved one. To talk made us vulnerable.

And we were only too vulnerable in our horrible prison. We had been granted our lives and a certain luxury, but we were deprived of light, air, and space. Our lodgings were so dark that the lamps were kept burning all day, and the scent of burning oil mingled with the thick, close smell of the rooms. All of us—Mahmud, his women, his slaves, my household and I—were crammed into four or five narrow rooms giving onto the central one. Armed eunuchs stood guard outside the door. I would almost have preferred to be locked up alone with Mahmud than with those thirty-odd people, all of them as heavy-hearted as we, stumbling over each other in misery.

We had been allowed to keep our chests, our jewels, our clothes, but that act of generosity was in fact a mockery—we had no use for embroidered caftans, diamond aigrettes, emerald necklaces. An imperial prince and a favorite kadin don't amount to much in prison. And yet in the days of the Cage, princes had been forced to make do with our lodgings for decades at a time. They had not died of it, for they knew nothing else. But Mahmud and I had lived in freedom and could not easily accustom ourselves to having lost it. Moralists and novelists would say that we still had hope left. In actuality, there is an entry in my diary which makes it clear that my separation from Selim had robbed me of hope as well.

I've just come from my daily visit to Selim. Where is the intimacy I long for? How can we speak in the presence of those venomous spying eunuchs? Now I am alone, but I can hear the reedy sound of his ney. Sineperver chose her vengeance well; it is all the more cruel for its apparent lack of harshness. I am well treated, well fed—and kept apart from Selim. Yet I am close enough to suffer from his very proximity, and the music he plays breaks my heart. A prison, with him, would not be a prison. If we were together I might forget, in the sunlight of his company, the pain of this stifling, futureless life.

We had some news of the outside world. Selim's supporters outside the walls, and my Ali Effendi, who lived in town, whispered to accomplices, who whispered in turn to Billal Aga or Idriss, who whispered to us whenever our guards' vigilance suffered a momentary lapse. For once the law of the Orient by which there is no wall thick enough to keep a secret played in our favor. The very walls of our prison had become a sieve for information. It added a little spice to our extremely bland existence; but the news was always so bad that it distressed us more than it entertained.

Musa Pasha and Atallah shared the power that treason had earned them. They worked on flushing out all hidden reformers and repealing all the reforms already enacted. A few weeks were enough to destroy the results of the previous eighteen years. A line had been drawn across Selim's reign and the country had returned to the old system of his predecessors.

Disorder and anarchy had settled at the front in our war with Russia. The janissaries' aga, who disapproved of the insurrection against Selim, had been massacred by his own officers. The Grand Vizier, indignant at the treachery of his aide the Caimacam, was deposed and escaped death only through flight. Baraïktar backed out of his commitment to Selim's enemies and led his troops back to his fiefdom of Ruschuk in Bulgaria. Amputated, deprived of its leaders, the army fell apart so quickly that the planned offensive against the Russians had to be abandoned.

The news wounded Selim in his patriotism, but his heart bled when he heard that Sebastiani was negotiating with Mustafa.

Forced to maintain the Franco-Turkish alliance, the French ambassador had emerged from mourning to establish cordial relations with the usurper. Then the hyenas began to fight among themselves. Atallah, the Sheikh-Ul-Islam, and the Caimacam, Musa Pasha, each came to feel that the other was in the way. Mustafa and Sineperver showed themselves incapable of maintaining order in their own camp. Intrigue, plots, assassinations, were her field; government was another matter. After demonstrating limitless ambition in her quest for power, she had taken to demonstrating her inability to wield it. After simmering for a time, the rivalry burst into the open. Backed up by Kabadji Mustafa and his Yamaks, Atallah obtained the deposal of Musa Pasha, as the empire fell back into the old ruts of corruption and intrigue.

Thereupon France tried to make us sign a shameful peace with the Russians. Bonaparte, far from fighting Czar Alexander, as Selim had wanted him to do, had gone over to his side—to the detriment of the Turkish Empire. They had met on the Niemen at Tilsit, and there the two of them had carved up the map of Europe. Betrayed and furious, the population of Constantinople rioted and threatened to burn the French embassy. Sebastiani was almost torn to pieces. He was saved only by the intercession of Atallah himself.

In fact, Bonaparte had simply served up the Turkish Empire to Russia in the secret articles of Tilsit, which we heard of even in our prison. "The West for me, the East for you," he had apparently told the Czar, his accomplice. Not satisfied with merely betraying Selim, his faithful friend, by failing to come to his aid when he was deposed, Bonaparte had then betrayed the Turkish Empire, his faithful ally. Selim had admired Bonaparte far too much, had believed in him far too well, not to be deeply wounded. I was not surprised. I boiled with hatred. From the bottom of my prison, which was beginning to seem permanent, I vowed that if ever I recovered freedom and power I would do my best to cause the downfall of that man who was the bane of our empire, of Europe, of his century.

One evening during my daily visit to Selim, the door to his drawing room opened to admit Mustafa IV, preceded by his eunuchs and Ristoglou. The reigning Sultan, struggling with the current troubles, had come to seek the advice of the fallen Sultan. Just like that. This incongruous step arose from the mixture of embarrassment and affection Mustafa visibly felt toward Selim. Despite what had been done in his name, despite the influences on him, the weak Mustafa retained a certain respect for Selim and confidence in his judgment. Anxious to moderate his successor by his own experience, Selim advised him not to rear up against Bonaparte: If the latter claimed that the treaty of Tilsit was to the advantage of the Turkish Empire, why not take his word for it? Pretend that we did not sense a trap and accept the mediation Bonaparte suggested—or demanded. Bonaparte would thus be forced to either hold to his promises or uncover his guns.

Mustafa thanked his teacher with deference and left as casually as he had come. The interview, and the problems discussed, inspired the philosophical bent in Selim: "So many men want power, so many are prepared to kill for it. If only they knew what power brings—the responsibility, the load that must be borne without a moment's rest. Mustafa, despite his protests, was delighted to become Sultan, and now there he is—anxious, lost, indecisive. And I, wretched prisoner that I am, I don't envy him the place I used to occupy."

Selim's advice turned out to have been excellent. An armistice was signed between the Turkish Empire and Russia. Then Czar Alexander disowned it. The armistice no longer suited him because Bonaparte—now we had proof—had tempted him with the possibility of putting his hands on Constantinople, the century-old dream of his dynasty.

The Turkish Empire could do nothing but prepare for war. Selim lapsed into pessimism. The government and the army were poisoned with anarchy and intrigue, and he doubted the possibility of victory.

That summer of 1807 was a trying time. We had no daylight under the eaves of the harem; but the sun, beating on the lead roofs, turned our rooms into furnaces. We were suffocated by the heat day and night. There was not a breath of air, not an instant of respite. We were not even allowed to open the door to the hallway to create the illusion of a draft. A thick dust further darkened the atmosphere and made us cough. Breathing was difficult, and every movement a great effort. The burning temperature, the unbreathable air, the darkness, the detention, the isolation, sometimes brought me close to madness. I sat sunk in hebetude, watching columns of dust swirling in the shafts of light from the ceiling; unattached, my mind wandered. I wondered how long I would be able to hold up.

Nevertheless I made every possible effort to maintain my physical appearance. I dressed and scented myself with care, and often had rose water sprinkled on my hands and face to wash away the sweat. And if I did sink into hebetude, I still sat very straight. And if the darkest thoughts drifted through my mind, I kept them to myself. Keeping up appearances was the only effort I could make for Mahmud, in order that he have before him at all times a flattering image of his mother, in order that he never know that I despaired of ever escaping the leaden weight of our imprisonment, in order that he have a good example; for Mahmud himself was letting go and, sinking under the same weight as I, losing the composure I had always admired in him.

He sought escape in debauchery, freeing his imperious sensuality with the many women generously supplied by his sister Princess Esmee. Having conspired energetically to place her brother Mustafa on the throne, she nevertheless retained some affection for her younger brother and sincerely tried to soften the conditions of his detention. She sent him his favorite dishes and chose for him the prettiest girls of her slave pool, which she constantly renewed. But that was no longer enough for Mahmud. He began to drink, depleting the stocks of the cellar lavishly maintained on orders from Sineperver. Mustafa's mother did not disguise her intentions of making of Mahmud a drunkard and an incompetent. She was slowly killing my son, as surely as if she had had him strangled, and far more cruelly. I could do nothing to prevent it. I was far too distressed to show energy. But one day I lost my temper at last and shouted:

"Are you really so desperate that you have to commit suicide?"

"But, Mama Nakshidil, I'm not desperate. I'm bored. I'm simply making use of the only distraction I have." He had straightened up to tell me this, and I believed him. My surprise and my immediate relief made my eyes sparkle.

He had emerged from drunkenness for a moment, and continued: "Don't be afraid—it'll take more than that to kill me. Despair . . . I don't know what it is. And neither do you," he added, looking at me. "You don't speak, but it is clear nonetheless. How could I despair when you are the living image of endurance?"

So my efforts were not in vain; so the mask I wore happily misled my own son.

Selim, a prisoner in his own apartments, had in a way returned to the existence he had led for so long in the Cage. Once again he devoted his days to music and poetry. I often heard him play his flute, whose melancholy swayed me and pierced my heart. I have kept a poem he wrote and slipped, one day, into my hand:

> To win? To lose?
> What are such things? I wonder.
> For all belongs to Him, all stems from Him, all is His.
>
> My coming, my leaving,
> Am I the cause of them?
> Even what I think reason flees from me:
> What was it I owned so much in this world? I wonder.
>
> This life? A mysterious entity.
> This sky? A tent
> With its settled stars and its wandering torch.
> The Universe is poured around me by a generous God.
> These dark pages? The fragments of the work.
> What was it I owned so much in this world? I wonder.
>
> Flesh? Mortal. Life? Fleeting.
> Possession? A passing acquaintance.
> Let the name of Creature be sufficient,
> And submission our only duty, for
> What do we own in this world
> That is not His?

Selim fell back on the mysticism that had always attracted him; and I could not follow. He explored the secrets of the Sufi thinkers, and his meditation on the fringes of the Muslim faith took him high above his prison, high above his surroundings and his flesh. He accepted his downfall just as he had accepted power. He accepted his life as he would accept death.

Selim's serenity was an inspiration for me. He knew that words, that encouragement, were useless to me in my lassitude. His example, however, was not, and its light pierced the dirty fog in my soul. He inspired in me the will to react.

The arrival of the first rains of autumn brought us a measure of relief. I emerged from apathy and unreason and tried to find something on which to fix my mind in order to avoid slipping back. I had been allowed to keep my books. Misfortune and idleness brought me back to them. The French classics—Corneille, Racine—which had never inspired me, now became passionately interesting. Trembling, I shared the destinies of their heroines, those epic, violent figures, admirable even in abjection or madness. Boredom and the need to occupy my mind led me to learn tirades, which I first recited like a parrot and then learned to declaim like an actress. I became more and more involved in the game and spent entire days outside myself, transformed into *Phèdre*, shouting her guilty love and her anguish to a bewildered Mahmud:

> "Hippolyte!
> In his bold gaze my ruin is writ large.
> Do as you will. My fate is in your hands.
> My whirling mind has left me powerless."

My pen flies on the paper, and I could darken entire pages with the verses of those tragedies. Almost ten years have elapsed since then, and thousands of Alexandrines still trot through my memory.

I felt supported by the love of Selim, that love which both galvanized me and tore at my heart, and which, far from weakening, had acquired a new dimension. Returning from one of those visits to my beloved that were my daily dose of life and yet left me torn and frustrated, I took up my diary and wrote:

He seems satisfied, with my proximity, with the happiness of seeing me briefly every day. I am not as detached. My nature cannot be content with disembodied love. I miss our intimacy fiercely. I envy those of his kadins who are with him at all times. I envy Refet, who, after having been neglected for so long, now enjoys the privilege which has been taken from me, lives at his side. Does she receive his favors? Am I jealous? Perhaps—and yet I would be sorry indeed to give Sineperver the incomparable satisfaction of awakening in me a feeling I buried long ago.

One of my slaves had a talent for miniature, an art she had learned in the harem's school. The girl spent days bent over her ivory, trying to reproduce my traits by the dim light of the drawing room, while I sat immobile, wearing the most graceful expression I could muster. I gave the portrait—a rather good likeness—to Selim, so that he would not forget me for an instant, even when he looked at his other kadins. Selim understood the allusion, smiled, and hung the miniature from his neck on a cord of blue silk—"the color of your eyes, Aamé."

Continuing my solitary apprenticeship as tragedienne with renewed ardor, I slipped into the soul of Camille, bent on asserting her right to happiness, and into that of Pauline, the faithful wife of Polyeucte:

> I still would love him were he false to me.
> And if at so much love you're stupefied,
> My duty does not turn on *his*. He may
> Fail in it if he will. *I* must do *mine*.

I asked Mahmud to read with me, but he did so in a morose monotone. Tragedy bored him. Everything outside of women and drink bored him. And even those things palled, although he could not tear himself from them. It was Selim who made him climb out of the abyss. He was determined to correct Mahmud's character. It was not in Selim to deliver the speeches of a noble father. He proceeded instead with a light but decisive touch. One day when he saw Mahmud beating a eunuch for a peccadillo, Selim stopped him.

"When you have been through the furnace of the world, you will not lose your temper like this. When you have suffered as I have, you will feel compassion for the sufferings of others, even those of a slave."

Then Selim rekindled the love of study Mahmud had shown as a child, which had been stifled by imprisonment. The renewal of his desire to learn, inspired originally by his father, came just in time— at a moment when Mahmud, weary of women and debauchery, was beginning to feel his own disgrace acutely. He abandoned his bottles and his women, to throw himself with a sort of rage into the study of history, politics, law, economics, military science.

Sineperver, when informed of this, thought it a passing phase.

Blinded by hatred, she failed to see the threat in Mahmud's new resolve. That was her mistake; for Mahmud's thirst for knowledge, his obstinate reflection, was eventually to destroy her son and carry mine onto the shield of history.

Mahmud's readings were powerfully stimulated by the lessons of Selim. The latter had taken to instructing him in politics every evening, sketching historical tableaux for the attentive young man. He described events, men, and affairs past and present from the vantage point of eighteen years of supreme power. He spoke of his own goals, of the reforms he had begun and failed to finish. He listed without complacency the errors and the failings of his reign, and warned Mahmud of the pitfalls of power. The eunuch spies listened, and sometimes, when their impassiveness failed them, I could read interest and even emotion on their features. Selim's speech and his vision were beyond them, but they were instinctively touched by his honesty and his faith, by that serenity of his in which one could discern neither regret nor bitterness. Without knowing it, Selim was gaining partisans among his jailers.

Thus, night after night, Selim trained Mahmud, as if the latter were destined to continue what the former had begun. I myself had taken to filling out those lessons in order to reveal to Mahmud all that was hidden behind Selim's humility: the depth of his efforts, the tenacity that had made him hold his course against wind and tide, and the successes of his program—which, although eradicated by Sineperver and her henchmen, had left their mark on the empire. I too educated Mahmud as if he were Selim's successor. Although he was indeed heir to the throne, his time was normally to come only after Mustafa's death, which seemed very distant. And then it was unlikely that Sineperver would allow my son to remain in freedom or even in life once Mustafa sired a son, who would succeed him if not for Mahmud. To reassure me I had only Euphemia David's prediction, which I dwelt on several times a day: "Your son will reign, and his reign will be filled with glory." It was small reassurance at a time when nothing promised any change in our situation. Indeed it seemed that it could change only for the worse. And yet it was during this hopeless period that I became certain

Mahmud would reign. I was so convinced of it that I felt the necessity to rush his training. It was an absurd conviction, and I have never been able to explain it to my satisfaction. And in fact, Mahmud was becoming imbued with the consciousness of responsibility, and gradually acquiring the maturity, the wisdom, and the patience he lacked, those necessary complements to the knowledge he was storing up in his solitude.

The winter, when it came, was terrible. We suffered from the cold as badly as we had suffered from the summer heat. Snow piled up on the glass piercing the domed ceiling of our drawing room, and now we lived in total darkness. The braziers filled the apartment with thick smoke which made us cough and spit. One could not sit close to them for the heat, and yet one shivered three feet away. We moved about in a sort of fog, and the acrid smell of burning coal impregnated our clothes and even our food. The constant passages from heat to cold, the smoke and the unhealthiness, made me ill. My lungs were affected. Breathing was painful, I was racked by a dry cough, I choked and weakened. I remained on my back for entire days, panting, desperate for air, too exhausted to rise.

I learned of Sebastiani's departure. Disillusioned, exhausted, crushed by the failure of his mission, wasted by sorrow and disease—it was said he had scurvy—he had asked to be recalled. Mustafa buried him in gifts, but Sebastiani made it clear to everyone that his most precious possession was the last message of friendship he had received from Sultan Selim. He had been powerless to help us, shackled as he was by the orders of his master, Bonaparte, who had betrayed us. But it was a friend who was leaving us, a friend whose personal prestige might have been a help to us if the opportunity arose. Sickness increased my vulnerability, and I felt more abandoned than ever. How many more winters, how many more summers, would we have to endure our prison?

It was then that a ray of hope appeared in our smoky Cage, some news which Mahmud whispered into my ear one evening as he leaned over my sickbed.

From his fiefdom of Ruschuk, Baraïktar had managed to send us a message, which Billal Aga had whispered to Selim. Baraïktar had launched an underground war to put Selim back on the throne. He had formed a secret committee—called the Committee of Ruschuk—in which were assembled military people, functionaries, reformers who had escaped the purge, and even some conservatives and ulemas who were disgusted with the internal quarrels around the throne. The plan was for Baraïktar's army to march on Constantinople to overthrow Mustafa. The danger was that the latter might assassinate Selim and Mahmud once the alarm was sounded, in order to ensure his inviolability by remaining the only living member of the Ottoman dynasty. And the problem lay in finding a way of moving Baraïktar's troops without awakening Mustafa's suspicion.

All the information we received pointed to the growing lassitude and dissatisfaction of the population, which had begun to realize it had been misled. Mustafa's weakness and incompetence were criticized everywhere, and he was accused of devoting himself, in times of war and shortages, to nothing more than his own pleasure. He was reproached for surrounding himself with corrupt men who thought only of amassing riches at the expense of the state, like Atallah, or like Kabadji Mustafa, the leader of the Yamaks who terrorized the population. In short, people missed Selim; his kindliness and his justice were spoken of with nostalgia, and many hoped for his return.

The turnabout of public opinion encouraged the Committee of Ruschuk to haste, but Selim's life was more threatened than ever. We were stuck between the hammer and the anvil, between the hope of deliverance and the terror of making a false maneuver which would cost us our lives. I felt helpless—a most painful situation for me—in the face of events of which we were nevertheless the cause.

In March of 1808 the army started preparations for the coming campaign against Russia. The presence of the Grand Vizier in Adrianople was the opportunity the Committee of Ruschuk had been waiting for. A messenger was sent to corrupt him. Reduced to impotence since Atallah and Kabadji Mustafa had gained power, the Grand Vizier lent an attentive ear to Bejid Effendi, the ablest member of the Committee of Ruschuk. The latter kindled the Grand Vizier's resentment, enticed him with the promise of keeping him in his post and reestablishing his legal power, and won him over to Baraïktar's cause. The Grand Vizier committed himself to joining his troops to Baraïktar's when the moment came. Meanwhile he provided Bejid Effendi with all the credentials and viatica necessary for him to operate within Constantinople itself. Bejid Effendi slipped the worm into the fruit as soon as he arrived: He encouraged Mustafa's and Sineperver's suspicions toward Atallah's and Kabadji Mustafa's growing power, advised them to lean on their most faithful supporters, and guided their choice toward the secret affiliates of the Committee of Ruschuk, whom he managed to place in key posts. Within a day he had succeeded in having himself appointed Treasurer of the Empire.

I was astonished both by Bejid's daring and by Sineperver's naiveté. It was not surprising that Mustafa should be taken in by the flattery and the insidious operations of Bejid; a weak man devoted wholly to women and to feasting, the Sultan was notoriously shortsighted, and the hope of being rid of those who had tyrannized him ever since his accession was enough to put his qualms to sleep. But how could Sineperver let herself be duped so easily? Though she was ruse and ambition personified, her intelligence was nevertheless limited by her pettiness. In her schemes the means took precedence over the ends. Her notion of politics was limited to intrigue and corruption. The vanity of power was far more important to her than the exercise of power. Now that the higher spheres were riddled with our partisans, we could keep a close watch on Sultan and Valideh. On the other hand, it also made us more vulnerable. One look, one clumsy word, would cause them to react, and their reaction would be all the more violent for their awareness that danger lurked very close at hand. It was the same net which closed around Sineperver and Mustafa and us.

Spring, in our prison, took the form of still-freezing nights and now-stifling days. My health had grown better, but morale was still low. I could imagine the profusion of flowers in the Seraglio's gardens, the songs of the birds, the sweetness of evening out of doors, the first stars. The outside world was at once so near and so inaccessible. Our only links to it were rumor and the echoes which reached us from the din of Mustafa's celebrations.

Deprived of light, deprived of air, deprived of spring, we felt our imprisonment cease to be merely a trial and become utterly unbearable. As long as there had been no possibility of escaping our fate, I had borne our incarceration with a sort of morose passivity, though not with resignation. Now there gleamed on the horizon a faint hope which, alternating with terror, kept me in a state of constant tension; I wanted to leap, to burst, to break the walls surrounding me. Formerly I had not counted the days, for there had been nothing to hope and wait for. Now I looked at my watch every hour, as if that gesture might accelerate the passage of time. I was awaiting deliverance . . . or death. I was on tenterhooks. Only my daily visit to Selim enabled me to control my exasperation, for I wanted to look well, and spent hours trying to dress with taste, covering myself with jewels and scent. Love had become my only discipline.

One evening's whispering session informed me that Bejid had suggested to Mustafa that he call for Baraïktar to deal with Atallah and Kabadji Mustafa and rid him of their yoke. Mustafa had not beaten around the bush. He had answered that he would call Baraïktar when the time came, and calmly announced his intention to kill Mahmud and Selim beforehand as a precautionary measure. Bejid managed not to twitch, and respectfully agreed that the time was not yet ripe.

Selim and Mahmud had narrowly missed being killed—and I with them, for there was no doubt that Sineperver would have included me in the massacre. The retrospective fear and the realization that we were surrounded by danger literally made me shake. For hours I was convulsed with uncontrollable tremors and finally Cevri had to give me a sedative to make it stop.

Thereupon Baraïktar lost patience with the endless postponements, and without warning anyone, set off toward Constantinople at the head of sixteen thousand men. My heart stopped when I learned of it. Death was at our door. Then Baraïktar announced that he was simply coming to join his troops to the Grand Vizier's army in preparation for the Russian campaign. Mustafa and Sineperver swallowed the lie whole. Once again I could breathe, but it had been a near thing.

June and July crawled by in silent, anxious expectation. Then, suddenly, everything stopped. We received no news, as if our lines of communication had been severed. Perhaps a coup was being organized in total secrecy, excluding even our informers?

It took all the efforts of reason to prevent my imagination, inflamed by imprisonment, idleness, and heat, from running wild. Yet the instinct I had acquired in the Orient told me that something was brewing. I felt it in all my joints. But what? When? And at what cost? Every day the temperature of my spirit rose with that of the summer.

CHAPTER 21

—————•❦•—————

IN THE AFTERNOON of July 14, we were roused by the sound of
cannon fire. Was it Baraïktar arriving with his troops? Was deliverance—or death—on its way? No; the rumble issued from another
direction. Suddenly news started coming in again, bringing outrageous and contradictory rumors. What was going on? Our anxiety
was matched only by our confusion. The cannon fire resumed the
next morning. Numerous families summering on the Bosporus took
refuge in the city, bringing news of an artillery battle around Rumeli Fanar, the headquarters of Kabadji Mustafa and his Yamaks.
But no one could tell us who was fighting whom.

The echoes of the battle came to a stop two evenings later, and at
last the picture became a little clearer. Three days before, a hundred
men led by a certain Hadji Ali had slipped into Rumeli Fanar at
night and surrounded the house of Kabadji Mustafa, ordering him
to give himself up in the name of the Sultan. When he had
emerged from the house, puzzled and half asleep, they had cleanly
slit his throat. The Yamaks, drunk with vengeance, had chased

them into an impregnable fortress, and then bombarded them without cease or success.

Weary and leaderless, the Yamaks had finally backed off, and Hadji Ali's little troop had managed to slink away and disappear.

Who was it who had sent him on his mission? Who had ordered the murder of Kabadji Mustafa? Either, as our friends whispered, the Committee of Ruschuk or, as it was claimed in town, Sultan Mustafa himself. Knowledge of the situation at the headquarters of the Grand Vizier and Kabadji Mustafa would have helped to clarify the picture, but strangely enough, no couriers were arriving from Adrianople. Were they being held back? By whom? And why? What was happening at Adrianople?

The bomb exploded, in our prison, on the morning of July 18. On Ali Effendi's information, Idriss told me that Baraïktar and the Grand Vizier, at the head of thirty thousand men, had just arrived in Silivri, twelve miles from Constantinople. In town imaginations ran amok, trying to find an explanation for the ill-timed movement. We even heard rumors that peace had been made with the Russians.

Then our informers announced that Mustafa, in despair, had assembled his advisers, whose talk only increased his panic: Leaderless, the Yamaks would be of no help at all, and most of the janissaries were in the army of the Grand Vizier. Mustafa was reduced to negotiating with Baraïktar. What did the latter want? What was the Grand Vizier doing in all this? For the second time Mustafa proposed to have Selim and Mahmud assassinated as a preliminary precaution. The viziers, who were secret members of the Committee of Ruschuk, labored to convince him that he must first sound out Baraïktar's intentions. Life in our prison seemed suspended. We dared not move, speak, or think. We hardly dared breathe. Our whispering retainers brought fresh news every hour, which we relayed to one another without comments or predictions, under the surveillance of the eunuch spies, who we felt were doubly watchful.

In the evening a message from Baraïktar was brought to Mustafa, a message of fidelity and devotion. Mustafa chose to be reassured and left for Silivri on the pretext of kissing the sacred Standard of the Prophet, which the Grand Vizier was bringing back with the army. Baraïktar threw himself at his feet and swore that his only motive was to defend Mustafa and rid him of those who oppressed him. Mustafa believed him. His relief was as great as the fear he had felt that morning. Fully reassured, he returned to the city—but not alone. The united armies of the Grand Vizier and Baraïktar followed him in and pitched their camps under the walls of Constantinople, at Davutpassa. There, twenty years earlier, Selim had handed the Standard of the Prophet to a young unknown officer, Mustafa Alemdar, who was then given the title of Standard-Bearer—Baraïktar. Salvation and danger followed him hand in hand—for Baraïktar's proximity made the situation explosive.

On July 20, Baraïktar entered Constantinople with five thousand men, installed himself at the Sublime Porte, the Grand Vizier's palace facing the Seraglio, and produced a Hatif Sherif, a decree signed by Mustafa, delegating full powers to him.

His first act was to dismiss Atallah and confiscate his vast and ill-earned fortune. Without waiting to hear more, Atallah hurried off into exile, happy at least to be alive. Baraïktar followed with a massive purge in the next few days: Viziers, ulemas, councillors, and officers among the Yamaks and the janissaries who were accused of having supported the former Sheikh-Ul-Islam were dismissed and replaced by the secret partisans of Selim . . . and Baraïktar.

Was it really possible that Mustafa should continue to believe blindly in Baraïktar's loyalty? Apparently yes—incomprehensible though it was, even from as stupid a man as Sultan Mustafa. As for Sineperver, was she really that drugged by the incense of Baraïktar's flattery, which he burned for her day and night? Lying hidden in the gilded lair of her apartment, she gave no sign of life. Perhaps she was ruminating in satisfaction at the disappearance of her rival for power, Atallah. Baraïktar was gaining ground by the hour. He told all the dignitaries and the ambassadors who flocked to sound him out that he would return to fighting the Russians as soon as he had accomplished his mission for his venerated master Sultan Mustafa. The population had been reassured by the fact that his troops had strictly followed his orders to abstain from any looting or rowdiness, and calm returned to the city.

The Grand Vizier was rubbing his hands with pleasure, for Baraïktar had at last cleared away those who had made him suffer such humiliation; and now he looked forward with great excitement to the fulfillment of Baraïktar's promise to restore his full powers. Mustafa was swimming in happiness at the thought that he had found such a champion of his throne. In short, everyone was pleased, so pleased that Mustafa gave Baraïktar an enormous feast in the open air at Ortaköy, echoes of which wafted through the walls of our prison.

No one in town doubted that Baraïktar had rushed to Constantinople on Mustafa's orders, and perhaps Mustafa himself had come to believe it. Baraïktar played his role as Mustafa's unconditional supporter so well that I myself was shaken. I had known so much treachery that even though he secretly tried to reassure me, I came to wonder what games his ambition was really playing. Having reached the summit of power thanks to Mustafa's weakness, he might well be tempted to remain there and govern, under Mustafa, with far more authority than he would ever have under Selim. I had to remain silent while my doubts gnawed at me. I could share them neither with Mahmud, who now lived only in the expectation of a denouement, whatever it might be, nor with Selim, who trusted Baraïktar—and who, besides, had already drunk the cup of treason and disloyalty to the dregs during his own reign. If Baraïktar remained loyal to us and planned to act, then we were in mortal danger. Should he betray Selim, he would ruin our only hope of ever seeing the end of our incarceration. Both alternatives made me tremble. The visit Ristoglou then paid us did nothing to allay my fears. He came under false pretexts, and the sort of jubilation I detected in his manner gave me the shivers. What, other than the knowledge that our fate was soon to be sealed once and for all, could have inspired such joy in him?

Thus I swayed between terror and despair when, one evening during our brief daily meeting, Selim managed to slip me a message he had just received from Baraïktar. The latter was preparing nothing less than an invasion of the Seraglio in order to free Selim and Mahmud. Everything depended on a single necessary condition: Mustafa's absence from the Seraglio. With the Sultan away, the Seraglio would defend itself only halfheartedly. Furthermore, in the event of danger only Mustafa could give the order to massacre his brother and his cousin. We knew that with the return of spring and order, Mustafa would resume his peregrinations from palace to palace on the shores of the Bosporus with his women. Baraïktar begged us to be as cautious as possible until the given day, to remain on our guard, to be silent, to show no emotion, to beware of everything and everyone, and especially to touch no food except that prepared for us by the most faithful of our slaves. Had Baraïktar got wind of preparations for an attempt on our lives?

His message reassured me as to his intentions and brought my anxiety to an unbearable climax. I came to wish that it were already all over, even at the cost of our death. My resistance had been exhausted, and my reason was sinking in that interminable wait filled with unexpected developments and coups de théâtre. Better death than madness.

On the morning of July 27, a spy informed the Grand Vizier of Baraïktar's real intentions and his imminent plan of action. The Grand Vizier rushed to tell Mustafa of the plot, and Ali Effendi relayed the news to us through Idriss. The torture of uncertainty lasted several hours. I expected the messengers of death to appear at any moment. But no! Mustafa did not hesitate in the choice between the bitter truth brought by a devious functionary and the assurances of his faithful champion. He sharply dismissed the Grand Vizier, ascribing his calumnies to jealousy.

The noose around us loosened—but not for long. The Grand Vizier tried his luck with Ristoglou, who was not as naive as his master, and exhorted him to the massacre of Selim, Mahmud, and the members of the Committee of Ruschuk, whose names had been supplied by the spy. The operation, said the Grand Vizier, ought to be carried out that very night, when Baraïktar had returned to his camp outside the walls at Davutpassa and the gates of the city were closed. Ristoglou laughed in his face: Polluted by intrigue, Ristoglou suspected it in any politician such as the Grand Vizier, but failed to recognize it in a mountain warrior like Baraïktar. In short, that fierce soldier had revealed himself to be a matchless actor, far more able than the old fogies of the Seraglio, professionals in duplicity though they were. Furthermore, upon dismissing the angry and discouraged Grand Vizier, Ristoglou sent a messenger to Baraïktar to inform him of all the "fabrications" being told about him, and to warn him against the Grand Vizier!

Baraïktar immediately let us know of this through Billal Aga, adding that he could not postpone action any longer. Mustafa, Sineperver, and Ristoglou could emerge from their innocence at any moment. Their awakening had to be prevented, and the machinery of the plot set in action before they could react and have us all massacred. However, it was absolutely necessary that Mustafa leave the Seraglio. Time was against us, and Mustafa kept postponing his departure to go gallivanting in his summer houses.

The memory of July 28 is so painful that I lack the courage to write about it. It would only turn the knife in a wound that remains open, eight years later. Once again I shall quote my diary, without reading it.

Friday, July 28, 1808: I must, they say. I must eat, I must sleep, I must take some rest. I cannot. I have to write. I have to organize my thoughts—that, perhaps, might help me to accept. They have at last brought me my writing desk, and now they have left. Now I must. Friday, July 28, 1808—I write the date with difficulty, with revulsion, but I must. I must travel back through the last hours.

I awoke at seven, after little sleep, and dressed. Outside, the sun was already coursing through radiant skies. The heat, as usual, would be stifling. Billal Aga came to tell us that Mustafa was about to leave the Seraglio with his women and his musicians, on his way to the imperial yali of Besiktas, on the Bosporus, on this side of the Christian quarters. A few minutes later I heard the cannon salvos saluting the passage of the imperial barges through the Golden Horn. Sineperver had stayed behind in her apartments.

Was this to be the day we had been awaiting so long, and with such apprehension? Was this the opportunity Baraïktar had been awaiting in order to free us? I drank cup upon cup of coffee, feeling as tense as a bow.

Around noon Billal Aga slipped into the apartment to tell us of what he had just seen from Selim's windows. A troop of soldiers, led by Baraïktar, had skirted the walls of the Seraglio and penetrated the Grand Vizier's palace. Soon afterward the latter had been taken prisoner and led away. Had Baraïktar simply wanted to get rid of his denouncer, or was this the first step of the vast operation that would lead him to the door of our prison? The exhausting torture of waiting began.

Two hours later we heard a loud clamor rising from the city. It seemed that the population had taken to the streets, but we did not know the reasons for their demonstration.

At three in the afternoon Billal Aga informed us that Baraïktar had invaded the Seraglio's First Court. He was engaged in discussions with the Kapu Agassi, the head of Mustafa's white eunuchs. The latter had shut the gates of the Second Court, and Baraïktar threatened to knock them down. We were quite as close to death as to freedom.

Another hour passed, and Billal Aga burst into our drawing room again, his features contorted with terror. He had just come from the Golden Road, where he had seen Mustafa returning from the selamlik. In a tremendous muddle of words and images, he described seeing Mustafa doff the disguise of a peasant's abaya and stride hurriedly toward the apartments of his mother, Sineperver. So Mustafa had returned! Only a miracle could save us.

Mahmud, his old tutor, Amber Aga, Cevri, and Idriss were with me in the drawing room. It was now past five o'clock. Suddenly the sound of voices and hurried steps brought us out into the corridor. Hiding, we saw Mustafa walking with half a dozen men toward Selim's apartment. A few minutes later the silence was pierced by a terrible scream, the horrified shouts of a woman; it stopped, then started again, doubled by the voice of another woman. Then came sounds of a rapid, brutal struggle, and more death cries. I tried to rush there, but Mahmud grabbed me, held me back, and gave an order to Idriss, who dashed away in the direction of

Selim's apartment. We heard the distant sounds of a battering ram, and Idriss returned at a run, haggard, shouting over and over again: "The Sultan orders you to hide. They're coming to kill you!" Amber Aga and Idriss drew their daggers; Cevri rushed over to the little cabinet where the bathwater is heated, and returned with a caldron filled with glowing coals. Sounds of a stampede rose from the nearby staircase, and then they appeared, their sabers drawn, Mustafa's ugly henchmen, the very same ones who . . . Mahmud tried to flee; one of the men threw a dagger, which hit him in the arm. I saw blood spurt from the wound, I saw Cevri throw the burning coals toward the attackers. They leaped backward, screaming. Wounded, Mahmud jumped into a cubbyhole off the room. Mustafa's men regrouped and charged again, throwing us aside to rush after Mahmud. An animal cry burst from my throat. Then Cevri grabbed me, lifted me off my feet, dragged me, screaming, to the closet where the carpets are kept rolled in summer. I stopped screaming; I had become an object, a statue which Cevri threw onto the layers of wool and covered with a carpet. The door was shut. I was alone in total darkness. The whole scene had lasted only a few seconds.

I was alive. The carpets in which I burrowed had been sprinkled with pepper to stave off the humidity, and my nose itched; but I would die if I sneezed. I breathed as little as possible so as not to inhale the pepper. I was alive and even comfortable in my woolly cocoon. I would have liked to stay there forever. My thoughts lurched at the very limits of consciousness, and I was flooded with my earliest memories—of Martinique, of childhood. From time to time my beatitude was torn through by a terrible pain, a pain which bore two names: Mahmud and Selim. Yet what I felt most strongly was the smell of the pepper, and the fringe of the carpet tickling my cheek.

I don't know how long I remained there. But at last the door did open, and I heard footsteps, and Cevri's voice: "It is I, mistress, don't be afraid." I wanted to stay there forever. I didn't move. I gave no sign of life. Cevri then threw herself on the pile of carpets, tore them aside, uncovered me. I was blinded by the light of the torches. At Cevri's side I recognized Billal Aga, Idriss, other eunuchs. Cevri leaned over me, forced me to rise. My clothes were covered in pepper, and I had a violent sneezing fit. At last it subsided, and then I looked about me, dazed. Cevri and Billal Aga were crying. My eyes questioned them. Billal Aga bowed very deeply and,. his voice shaking, said:

"His Highness Sultan Mahmud has sent me to take care of the Valideh."

I didn't understand. My mouth could open only to one name: Selim? Billal Aga dropped his head, racked by sobs, and now I understood. Selim was dead.

When he calmed down, Billal Aga again said: "Sultan Mahmud has sent me to take care of the Valideh." I took pity on that half of me which refused to understand, and explained: I was, as the mother of Sultan Mahmud, the Valideh.

Billal Aga stammered on: "Would the Valideh do me the honor of following me to shelter. There is still danger."

Cevri took me by the hand, and dragged me off once again. I walked through the apartments where I had spent fourteen months as a prisoner. We followed the Golden Road to the harem's mosque, where Billal Aga left me in the care of Cevri and Idriss, who had about a score of eunuchs.

There I was, standing in that room, surrounded by people protecting me. I thought of Selim without pain. Images of our life together, of our happiness, rolled by as in a book. Our meeting in the Cage, our visit to the abandoned palace at Beylerbey, my first outing to the bazaar, our first night of love in the Kiosk of Osman, the picnic at the Grand Signor's Ladder with Selim, picking wildflowers ... summer nights through which we would whisper in each other's arms among the scented bushes, winter nights making love by the fire, autumn nights when the rain shut us in with each other, spring nights talking and kissing on the balcony under the stars. The rare torches barely lit the narrow mosque, and the glazed tiles on the walls threw green reflections on us. I tried to force myself to imagine what life would be like without him, but could not. It was not conceivable. Strangely enough, I did not wonder about the circumstances of his death.

Suddenly the Seraglio was shaken by cannon fire. I didn't react. These salvos, they told me, saluted the accession of Sultan Mahmud. Then a clamor rose, grew, rumbled through the high, narrow windows of the harem's mosque: "Long live Sultan Mahmud! Long live Sultan Mahmud!" I was told these were the voices of Baraïktar's soldiers.

Soon afterward there were hurried steps and shouts in the corridor. Idriss and his eunuchs were on the defensive, their weapons ready. As they drew closer I recognized Mustafa's voice, by turns furious and imploring:

"How dare you raise a hand against your Padishah!"

A woman's voice, Sineperver's, rang out hysterically over his:

"May he be damned forever, that Sultan Mahmud! May she be damned, Selim's whore! May they die! May they suffer! May they know the fires of hell! May they be damned, damned, damned now and forever!"

Sineperver's maledictions echoed in the corridor for a long time afterward. Damned! Forever damned. They had passed. They had been vanquished. They had been taken prisoner.

Again we had to wait, but I hardly cared. I no longer expected anything. My eyes were locked on the naive Iznik images of the Holy Cities of Mecca and Medina on the walls. I was absorbed in the details of minarets, mosques, houses, ramparts, the black stone of the Kaaba . . .

Night had fallen when the door opened to admit Billal Aga. "His Highness the Padishah awaits the Valideh," he said. I followed him along the Golden Road. Eunuchs carrying a stretcher came from the opposite direction. In front of me, Billal Aga shuddered and stopped in his tracks. I went up to the stretcher. I recognized the bloodstained yellow silk cover; it used to be in Selim's room. I drew it away to find the corpse of my beloved. His green robe and his short embroidered coat were torn and darkly streaked. Half his black beard had been torn off. The open wounds on his face had stopped bleeding. Despite his suffering and the horror of his end, his face had found in death a peaceful expression. He had reached at long last the peace he aspired to all his life. I kissed his cheek, which was already cold. Around his neck I saw the blue ribbon, and I removed the miniature, my portrait. The glass had been broken in the struggle, and it was spattered with a few drops of blood. I kept it in my hand, drew the cover over Selim's remains, and set off again behind Billal Aga.

There was a crowd of soldiers and dignitaries on the terraces of the selamlik. We crossed the threshold of the Hall of Circumcision and at last I saw Mahmud. He came toward me, took me in his arms, held me close without a word. We were surrounded by men, and my first impulse was to put on my veil, but Mahmud gently drew my hand away.

"Don't veil yourself, Nakshidil. It is the Valideh's prerogative to appear unveiled before anyone."

At last I dared look at Mahmud. He was in a pitiful state, his wounded arm clumsily bandaged; his clothes were torn and bloodstained. Despite his appearance he exuded an impressive authority—even majesty. It was with a sort of pride that he introduced the men around him, those who had saved us: Baraïktar, Bejid Effendi.

I smiled like an automaton, watching these men bow before me in a fog. The introductions were almost over when, from the ranks of spectators, Ali Effendi rushed forward, fell to his knees, kissed my feet, sobbing with joy, with grief. By what miracle was my Ali Effendi here? I drew him up, consoled him. His familiar presence soothed me. Very soon he gathered his spirits and turned back into the Ali Effendi I had always known, zealous, opportune, taking care of everything. He took me to a sofa, sat me down, ordered a meal, forced me to eat. I wasn't hungry, but suddenly I was happy to eat.

Dignitaries, messengers, military men came and went without cease. Mahmud, standing in the midst of his subjects, spoke, listened, decided, distributed directives. Beside him Baraïktar barked brief, sharp orders. I did not tire of watching Mahmud, as if I had never seen him before, as if it were a miracle to see him. And it was. God had saved him, and there he was, my son—the Sultan.

It was already late at night when the room emptied and he joined me. For a few moments there was silence between us, a silence we dared not break to speak of Selim. We had to hold together, if only for each other. Forcing myself to keep an even tone of voice, I invited him to share my meal. It was a good idea; he threw himself like a starving man on the dishes brought by Ali Effendi. Our apprehension lessened while we ate; he asked how I felt and what had happened to me. I told him how Cevri had saved me from our aggressors, how she had borne me away and hidden me under the carpets. I emphasized the anecdotal, distracted him, reassured him.

He had fallen asleep, crushed by fatigue, lulled by my story. I laid him down on the sofa and covered him with a light blanket, as I used to do when he was small, and called Ali Effendi to bring me my quills and my paper. In my hand I still held the miniature stained with Selim's blood. I wrote: Friday, July 28, 1808.

The following morning I called Baraïktar and Billal Aga to the Pavilion of Circumcision and asked Mahmud to have the dignitaries, the military people, and the eunuchs leave. Once I was alone with the three men, I said: "You are the principal witnesses to what happened yesterday—I want to know exactly what it was. I want to know exactly how Sultan Selim died. Don't spare me a single detail." Mahmud seemed deeply surprised, and Billal Aga, somewhat embarrassed, hesitated. "I died with Sultan Selim," I told them, "and I have a right to know how."

Baraïktar was not a man to ask questions. He began: "Early yesterday, as soon as I heard that Mustafa had left for Besiktas, I struck my camp at Davutpassa and entered Constantinople with fifteen thousand men. The population cheered loudly when it saw the Standard of the Prophet, thinking I was bringing it back to the Chamber of the Sacred Cloak. I left most of my troops on the square of At Meydan and took a small detachment to the palace of the Grand Vizier, whom I arrested. I tore the Seal of the Empire from him with my own hands.

"Then, still carrying the Standard of the Prophet, I came to the gates of the Seraglio. The janissaries stationed in the First Court fell to their knees before the sacred relic, and thus I was able to enter the Seraglio. No difficulty arose until I reached the Second Court. There the Bostandgy baj had barricaded the gates. I began to negotiate. The Kapu Agassi was ready to give in; the Bostandgy baj was not. He would open the gates, he shouted, only on Sultan Mustafa's order. Then I lost control of my temper and made the fatal mistake of revealing my true intentions. The Bostandgy baj was standing atop the ramparts, and I shouted back to him: 'This has nothing to do with Mustafa! It's Sultan Selim that you must ask for orders, you vile slave! Sultan Selim is our only master! We've come to free him from his enemies and place him once again on the throne of his ancestors!'

"At that moment the Kizlar Aga Ristoglou appeared on the ramparts. He pretended to give in to my demands. He claimed that Sultan Selim was going to be taken out of his prison and delivered to me. What I failed to count on, however, was Sineperver's presence in the harem. I have been told that she sent a messenger to fetch Mustafa at Besiktas as soon as she heard of the arrest of the Grand Vizier and the movements of my troops around the Seraglio. Sultan Mustafa left his women and his musicians, threw a peasant's abaya over his caftan, jumped into a passing boat, and had himself put ashore on the beach below the Seraglio gardens. Thus while Ristoglou negotiated with me in the hope of gaining time, Sultan Mustafa was already within the walls, conferring with his mother. It is on her advice that he prepared to commit his crime. He gathered a few eunuchs and dignitaries around him and rushed off to Sultan Selim's apartment."

Baraïktar fell silent. After a long interval, Billal Aga began his story.

"When they broke into his yellow-and-silver room on the second floor, Sultan Selim was in the midst of his prayers. With him were Refet, a gedikli named Pakiseh, and I. When he saw his assassins burst in with daggers drawn, Sultan Selim stood up.

"'Are you the executioners?' he asked.

"'You are the cause of all these troubles," answered the eunuch Nezir Aga. Sultan Selim turned to Mustafa and asked to be allowed to finish his prayers. Mustafa did not answer. The men had been held back for a moment by Sultan Selim's calm. Now they began to close in on him. At that moment Sultan Selim saw Idriss running up behind them. He drew his dagger, and ordered Idriss to put you, Sultana Nakshidil, and Sultan Mahmud in safety. Before the final assault, Sultan Selim said, 'Allah is great.'

"The gedikli Pakiseh threw herself between Sultan Selim and the attackers. A dagger stabbed her hand, and both she and Refet began to scream. The first saber thrust split his cheek, but Sultan Selim's own dagger dispatched two eunuchs who had lunged at him. Mustafa tried to stab him, but a blow of Sultan Selim's hand threw him aside—Sultan Selim's diamond left a mark on Mustafa's cheek. But there were too many of them, and despite the skill and the courage with which he defended himself, Sultan Selim soon fell to the swords of Mustafa's henchmen. Ristoglou, who had returned in haste, was the most enthusiastic of the assassins. Sultan Selim had been stabbed more than twenty times when Mustafa's favorite eunuch came to finish the job with the silk bowstring. I tried to intercede; I threw myself on my master's already inert body. I wanted to protect his neck, but my hands were cruelly mangled."

Billal Aga, choked with emotion, interrupted his story. He began to cry softly. Baraïktar finished for him.

"It must have been at the very moment when Sultan Selim died that I understood something had gone wrong. I decided to knock down the gates of the Second Court with battering rams. But Mustafa had foreseen the move. In order that I be immediately informed of the failure of my coup in the event of my managing to invade the Seraglio, he had Sultan Selim's corpse placed well in sight within the throne room; at the same time he sent his assassins off to your apartment, Sultana."

I turned to Mahmud. "What happened to you after Cevri slowed them down with the hot coals?" I asked.

"I was wounded in the arm," Mahmud answered. "I managed to

dive into a cubbyhole off the drawing room. Luckily this cubbyhole was the only room with a window, if you can call it a window. I slipped through, cutting my arms and hands on the broken glass, and found myself on the roofs of the harem. I darted up and down between domes and chimneys to evade my pursuers, who were still close behind. The light was failing, and I took refuge in the shadows of a narrow recess. There I waited for them to give up the search. When I could no longer hear their footsteps, I left my hiding place and began to wander the rooftops, not knowing where to go or what to do next. Finally I came to a portion of the roof overhanging the little courtyard of the white eunuchs' kitchen, where several people were gathered. My shadow on the ground beside them drew their attention. An old iman, who luckily had remained faithful to us, recognized me immediately. The men in the courtyard tied their belts together and threw the improvised rope up to me. I tied one end around a chimney and slithered down. The old iman took me to the nearby apartment of the Kapu Agassi, the chief white eunuch, where he dressed my wounds in makeshift bandages. I was dusted off, cleaned up a little, and given a pair of slippers, for I had lost mine in my flight. Then suddenly the old iman bowed low before me, kissed the soiled and torn edge of my robe, and, trembling, uttered, almost incomprehensibly: 'Long life to Sultan Mahmud!'

"Completely puzzled, unable to understand what was expected of me, I followed the old iman to the Third Court—it was already in the hands of your soldiers, Baraïktar—and let myself be led to the porch of the throne room. Only there did I understand. Sultan Selim's mutilated corpse, half hidden by a bloodstained cover, lay on a long slab of porphyry. Next to it knelt a sobbing man—you, Baraïktar."

"It was I, Padishah," continued Baraïktar. "I had rushed through the open Gate of Felicity shouting, 'We want Sultan Selim!' Then I came face to face with Ristoglou. Pushing the corpse with his foot, he spat, 'Here he is—your Sultan.'

"So I grieved over the remains of the master I had been unable to save. While I cried I heard one of my lieutenants, Ramiz Pasha, say, 'It is not right, Baraïktar, to cry like a woman. Better to avenge Sultan Selim.'

"Spurred, I stood up, my saber already in hand. At that moment the old iman stepped forward, leading Sultan Mahmud by the hand."

"And then you asked, 'Who is this?'" interrupted Mahmud, a hint of acid in his voice. "It's true you'd never seen me before. Then the old iman said, 'He is our lord, Sultan Mahmud. The throne is his. I have already pledged allegiance, and you must do the same.'"

Baraïktar, who could never be stripped of his composure, continued his story. "I fell to my knees before my Sultan and told him: 'My lord, I had come to put your cousin back on the throne. Now that my eyes—may they be blinded—have beheld this sight, let me console myself by placing you on the throne!' Then all my soldiers acclaimed Sultan Mahmud with a formidable ovation.

"I wanted the immediate execution of Mustafa and the traitors who had served him, but Sultan Mahmud silenced me. 'I shall not begin my reign with vengeance, but with justice,' he told me. 'Arrest them, but don't harm them.'"

Mahmud finished: "It was nevertheless necessary to find Mustafa and Sineperver. Frantic searches were conducted throughout the Seraglio. Finally they were found hiding in the Mabeyn, my father's old apartment, which has been shut since his death. They were arrested and led off to their temporary prison."

I already knew the rest: The Bayran Throne was taken out and set down at the Gate of Felicity; and there, in the presence of Baraïktar's soldiers and the few available dignitaries, my son, Sultan Mahmud, was hastily and unceremoniously placed on the throne.

PART 5

THE VALIDEH SULTANA

CHAPTER 22

———————⟡⟡———————

MAHMUD HAD forbidden the popular celebrations which normally follow the accession of a new sultan. The empire, he decreed, was in mourning for Sultan Selim. And so it was, in all sincerity.

His burial took place amid general sorrow. An immense procession, led by Mahmud, followed his remains—wrapped, according to custom, in a simple white shroud—to the Laleli Mosque, the Mosque of the Tulips, far beyond the bazaar. Selim had wanted to be buried there, next to his father Mustafa III.

I did not attend the funeral—none of the harem could—but from the windows of the Hall of Circumcision I saw thousands of barges ferrying the population through the Golden Horn to the Laleli Mosque. The homage to Selim most genuinely popular in spirit was given in the coffeehouses of Constantinople; there the humble citizens thronged around the storytellers and, crying and lamenting, listened to the dramatic (and considerably embellished) tale of his death.

Constantinople cried, and my own eyes remained dry; the population which mourned Selim with such sincerity was the very same one which had contributed to his downfall. The fickleness of nations is legendary, and that particular one had been skillfully misled by Selim's enemies. And then it is a law in the Orient that a man in power, no matter how feared, how hated, is immediately redeemed by his misfortune and downfall. Selim's death had transformed him from a cursed and reviled master into a popular hero. This idealization, however, could not return him to life or to me. Had the people not risen against him, he might still be alive today. A few weeks later I made the following entry in my diary:

The sorrow of Constantinople leaves me unmoved. I am indifferent to everything—to the mourning of an empire, to the fleeting days, to events, to a glorious spring, to life itself. Indifferent, perhaps, even to Mahmud. Why don't I put an end to my days, swallow a cupful of poison as Selim wanted to on the evening he lost his throne? Nothing would be easier—but then I am quite as indifferent to death as to life.

I live only within my dreams. Confused images of Selim arise and recede before me. My memory tries to fix their smallest details, and I linger over them as long as possible, lost in my past, frozen in a sort of catalepsy.

I feel hollow, as if my blood and my sap had been drained from me. As if my heart had stopped beating. And yet I sleep, I rise, dress, eat, go about my business, according to my unchanged schedule. I maintain the discipline I forced on myself in prison, though now my prison is nothing more than myself and my memory. Why do I impose these tasks on myself? I wonder. Perhaps I do it through instinct, unthinkingly. In short, I live as an automaton.

And it was that same automaton who had become: "most illustrious and chaste Princess; crown of continence; reigning sovereign; lady of noblest extraction, gifted with the purest of qualities and celestial character; diadem of her sex; mistress of the holy places, risen to the most sublime glory; star of the seventh heaven, and full moon among the stars; mother-of-pearl of the empire; foremost gem of the imperial crown."

These were just a few of the Valideh's titles. Since I was the Sultan's adoptive mother only, Mahmud had been compelled to issue a Hatif Sherif to raise me to the Valideh's position. I was granted it officially in a solemn ceremony similar to that which had welcomed Mirizshah and then Sineperver. The entire harem awaited me in the Court of the Valideh, with, at its head, the new Kizlar Aga, whom Mahmud had recently appointed—Ali Effendi himself, beaming, dressed in a red pelisse trimmed with black fur and a white turban which almost doubled his height. He introduced my household: the Bearer of the Seal, the Mistress of the Robes, the Preparer of Coffee, the Mistress of Sherbets . . . and my Treasurer, kind Idriss; though no genius, he was the most honest eunuch on earth, an essential quality for the post.

Then Mahmud brought me to the Valideh's apartments, which I knew so well. Almost nothing had changed there since I had decorated them for Mirizshah, but I noticed that Sineperver had indulged her pettiness as far as to have the dedicatory inscription to Selim's mother erased.

I hoped that Vartui, in Allah's paradise, could see her dearest hopes fulfilled. Henceforth I was the second-highest personage of the empire and the Mistress of the Imperial Harem. I had the use of an immense fortune and thousands of slaves. I stood at the very summit, as mother of the reigning Sultan, and Euphemia David's prophecy had been fulfilled to its end: the steps rising to my son's throne were soiled with the blood of Selim.

I was condemned to live in the room next to his, that room where he had welcomed me so often and where he had been assassinated. I went there that same evening, after the ceremony, when at last I was left alone. I took the corridor I had had built so that Mirizshah could communicate with her son. Selim's yellow-and-silver room seemed intact, the same room I had always known; all traces of the violence had been erased. But it was an empty, deserted, desolate room. I myself had been raised to the highest position in the empire; there was not a woman who did not envy me; I was only thirty-five years old, and I felt exactly like that room, empty, deserted, desolate. I understood then that even if I lived many years more, my life had in fact come to an end on the twenty-eighth of July, cut off by the sword thrusts that had pierced Selim.

As if to point out the vanity of honors, Mahmud ordered me

never to move about, as was my habit, without an escort of armed eunuchs. Some of Mustafa's partisans were still hiding in the Seraglio, and even the harem was less than safe in those first days of Mahmud's reign.

Baraïktar, who had been made Grand Vizier immediately after recognizing Mahmud as Sultan, carried on the business of purifying the Seraglio, and execution followed execution at a good pace. Ristoglou, for his decisive role in Selim's death, was the first to be submitted to capital punishment. He was beheaded, and because of his high rank, his head was displayed on a silver platter. He was the forerunner of a long procession to pass through the hands of the executioner, for none of those who had supported Mustafa or dabbled in Selim's assassination were spared. They were hunted down in every corner and dragged before the executioner in the First Court. The heads of the Bostandgy baj, who had refused Baraïktar access to the Second Court, of the Yamak and janissary officers who had participated in the revolt against Selim, were soon placed with those of his assassins in the niches at the Imperial Gate, or, according to their rank, stuck on pikes before the Middle Gate.

Mahmud's wish was that his reign be one of reconciliation; but Baraïktar's thirst for vengeance was so strong, and his repression so fierce, that in the end Mahmud was forced to take his first steps as a ruler on a carpet of cadavers.

After Mahmud had ordered Baraïktar to spare Mustafa's life that first night, the latter had been locked up in the same apartment that had been Mahmud's prison and mine. Sineperver and Princess Esmee had been shunted off to the Old Seraglio.

As for Mustafa's kadins, they had literally vanished into thin air. No one, in the confusion of those weeks, could have said where they were. Had they been packed away in the Old Seraglio on Baraïktar's order? That was the general assumption, but no one knew for certain.

Baraïktar punished, and Mahmud rewarded. Cevri, whose presence of mind with the hot coals had saved his life in the tragedy of July 28, was awarded a substantial pension and named Khaya Kadin, superintendent of the harem, the post once occupied by Vartui.

It was a position an illiterate slave like her could normally never have aspired to. Though she lacked subtlety, Cevri was gifted with extraordinary energy ... and a build which could not fail to inspire awe in her flock.

The families of the reformers who had been assassinated or dispossessed when Selim was overthrown saw their possessions and their honors restored. I directed Mahmud's attention to Refet and Pakiseh, those women who had tried to save Selim's life at the risk of their own. Refet was given a sum of money and a yali at Besiktas, where—an unprecedented honor—she was allowed to retire, rather than be forced to rot in the Old Seraglio, the fate usually reserved for the kadins of a defunct sultan. Pakiseh's hand was given in marriage to a young and dashing aide to Baraïktar, and she was furnished with a handsome dowry for the occasion.

Mahmud's enthronement on the evening of July 28 had been somewhat hurried, owing to the circumstances, and it was decided that his official coronation would take place with full pomp on the concourse of the holy Mosque of Eyub, a place of pilgrimage outside the walls, at the end of the Golden Horn.

I kept Mahmud company while he dressed for the ceremony in the room of his father, Abdul Hamid, where he had chosen to live. He had already slipped on his sleeveless ermine-trimmed caftan, and was preparing to don his turban. Our eyes met in the silver mirror held before him by a eunuch.

"I knew that one day you would be Sultan," I said. "I was sure of it even in the most desperate days of our imprisonment. And now I know that you shall succeed and that you shall be a great Sultan."

"I don't 'feel' the future like you," he answered with a smile.

"But I always wanted to help Selim and now I want to continue his work. You are so young, and yet you have already walked through a hail of events and tragedies. At least the trial, hard as it was, will have tempered you."

"Perhaps—but still I need you so, Mama Nakshidil." He had turned around and taken my hands in his. He held them very tight, his eyes staring into mine.

"You need me, Mahmud? What could I do for you? I did my

best, what I thought best, when you were a child. Then Selim trained you. You are ready. What could I give you now, my son?"

"Love and strength—the two virtues that mark you most deeply. With them you sustained Selim, and with them you will sustain me. Don't lose yourself in your grief, Mama Nakshidil. Don't abandon me."

Emotion was rising in me like a fever, but it was not the time to cry. "That old witch Euphemia David was right yet again," I said, as lightly as I could. "She did tell me my son would be a powerful ruler."

"A ruler, yes—but not powerful yet!" Mahmud had returned to the mirror to affix the three aigrettes to his turban. He continued in French, so that the eunuchs would not understand.

"I shall be powerful only when those who put me on the throne, and now keep the power for themselves, are gone."

I did not answer. I knew that one day my son, Sultan Mahmud, would be powerful indeed.

I admired his looks. Although not very tall, he was well proportioned, and his body, conditioned by sports, was all muscle and agility. He had inherited the hazel eyes of his mother, the French kadin, and wore a short black beard. The reserve and dignity of his orphaned childhood had grown into impressive majesty. Even I was awed by his gravity and his authority, which were startling in a man so young. I could see the respect he inspired in his servants—a respect which included an obscure fear. It was not likely that anyone would joke in his presence or contradict him. His straightforward gaze seemed to pierce one. And yet his stony expression could easily shift into a disarming smile, the smile of a charmer. He was subject to terrible rages, but in general he never lapsed from the icy courtesy he displayed to everyone, from the Vizier down to the lowliest of slaves.

He left after bidding me goodbye. There was a hedge of janissaries, in purple uniforms, stretching all the way to the Eyub. Mahmud was renowned for his grace and his agility on horseback. He rode a white purebred with a saddle and a harness of gold inlaid with rubies and turquoise. The Sword-Bearer rode at his right side, carrying the Sultan's ceremonial weapon sparkling with diamonds. On his left, the Master of the Wardrobe threw coins to the people. The household dignitaries followed, in the midst of a trotting throng of pages, messengers, and guards.

The Valideh did not attend the ceremony. The hints of summer had drawn me to the Seraglio gardens, and my steps guided me to the Kiosk of the Pearl, the guardian of so many memories. While Mahmud received the simple iron blade of his ancestors, over there in the Eyub, I stood on the balcony where I had so often lingered with Selim, dreaming of Selim, seeing him, hearing him. Suddenly my attention was drawn to some shapeless sacks lolling in the water, some of them washed up on the shore below the Seraglio walls. Intrigued, I called the gardeners who were at work around me and asked them to inspect the strange flotsam.

From my balcony I watched the gardeners walk down to the first sack, split it open with a knife, and discover a woman's corpse, hideously disfigured by days in the water. The greenish skin of the face and limbs fell away in shreds. The eyes were no more than black holes, and the lipless mouth was open on an atrocious smile. Long black tresses were plastered to her body like dark tentacles. There were twenty-one other sacks floating sluggishly in the ripples, twenty-one other corpses of women. I needed no further explanation; the women drowned in the Bosporus were Mustafa's twenty-two kadins and favorites, whose disappearance had remained unexplained. Baraïktar had not hesitated to commit that senseless act of cruelty against innocent women whose only crime was to have belonged to Mustafa.

Paralyzed with horror and revulsion, my heart in my mouth, unable to tear myself away from the nightmarish vision, I stood there until Mahmud, returning from the ceremony, came to look for me. His face was a terrifying mask of rage. For a moment I thought he had already heard of the poor drowned women. I was wrong.

"Baraïktar!" he spat. "I won't ever forgive his extraordinary impudence. Sacred tradition holds that on the day of the coronation of a sultan, all those present at the ceremony have to come unarmed.

Even the janissaries and the guards replace their weapons with white sticks as a sign of peace and faith. And yet Baraïktar appears in war uniform, armed to the teeth and surrounded by his personal guard of three hundred men, all of them with rifles, sabers, and yataghans. It was a useless provocation, a sacrilege in a holy place, and a personal insult to me. It caused indignation not only to me but to the entire gathering. Why this absurd display of force? Did the Grand Vizier Baraïktar simply want to make a show of power? You don't say anything, Mama Nakshidil. You seem horrified."

Silently I showed him the cadavers of Mustafa's twenty-two odalisques. Mahmud understood immediately, and his rage against Baraïktar lost all measure. He began to shout insults at the absent Grand Vizier, promising vengeance.

"Instead of shouting, Mahmud, you would do better to take steps and make it clear to Baraïktar that he cannot indulge all his whims."

"And how can I do that?" Mahmud asked bitterly. "Baraïktar governs in my place. Baraïktar has put all his own men in the key posts without consulting me. Baraïktar holds the whole machine of the state in his hands. Baraïktar holds all the power himself."

"Baraïktar put you on the throne, and he is faithful to you."

"Do you really think so, Nakshidil? He made me, and he can just as easily destroy me. He never meant to give me the throne. He chose me on the spur of the moment, simply because he had no other prince close at hand. He keeps me because he thinks me docile."

"You have your own supporters; you have the sacred power you were invested with this very day."

"I know," he said, before ironically intoning the list of his titles. "I am now 'the Emperor of the powerful Emperors, the support of the great men of this century, the distributor of crowns, the shadow of God on earth; the protector of Mecca and Medina, the holy places, the cradle of faith, and of Holy Jerusalem; the sovereign of the three great cities, Constantinople, Adrianople, and Brusa; the master of Damascus, the scent of paradise, of Tripoli, of Syria, of Cairo, alone of her kind; of all Arabia, of Africa, of Iraq, of Basra, of

Baghdad'—an unknown, a product of the Seraglio, whom the entire empire, including Baraïktar, thinks of as an ignorant, indecisive, inexperienced young man. In other words, I am nothing."

"You shall be something, you shall be a great Sultan, and I will be at your side to help you become one."

Mahmud was not entirely mistaken. The laws of the Seraglio, though considerably softened by Selim, had made of him an unknown. Besides Selim and myself, none had had the opportunity to gauge his ability and his knowledge. Only a few reformers, a few of Selim's collaborators, had known him well, but they were all dead, massacred by Mustafa's men. Mahmud had participated in no political or military activity. He had been given no opportunity to make himself known to his empire. And now, at the age of twenty-three, he saw everything raining down upon him in dramatic circumstances: a throne, an empire in disarray, millions of subjects who knew nothing of their new Sultan . . . and Baraïktar. My son was alone to face this avalanche, and I could not leave him like that; I had to shed my indifference, emerge from my lethargy.

"I will be at your side," I had promised, and I swore to myself I would keep that promise. I did not stop to wonder whether I was satisfied to be thus returned to the present. My instincts as well as my duty commanded me to help Mahmud. But he was much harder to help than Selim. He did not lack self-confidence, nor application or determination. And then he was so withdrawn, so difficult to get through to, to reach, even for me. I had to help him, but how could I? That crucial and urgent question brought me back, independently of my will, into reality.

The foremost problem was Baraïktar. Once he had been poor, and now he suddenly found himself smothered with honors and riches. He was only a man, a fallible creature subject to the temptations of perversion and corruption. Furthermore, he was a man who had devoted himself to a master, a single master, Selim. Now that the latter had died, Baraïktar refused any new allegiance. He was a man without a master, intoxicated by the heady air he breathed at the summit after an amazing ascent.

He grew irritated when he felt in Mahmud an unspoken resistance to his dictates. Although stripped of power, Mahmud by his very person was a presence, a weight on Baraïktar's own power. He tried to intimidate Mahmud. He made a ceremonial visit to an obscure descendant of the Great Conqueror, Genghis Khan, who lived in poverty in Constantinople, and covered him in honors and gifts. Mahmud, like myself, understood the hint: If the Sultan did not show himself more flexible, there was always the possibility of inventing a new dynasty. . . . And there Baraïktar had gone too far.

I then thought of Vassilo, Baraïktar's beloved wife, who was now enthroned in the closed quarters of the Grand Vizier's palace. I liked to imagine that our first meeting, two years before, and the friendly complicity that had arisen between us, had played a part in Baraïktar's efforts for Selim. I received Vassilo in the sitting room I had designed for Mirizshah. She was graceful, fragile, young-looking; but I knew that the air of youthfulness was not to be trusted. I opened fire immediately:

"Is your husband the savior of my son, or his tyrant?"

"How can you ask, Sultana? Didn't my husband put Sultan Mahmud on the throne?"

"Then why does he invent other pretenders? Why does he cultivate, for instance, that absurd descendant of Genghis Khan?"

Vassilo bowed her head and thought for a moment before launching her counterattack:

"My husband follows faithfully the politics of Sultan Selim—blessed be his memory—and has no other goal than to bring to fruition the work of his master. That is proof enough, Sultana."

She was right. Baraïktar followed in Selim's footsteps, having taken up the entirety of his program for reform. And yet . . .

"I cannot be satisfied, Vassilo, when your husband, through presumptuousness and brutality, offends the janissaries, the ulemas, and many of Sultan Selim's old partisans. Why does he insist on making enemies where he used to make friends?"

Vassilo weakened. She told me how Baraïktar had changed recently, and confessed that she suffered from it. He no longer listened to anyone—not even to Vassilo, although he remained completely attached to her. She thought that someone had cast a spell on him, that he was a victim of the evil eye. Evil eye or not, I continued:

"Vassilo, listen to me. Your husband's interests lie in the same direction as the Sultan's. Their only goal is the regeneration of the empire. My son has no other support than Baraïktar, and Baraïktar will not find any support more solid than the Sultan. Why must he alienate my son with his intransigence and his insolence? I beg of you, Vassilo, bring your husband back into the path of honor and devotion to the Sultan. Bring him back to reason."

She promised warmly, but I felt her pessimism. She was no longer confident of her influence over her husband, of her ability to steer him away from his race down the path of disaster. At the summit of power, he seemed to incur deliberately the enmity of every party. Recently there had been a revolt at Ruschuk, and in order to crush it, Baraïktar had sent most of the troops who ensured his power in Constantinople. That unexpected and incomprehensible explosion within Baraïktar's own fiefdom reminded me too much of the rebellion of Ismaël Aga, which had been organized, financed, and directed from Constantinople itself by a conspiracy— that first conspiracy against Selim, which Baraïktar had nipped in the bud by beheading his chief, Ismaël Aga. The Ruschuk revolt smelled of a plot, and I told Vassilo as much. To my surprise, she agreed.

"I told my husband, but he chose not to believe me. His partisans tried to warn him, and encouraged him to take preventive measures. He only laughed at them. Yes, Sultana, the empire bends before Baraïktar, and yet he has never been in greater danger."

I was surprised that a young Albanian peasant woman should have an understanding so much deeper and clearer than that of her husband, the Grand Vizier. But are women not more intuitive than men? Vassilo let herself go, and opened her heart to me. She feared for her husband. She faced the future with lucidity and foreboding. She felt the hatred of the people rising against Baraïktar, and guessed that his enemies were growing in number and organizing on fertile plotting ground.

"Whatever happens, I shall remain at his side, and if need be I shall die with him. I love him, Sultana, and I shall love him to the very last."

My interview with Vassilo only reinforced my admiration and my sympathy for her. But it also disturbed me, all the more because I did not know what to do.

That year Ramadan, the Muslim Lent, ended in mid-November. I was relieved to see it go, for it is a period that invariably generates agitation among the people. They are not allowed to eat from sunrise to sundown for forty days, and the need to eat at night deprives them of sleep—and all this bares the nerves, and encourages aggressiveness and quarrels.

One afternoon Ali Effendi came to tell me that there was some trouble in the city. Following the custom, the Grand Vizier, surrounded by his guard, had gone to visit the Sheikh-Ul-Islam, whose palace was surrounded by a crowd of onlookers. Baraïktar gave orders to have the bystanders dispersed and given a drubbing. There were several wounded. I had lived through hundreds of such incidents, and did not pay this one any particular attention. A few hours later it was Mahmud who came in. The "wounded" of Baraïktar's drubbing now sat in the coffeehouses, embroidering on the accounts of brutality and delivering incendiary speeches against Baraïktar. The city was simmering. I was accustomed to that as well, and did not worry. Then came cries of "Yangum war"—"Fire"—and the drumrolls sounding the alarm. Several blocks of houses were burning in the vicinity of the Grand Vizier's palace. Fires were, alas, too frequent to upset me. I left for my daily inspection of the harem. When I returned to my sitting room I found it stinking of smoke. I rushed to the window. Beyond the walls of the Seraglio, the palace of the Grand Vizier was in flames. It was the evening of November 14, 1808. I saw, I understood, and—at last—I worried.

I saw the outbuildings burning like firebrands; the janissaries were spreading flammable matter to feed the blaze. I saw the Grand Vizier's guards rush to put out the flames; I saw them killed under the blows of the janissaries. I could see the fire gaining ground, and the wings of Baraïktar's palace catching one by one. I saw the fleeing occupants of the palace—scribes, employees, guards, slaves—caught and killed, their throats slit by the janissaries who surrounded the building. I heard the cries of the dying, the crash of roofs caving in, the roar of the fire. The palace of the Grand Vizier was now a gigantic incandescent mass, an infernal bonfire cheered on by the vengeful crowd of Constantinople.

There I stood, turned to stone, when Idriss came to tell me that soldiers had invaded the Seraglio's gardens and were headed for the selamlik. My first reaction was lassitude. Not again . . . But yes. Again. I no longer cared what happened to me. I did not care if I lost my life. I couldn't care less about the fate of Constantinople or the empire. I simply did not mind anymore. But there was Mahmud. The fire of a familiar terror coursed through me. Were the soldiers Idriss had seen friends, or enemies? Mahmud! I ran to the Hall of Circumcision, where he liked to work. He was there. He reassured me. The soldiers had come to protect us. They had been brought from Scutari by Cadi Pasha, the former head of the Nizami-Jedid, once Selim's champion and now Baraïktar's.

"And what of Baraïktar?" I asked.

"He escaped the fire with his wife, Vassilo. He has left for Adrianople to get reinforcements."

"Is it a revolution, then?"

"Barely a revolt. And a strange revolt, at that—without a watchword, without a leader. It's just that spirits are overheated by the fast of Ramadan. The people are exasperated with Baraïktar. The janissaries, as usual, have joined in the fun. But don't fear, Nakshidil. Measures have been taken, our troops are on alert, and the Seraglio has better defenses than a fortress."

I believed him so well that I was completely reassured. Though so young, Mahmud had an extraordinary knack for inspiring confidence in others.

I was awakened at dawn by the sound of rifle fire. Our defenders had fired from the Seraglio walls on "assailants" who turned out to be not rebels but just people who had come for a look. Then came cannon fire, the echoes of which shook my walls. The Capitan Pasha, the admiral, a faithful follower of Baraïktar, had sailed his fleet around the Seraglio to shell the palace of the janissaries' aga. Then everything calmed down; the eve's excitement had waned, and the population hid in their houses; the janissaries, cowed by the Capitan Pasha's shells, were silent in their barracks. Baraïktar was approaching Constantinople at the head of his reinforcements, and the news of his impending arrival instilled panic in the rebels and increased tenfold the ardor of Cadi Pasha's troops defending us. When evening fell, Mahmud assembled his advisers in the Hall of Circumcision and expressly asked me to attend the meeting. There were half a dozen of Baraïktar's partisans, those who had been with him from the early days: the Capitan Pasha, Cadi Pasha, Bejid Effendi, who had played such an important part within the Committee of Ruschuk, etc. The insurgents were demoralized and hesitant. Mahmud suggested a general amnesty. Cadi Pasha violently opposed such appeasement. Where Mahmud wanted reconciliation, the admiral wanted a merciless repression that would put a definitive end to the janissaries. The argument grew louder; Cadi Pasha would not abandon his intention of conducting a punitive incursion the next morning. Mahmud formally forbade it. Cadi Pasha declared that he would ignore the veto and defend Mahmud in spite of himself; if he was not allowed to protect the interests of the Sultan, at least he would protect those of the empire.

"Tomorrow morning," he continued, "I shall leave the Seraglio at the head of my troops and I shall cleanse Constantinople of the janissaries."

"I forbid you," said Mahmud.

"I have orders from Baraïktar Pasha."

"You're lying, Cadi Pasha. Baraïktar cannot have given you any such order. No one knows where he is."

"I shall act as if I had his order."

Mahmud began to draw his dagger. I saw murder in his eyes. I barely had time to place my hand on his arm to restrain him. Cadi Pasha forged ahead:

"I shall take advantage of the purge to eliminate Sultan Mustafa in order to prevent once and for all any possibility of a plot against our Padishah."

His voice white with rage, Mahmud answered: "I swear to you, Cadi Pasha, that if you touch a hair on the head of the former Sultan, my brother, I shall kill you with my own hands."

Cadi Pasha saw that Mahmud was in earnest, and fell silent. A few hours later, when we were alone, Mahmud told me very calmly that he would have Cadi Pasha killed in the night. For a moment I was dumb from astonishment.

"At least wait until tomorrow, Mahmud. Let him be for a moment, if you can stop him only by a crime. Let Baraïktar's partisans attack the janissaries, let the various factions fight each other. Then we shall see; then you may decide and take action."

"I won't allow him to ignore my authority," said Mahmud. "It is an authority granted by Allah, and they must learn that they cannot defy it with impunity."

Mahmud was right, but he was also in the grip of his youthful impetuosity.

"And you must learn, Mahmud, that patience is the only defense against impotence. You are boiling because you are being denied your legitimate power. Be patient. One day, soon, you shall grasp and hold that power."

Mahmud gave in to my arguments with ill grace. He thought it over during the night, and even changed his mind; and in the morning he came to wake me, and told me that he would join Cadi Pasha's troops and place himself at the head of their sortie.

"That way I'll turn the operation to my advantage, and I'll be rid of the janissaries forever."

At that point I lost my temper. Besides, I had a horror of being wakened inopportunely.

"Listen to me, Mahmud. If you get mixed up in this affair and Cadi Pasha wins, you will have shown that you are nothing but a puppet in his hands. On the other hand, if the janissaries win, they'll do everything to chase you off the throne. Stay out of it, and wait."

He had to agree that I wasn't wrong. My son was struggling with a most complicated situation. He was only twenty-three years old and had no one but me to guide him.

At eight o'clock Cadi Pasha and his four hundred thousand men marched off on their punitive expedition, leaving the Seraglio by the Imperial Gate. The strong points of resistance were rapidly overwhelmed, and the janissaries fell back in disorderly retreat. But the vengeful soldiers, seeing themselves masters of the situation, gave in to the temptation of looting, broke into houses, and indulged in all the usual barbarities; so much so that the population of the city, which had been rather quiet the day before, rose up against the assailants and threw them back with stones, boiling water, and boiling oil, amid the hysterical shrieks of the women, the wailing of the children, and the curses of the old men.

This unexpected help from the population spurred the janissaries on, and soon there was a spectacular reversal of the situation. Now it was Cadi Pasha's soldiers who were pursued; finally they found themselves cornered by the infuriated crowd in the square of At Meydan, while the janissaries retook their barracks from Cadi Pasha's men and put them to the torch. Cadi Pasha, with the remains of his troops, barely managed to reach the Seraglio's First Court and swing the heavy gates shut against the enraged hordes on his heels. Disorder and violence reigned everywhere.

Drawn by the smell of gold, the vociferous crowd rushed to the smoldering ruins of the Grand Vizier's palace. Soon a group of men emerged from the pile of blackened beams and smoking joists, bearing something far better than gold: the corpses of Baraïktar and his wife. Contrary to what we had heard, neither Baraïktar nor Vassilo had been able to flee the palace. Instead they had taken refuge, with the enormous treasure Baraïktar had accumulated, in a stone tower, protected from the fire and the attackers by a triple rampart of iron doors. They had escaped the flames and the rage of the rebels, only to be asphyxiated by the smoke. Keeping her promise, Vassilo had shared the fate of the man she loved to the very end. . . .

The discovery of Baraïktar's remains drew an immense clamor of joy from the insurgents outside the Seraglio. In the First Court, however, among Cadi Pasha's soldiers, it caused rage and despair. They had been cheated; they had been told that Baraïktar was safe, that he was gathering reinforcements, that he was on his way to support them. And he was dead, and they were cornered with no way of escape. While part of the force continued to fire on the insurgents from the Seraglio walls, another turned against its leader, Cadi Pasha, shouting for his head.

Until then I had remained, on Mahmud's orders, in the shelter of my apartment, listening from afar, kept abreast of developments every minute. At three in the afternoon Mahmud sent for me from the Tower of Justice, his observation post. I returned to the platform from which I had witnessed Selim's coronation, from which Selim and I had watched the British fleet sail toward us. In silence, Mahmud gestured over the city. Constantinople was in flames. I had seen several fires, but none had been closer or more terrible than this one. The janissaries had set fire to their own barracks; the flames had spread to the neighboring quarters, linked up with the still smoldering embers of the palace of the Grand Vizier, touched them off again, and traveled outward in every direction. The areas around the square of At Meydan, the Mosque of Sultan Ahmed, the basilica of Saint Sofia, the Sublime Porte were an inferno. A wall of smoke and flames surrounded the Seraglio. The roar of the fire and the din of collapsing houses were so loud that they covered the shouts of the insurgents and the soldiers of Cadi Pasha who had turned against him. We were besieged by fire and rebels, and our troops, Cadi Pasha's, were in mutiny.

"And now?" I asked Mahmud.

"Now, Nakshidil, it's my turn. My turn has come."

Mahmud summoned Cadi Pasha and ordered him to put an end to the fighting. Cadi Pasha, who had been so sure of himself the day before, so arrogant, so insolent, now reeled under the weight of his defeat. He bowed to Mahmud in submission.

At that very moment a shout came from the crowds of insurgents outside the Seraglio, a triumphant, rhythmical shout:

"Long live Sultan Mustafa! A thousand years to Sultan Mustafa!"

I had already heard those words—on the day Selim was overthrown. Once again the revolt had found its banner, if not its master, and had become a revolution. . . . I can still see us, the three of us standing in silence, listening, on the terrace roof of the Tower of Justice. Cadi Pasha was haggard, Mahmud impassive—not a single muscle moved in his face—and I myself livid with fear and rage. But rage dominated fear, and soon I pulled myself together. Turning to Mahmud, I said:

"I have often wanted to ask you to kill Mustafa in vengeance. I always held my peace. Now I ask you to do it, I demand that you do it, because the interests of the empire are at stake. Yesterday you refused, and I understood. But now you should not—you cannot— shirk it. It is not a question of you or of me, but of the empire. In the name of Selim, whose work only you can carry on, I beg you to have Mustafa killed this very minute!"

I delivered this speech in a calm voice, in the midst of the terrible din of the fire and the riot. Mahmud listened with attention, without saying a word. Then, locked in the silence of his conscience, he pondered the matter for a few minutes, and turned to Cadi Pasha.

"Yesterday you asked me for Sultan Mustafa's life, and I refused. Today I order you to have him executed. Stop the fighting, and kill Sultan Mustafa. Go."

Once Cadi Pasha had left, Mahmud turned to me:

"Come, Nakshidil; there's nothing more we can do here. The riot is over."

I couldn't believe my ears. I followed him to my apartment. Without haste he took my writing chest of gold and agate, a present from Selim, and began to compose a decree, addressed to the Aga of the Janissaries. In it he announced the deaths of Sultan Mustafa and Grand Vizier Baraïktar; he ordered the Aga of the Janissaries to recall his troops and send them to fight the fire; he declared a general amnesty; and he enjoined the janissaries and the ulemas to come and pay homage to him. He signed the Hatif Sherif and told Ali Effendi to deliver it. Green with terror, the latter had no choice but to comply and left to face the riot, armed only with the Sultan's decree.

A eunuch came to tell Mahmud that Mustafa had been executed. With several eunuchs, Cadi Pasha had dragged him from his prison—the prison that had been ours—and brought him to a corner of the Third Court. Cadi Pasha himself had placed the silk bowstring around Mustafa's neck. Mustafa had lived as a weak man, and he died as a coward, begging for his life.

The soldiers who were still faithful to Cadi Pasha held their fire, and the fighting came to a stop. Mahmud gave orders that would enable Cadi Pasha and Baraïktar's most important aides, whose heads the insurgents were after, to leave the Seraglio without interference. Then we waited. Mahmud sat immobile, his head bowed. Only his lips moved.

"What are you doing, Mahmud?"

"I'm praying, Nakshidil. I'm praying for the empire."

An hour passed. A eunuch came to inform Mahmud that the delegations of janissaries and ulemas were waiting to pay homage to him in the throne room. The Aga of the Janissaries had not come. He was leading his men in the fight against the fire. Vigorously contained, it was at last in retreat.

Mahmud went to the throne room. He was still there when cannon volleys rang out from every fort of Constantinople, announcing the end of Ramadan. Custom held that the Sultan must appear under the Iftariye, a bronze canopy on the terrace of the selamlik, which dominates the entire city. Mahmud appeared, surrounded by janissaries and ulemas. From the terraces of the city the people were able to see their ruler from afar under the golden canopy, a thin silhouette brilliantly lit by torches. As Mahmud had declared, the revolution was over.

I had surprised myself by being so little afraid; for me it had been quite unlike the "other" revolutions, which I had lived through in terror. As I have said, Mahmud inspired confidence. His young presence radiated a feeling of protectiveness. And perhaps my sensitivity had been dulled by all the emotion of my past; no doubt a great part of it had died with Selim. I no longer reacted to danger. I had reacted only at the sight of a transfiguration, that of my son. The impulsive young man who that very morning had wanted to tag along behind a master was now a man calm, cool, decided, and daring, a firm man whose orders were not disputed. And the transformation had taken place before my very eyes, at the top of the Tower of Justice.

I had already seen him like that once before, on the tragic night he had come to the throne. But then the triviality of his power, the contempt in which Baraïktar held him, the difficulties of his task, had somewhat restored in him the weaknesses of his age. Today again he had brutally chased them from his character, and this time I was certain the change was to be permanent.

When he returned from the ceremony of the Iftar, the end of the fast, I was unable to restrain myself from asking:

"Why did you call me to the Tower of Justice? Of what use did you think I would be?"

"I needed your presence. I knew the man you wanted me to become. And I became him, thanks to you, for you, before you."

CHAPTER 23

———————◆━◆———————

Of a common accord, Mahmud and I decided to move out of the Seraglio. There were too many painful memories, too many tragic memories there to haunt us. For his own use Mahmud restored the palace at Beylerbey on the Asiatic shore of the Bosporus—the same palace where, one winter afternoon, Selim had declared his love for me. He returned to the Seraglio only to work. He gave me a yali at Besiktas, on the European bank, almost opposite his palace. In a large park with beautiful centuries-old trees there are several wooden villas, the summer houses of former sultans. Mustafa had often come there with his women—he had been there, in fact, on July 28, until his mother Sineperver called him back to the Seraglio in haste. My yali skirted the Bosporus. After so many years spent in the cramped and often lugubrious apartments of the Seraglio, I enjoyed, at last, space, light, and air. I renovated the rooms for sobriety and clarity, qualities which did not exclude the delicate touches of luxury. Europe, represented by large mirrors, crystal chandeliers, and porcelain objects, mingled with the Orient in the shape of large flowered carpets, draperies, and sofas upholstered in pastel silks, woven with gold or silver. I had renounced the brocaded velvets, which I found too heavy. I had the windows widened, and added verandas and balconies so as to have the widest view possible on the gardens and the sea.

I was officially the Mistress of the Harem, and its government forced me to return to the Seraglio nearly every day. I instituted a discipline the harem had never enjoyed until then. The Kizlar Aga, my Ali Effendi, had found his vocation in managing the harem's affairs, and seconded me ably, directing our little world with commendable briskness. My Norman atavism resurfaced as I set about tracking down laziness and carelessness, demanding order and cleanliness, imposing the satisfaction of work well done. In short, I had become a perfect mother abbess. I fulfilled all my duties—inspections, settlements of conflicts and arguments, restoration and upkeep of the buildings, discovery and development of the harem girls' talents, organization of feasts and celebrations—with the dedication I devote, by nature, to all things. Never had I imagined that there could be so much work, and never had I thought that I would find it so interesting. Seen from above, the harem was a microcosm, a miniature world, an inexhaustible source of observations and education in human nature. And then the Orient has that incomparable talent for transforming daily existence into a theatrical spectacle where the smallest incident becomes a fascinating story. The Orient can be quite tiresome at times, but it can never be boring.

I followed political developments only intermittently. Now that Mustafa was dead, Mahmud remained the only living member of the Ottoman dynasty, and as such he was inviolable. But he did not lack adversaries. Sineperver still lived. She was responsible for Selim's death, and she had wanted Mahmud and me killed, but still I did not wish to imitate her by asking Mahmud for her head. Her son was dead, her ambitions and her hopes shattered, and it was revenge enough to know that she was stagnating in solitude, grief, and bitterness. The janissaries, for whom Baraïktar's death had been a triumph, dominated the government of the empire, but their time would come. Mahmud, while praising and pampering them, had confided his intentions to me:

" 'Kiss the hand you cannot cut off,' says an Arab proverb. That is exactly what I am doing, Nakshidil. I stroke the janissaries, I lull them to sleep—and one day, when I am stronger than they, I shall get rid of them. I'll wait—a year, ten years, twenty years if I have to. I have time. And one day I shall kill every last one of them. For reasons of state."

And I knew he would keep his word. Baraïktar's principal collaborators—Cadi Pasha, the Capitan Pasha, Bejid Effendi—whom Mahmud had helped escape from the Seraglio, had been captured a few weeks later. Mahmud had let them be executed. Had he wanted to eliminate a group of people who had humiliated him, or had he invoked reasons of state? I did not ask him about it.

We saw less of each other. Forever on the move from Beylerbey to the Seraglio and from the Seraglio to Besiktas, Mahmud was often unreachable. Perhaps his incessant peregrinations were a deliberate attempt to escape from everyone. When he came to visit me I never questioned him about politics, knowing that I mustn't. He himself did not seek my advice on any matter, and I understood and accepted.

Mahmud needed to develop on his own. He did not want to owe anything to anyone. He was young, and only later on in life has one the experience to accept advice, to tolerate being indebted. I let him try himself, put himself to the test, and limited myself to keeping up his household. With the weight of my experience, I had advised him in the liberalization of the harem he had undertaken. Henceforth the ladies would be allowed to leave the Seraglio and walk in town, as long as they were veiled. The kadins of departed sultans and the old women were no longer relegated to the Old Seraglio—a prospect that had haunted me—but were allowed to retire to a residence of their choice.

For reasons of economy, Mahmud thinned out his own harem, and a number of girls were returned to their families. This decision, which was attributed to Mahmud's notorious avarice, had in fact a name: Besma, a simple bath slave with whom Mahmud had fallen as always, passionately in love, to the exclusion of all others. So I had to listen to the neglected odalisques who turned to me for consolation; I sympathized with their sorrows and did my best to keep them entertained.

I also had to take care of Mahmud's children. He had fathered a first daughter, Fatma, and then a second and a third. I did not fully share Mahmud's happiness and pride. For me children remained strangers, and I was not entirely comfortable with them, perhaps because I had not had any of my own. Nevertheless the imperial brood took much of my time, for I had to find nurses, take care of lodgings, watch over their precious health, and so on.

In December 1809 I was drawn out of my placid existence by news which Mahmud brought to Besiktas in person. Napoleon had divorced my cousin Josephine. The account sent by our ambassador in Paris brought tears to my eyes.

The scene had unfolded at the Tuileries palace, in the throne room, where Josephine had appeared in court costume, her diadem on her head, but pale and teary, supported by the two children fathered by Alexandre de Beauharnais. She had taken her seat on the throne and, with trembling hands and voice, read a declaration before her family by marriage, those Bonapartes who hated her, and the assembled courtiers and ambassadors.

"With the permission of our dear and august husband, we declare that, having no hope of producing a child who would satisfy the needs of his politics and the interests of France, we are happy to give him the greatest proof of attachment and devotion that can be shown. . . . "

On those words Josephine had burst into tears, and unable to read any further, had handed the message to her secretary, who finished it:

"We consent to put an end to a marriage which is an obstacle to his happiness and compromises the interests of France."

Bonaparte had pushed his cruelty as far as to force her to announce her own downfall to that mocking assembly, over which she would no longer reign.

He had then exiled her to the provinces, far from the Paris she loved above all else, having decreed that her presence in the capital was inconvenient and therefore forbidden.

Suddenly my hatred of Bonaparte flared up again, fed by old resentments as well as recent ones—the invasion of Egypt, his treason at Tilsit, his betrayal of his friend Selim. It was because of Selim's faithfulness to me that he had been attacked, because of me that he had been accused of sterility, and he had kept me though it had almost cost him his throne. Whereas Bonaparte discarded Josephine as if she were a good-for-nothing chambermaid. In prison I had sworn that if ever I recovered my freedom and my power, I would take my revenge on that man. I appealed to Mahmud:

"Something must be done. That man—that evil man, that tyrant—must be destroyed." Fury had robbed me of reason and moderation.

"Destroy Napoleon!" he answered. "Napoleon has reduced Europe to servitude. He has made vassals of Germany, Italy, Switzerland, Denmark, Sweden, Holland, Portugal, and Spain. He has just crushed Austria. He has made a friend of Russia—more than a friend, an accomplice—as we know only too well. Only England still resists. And for how long?"

"Let us make an alliance with England, then."

"In order to have Napoleon on our back with his invincible armies?"

"In the end, Mahmud, you admire Bonaparte just as Selim did."

"I don't admire him the way Selim did. Nor do I hate him as you do. I think only of the interests of the empire."

"Is it in the interests of the empire to let Bonaparte gather power over all Europe before he turns his attention to us? Don't be mistaken, Mahmud. We are in his line of fire quite simply because we exist, and everything that exists must be subjected to his power."

"I know as well as you that Napoleon is a threat to the world in general, and to us in particular. But we are not strong enough to rise up against him. We must wait for the proper moment, for the opportunity."

"Wait! To wait! It's the only word I hear in Turkey!"

Mahmud smiled. "Wasn't it you, Nakshidil, who once counseled patience? I followed your advice, and did well by it. Now it is your turn to follow it."

After that I became half obsessed with waiting for the opportunity to harm Bonaparte—but it never seemed to appear.

The war between Russia and Turkey had resumed in the spring of 1809. In fact, the hostilities had never really ceased; for a long time, however, they had consisted of sporadic skirmishes rather than real campaigns. Our empire was undergoing the revolutions I have described, and Russia, unsure in the midst of the confusion of European politics, had not taken advantage of the convulsions that had weakened us. . . .

The campaigns of 1809, 1810, and 1811 were disastrous for us. We were in retreat in the Balkans, in the Caucasus—everywhere. It was then that I received a new letter from Mother Marie-Agnès. Our correspondence, interrupted at the time of my imprisonment, had resumed. Her first letter had expressed her compassion after Selim's death. She had written these prophetic words:

> "In your distress God is your only recourse—but will you recognize His might? I wonder: You could easily be blinded by sorrow. You don't believe me yet, for since Sultan Selim's death you see your existence as a tragic burden. Nevertheless you will return to life little by little, drawn in by whatever you can and must do for others. I am thinking in particular of your son, the new Sultan."

Her next letter, dated late in 1811, was somber. Gone was the enthusiasm she had shown for the French victories of 1805.

> Is there a limit to the Emperor Napoleon's arrogance? In order to flatter him, Austria has gone as far as to grant him an archduchess after his divorce from your cousin Josephine. Imagine! A daughter of Caesar's married to a former Corsican lieutenant! Russia, now his ally—some say his accomplice—follows him blindly, weakly. Prussia—occupied, amputated, ruined—is out of the picture. In Portugal and Spain his troops score victory after victory over the recently landed British forces. England herself is powerless—struggling with a royal crisis caused by the madness of King George III, isolated, without friends or allies, strangled by the Emperor Napoleon's continental blockade. Napoleon's relatives reign

in Spain, in Holland, in Westphalia, in Tuscany, at Naples. One of his companions in arms will soon rule in Sweden and Norway. The monarchs of Europe are his vassals—if not his valets. What is left for him to conquer? What is there left to subjugate? Nothing, apparently—and yet it is clear to everyone that he will never stop his warring. Drained France and trembling Europe wonder where he will strike next.

His self-assurance has recently been reinforced by the birth of a long-awaited son and heir, borne him by his second wife, Archduchess Marie-Louise. He has reached the summit of glory, and everything smiles upon him. Yet the people mutter that he was wrong to dismiss your cousin Josephine, because she was his lucky star. Without her, they say, his proverbial luck will desert him. Since superstition is something I am forbidden, I prefer to think that one day God will punish him for the fate he has imposed on His servants. Bishops and priests who have dared oppose Napoleon's decrees are pursued and thrown into prison. He has gone as far as to have our Holy Father the Pope deported and imprisoned at Fontainebleau.

I think you will be less affected by his misfortunes than by those of your cousin Josephine. Naturally she has been allowed no part of her former husband's apotheosis. She is not allowed anywhere near Paris. She languishes in the country, alone, devastated. You probably have not heard that a few years ago your younger sister Alexandrine—almost a stranger to you—married a neighbor from Martinique, Charles Guillaume Marlet, whom you might remember from your childhood. Your father died while you were in prison, in May 1808. I did not have the heart to tell you earlier, believing that the death of Sultan Selim was sadness enough for the time being. . . .

For a long time already my father had been almost dead for me; my distant memories of him had receded little by little into the mist. Nevertheless the contraction of my chest, the tears that rose to my eyes upon reading Mother Marie-Agnès's letter, showed me that I had not forgotten him. Yet I was even sadder when I thought of Josephine. She had been my friend, and in the bottom of my heart she would always remain my friend. Current events and the renown of her husband had kept her in the forefront of my thoughts. Her fate caused me acute distress.

I had to fight my impulse to contact her. At times I even thought of trying to have her brought to Constantinople. Mahmud encouraged me in these thoughts, but in truth they were no more than vague desires in which I could not allow myself to indulge. Despite my affection for Josephine and my urge to help her, I knew that our paths could never cross again. I had chosen my destiny, and I belonged to Turkey.

While Josephine wilted in the depressing chateau she had been assigned, I wasted away in my yali at Besiktas. The birth of Bonaparte's heir had discouraged me, as it had discouraged all of downtrodden Europe. Now that the future of his dynasty was safe, it seemed that nothing could put an end to the tyrant's power.

Thereupon Mahmud informed me of the presence of Count d'Antraigues in Constantinople. He left a trail of intrigue and plotting wherever he went. Six years earlier, his arrival had triggered an assassination attempt on me and Zinah's death. What were his intentions now? Whom would he attack this time?

Three days later Ali Effendi gave me a packet of letters which had mysteriously made their way into his hands. They were addressed to "Her Highness the Valideh of Turkey." The first was a short note:

The bearer of this letter has my full confidence. He speaks in my name, and what he will say must be believed to come from me.

It was signed "Talleyrand," and I easily recognized his scrawl, which I had seen on his letters to Selim. The second was an anonymous letter.

You cannot be approached or spoken to; therefore it is best to write to you. Your desire for a general peace is known, as well as the power you hold. It is also known that you regret your former support of Bonaparte, and that you seek the downfall of the tyrant of Europe.

Then came the announcement that Bonaparte was preparing, in deep secrecy, an invasion of Russia, his ally. Discreetly, on false pretexts, he was assembling the greatest army ever seen, in order to attack his friend Czar Alexander—while burying him in praise and insisting on the solidity of their alliance. Bonaparte meant to take advantage of our war on Russia, which kept a large part of her forces tied down on our front. Wedged between two walls of fire, Russia would be crushed, occupied, and reduced to a vassal state by Bonaparte. Then he would turn to our empire, the only remaining independent continental power. The letter continued:

> Since the distant days of the Egyptian war, the Turkish
> Empire has been Bonaparte's goal and ambition. Conquering
> it will provide him with the worldwide empire he covets.
> Once Russia has been defeated, he will attack Turkey in
> order to fulfill a long-standing dream. You are entreated, you
> are begged, to prevent this crime against history. The Sultan
> listens to you. Warn him, open his eyes to the dangers
> threatening his possessions and his empire itself. Act now,
> for his welfare, for the welfare of the empire, for the welfare
> of Europe.

The letter was not signed, but I did not need to rack my brain to know that it came from Count d'Antraigues. He inspired only mistrust and revulsion in me, for I knew there were no limits to his perfidy. Nevertheless I was forced to believe those incredible assertions. Bonaparte had already proved, at our expense, that he could turn against his most faithful ally, and Talleyrand's note was a guarantee for d'Antraigue's credibility. As Bonaparte's minister of foreign affairs he might betray his master, perhaps in fear of the latter's ambition and the disasters it might cause; but he would never have invented such an enormity. Mahmud, when informed, believed d'Antraigues as firmly as I. "Act," said the letter—but what could we do, what could I do? We were bogged down in our war with Russia, and too weak to think of fighting Bonaparte. We were powerless, as before—as always, I wanted to add angrily.

It was then that I was told of the arrival in Constantinople of Queen Marie-Caroline of Naples. The sister of the Queen of France,

Marie-Antoinette, wedded to a Bourbon, the King of Naples, she had been Bonaparte's most constant, most determined and energetic adversary. The British who came to her rescue had taken over her kingdom the way they had taken over Egypt; and because she resisted, they had finally exiled her. She was on her way to return to her native Austria, but the occupation of three-quarters of Europe by her enemy Bonaparte had forced her to make a long detour through Turkey and Russia. It was said she had a woman's weaknesses in a man's character, that she was cruel and voluptuous. Curiosity and the urge to honor a luckless adversary of Bonaparte led me to receive her.

I waited for her in the Seraglio, in the sitting room on the first floor of my apartments. The austerely dressed woman who was shown in was naturally majestic and haughty. She must once have been beautiful, and I recognized in her features traces of those of her sister, Queen Marie-Antoinette—though the latter's had been more harmonious and less masculine. Her sixty years of trials had muddied her complexion and her eyes, and furrowed her long face. All in all she reminded me of an old horse—though a thoroughbred. She looked me up and down before dropping the remark: "Madame, I am told you are French."

I must have seemed quite disconcerted, for she smiled before continuing: "Don't be surprised. Count d'Antraigues is one of my friends. He has told me about you—and there is no need to fear. In my long life I have accumulated so many secrets that I forget to repeat them."

I looked at this old queen, whose grace had not been altered by failure and bitterness. She faced my gaze, and said, "My enemies used to say I was the devil. In any case, I am his grandmother—ever since my granddaughter married Bonaparte. Yes, Madame, you have before you the devil's grandmother—by marriage."

So we spoke of the devil. Marie-Caroline did not for a moment deny his genius. But would he have got so far had he not had utter nonentities for adversaries?

"Cowards, Madame. All my cousins the kings, and the ministers, the generals ... all cowards and no match for Bonaparte. Believe me, I have spent less time fighting him, my enemy, than I've spent fighting them, my allies. Now I am too old. It is for you to continue the struggle."

"For me! I am isolated in the harem of Constantinople! How could I succeed where Your Majesty, an absolute queen, related to all Europe, has failed?"

"When I fought Bonaparte he was just beginning his career. You shall step in now that his career is coming to an end."

"Coming to an end! He dominates all of Europe, and he has just founded a dynasty."

"Precisely. Bonaparte has seen too many victories and too much tyranny. He is bloated. He has reached the summit, and now he can only go down."

"And how can I contribute to his downfall? I have no armies at my disposal such as Your Majesty had."

Queen Marie-Caroline's eyes lit up with a warm glow. "My child, those are illusions. Kings and generals do nothing. I am in a position to know. It is details, small facts, that make history. A single cog can halt a perfectly well-oiled machine. And you must be that cog. You can do it. You must think; you must use your imagination. Wars are won not with regiments but with ideas. Think of an idea!"

And finally I did think of one, if only because Queen Marie-Caroline had made me feel ashamed of my discouragement. I even called Mahmud—breaking my rule—to tell him of it.

"I've thought about it, Mahmud, I've looked at the question from every angle. There is only one thing to do: Make peace with Russia immediately."

"You can't be serious, Nakshidil. The Russians have beaten us, but we still have reserves. A peace signed now could only be a shameful and useless one. Furthermore, if Napoleon attacks Russia and beats her—which is bound to happen—then we shall obtain a more advantageous treaty."

"If Russia is beaten tomorrow, Turkey will be beaten the day after. Bonaparte is counting on our war with Russia. If we make peace with her before he attacks, he will have fallen into his own trap."

Mahmud was beginning to see my point. Yet there were apparently insuperable difficulties. We had to beware of the conservatives who led the government; their narrow vision would allow them to see only a shameful peace, and they would rise against the project—if not against Mahmud himself. I could already hear the janissaries gleefully beating on their upturned caldrons and opposing the Sultan's "cowardice." We had to beware of Bonaparte, whose agents swarmed all over Constantinople; as soon as he learned of our first step toward peace, he would realize he had been tricked and swoop down on us. We could act only in the most hermetic secrecy, without informing anyone—especially the Divan. Finally we had to convince the Russians that we wanted to negotiate out of a sincere desire for peace, and not because we were beaten. As soon as we made overtures they would think we were cornered and try to take advantage—all the more so because the Czar's government and staff, blinded by Bonaparte's assurances, swore by France's friendship. How could we contact our enemy the Russians quickly and discreetly?

"You must find a way, Mahmud, and you must find it soon. Remember—if Russia is beaten tomorrow, Turkey will fall the day after."

It was then that Mahmud remembered an old Neapolitan ambassador vegetating in Constantinople, the illusory representative of the kingdom that Queen Marie-Caroline had lost; and this ambassador had a colleague in Russia, at Saint Petersburg, where the Czar, out of politeness, allowed him to represent a kingdom which, to all intents and purposes, no longer existed. We needed to persuade the Constantinople Neapolitan to write the Petersburg Neapolitan a letter, dictated by Mahmud, insisting on the urgent necessity of a Russo-Turkish peace; and then ask the Petersburg Neapolitan to show it to the Czar, and hope that the Czar would understand its relevance and act in consequence. It was like throwing a bottle to the sea. There was nothing else that we could do, however. We cast the message to the waves, and waited for a response—in vain. It seemed that it had never reached the shore.

The Balkan campaign began early in 1812. Russia and Turkey were still at war, and peace had never seemed more distant. Nevertheless we learned that the Czar had sent a diplomat to the Russian lines, ready to open negotiations with us if the necessity arose. The Czar had pushed forward a pawn—but a prudent, uncompromising pawn. Our message had been received, but the Russian ruler did not want to commit himself. We imitated him and sent our own negotiator to our lines, to have him there in case of need.

Thereupon Mahmud received a personal message from Bonaparte. In it he declared—in slightly veiled terms—his intention of invading Russia, and proposed an offensive alliance. We were earnestly asked to join the European coalition he was about to unleash on Russia—or else. In exchange, Napoleon offered to return to us all the provinces Russia had conquered in the last decades. Napoleon was so certain of our response that he counted on an attack on the Russians' southern flank by the Turkish army, led by Mahmud himself.

The possibility of recovering our lost territories from our hereditary enemy was most tempting. But I reminded Mahmud: "Remember—Russia beaten tomorrow, Turkey beaten day after tomorrow."

A wily man, Mahmud sensed Bonaparte's intentions. Instead of falling into the trap, he relayed to the Czar, through the Neapolitans, the text of Bonaparte's proposals. The Czar reacted immediately. A new defeat he had inflicted on us in the Balkans furnished him with the opportunity to propose an armistice, which we accepted eagerly. The negotiators that both sides had kept in reserve for months met at Bucharest—then under Russian occupation—and opened the negotiations. But what negotiations! They were quite official, and their goal was to explore the possibility of an eventual peace; they did not take into account our secret goal of obtaining peace at any price; and finally, they did not worry anyone, neither the Divan nor the Francophile Russians, nor even Bonaparte, for they seemed to have no chance of succeeding.

In short, we marked time, and time was running out. Bonaparte increased the pressure on us: If Turkey did not enter his coalition she would be considered an enemy and treated as such. We also knew that he was progressing in his preparations for war with Russia. It was imperative that we make peace with Russia before he attacked her; otherwise that peace would be useless, and our fate sealed. At Bucharest the negotiators progressed at the pace of turtles; ours was tangled up in the vacillations of the Divan, and his Russian counterpart had to deal with a hesitant Czar. Meanwhile the day of reckoning was rushing toward us. Something had to be done, or we wouldn't come to a settlement in time.

I harried Mahmud, but neither he nor I could act. One day, I said, "There is only one thing to do: You must negotiate in person, above the Divan, above the diplomats."

Mahmud was stunned. Could the Sultan, under the watchful eyes of the court day and night, negotiate with the Russians in secret? And negotiate where, and with whom—with which Russians? And yet the idea pleased Mahmud, who answered, "All right, then, I shall negotiate with Kutuzov."

It was my turn to be stunned. Kutuzov was the Russian generalissimo. How did Mahmud plan to approach him, to meet him? Why Kutuzov, the general who commanded the armies fighting us, the veteran of Russo-Turkish wars? He was an old, headstrong daredevil. He had been known to disregard the orders of his master the Czar when he thought them contrary to the interests of his motherland. It was that reputation which led Mahmud to settle on him. He would see the generalissimo in person to negotiate a peace treaty.

However inconceivable it was that the Sultan should receive the commanding officer of the enemy armies in the midst of a war, nothing would stop Mahmud once he had made up his mind. He sent his personal secretary with a hand-picked escort. Thanks to the truce, the secretary was able to travel through the lines and reach Bucharest, where he had a private audience with Kutuzov. The Russian was handed an urgent letter from Mahmud. Convinced, he agreed, and let himself be taken away in a curtained coach. He had announced that he was ill and unable to receive anyone. No one was surprised. Kutuzov's "illnesses" were legendary, a laughing-stock to his armies. A libidinous, lazy man, he liked to lock himself up for several days at a time to indulge in drink and debauchery with a lovely Circassian girl who traveled with him everywhere—or a lovely Circassian boy, according to the nastier gossips. A week after his departure, Mahmud's secretary returned to Constantinople with his "parcel" under his arm. The parcel, Kutuzov, was unload-ed from the coach and placed in one of the pavilions of my garden. Mahmud had decided to meet Kutuzov in the middle of the night at my palace at Besiktas, where he wasn't watched as closely as in the Seraglio.

The man brought to my sitting room, puffing and panting like a whale, was very fat, apoplectic, hirsute, and one-eyed. The eye sparkled with malice. His uniform was unbuttoned, and he had a little cap rammed askew on his head.

"What a trip!" he said to Mahmud. "Your Highness, if I may say so, doesn't believe in wasting time. . . . But what do I see here?" he added, his eye lighting up with gluttony. Having heard of his pro-digious appetite, I had ordered a considerable buffet from the kitch-ens.

"And champagne! I prefer vodka. There is nothing better than vodka. But champagne will do. After all, there is a war on. . . . "

Mahmud was not able to get a word in until Kutuzov was propped up with a glass in one hand and a chicken wing in the other. The conversation was held in French, for the matter at stake was too important to be crippled by protocol and translators.

"General, we have no time for subtleties!" said Mahmud, before explaining the situation that had obsessed us for weeks: the immi-nence of Bonaparte's invasion of Russia; the defeat of Russia, trapped between two fronts by Bonaparte's attack in the west and our war in the south; the subsequent defeat of Turkey; and the necessity to avoid the above by signing a peace treaty immediately.

Kutuzov listened closely to Mahmud's explanations, thought for a long moment, and answered, "I know all that only too well. I feel as sorry for my country as Your Highness feels for his. But I can do nothing against the hesitations of my Czar and the slowness of your Divan."

"That is why I sent for you, General—so that we can make peace immediately, independently of my Divan and your Czar."

Kutuzov's blue eye stared piercingly at Mahmud for a long moment before he muttered, "All right, Sire. I shall disregard my master's instructions, though I shall fall into disgrace. And you and I shall make peace."

I stepped in: "Yes, but not peace at any price; my son, the Sultan, will not sign a shameful peace."

Kutuzov proposed that both sides remain in their current positions. I demanded the restitution to Turkey of the Rumanian provinces occupied by Kutuzov. He had them, he replied, and he would keep them.

"No Rumania, no peace," I said. "Turkey may be lost, but Russia will be lost before her."

Kutuzov burst into laughter. "May God preserve Russia from having to negotiate too often with the likes of the Valideh! You shall have your peace within a week on your conditions. I don't like it, but I'll have to do it for my country."

I felt deep sympathy, almost a sort of tenderness, for the old fox. I asked, "And what will happen then, General?"

"Once we have signed the treaty, the Czar will be furious, and he'll send me away in disgrace. I'm used to it. Then Napoleon will invade Russia. The generals around the Czar are inexperienced young dandies whom Napoleon will defeat with ease. Invincible, he will march on into the heart of Russia. But in the end he will not win. Thanks to the treaty Your Highness and I will sign, and thanks to the size and inexhaustible resources of Russia, we shall have the last word—but not before the defeat, the ruin, the death of my country."

Mahmud encouraged him: "You shall save your country, General, I am sure of it."

"The Czar already hates me. He will never call on me. I shall rot on my estate, old, disgraced, and forgotten."

Kutuzov left for Bucharest that same night. I had ordered his coach stocked with enormous amounts of food and champagne, for which he showed me boundless gratitude. With him he took a rough draft of our treaty and Mahmud's written instructions to our negotiator to put the final touches on the treaty and sign it as soon as possible. To the grace of God! We could only hope that Kutuzov would not be prevented from signing, that Bonaparte would not learn of the treaty—nor the Divan, which, in those days of May 1812, was favorably discussing Bonaparte's proposals. A "leak," a single one, and we would have a revolution on our hands. To the grace of God!

One morning I went to visit the apartments of the Valideh, which had been relinquished to the masons and painters. As I have said, though I no longer lived in the Seraglio, I still took care of its maintenance, and regularly came to supervise the work I had ordered.

I was standing in the green-and-gold sitting room I had decorated long ago for Mirizshah. A painter worked at its walls while his companions busied themselves in the neighboring rooms. Satisfied with my inspection, I was already on the threshold of the next room when I heard these words:

"One moment, Mademoiselle Aimée Dubuc de Riverie!"

I stopped dead in my tracks, as if pinned to the spot by an arrow. But already the painter who had been coating the woodwork moments before was at my side.

"Franchini, dragoman at the French embassy, at your service," he said.

The dragomans were the secretaries and interpreters at the embassies; Franchini was the double agent who, years before, had warned us that his master Sebastiani, fearing arrest from Selim, was preparing to flee.

The first question that came to my mind was to ask him how he had managed to enter the Seraglio. With a burst of laughter, he told me that the Seraglio crawled with eunuchs whose corruption was a godsend to spies such as he. There were many questions on my lips, questions he did not avoid. In fact he answered them with arrogant eagerness. How did he know of my existence? How did he know my name? The British and Count d'Antraigues were not the only ones who were well informed. . . .

I asked him what he wanted of me, and in response he launched into a tirade both didactic and insulting, in which he accused me of being a traitor to my country, France. After his sermon, he brutally laid out the terms of his blackmail. I had to obtain from Mahmud that he cease negotiations with the Russians, that he rally to Bonaparte and attack Russia on the Balkan front. Otherwise the secret of my identity would be divulged to the entire world. Aware of the trump he was holding, Franchini then gleefully enumerated the "regrettable" consequences such a revelation would incur here in Turkey. Were the janissaries and ulemas to learn that a Frenchwoman, a Christian, a giaour, governed the Sultan and the Seraglio, there would be an inevitable revolution that would overthrow Mahmud.

I tried to defend myself, assuring Franchini that I had no influence on Mahmud, but he only laughed at my protestations. I then threatened him, suggesting that I could summon people who would make him disappear on the spot. Knowing our expedient habits, he said, he had taken precautions; if he failed to return to the French embassy, others would take care of publicizing the truth about the Valideh.

He granted me two days in which to reflect, after which I was to meet him in the Princes' School; it was not in use at the time, and seemed to him a fitting place for our next rendezvous.

It was with feelings of impotence and infinite lassitude that I returned to Besiktas. Several times in the past my presence had been a liability to Selim, and now I was a danger to Mahmud. Would the struggle never cease? I no longer had any taste for defending myself, but I had to fight, if only for Mahmud. I could not think of confiding in him, for it would have put him in the cruel position of having to choose between his mother and his policies. Nor could I ask anyone for advice, for what advice was there to give? Why then did I summon Pierre Ruffin? Was it because he had always been the pillar of the French embassy? Because he had the reputation of an honest man? Because, in my distress, I needed to confide in someone? At any rate, he came to see me in my garden at Besiktas on the following day. His impeccably pressed black clothes bore traces of wear. A drab stalk, he still had that air of a sad clergyman which had struck me one evening at the Palais-Royal twenty-four years before. Age had barely touched his bony face. He crossed and uncrossed large, nervous hands protruding from sleeves that were an inch too short. I spoke to him in French:

"Monsieur Ruffin, it is an urgent matter which led me to send for you."

"I am at your orders, Madame," he answered, showing no surprise at the fact that the Valideh had addressed him in his own tongue.

I had planned on revealing my identity; at this point I had nothing to lose. But in fact he had known of my existence in the Seraglio since the distant days of the Egyptian war.

I voiced my surprise that he had never publicized the fact or sought to make use of it. He answered that the secret was mine, and not his to dispose of. With these words he earned my confidence, and I told him of my encounter with Franchini.

Ruffin was sincerely indignant. "Such methods, such men, pollute my country," he said. "The government of the great Napoleon has no use for them and wholly disapproves of them."

Naive Ruffin! I did not tell him that the "great Napoleon" was not averse to spying and expediency. He did not think that his ambassador approved or even knew of Franchini's initiative. But the latter was obeying Bonaparte's orders: it was necessary that Turkey be made to join the French camp, and to this end the ambassador would use all his weapons, even those most distasteful to him, and would go so far as to cover Franchini in gold for his brilliant success; and there was nothing Ruffin could do to prevent him.

I tried to explain to Ruffin why I supported Mahmud rather than France, but he interrupted me. "There is no need to continue, Madame. I understand your position very well. Only a shifty double agent like Franchini could accuse you of treason. You have chosen

Turkey, your adoptive country, which I love as much as France. I know what a help your presence and your advice were to Sultan Selim, and are to Sultan Mahmud. You are faithful to those you love, and I respect you for it, just as I am faithful to Emperor Napoleon, my master and your enemy."

Despite his sympathy, Ruffin left me with an admission of his powerlessness. I was still in a bind. If I prevented the signature of the treaty with Russia I might be endangering the very existence of the empire. If I allowed the signature, my presence in the Seraglio would be revealed to the entire world, and in that case it was Mahmud's life that was in peril. The dilemma tortured me so deeply that I could see only one solution: to leave—leave Turkey, my house, Mahmud. My departure would remove the political obstacle and the danger to Mahmud. If I left, Franchini could reveal my secret to whomever he wanted; it would no longer matter in the least. I would find a way to force Mahmud to let me leave.

But where would I go? There was no question of returning to France under Bonaparte. To Martinique then, to a world grown foreign to me, among relatives who were strangers? And how would I adapt again to a world that had been mine so long ago? It was only when I thought of leaving the Orient that I realized to what extent I was its prisoner. At first the Orient had rebuffed me, as it rebuffs any newcomer, by its hermetism, its contrasts, its singularities. Then, little by little, it had seeped into me; its habits had won me, its seduction entrapped me. I could no longer imagine leaving it. The Orient would not release its now willing prey. And yet I had no right to think that way—my son's future forbade it.

Where would I go? There would be time to decide later. First it was necessary to leave as quickly as possible, and notify Franchini so as to defuse his bomb.

On the following day, I went to the Seraglio at the appointed hour. Shedding my retinue, I walked alone toward the Princes' School, on the second floor above the Black Eunuchs' Court, where Mahmud, as a child, had been the last imperial prince to study. This deserted, allegedly haunted place was made even more sinister by its dereliction. There was no one, not a sound, and I traveled through the dark rooms with an ineffable feeling of oppression. And suddenly, as I stepped over the threshold of the last chamber, I saw them—several bodies lying on the ground. Franchini was there indeed, but his throat had been cut, and he lay among eunuchs, no doubt his accomplices, who had met the same fate. I could see there had been a struggle, for there was blood everywhere—in the matting on the floor, on the walls, on their clothes. I was glued to the spot, paralyzed with horror, when a sound behind me made me leap: It was Mahmud!

I threw myself into his arms and burst into tears. I cried convulsively, from nervousness, fear, relief, and horror. My son held me tight in his arms. The explanations came later.

Kind Ruffin, upon leaving me the day before, had rushed to Mahmud to tell him all that I had planned to hide from him. Mahmud, informed of the time and place of my rendezvous with Franchini, ordered his henchmen to lie in wait for the double agent and eliminate him along with his accomplices.

"Why didn't you warn me, Mahmud? Why did you frighten me so?"

"So as not to raise Franchini's suspicions until the very last minute—and to punish you, Nakshidil," he said tenderly. "To punish you for not having confided in me and for having thought of leaving me. What is the point of protecting my empire if I cannot protect my mother? Have you thought for a moment about what I would do without you? You wanted to spare me, and in order to do so you were prepared to deal me a blow that would have destroyed me."

My fears had not left me entirely. Hadn't Franchini promised that if he came to harm, others would divulge my secret in his place?

Mahmud did not share my anxiety. According to him, Franchini's mysterious disappearance and the Sultan's possible role in it would inspire salutary fear and respect in his accomplices, and keep them in check, at least for a time. We needed only time enough to sign the treaty with Russia, which would make an alliance with Bonaparte impossible. After that . . . we would see!

On Mahmud's orders, the bodies of Franchini and his eunuchs were buried, with the pay of their treason, under the floor of a shed at the entrance of the Black Eunuchs' Court.

Kutuzov kept his promise. On May 18, 1812, a week after his return to Bucharest, a peace treaty was signed between Turkey and Russia. Rumania was returned to us. The Czar flew into a rage, sent Kutuzov away in disgrace . . . and ratified the treaty. On the very next day, Napoleon crossed the Niemen at the head of the Grande Armée and began the invasion of Russia.

It had been agreed that the Treaty of Bucharest would remain secret until the Russian troops that had been used against us were transported to join the army fighting Bonaparte. The latter sent courier after courier, urging us to join the coalition against Russia. We wanted to postpone the avalanche—that is, Bonaparte's discovery of the treaty—for as long as possible. But the treaty itself was beginning to seem useless. Despite the advantages with which it provided Russia, it seemed that nothing could stop Bonaparte's advance. He took Vilna, then Smolensk, toppled the Russian army at Borodino, and entered Moscow in triumph. Once again we wondered anxiously whether he would win, as he had always won in the past. It seemed that nothing would ever stop that devil of a man. In the meantime we ran the risk of finding ourselves among the vanquished, and that would spell the end of Mahmud—and the end of Turkey itself.

To top it all, a plague broke out in Constantinople, and within a few weeks killed more than a hundred and twenty-five thousand people.

Confined to Besiktas, I spent long hours strolling through my peaceful gardens, wondering at the fact that nature, here around me, should give birth to miracles of beauty, while a little farther away in town it did nothing but destroy, covering bodies with pustules and ravaging entire families.

My duty as the Valideh was to organize relief efforts, but I could not feel deeply moved by the people's suffering, terrible and near though it was. My long trials had hardened me, and I was no longer afraid of death. I trembled, however, for Mahmud. Despite my pleas, he went every day to visit those neighborhoods most affected by the epidemic, to speak and lend comfort to his subjects, who were numbed with horror. He walked fearlessly among the victims, radiant with a legendary aura, that of the invincible Sultan.

Yet tragedy struck him cruelly: his two sons, Bayazid and Murad, both of them barely a year old, died within a week of each other. Mahmud left the Seraglio daily to defy the plague, but the plague had slipped into the unhealthy Seraglio and chosen the first two of his heirs.

The kadins and the imperial children were evacuated and split up among various palaces. I was put in charge of Mahmud's last-born, tiny Eminee. The baby, only a few weeks old, amused me: she was the image of Mahmud—the same piercing eyes, the same pout, the same stubborn brow. And for the first time I felt something akin to tenderness for a child.

Mahmud grew even more withdrawn, more severe, more inaccessible with the death of his children, the daily spectacle of the plague, the catastrophic news from Russia and Bonaparte's threats. He came to Besiktas every day; however, it was not me but my flowers he wanted to see. Only the contemplation of those short-lived but inexhaustible marvels could relieve him of the tragic gloom in which he lived. We walked side by side, in silence, stopping to look at a flower bank, a flower bed. It was there, in the dahlia-bordered alley, that one afternoon Mahmud was handed a message by a eunuch. He unsealed it and began to read, and I saw his expression change from disbelief to radiant joy; and then that severe, self-controlled man suddenly began to dance an absurd jig, waving his arms, jumping up and down, trampling my flowers, his caftan billowing in the wind. Even in his childhood I had seen such explosions of joy no more than once or twice. "Napoleon has evacuated Moscow!" he cried. "He's begun his retreat. He's beaten. Kutuzov himself wrote me."

The Czar, who faced total defeat, had called him out of disgrace—to everyone's great surprise, Kutuzov's included. He lacked able commanders, and put Kutuzov at the head of the Russian defense. At first Bonaparte beat him at Borodino. Kutuzov had to retreat and allow Bonaparte to seize Moscow. But Bonaparte found himself the prisoner of a desert of ashes. Moscow burned for three days and three nights. All Russia had been set ablaze by the hand of her own sons. The scorched earth could no longer feed Napoleon's troops, and winter—General Winter, as Kutuzov called her—Russia's most precious ally, was on her way. Bonaparte found a copy of the Treaty of Bucharest in the archives captured at Moscow. Simultaneously he learned that the Russian army fighting us on the Balkan front was now free and on its way to link up with Kutuzov's force. He understood that he had been duped, and that winter would leave him no chance of victory. He gave up the fight and started to withdraw from Moscow.

"What else does he say?" I asked.

Mahmud handed me the letter. The last paragraph read: "I pay tribute to the courage and clairvoyance of Your Highness. Through your brave initiative you have contributed to saving the freedom of Europe. For it is clear that in beginning his retreat, Bonaparte has taken the first steps toward his inevitable downfall. It is thanks to Your Highness that Russia is saved."

"Turkey too is saved," murmured Mahmud as I returned the letter to his hands.

"And Selim is avenged," I added, "and my cousin Josephine." Mahmud had allowed me to keep the promise I had made in prison. Even if my part in it had been minor, he had let me contribute to Bonaparte's ruin.

After marking Constantinople with its seal of mourning, the plague finally subsided. More good news followed: Bonaparte had lost a part of his army while crossing the Berezina, and the rest of his forces were being shredded by the razor-sharp Russian winter. Yet in Germany he fought like a devil, inflicting defeat after defeat on the European coalition, which had now turned against him. The eagle was wounded, but his beak was still sharp. I wanted to see him crushed, but I was no longer certain that I would. One day in the winter of 1813 I was racked by a violent fit of coughing, and I spat up blood. My Greek surgeon tried to reassure me—in vain. I had no illusions as to the nature of my illness; it was consumption. My Dubuc grandfather had died of it. My incarceration in the humid, badly heated apartment under the eaves of the harem, my illness in the winter of 1806–1807, had no doubt encouraged the growth of the disease in an organism worn and weakened by trials. It had been hatching for a long time, unsuspected, before it finally revealed itself.

Contradictory emotions began to battle within me as soon as I became conscious of the gravity of my situation. How long would I live? A year, two years; at most, five.

As I have said, I was not afraid of death. That fear had been taken from me with Selim; sometimes I even wished for it, so that I might join him. And yet I was only forty, and I found myself trying to reason in secret with death, trying to mollify it. Could it not wait a little? Just enough to let me witness Mahmud's success and the restoration of the empire under his scepter? And why should it drag me away before I had seen Bonaparte's downfall?

That last event, however, was striding closer with the energetic gait of History. The allies invaded France, from which Napoleon had so often marched to invade Europe. He tried to stop them in a remarkable campaign, but this time the eagle's wounds were fatal. The allies marched into Paris, to be greeted as liberators by the population. Bonaparte abdicated at Fontainebleau and was sent into exile on the island of Elba. The guns fell silent, and the Treaty of Paris put an end to a war through which Europe had suffered for twenty-two years without interruption.

I thought I would be the first to leave; but Josephine died before me, on May 29, 1814. I had learned that she had escaped Bonaparte's disaster—which was only fair—and then the next mail informed me of her sudden death. Pneumonia had swept her away in three days. She had caught cold one evening, walking through her gardens with the Czar, wearing a light dress with a large décolletage. I could imagine Josephine determined to seduce, baring herself a little too boldly, and dying as she had lived—by frivolity.

For me Josephine was no more than a faded image, alive only in my childhood memories. And yet our destinies, though separate, had remained linked ever since the day when Euphemia David had read them together in the palms of our hands. I had followed her career with interest and kindness, and I had never been jealous of her. She had known the lights of the stage of History, and I the shadows of the Seraglio's secrecy; and both our fates had suited us. Yet my own life, though more tragic, had been fuller than hers. I had loved and been loved. Admittedly Josephine had grown to love Bonaparte in the end, long after marrying him, and he had loved her insofar as he was capable of love. Nevertheless he had turned her away and dethroned her. She had only begun to rebuild her life when death cut her down. I lived on, though I had died with Selim. As Euphemia David had predicted, Josephine must have longed often for the Martinique of our childhood. As for myself, I had no regrets.

I was particularly moved by one detail which our ambassador in Paris wrote of in his letter. One English general among the victors knocked at Josephine's door and asked the favor of being received. She invited him to dinner. When the English general arrived, on the appointed day, Josephine had been dead for barely two hours. The Englishman's name was William Fraser. He was Josephine's first fiancé, the one whom Euphemia had predicted she would not marry. They had not seen each other since; and death had come to her door a little earlier than he.

Death struck many in those days, Kutuzov among them. Russia had finally given him recognition. Kutuzov had liberated his country, and, his task accomplished, he passed away. Queen Marie-Caroline of Naples followed him. She had finally reached Vienna, her city of birth and now her land of exile, and died on the day before she was to meet her great-grandson, the devil's child, Napoleon's son.

Count d'Antraigues was assassinated with his wife, Saint-Huberti, the actress whose performance of Phèdre I had seen in Nantes. They were murdered by their valet, who then committed suicide over their corpses, adding another layer of mystery to d'Antraigues's life—a suiting end for a spy.

Mother Marie-Agnès added her news to this hail of events:

Thus the prodigious adventure has come to an end. At last Napoleon has been dragged off the stage of History, to vegetate in the ridiculous kingdom of Elba. Exhausted, ruined, in mourning—there is not a family here that does not grieve for its dead—France is emerging at last from the nightmare of war and occupation, happy again in the hands of its legitimate kings. Europe breathes freely: The kings Napoleon deposed have returned to their thrones, and the others are slowly forgetting the fear in which he held them for fifteen years. They have met in congress in Vienna to rebuild the world he ruined. Silence and peace have replaced the roar of cannons . . . and I have no doubt that an era of mediocrity will follow the terrible genius with which Napoleon stamped his time. I pray ceaselessly for your cousin Josephine. Eternal rest will erase the bitterness she lived on this earth in spite of—or perhaps because of—her high position.

The war in Europe seriously impeded communications for a time, and therefore I learned only recently of your mother's death, which took place three years ago and of which I now inform you with great sadness. She was followed shortly by your brother Pierre, whose christening you once told me of, who died at the age of thirty. He suffered the same disease as you. The letter in which you told me of your illness caused me such distress that I had to wait to recover my serenity in order to mention it to you. I am old and alone, and because of my infirmities I am of no use to anyone. I am a burden to others, and still God does not call me to His side. You are young, loved, powerful, you still have everything before you—and it is you God has chosen. His ways are mysterious, and we can only bow before His will. I know that courage is something you do not lack; I can only pray God to grant you resignation. I deeply regret that the circumstances will not allow you the comfort of religion in your last hours. At least you will continue until your last breath to think of others as you always have, to think of ways to alleviate their suffering. Rest assured that my prayers, my thoughts, and my everlasting affection remain with you at all times.

Mother Marie-Agnès had sinned through optimism in assuming that Bonaparte had made his exit from history. Soon the devil leaped out of his box, landed on French soil, and reclaimed his throne. War broke out again—luckily not for long. Bonaparte was crushed at Waterloo and forced to abdicate a second time. A second time France was invaded, and the Bourbon monarchy reinstated. Bonaparte was locked away on Saint Helena, and we hoped that at last we would no longer hear anything about him but his legend. In Constantinople, the hero of those uncertain times had been none other than Pierre Ruffin. Faithful to Bonaparte, he had refused to lower the tricolor flag when the Bourbons' banner decorated with fleurs-de-lys replaced it as France's national emblem. The French colony, eager to pay court to its new master from afar, had tried to imprison Ruffin; faced with Mahmud's refusal, they then tried to tear him to pieces. Mahmud's police rescued him from the clutches of his compatriots in the nick of time. The new ambassador dispatched by the King of France quickly dismissed Pierre Ruffin from the diplomatic corps. He decided to return to France after having lived in Turkey for forty years. I asked to see him before he went. It was a destroyed man who came to me. He began by telling me how touched he was by the honor of my invitation.

"And I honor faithfulness in you, Monsieur Ruffin, your faithfulness to your Emperor, though I did not like him. You once told me that you respected that quality in me. Let me return the compliment. But why do you have to leave Turkey?"

"My compatriots here hate me. I can no longer be of use to my country here in Turkey. I cannot stay."

"You are more courageous than I. I have not lived in Turkey as long as you, and yet I know I will never be able to leave. I could not face the prospect even when Franchini's intrigues forced me to consider it. I could not live anywhere else even if I wanted to. The Orient has had the better of me, just as it has, over the centuries, of all the foreigners who have known it."

"You and I, Madame, will always remain foreigners here no matter what we do; but in the meantime we have also become foreigners to the West. Nevertheless it is better here; for the Orient has the secret of accommodating uprooted people like us. I will miss Turkey, believe me. . . ."

"Then stay! The Sultan, my son, will be happy to see to it that you are comfortable."

"I cannot. If there is one thing the Orient cannot abide, it is failure. You succeeded, Madame, and therefore you have a place here. I lost face, and therefore I cannot stay, in spite of the kindliness of His Highness."

"Where will you go?"

"I have some land in Provence. I shall settle down there and grow flowers—like your flowers here. I shall think of you, of this garden in Besiktas. I shall miss you . . . even though I should hate you."

I started.

"Yes, Madame, I should hate you, for you are the cause of the Emperor's downfall."

"You're exaggerating, Monsieur Ruffin. It is the European armies that defeated him."

"You were the beginning of his end." Ruffin had understood the decisive importance of our treaty with Russia on the eve of her invasion by Bonaparte. "You were the cog that ruined the Great Emperor's machine."

Strangely enough, Ruffin used the same image—the cog—as Queen Marie-Caroline to describe my part in the affair.

"Without you, Madame, the Emperor would have conquered Russia—and," he added, lowering his voice to a whisper, "perhaps he would then have conquered Turkey."

"You are wrong, Monsieur Ruffin. It is Sultan Mahmud who made peace with the Russians."

"The Sultan is still too young to attribute his success to another than himself. But I recognized your touch in the boldness of that move. It is you who shaped that peace that was so catastrophic for my Emperor."

"In that case, History will not think very highly of me. And what do *you* think History will say of me?"

"Nothing, Madame. Posterity will know nothing about you."

"You don't mean it! Franchini, d'Antraigues, Queen Marie-Caroline, yourself, the British spies—many people know of me. Even the British papers wrote about me."

"Those who really knew who you are have all died. The others have only suspicions. There will be rumors, perhaps even novels—is your life not fit for a novel?—but there will be no certainty. In the Seraglio you shall be remembered as Kadin Nakshidil, and you shall be honored as such. A Frenchwoman who rules over the Seraglio is an anomaly, a heresy. Aimée Dubuc de Riverie will never have existed—it will have been impossible for her to exist!"

"I would only have to publish the memoirs I am writing."

"You won't do it. You already enjoy the thought of the mystery that will shroud you."

I had a present for Ruffin; I had it brought in. It was the bust of Bonaparte that the latter had sent to Selim, and which Selim, against my wishes, had kept in his drawing room. When it was given to him I saw two big tears roll down Ruffin's cheeks. I too had tears in my eyes.

"Thank you, Madame. And farewell. Farewell to Turkey."

CHAPTER 24

———⊶✦⊷———

EVER SINCE Bonaparte had left the stage, the world seemed exhausted and silent. Of course the powerful carried on with their politics, and History rolled onward. But everywhere calmness and mediocrity had succeeded to genius and turbulence. I did not miss the Napoleonic tempests—God forbid!—but I was no longer interested in the news of the world. As for Mahmud, he took advantage of this lull in History to launch a series of reforms he had been planning for a long time. They had long been postponed by various events, and now they swept over the empire like a young wind. Modernization was the order of the day, everywhere: in the administration, in the army, in the national customs; a methodical, irreversible modernization. Mahmud reinforced his authority by centralizing power shamelessly. He stripped the warlords of all power. He put strict limits on the pashas and the provincial governors. He dismantled the privileges of feudal cities and dynasties. There was no lack of violent protests. Then Mahmud would send for the executioner—and when he couldn't, he sent the assassins. The pyramid of severed heads grew as fast as opposition diminished. Simultaneously he imposed a revolutionary religious tolerance. He allowed the Christians to worship freely, put controls on the Wakfs, the prodigious fortunes of the Muslim clergy, and finally decreed equality before the law for Muslims and Rayas—the Christians and Jews of Turkey, who until then had been subject to all sorts of humiliations.

One morning, when he came to see me at Besiktas, I took a step back in surprise when I saw him walk in. He had dressed in the European fashion, in black, with a gold-buttoned frock coat, straight trousers, and a military cape. The turban had been replaced by a red fez, decorated with a diamond aigrette—the only concession to the past. "The days of brocade, of caftans, of feathers are over," he announced.

He had just published a decree ordering the officers of the ministries and members of the government to wear, in the future, the same dress as he. This sartorial revolution met with more resistance than any other reform: One does not allow oneself to be dragged into the nineteenth century without protesting a little. But no one shied away. The empire had learned that the Sultan's orders were not to be taken lightly.

Mahmud's daughter, little Eminee, almost three years old, walked circles around her father, surprised and puzzled. I had become attached to the child ever since she had been put in my care during the plague of 1812. She seemed very disappointed that her father no longer gleamed with gold and diamonds.

I was proud of Mahmud, of his actions, of his reforms, and I told him as much. He silenced me.

"Everything I do, Nakshidil, I owe to your education and Selim's teachings. Do you remember his lessons, each evening, when we were in prison? I haven't forgotten a word of them. It is Selim who speaks in my voice, it is he who dictates my decrees and reforms."

The knowledge that the sacrifice of my beloved had not been in vain was very dear to me. Yet Mahmud had forgotten one of Selim's teachings: clemency.

"Is it really necessary to cut so many heads, Mahmud?"

"Selim showed me the way, but he failed. The Sultan cannot

allow himself another failure. The empire can no longer wait. If I want to be known one day as the Reforming Sultan, I must first be known as the Sanguinary Sultan."

Seeing my mood darken, Mahmud invited me to a stroll through Constantinople incognito. He had acquired this habit of his predecessors, and was eager to show me the transformations of the town. The court barges brought us to the Seraglio, and there we put on our disguises. There was no question of strolling through the streets in European dress without drawing attention. Mahmud, grumbling, was forced to don the robes, the caftan, and the turban of a respectable burgher. Each leg of our excursion brought back a flood of memories—Ali Effendi draping me in a black abaya, Ali Effendi opening the secret door in the Seraglio wall, through which we slipped unseen. And then that itinerary through the narrow streets where, the first time, Selim had had to hold me up because I had grown so dizzy in the midst of the crowds and the noise after years of confinement.

I noticed some definite changes: Several streets had been widened and many small wooden houses with charming balconies had been replaced by stone buildings.

We stopped for a moment on the terrace of the Mosque of Sulemanye. Mahmud pointed out to me in the distance the spires of two churches the Christians were building in their quarter, a sign of the new policy of religious tolerance. Then Mahmud proudly showed me the bridge he had just finished building over the Golden Horn to link the old town with Pera and Galata. This innovation made life much easier for the inhabitants of Constantinople, and yet Mahmud had been publicly insulted at its inauguration, precisely because of his religious tolerance. I had already heard of the incident, but I let Mahmud tell me about it again. While he was crossing the new bridge a dervish had leaped across his path and cried: "Stop, Sultan Giaour!" Giaour—Christian—the worst insult for a Turk: Mahmud had last had the epithet hurled at him in his childhood by his brother Mustafa. This time he did not let it affect him.

"That is not how they'll succeed in stopping me. I will break those who stand in my way as easily as I had that insulting dervish executed. I shall pursue my policy of tolerance, even at the cost of intolerance."

That speech would be useful to me in the future. I was constantly bombarded with petitions and appeals, because it was assumed that I took an interest in politics—which I didn't—and that I had influence, which, if I had, I did not use. And then it was not easy to approach Mahmud. One day a Jewish employee of the bank, who came to Besiktas at regular intervals to inform me of the state of my savings, transmitted to me a message from his fellow bankers, the illustrious Rothschild brothers. They wanted me to lodge a request with the Sultan to lift the restrictions on Jewish immigration to Palestine. I mentioned it to Mahmud that evening while we stood on the terrace of the Mosque of Sulemanye. He resolved to grant the request.

"All my subjects are equal before the law, the Jews as well as the others. If they want to settle in the land of their ancestors, so be it."

Later we strolled through the bazaar. I found it unchanged, with its vaulted ceiling, its stalls, its merchants, its crowds. I even recognized the coffeehouse where I had once sat with Selim. We stopped there, Mahmud and I, and ordered—for the sake of appearances— "harem delights," those ices, dondourmas, I had liked so much the time before. Then, like the burghers seated at the tables next to ours, we exchanged family gossip. Princess Hadidgeh, Selim's sister, had settled down at last, now that her lover had been sent back to his native Germany. She had raised a storm, shouted, cried that she was being robbed of life itself, and calmed down only when Mahmud promised to pay her fabulous debts. Now she dedicated herself to the upkeep of her palaces—an activity more discreet than the upkeep of her love affairs.

To my extreme annoyance Mahmud had rescued his sister Princess Esmee from the Old Seraglio, and restored her gigantic fortune and her favor. She had participated actively in the revolutions against Selim, and even against Mahmud, but the sympathy between brother and sister had survived all her machinations. Now that Esmee had returned to freedom she recovered her sparkle and resumed her extravagant behavior. She had ordered a large chara-banc of gilded wood, in which she piled up the prettiest of her slavegirls before going out to drive through the Christian quarters. Whenever a respectable-looking stranger noticed the swarm of lovely creatures half hidden by brocade curtains, Esmee would beckon to him, start a conversation, and more often that not the stranger ended up in Esmee's bed. I pointed out to Mahmud that this permanent scandal was detrimental to his prestige. He prom-ised to reprimand his sister harshly, but I knew he never would. He forgave Esmee everything because she amused him.

Mahmud told me that Esmee's mother, Sineperver, was going blind in the Old Seraglio. The news sparked neither satisfaction nor pity in me. Ever since that woman, the cause of so much trouble, had been reduced to powerlessness, I had taken my vengeance in only one way, perhaps the most cruel: indifference.

It was getting late, and the stalls of the bazaar were beginning to shut down. The day had been long, I was tired—my disease sapped my strength—but there were still things to be done. Without ask-ing questions, Mahmud followed me to the Mosque of Mohammed the Conqueror. There, behind the school for theologians, was a gar-den where rose the turbehs—the pavilion-tombs—of several sul-tans; it was a place where I had come to walk more than once. I drew Mahmud to the wildest corner of that poetic jungle, into a tangle of hawthorn, acacia, iris, and syringa.

"It is here," I said, as softly as I could, "that I wish to be buried."

"Don't say that, Mama Nakshidil. You're much too young." He seemed annoyed by my whim.

"I have the disease that killed my grandfather and my brother. I am fatally ill; I don't have long to live."

"I don't believe you. It's impossible. I don't believe it." His first reaction was revolt; it had been the same when, as a child, Mah-mud had seen me come close to dying of poison.

"Believe me, my son. If I trample my shame in order to tell you my secret, if I break for you my silent pact with death, if I over-come my pain at causing you pain, it is only because time is so short."

He bravely controlled his emotion, and only a blink of his eyelids and a fleeting pallor betrayed him. I asked him permission to begin the construction of my turbeh immediately. He assented, of course, and promised that we would come to oversee the work together.

"No, Mahmud. You'll come alone. Today is my last outing. I have seen again the Constantinople of yesterday, of my happy memories, and I have seen the Constantinople of tomorrow, of your reign. That is enough for me. From now on I shall stay at Besiktas, for I have neither the strength nor the desire to go out."

I was already too exhausted to walk home. Mahmud stopped a tayvan, a rental charabanc, and together we rode back to the walls of the Seraglio.

While I put order in my affairs, troublemakers sowed disorder in those of the empire. A revolt broke out in Asia Minor, followed by another in Serbia. The secret societies of the Greeks prepared their uprising. Several times various incidents had forced Selim to interrupt his reforms, and now it seemed that Mahmud was condemned to know the same frustrations. Would he then never enjoy the peace necessary to the restoration of the empire? I was weak and discouraged—unlike Mahmud. It was he who gave me back my confidence.

"There have always been revolts in the empire, and there will be more. I shall crush them. If I don't succeed, I shall lose some provinces. And so what? Nothing will stop my reforms, nothing! I shall turn this empire into a modern state even if I have to lose some of it on the way. That is what is most important."

"And what about the opposition, Mahmud! The janissaries will never let go!"

"I have told you, Nakshidil. One day I shall eliminate them. Physically. All of them. I can wait; I have time."

He was right. Unlike me, he had time on his side. "I had forgotten that you are young, Mahmud, while I am old."

"Old, Nakshidil! Look in the mirror and tell me whether you are old!"

He wasn't wrong. My face, though hollowed by my illness, was still smooth. There was no white to take the luster from my golden hair. The light fever of consumption, which never left me anymore, lent a flush to my cheeks and a sparkle to my eyes. I did not look old, perhaps, but my spirit had lost all youth. I was a woman of yesterday, and a difference of twelve years was enough to make my son a man of tomorrow. I gladly left to him the cares of politics and his reforms . . . and his troubles. I no longer had the heart to take interest even in the latter.

In order to entertain me, Mahmud invited me to the opera. Recently he had acquired the notion of learning to play the piano, and had imported to Constantinople the brother of the composer Donizetti for his lessons. Between two sets of scales, the instructor decided to stage, with the help of a touring Italian company, an opera, the first performance of which was to be given for his imperial pupil. All the harem was invited to the Sultan's Hall for the occasion. I knew that the opera's first night was to be the last time I appeared in public, and though it was a great effort for me I dressed with special care, not only to honor Mahmud but also to leave a suitable impression in the harem. I sent for my jewel chests, which I had not touched in years. The excitement of my "granddaughter" Eminee made up for my own lassitude. She opened all the drawers one after the other, and dug her chubby little hands into the diamonds, the emeralds, the rubies. She threw necklaces and bracelets onto the carpet and rolled in chains of cabochons. Showing the jewels to the child was like passing my life in review: the Persian earrings Vartui had given me after I had met with Mirizshah's approval, the dove-colored ruby from my first night with Abdul Hamid, Selim's black-and-white pearl, and even the modest coral necklace that my aunt Elizabeth de Bellefonds had given me in another existence, and which had followed me ever since. Soon, upon my death, these jewels would return, according to custom, to the Sultan's treasury. Mahmud and his successors would "lend" them again to other women; kadins, favorites, and perhaps another Valideh would wear them. I showed Eminee her father's last present: an enormous faceted diamond, pear-shaped, which had once belonged to . . . Bonaparte. "Madame the Emperor's Mother," in exile and penury, had been forced to sell the gem. That old scoundrel Ali of Tepeleni, the Pasha of Iannina, had ordered his agents to buy it, and sent it as a conciliatory present to the Sultan, having learned, the hard way, to treat him gently. "This spoil of your enemy is yours by right," Mahmud had said when he gave me the stone. I turned it and made it sparkle before the child, who watched, fascinated and without stirring, the seven colors in it. Suddenly Eminee snatched the diamond and ran to hide it under the pillows of the sofa. It took several eunuchs and a frantic search to find it.

At last I was ready: all in black and silver with only pearls for jewelry, streams of tears in which sparkled Bonaparte's lonely diamond.

I was the last to enter the Sultan's Hall, and Mahmud himself led me to my sofa. A little stage had been erected facing his throne, and men—musicians, singers—were to participate in the show. A light golden lattice had been raised in front of the dais where I sat with the women. The opera, *The Italian Maid in Algiers*, was by a young composer who was all the rage in Europe, Gioacchino Rossini. From the very beginning the plot awoke an old memory. It was the perfectly true story, which I had heard among the pirates, of that Italian woman who had so bewitched the Dey of Algiers that, after putting her charms to good use, he had returned her to her family with rich presents. I smiled at the sight of imposing Baba Mohammed, who had made a present of me to Abdul Hamid, transformed into a sort of operatic sultan. The audience was convulsed by the comical representation of a harem. Everyone was there: little Ali Effendi, tottering under his enormous turban, his mischievous eyes darting about, surveying his flock; Cevri, massive and still; Idriss, frowning, doing his best to understand the plot of the opera. And Mahmud's kadins, his odalisques: his fallen favorite Besma, the former guardian of the baths; and the siren Husmumelek, his first flame, given to him by his sister Princess Esmee. Esmee herself was seated next to me, outrageously painted, and smothered in an excess of jewels. I looked at them all as if they were strangers; and indeed they might as well have been, so foreign to their universe did I feel, so detached from life. They stole glances at me in which I read reverence and almost awe. They watched me the way one watches an exotic idol, an undecipherable legend, or death itself: The news of my disease, no doubt, had spread.

I turned to Mahmud. I laid my eyes on that man whose upbringing I had directed, who was my child, my work. I saw in him the gravity that had so impressed me the first time we met—when he was only three years old. Mahmud was obviously a leader of men, a creature born to rule. He was wary and suspicious of everyone, and perhaps it was for the better. Had Selim not failed by trusting too easily? But I wondered whether Mahmud, that energetic, determined, stubborn man, was not also lonely. I knew that he drank more and more. Was it the loneliness of power that drove him to champagne? It seemed that even love had lost the power to break through his isolation. Ever since his passion for Besma had died, he showed no preferences among his women. He honored them all, conscious only of the fact that he was the last of his dynasty, whose duty was to prolong it and therefore father children.

I had perhaps contributed to the formation of a great ruler, but not a happy man. It was too late to correct this deficiency or even to repent for it. I convinced myself that Mahmud valued glory over happiness, and that none had ever known the two simultaneously.

I had hoped that my last appearance in public in the harem would be a brilliant one. But I was racked by a long coughing fit, and then spat up blood. The show had to be interrupted and I was carried out, like an invalid, distraught and panting, in the midst of the harem's whispers.

And so I regained my isolation, from which it was clear I ought never to go out again, even for an evening. I devoted my time to my flowers—and to the most beautiful among them, my little granddaughter Eminee. I had not had a garden since my childhood in Martinique, I had never had a child, and I discovered these twin joys at the gates of death. I planted trees and educated a child, knowing I would not live to see them grow. Eminee already showed her father's indomitable character and his insatiable curiosity. I spoiled her shamefully, and only she had—or had taken—the right to pick my most beautiful flowers. I hoped to die quickly, among my flowers, close to Eminee.

But those three wishes were denied. One night my yali at Besiktas burned to the ground.

The blaze was sparked by embers that someone had forgotten to put out and it found the wooden structure a choice prey. Weakened by disease, half asphyxiated by smoke, I was barely aware of the disaster. When I found myself outside, in my garden, practically unconscious in the arms of Idriss, my wooden house was burning like a gigantic torch. I barely saw the panicked slaves and eunuchs scattering. I barely heard the shouts and the crackling wood. In the turmoil Eminee, who was asleep in my room, had been forgotten. When she was remembered, it was too late.

I did not learn of her death until the following morning. I was assured that she had died quickly, painlessly, asphyxiated but not burned. It was not much solace. At first I was revulsed by the injustice of fate. I was condemned, I wanted to die, and yet I went on living against my wishes. Eminee had her whole life before her, and death had stolen her away. There was nothing to do but turn to God. Not the God of my youth—that friend I had invented, in whom I confided and whom I reproached—but Selim's omniscient and unfathomable God, before whose decrees one must bow even if they strike like lightning.

Now that my yali had been reduced to ashes, I was forced to return to the Valideh's apartments in the Seraglio. The imperial harem, which had held me prisoner for so long, would not let me go and would keep me to my last day.

Everything is ready for this date. My turbeh is finished. I have caused the remains of the French kadin to be brought there, in order that Mahmud's real mother be reunited with his adoptive mother, and I have ordered a fountain built against the wall of the turbeh, so that passersby will be able to refresh themselves, perhaps while thinking of me.

Everything is in order for Nakshidil Sultana, but not for Aimée Dubuc. I would like to die in the religion of my childhood, whose prayers have remained the medium of my God. I should like—as my mother would have—a priest to be present at my last moments, to administer the extreme unction. But I know that is impossible. Even Mother Marie-Agnès admitted it. A priest in the imperial harem, the mother of the Sultan, of the Caliph of Islam, dying a giaour, a Christian! The Seraglio would never live it down, and I have no wish to burden Mahmud with it—though, in a moment of abandon, I did mention it to him.

On the other hand, I have made my will. I simply left some gold to the poor of Nantes, as a tribute to Mother Marie-Agnès. I left my portrait to my sister Alexandrine; I had heard from Mother Marie-Agnès that she had been living in Chateau Dubuc since her wedding and our parents' death. I want to live in her memory through this present from beyond the grave. It is the miniature which I gave to Selim in prison, which I took from his body; it has not left me since.

That talisman, stained with Selim's blood, is here before my eyes as I finish these memoirs. I began them at Besiktas, and I had hoped to finish them there. Pierre Ruffin was right. I shall not publish them. I shall even hide them behind one of the green-and-gold panels of my sitting room. Perhaps one day someone will find them. Otherwise I shall remain a mystery, a mere story, a rumor, and people will even doubt that I existed. To the grace of God. The hiding place awaits my manuscript. I have only to write its title:

"Memoirs of Aimée Dubuc de Riverie, Valideh Sultana of Turkey."

EPILOGUE

Excerpts from *Chroniques des Frères Mineurs Capucins de Constantinople* (Chronicles of the Capuchin Brothers of Constantinople), Volume IV, page 399:

It was during a night of November 1817. Reverend Father Chrysostom, Superior of the Capuchin Monastery in Constantinople, had retired to his cell and knelt at the foot of the crucifix.

Gusts of wind shook the houses, which creaked and moaned. Winds from the Black Sea, sliding over the Bosporus, had brought with them storms and tempests.

Father Chrysostom heard urgent knocking at the monastery door; and soon the friar porter came in, pale and trembling, followed by two janissaries, one of whom stepped up to the Superior and handed him a firman. The Reverend Father, after reading it with surprise, rushed to the church, where he stayed for a few moments; then, escorted by the janissaries, he went to the port of Pera. The three of them climbed into a caïque manned by twelve pairs of oarsmen, which immediately pulled away and vanished into the shadows of the night.

Meanwhile, in a sumptuously decorated room with rich tapestries and luxurious carpets, a woman lay in agony on her deathbed. She seemed about fifty years of age, but she was still extremely beautiful, with very fine features. She was as thin and pale as a cadaver, and it was plain to see that she was living her last hours. A chandelier and candelabra with pink candles gave enough light to see what was happening within the silent room. Next to the bed a surgeon dressed in the Greek fashion often picked up the patient's wrist to feel her pulse; by the door, behind a railing, two black slaves stood waiting, ready to execute orders.

A few steps away, a certain man seemed prey to deep and poignant grief. He could have been about thirty years of age. His height was above average. A high, noble brow, and a gaze where one could read a long habit of authority, gave his features an imposing air of gravity. His dress was simple and of rare elegance. Signs and stifled moans he could not control testified to his anguish and the wrenching of his soul.

It was already past midnight when a slight noise was heard in the antechamber. A black man came in and, bowing to the ground, said, "He is here. Must he be brought in?"

The prince signaled assent. Father Chrysostom, whom the janissaries had just brought, was admitted into the room. The man who holds all power there dismissed everyone with a wave of the hand and, stepping to the dying woman's bedside, said:

"My mother, you wanted to die in the religion of your fathers. May your wishes be fulfilled! Here is a Catholic priest."

On those words the prince left. For the next hour the Capuchin Father bent over the dying woman and listened to the admission of her sins and to her repentance. He wept. The woman wept too. Then, when the infidel prince returned to his mother's bedside, the priest raised the Holy Host and placed it on her lips. At that moment the only witness, that august personage, threw himself to the ground, invoking the name of Allah!

In the meantime the news of Father Chrysostom's abduction had spread through the free quarters of Constantinople. By morning no one spoke of anything else, and each had his own theory about the mysterious disappearance. Some said that the monk had been imprisoned in the Castle of Seven Towers. Others went further and claimed that he had died in tragic circumstances. Yet others, impatient to know the truth, walked into the monastery, where, to their surprise, they found the Superior in the church, kneeling at the altar.

Alone with God, ignorant of everything around him, his brow pale and his eyes filled with tears, Father Chrysostom prayed for the soul of the Valideh, who had died in the night.

On Nakshidil Sultana's turbeh in the gardens of the Mosque of Mohammed the Conqueror, one can read the following epitaph, which, in all probability, was written, under the name of Sadik, by Sultan Mahmud II:

> A character of sun, pure and noble,
> Conquered the Orient by her simple Majesty.
> Thanks to her, nature grew yet brighter,
> Her resounding grandeur and fame
> Made of this country a garden of roses,
> The flowers are happy through her,
> They shall hold her memory forever
> The Sultan of the World, Mahmud II
> Is filled with her
> On the august head of his mother Nakshidil
> Prayers and earth are placed
> It is with tears of blood
> That I write here for memory
> I, Sadik, the date of her painful death
>
> 1817, or 1233 of the Hegira.

THE CAVE DREAMERS

A NATIONAL BESTSELLER BY
JEANNE WILLIAMS

THE CAVE DREAMERS is a vivid, passionate
novel of the lives and loves of the women
across centuries who share the secret of
"The Cave of Always Summer." From the dawn
of time to the present, the treasured mystery
of the cave is passed and guarded, joining
generation to generation through
their dreams and desires.

86488-6/$3.95 U.S.
86496-7/$4.75 Canada

An **AVON** Paperback